THE FIRST AMENDMENT UNDER FIRE

THE FIRST AMENDMENT UNDER FIRE

America's Radicals,
Congress,
and the Courts

MILTON CANTOR

Transaction Publishers
New Brunswick (U.S.A.) and London (U.K.)

Copyright © 2017 by Transaction Publishers, New Brunswick, New Jersey.

All rights reserved under International and Pan-American Copyright Conventions. No part of this book may be reproduced or transmitted in any form or by any means, electronic or mechanical, including photocopy, recording, or any information storage and retrieval system, without prior permission in writing from the publisher. All inquiries should be addressed to Transaction Publishers, 10 Corporate Place South, Suite 102, Piscataway, NJ 08854. www.transactionpub.com

This book is printed on acid-free paper that meets the American National Standard for Permanence of Paper for Printed Library Materials.

Library of Congress Catalog Number: 2016027010
ISBN: 978-1-4128-6341-4
eBook: 978-1-4128-6364-3
Printed in the United States of America

    Library of Congress Cataloging-in-Publication Data

Names: Cantor, Milton, author.
Title: The First Amendment under fire : America's radicals,
   Congress, and the courts / Milton Cantor.
Description: New Brunswick, New Jersey : Transaction Publishers,
   2017. | Includes bibliographical references and index.
Identifiers: LCCN 2016027010 (print) | LCCN 2016038321 (ebook) |
   ISBN 9781412863414 (hardcover : acid-free paper) | ISBN
   9781412863643 (ebook) | ISBN 9781412863643
Subjects: LCSH: Freedom of expression--United States--History--
   20th century.
Classification: LCC KF4770 .C36 2017 (print) | LCC KF4770 (ebook)
   | DDC 342.7308/53--dc23
LC record available at https://lccn.loc.gov/2016027010

Contents

Introduction		vii
1.	Nationalism and War: The Casualties	1
2.	Post-War Harvest: "Traitors to America"	21
3.	Judicial Tolerance of Intolerance	43
4.	The First Amendment: Crucible Years	57
5.	Freedom of Expression in Flux: The Twenties	69
6.	The Thirties: Evolving toward the First Amendment	89
7.	Stare Decisis: Old Responses to New Crises	131
8.	The Cold War Enters the Courtroom	165
9.	The Fifties: The Left under Assault	185
10.	The Warren Court: The Cloudy Judicial Landscape	207
11.	Red Monday	237
12.	"Exposure Purely for the Sake of Exposure" (Brennan in *Barenblatt*)	259
13.	Requiem for Precedents	287
Conclusion		307
Index		317

Introduction

This book proceeds from some commonly held assumptions: the belief that the tradition of law is deep rooted in the national mindset, that its operation, indeed its very vocabulary, defines the political community in which both people and parties exist, and that the law has played a pivotal role in giving meaning and cohesion to American society. Assuming that the law has had a profound role in shaping our identity and culture, this book explores over a half-century of court opinions in which the judiciary oversaw the law and its impact on the national culture. From the beginning, it was the Supreme Court that carved out a special niche within the judiciary and government. It would be the branch of government that clothed itself in the Constitution, with the definitive role of interpreting this Holy Scripture, including the First Amendment, defining its usage in the twentieth century.

Although on occasion lower federal court decisions will be reviewed, the primary focus will be on the High Court and the corpus of law regarding free speech over fifty-plus years. Seeking to do so, without a condescending oversimplification this study will at times present thick and in-depth examinations of cases that are of seminal importance. It seeks to draw out, in the context of fundamental rights, the significance of those rights prescribed in the First Amendment, especially that of free expression. It sees the Court as the central institution in reconstituting such rights and shaping the legal culture, and assesses whether and when it has nurtured or undermined such rights.

The story does not begin with the Founding Fathers, since the First Amendment that they authored made no appearance in case law before the 1900s and was not significant in free speech cases before World War I. But from that time forward, the reader will learn the evolving flux of First Amendment rights, how they came to maturity, how the judiciary (Justices Oliver Wendell Holmes and Louis Brandeis, in particular) initially breathed some life into the near-lifeless body of the First Amendment, and how a minority on successive tribunals came to see itself as a guardian of the rights of the people. Essentially a chronological account, this study will explore how the judicial majority, responding to the overwhelming convictions of the public and the political branches of government in a generalized atmosphere of crisis, affirmed existing curbs on free speech and how rarely did the justices become an anti-majoritarian voice within a system of majority rule.

Whether the matter at stake involved free speech for anarchists, socialists, pacifists, or communist defendants, the judicial majority's response to crises, on both state and federal level, occasions little surprise, because a recurrent response to the great national crises was duplicated in many courtrooms across the country. What becomes inevitable and central to our story is the two-fold explanation of why there should be no surprise, and how the protection of human rights and the perceived urgent need of the nation came into conflict and required adjudication, which is coupled with the judicial effort to find and maintain a balance between these intrinsically conflicting viewpoints. Such an effort was to be expected, David Low has observed, when courtrooms were besieged by cases freighted with conflicting interpretations and required to select among them. In a number of instances, this study will set forth judicial efforts to weigh cherished individual rights against social imperatives, such as the requirements of national security, two seemingly antithetical vectors in continuous conflict.[1]

This search for balance was established relatively early when Justice Holmes in 1919 unpacked the clear and present danger test in seeking to deal with speech that advocated unlawful action.[2] Implicit in his formula was an attempt to determine when limitations on free speech should be imposed and whether the strong presumption in favor of it should prevail over the alleged or possible threat to national security—by establishing the requirement of imminent danger as necessary to overcome the presumption. Reflecting the tenacious hold of this formula upon the judiciary, Justice John Harlan over a half-century later explored the balance "struck between that liberty ['liberty of the individual'] and the demands of organized society."[3] This balancing concept would constantly challenge courts to determine where to draw the line and when to permit or institute legal restraints on speech. In short, two seemingly antithetical vectors are in a constant tug-of-war, and it would create a great and lasting discord on federal tribunals, most pointedly on the High Court in legal controversies dealing with free expression.

The inclination to weigh competing interests to determine which should prevail would be undertaken by the Court on an ad hoc basis, and

Introduction

which competing necessity dominated depended on both the shifting sands of time and membership of the bench. Premediated decision-making, when confronted by crisis times, the reader will learn, usually did not uphold dissident speech, press, and persons, but came down in favor of draconian state and federal laws and prosecutorial zeal discouraging protection for such dissidence. Thus, before the climacteric of World War I, when labor violence and alien radicals seemingly threatened the social fabric, judicial antennae picked up vibrations of class struggle, and the law arguably became a most important means of social control, a function that Harvard's Dean Roscoe Pound has developed.[4] He was hardly unique in this regard. Three decades later, for example, Gerald Gunther states that Appellate Court Judge Learned Hand was very mindful of the world affairs—the Korean War, the Berlin Blockade due to the Cold War, etc.—rather than labor struggles influenced his weighing "the gravity of the evil" against the necessity of free expression.

Indeed, few judges and justices were unaware of the world outside their chambers. Consciousness of it in 1919 prompted Justice Oliver Wendell Holmes to observe that "the federal judges ... have gotten hysterical about the war."[5] And his colleague, Justice Louis Brandeis was fully aware of the parlous domestic social–political conditions at the time, comparing the nation's popular views to the Spanish Inquisition and the Know-Nothing movement of the mid-nineteenth century. He called the Red Scare a "disgraceful exhibition" of "hysterical, unintelligent fear."[6] And at the outset of the Cold War, Justice Hugo Black alluded "to the present climate of public opinion," a reference to the virulent anti-communism of that day.

Such recognition of outside social and political forces challenges the conventional understanding that the justices are presumed immune to or isolated from non-legal considerations, and expected to be neutral and obedient only to abstract legal and constitutional imperatives. They were not supposed to render decisions affecting speech or press on the basis of moral considerations, personal predilections, and/or popular reactions to the wisdom of free speech or press and/or conditions outside the courtroom. But to claim otherwise, to find that only impartial legal considerations determined the statutory or judicial outcome is a chimera. Accordingly, the crises background becomes a necessary component for the purposes of our story. Without context, examining the judicial search for a viable balance between individual freedom and social necessity would be to make the legal study abstract and unrealistic. Without it, then, one cannot understand why every

ix

state and federal statute aimed at curbing an alleged overseas menace passed the judicial balancing test across the first five decades of the twentieth century. Recognition of context, it follows, enhances the approach to civil liberties law and renders greater sense and clarity to the legal issues before us. Consequently, attention is given to legislators and administrators as well as the judiciary, to the impact of community norms and national public opinion upon judicial thought, including the role of foreign affairs as partially fathering such thought.

Non-judicial affairs abroad and at home, it follows, necessarily constitute the frame of judicial thinking. To offer one example, it becomes appropriate, when discussing Court decisions directly after 1918, to review the anti-anarchist and anti-socialist popular sentiment that ran rampant in American public culture prior to World War I. And it is likewise necessary to consider Lenin's dramatic return to Russia and the November 1917 revolution to fully comprehend the foundational impulse for America's post–World War I Red Scare that accompanied it. Nor is it a *non sequitur* to consider the fact that twenty-five years later, with Russia, the wartime ally restored as enemy of first resort, Cold War decisions by policy makers, and post-war events convinced the judiciary as well as the public that serious internal and external threats to national security abounded.

If the reader sets popular reactions and judicial rulings in such a historic framework, then the results are unsurprising, in fact preordained. It follows that a sensitivity to the historical background is clearly required. Disturbing news from abroad or critical opinion about the political branches of government was highly publicized and inevitably affected most Americans. Deviant opinions or behavior, or the threat of either, became "perceived as ... potentially hazardous to the social order, and its cherished creeds and symbols," as stated by McCloskey and Brill, and they enjoy little popular support. Only a relatively few Americans internalized First Amendment norms, especially in times of great or perceived crisis, whereas fear of radical conspiracy governed the popular culture. The urgent need to neutralize internal subversion and conspiracy shaped a set of cognitive limitations on protected rights that dominated the decades preceding and succeeding two world wars and that resonating through state and federal political branches. Considering the successive international crises, when the spores of radical ideology swirled around in the wind, most Americans, as well as the members of bench and bar, looked backward longingly to a simpler, more tranquil rural past, when Protestantism, conservative cultural and

Introduction

political values, and a simplistic hip-hop-hurrah view of democracy dominated. More pronounced in times of peril, these cultural imperatives push aside rational discourse and solidified a broad national consensus around democracy. It follows that popular hostility toward radicals, Communists, Communist sympathizers, and even liberal critics of American policies, was inevitable.

To elaborate, the Cold War was strikingly similar to the outbreak of European belligerency, whether in 1914 or in 1939, in that the old convictions reappear, *mutatis mutandis*, the belief that the nation is besieged from within as well as without a conspiratorial network of ideologues, spies, alien radicals, which would shred America's security and stability, and it fueled an extensive net of investigative practices and anti-subversion legislation on all levels of government. Could not the thoughtful student of these stressful times anticipate such activities and measures would carry the day?

In answering the question, there is on the one hand Justices William Douglas and Hugo Black who believed that social turbulence should not affect the First Amendment, and that the fundamental freedoms were not to be compromised. On the other hand, there were justices, such as Oliver Wendell Holmes and later, Felix Frankfurter and John Harlan, *inter alia*, who were not at all convinced that the constitutional scripture gave primacy to certain liberties like speech and, we will shortly learn, they would leave settlement of the question to the legislature, the body most directly representative of the people, rather than to the High Court. For these justices and their votaries, it was not their right or function to overrule harshly restrictive statutes, state, or federal. To do so, they believed, would mean going outside the traditional judicial boundary of the constitutional system. It would be to engage in "judicial activism," a scornful claim of those who argued that certain justices were intervening in the congressional realm of governance, and a term of opprobrium held by legal as well as political conservatives. Any other judicial activity, such as embracing a creative role, essentially a legislative function, was likewise considered anathema. For these avatars of deference to the legislature, their only function was to discover and apply "the law." They were simply to determine whether it comports with the Constitution.[7]

That the freedom to dissent consequently suffered disappointments and defeats in America's courtrooms is understandable. Judges, to reiterate, are human with human prejudices, J. A. G. Griffith reminds the reader.[8] They do not live in a social vacuum and are not inevitably neutral observers, impartially making legal decisions. They are at a far remove from being "mere instruments of the law," as Chief Justice John Marshall had contended.[9] The High Court, in its function to interpret and enforce the Constitution, tends to affirm preexisting legal concepts, and by so doing also imposes an element of social control. The majority of its members often tend to see themselves primarily as adjuncts of the law enforcement system rather than as protectors of our constitutional safeguards. They come to the bench with internalized ethical and moral considerations and prejudices. Furthermore, they come from a social and cultural background that reflected the conditions prevailing at home and abroad as well as in their life and work experiences. To provide substantive content to that arbitrary and governing motto of law, *Fiat justitia ruat caelum*, context is always critical. This phrase is no isolate. Judicial decisions are apt to be influenced by both context and conditions; and, accordingly most of its members were more likely to be prejudiced against certain alien and alienating elements in American society. Justice Benjamin Cardozo affirmed as much in his seminal law lectures. Legal precedents, he argued, were often abandoned, and other factors became primary factors in decision-making: the likes and dislikes of judges, the complex of instincts and emotions, habits and convictions that comprised them, be one the litigant, lawyer, judge.[10] Lawrence Tribe appears on the mark when contending that the Constitution "at every moment depends on extra-textual courses of meaning." The best that those on the bench can do is to maintain internal restraints on their preconceived biases.[11] Without denying the impact of analytical skills and judicial experience, it nonetheless may be argued that cultural and political attitudes are usually the best predictors of the outcome of a case.

Justice William O. Douglas, for one, phrased it admirably when offering up a futile admonition: "The problem of the judge is to keep personal predilections from dictating the choice and be as faithful as possible to the architectural scheme of the Constitution." But the prevailing ideology and political events combined to cast a large shadow over the bench. Those sitting on judicial tribunals, to reiterate, were men of their times and social culture, responsive to cultural and political opinions held outside their hallowed precincts—whether these opinions were those of government officials or of a popular majority. They were hardly cut off and immune from the national climate. Their interpretation of the law respecting speech was on the basis of personal views of its timeliness, virtues, and primacy in a given age. As Ronald Dworkin has cogently stated, they cannot say what the law is on most issues, without engaging their own viewpoints and principles, their own values of right and wrong, of what is just or unjust—rather than those embedded by the Framers or by *stare decisis* and earlier generations of judges.[12] And more often than not, affirming John Wirenius, they wove their own views of exigent social needs into the law in the guise of construing it. Sensitive to the atmosphere of chill across the decades under review, they inevitably heeded what Holmes once termed "the felt necessities of the time."[13] Over these years, court decisions reveal, the judges were men of their times, entwined in society and sharing its anxieties. Arthur S. Miller is startlingly direct when observing:

> Law is not "there," a separate and discrete entity apart from the warp and woof of society from which judges can select their basic principles in the sense that only one tenable principle exists. The corpus of law contains a multiplicity of premises ... It is not a science at all, but a series of temporary accommodations to deal with different situations.[14]

Because court chambers are not insulated from outside influences, popular opinion becomes an important signifier for the judiciary. Indeed, a symbiotic relationship between popular sentiments and judicial review may often be found, and as a result the courts were usually in accord with public views—or at least not antagonistic to them or far in advance of them. Consequently, the judiciary joined most Americans, especially in stormy weather, in perceiving radicals of every strain as a serious threat to the nation's security. To be sure, the court's response frequently came after the storms ended, after the guns of war had been silenced. But the shadows of war lingered and new threats seemed omnipresent. Hence, the response of the judicial majority would be to authoritatively *affirm* what had ever been the hegemonic legal, cultural, and community norms, those which in practice usually condemned rather than embraced diversity.

As to these norms, in 1950 for instance, Samuel Stouffer found that over seventy-eight percent of Americans would prohibit Communist Party members from the ballot and approximately seventy-five percent would prohibit them from speaking on the radio. In the mid-fifties, only twenty-seven percent of those polled would permit an admitted communists to speak in their community; only six percent would allow a communist to keep a job as a college teacher; nearly three-fourths would remove books written by a communist from the public libraries; over three quarters of the public would actually put him or her in jail; and the same percentile would report to the Federal Bureau of Investigation (FBI); "any neighbor or acquaintance" they suspected of being a communist. In effect, the First Amendment notwithstanding, the level of public tolerance of freedom of expression for unpopular or unconventional opinions is astonishingly low. In the early Fifties, only twenty-five percent of Americans would uphold the right of a public school teacher to express opinions that were opposed to those of the community. Unsurprisingly, well over half of Americans would refuse to hire a professor who held unorthodox political views.[15] Of greater significance for this study, judicial thinking and decisions reflected the national atmosphere of unreasoning apprehensiveness akin to panic were indicated by these startling figures.

Admittedly, there were occasional judicial voices truly and ungrudgingly committed to the maintenance of protected freedoms, although they were an endangered species, especially imperiled in times of international conflict. Louis Brandeis' observation, in a letter to a friend, "[d]uring a war... all bets are off," neatly encapsulated the judicial story. Consider how few judicial protestants there are on the bench in wartime or during the "war on terror," for which his quote remains appropriate. Clearly, this minority bloc on federal courts would respond in marked contrast to the neat and simple procedural formulas frequently offered by colleagues who intuitively understood that their primary function was to provide stability to the government. To reiterate, this should not suggest that acting in accord with the dominant social order reflected adversely upon their personal integrity. Indeed, we shall presently learn that there were occasions when the judicial breach had temporarily healed and a majority acted in defiance of the political branches and the popular will. By their sometime audacity, they rendered the federal bench a national adornment.

To observe that when great national crises confront us, the protection of protected rights and indeed fundamental legal principles tend to be eviscerated, may be seen in a more recent instance than that explored in the twentieth century. Consider, for example, the immediate response to the September 11 attacks, and the egregious popular and governmental surge toward conformity that it produced, taking the form of mass arrests of foreign nationals, and surveillance of Muslims, the compromised principle of individual culpability, that is, the proposition of guilt by association. Official and popular responses prompt a series of questions. Was not the reaction strikingly similar to the mass roundups, the preventive detentions, and deportations following the

Introduction

anarchist bombings of 1919? Did it not have a parallel to the secret hearings and deportations of radical and communist non-citizens three decades later? And in our time, were the warrantless wiretapping, suspensions of habeas corpus, secret trials, and deportations of Muslim aliens seemingly justified by the terrorist threat? Did not the preventive detentions of hundreds of Muslims after September 11 attacks have a striking parallel to the emergency detention provision of the 1950 McCarran Act? And do these federal actions, aimed at those having specific ethnic and religious affiliations, compatible with the Constitution? It prompts a complementary further question: would it not be the better part of wisdom to take an absolutist view of freedom of expression and assembly under the First Amendment rather than attempt to modify its unqualified language? May one not effectively argue that the court thereby departed from the Framers' blueprint for the governmental structure when qualifying this absolute mandate? Admittedly, and terrorism—excluding Stalin's application in Russia—was far more murderous than anarchism and communism (though in 1919, eight bombs were exploded by anarchists in eight different cities within the same hour). But, however inexact the parallel, the similarities remain striking.

In closing, it may be noted that the Founding Fathers had not been inclined to endorse populist views. To the contrary, they were on record as opposed to the *vox populi* and their understanding was that the Senate would function to impose limitations on democratic impulses. This tendency of the Framers prompts a further series of questions for us. Would they have affirmed or denied expansive protection to speech, even the speech of radicals and dissenters, and stand firm against the stormy oppositional popular climate? Would they do so in time of crisis when panic and similar emotions prevail? Would they, to use Isaiah Berlin's words, stand as a steadfast hedgehog among wavering foxes? Would they have approved the many political trials chronicled in this study? And do such trials have anything in common with celebrated earlier ones, such as that of Galileo in 1631? Or that of Joan of Arc in 1431? Or are such analogies hyperbolic and needlessly hypothetical?

Notes

1. David Law, "A Theory of Judicial Power and Judicial Review," *Georgetown Law Review* 97 (2009): 730. See also Barry Friedman, *The Will of the People: How Public Opinion Has Influenced the Supreme Court and Shaped the Meaning of the Constitution* (New York: Farrar, Straus and Giroux, 2009), 14.
2. Christopher Wolfe, *The Rise of Modern Judicial Review: From Constitutional Interpretation to Judge-Made Law* (New York: Basic Books, 1986), 193.

3. *Poe v. Ullman*, 367 U.S. 497, 542 (1961).
4. Quoted in Arthur S. Miller, *Toward Increased Judicial Activism: The Political Role of the Supreme Court* (Westport, CT: Greenwood Press, 1982), 314, n. 26.
5. Holmes to Laski, March 16, 1919, in Mark de Wolfe Howe (ed.), *Holmes-Laski Letters: The Correspondence of Mr. Justice Holmes and Harold J. Laski, 1916–1935* (Cambridge, MA: Harvard University Press, 1953), 190.
6. Brandeis to Susan Goldmark, December 7, 1919, in Melvin Urofsky and David Levy (eds), *Letters of Louis D. Brandeis* (Albany, NY: State University of New York Press, 1971–1978), IV, 444.
7. Among many possible examples of judicial deference, see Justice Harold Burton's clear affirmation of the doctrine in *Duncan v. Kahanamoku*, 327 U.S. 304, 66 S. Ct. 606, 90 L. Ed.688 (1946). On Congress "making" the law, see Miller, *Toward Increased Judicial Activism*, 33, n. 23.
8. J. A. G. Griffith, *The Politics of the Judiciary* (Manchester, UK: Manchester University Press, 1977), 31.
9. *Osborn v. Bank of the United States*, 9 Wheaton (22) U.S. 738, 6 L. Ed. 204 (1824). For the contrasting view, see ibid. Martin Shapiro touches on this argument in the *Courts: A Political and Comparative Analysis* (Chicago, IL: University of Chicago Press, 1981), 26–30.
10. Andrew Kaufman, *Cardozo* (Cambridge, MA: Harvard University Press, 1998), 215–21.
11. Ibid., 209.
12. G. Edward White, *Earl Warren: A Public Life* (New York: Oxford University Press, 1982), 359. See also Ronald Dworkin, *Freedom's Law: The Moral Reading of the American Constitution* (Cambridge, MA: Harvard University Press, 1996).
13. Oliver Wendell Holmes, Jr., *The Common Law* (Boston, MA: Little, Brown and Company, 1881), 1.
14. Miller, *Toward Increased Judicial Activism*, 113. On judges as influenced by the political branches as well as events around them; see also Miller, *Politics, Democracy and the Supreme Court: Essays on the Frontier of Constitutional Theory* (Westport, CT: Greenwood Press, 1971), 275.
15. Herbert McClosky and Alida Brill, *The Dimensions of Tolerance: What Americans Believe about Civil Liberties* (New York: Russell Sage Foundation, 1983), 54, 56, 74–7. See also Samuel Stouffer, *Communism, Conformity and Civil Liberties: A Cross-Section of the Nation Speaks Its Mind* (New York: Doubleday, 1955).

1

Nationalism and War: The Casualties

The dawning of the twentieth century set the stage for events of a half-century later and for shifting views of the First Amendment. On September 6, 1901, a self-proclaimed anarchist shot and killed President William McKinley. Although five European heads of state had been anarchist victims in this decade, it was only his assassination that aroused the nation's press and public. Inflammatory articles reminded readers that anarchist newspapers existed in their country and described nests of bomb throwers as being on the loose across America. Leon Czolgosz, the assassin, was a U.S. citizen, but he had a foreign-sounding name, which was sufficient cause for public and political outrage.

Recollections of the 1886 Haymarket bombing and riot were not out of the nation's memory and would shortly be recalled by the attempt of a young Russian-born anarchist, Alexander Berkman, to murder Henry Clay Frick, magnate of the Carnegie Steel empire. His highly publicized court trial in the summer of 1892 was not out of memory, and the public once more reawakened to the presence of radicalized aliens like him in its midst. The radical actions of immigrants, first targeted in 1797 and 1798 with the Alien and Sedition Acts, would be associated after 1900 with the 1886 bombings, the militant labor actions of Jewish socialists and German social democrats in Chicago, New York, and other major cities, and with radical aliens in the late nineteenth century. Nativist organizations, it inevitably follows, revived and highlighted the menace.

The High Court, as emphasized, was hardly insulated from public apprehensions. Oliver Wendell Holmes recognized as much even before being elevated to the Supreme Court. The idea that the law was neutral and that judges impartially imposed it, which was written by him in 1873, "presupposes an identity of interest between the different parts of a community which does not exist in fact."[1] Fifteen years later, a High Court Justice, Samuel Miller affirmed as much when he warned the graduating class of the University of Iowa that radicals of every persuasion "come here and form clubs and associations; they meet at night and in secluded places; they get together large quantities of deadly weapons; they drill and prepare themselves for organized warfare; they stimulate riots and invasions of the pubic peace; they glory in strikes."[2] Hardly suggestive of judicial impartiality, but understandable in Miller's day when society remained overwhelmingly rural and homogeneous; and characterized by traditions of stable family life, familiar religious conventions, and seemingly unchanging social values—which appeared to be threatened by a growing number of strangers and strange tongues and customs.

In short, public suspicions of radical aliens were predictable. They were always simmering just below the surface of a seemingly durable and emotionally comfortable social and political culture. The presidential assassination understandably trumped tolerance and was followed by actions of local law enforcement as well as ramped up federal efforts to deport suspect aliens. Considered bomb throwers after Haymarket and now assassins, anarchists were beaten and jailed, their homes raided, and their newspapers banned from the mails. The leading voices of American anarchism, Emma Goldman, known as "Red Emma," and Johann Most, a leading German editor, were arrested; many others were immediately deported. New York State enacted the nation's first anti-anarchy, anti-sedition law, the Criminal Anarchy Act of 1902, which made it a crime to advocate in speech or writing "the doctrine that organized government should be overthrown by force or violence ... or by any unlawful means." After defining criminal anarchy, the statute embellished it by warning: "Whenever two or more persons assemble for the purpose of advocating or teaching, the doctrines criminal anarchy ... such an assembly is unlawful ... and every person voluntarily participating therein by his presence ... is guilty of a felony."[3]

Under the statute, Johan Most, the head of the anarchist, violently anti-capitalist International Working People's Association and publisher of *Morgen Freiheit*, was found guilty of slander and endangering the public peace—in *State of New York v. John Most* (*People v. Most* (1902))—and his conviction upheld by the State's Court of Appeals.[4] His newspaper had published an article entitled "Murder for Murder," advising revolution and murder. The article, to be sure, had appeared a half-century earlier in *Pioneer*, a Boston newspaper, but was republished on September 7, 1901, the day President McKinley was shot, unfortunately for Most. The article shouted: "We say murder the murderers, save humanity, through blood and iron, poison and dynamite." All government is founded on murder, it proclaimed, and revolutionary forces sometimes have an obligation to kill "a professional murderer." To urge the death of government officials was too much for any judiciary to accept. Maintaining the familiar distinction between "free" speech and its "abuse," the trial court swept aside defense counsel's free-speech argument and found the article to be outside the limits of constitutionally protected expression. The above observation that judges hold human prejudices and also seek to maintain pre-existing social rules becomes immediately evident in the New York State Court of Appeals. Judge Parker Vann, for four colleagues, upheld trial court conviction in what was a precursor of judicial things to come: "The Constitution [does not] … sanction unbridled license, nor authorize the publication of articles prompting the commission of murder or overthrow of the government by force."[5]

In response to the menace posed by radical aliens and sweeping public apprehensions, Congress enacted an immigration law in 1903, the first to impose a political test for entry into the United State. It prohibited entry to "anarchists, or persons who believed in or advocate the overthrow by force or violence of the Government of the United States or of all government or of all forms of law," the template for the deportation of radical aliens as well as anti-communist and anti-radical measures in future decades.[6] Even "peaceable" anarchists—that is, philosophical anarchists—were barred from entry. Congress would expand this statute in February 1917 and would prohibit the entry not only to those who advocated overthrow of the government by force and violence but also to persons who "advocated the unlawful destruction of property, disbelieve[d] in or [were] opposed to organized government," or belonged to organizations having such views; that is, the principle of guilt by association.[7] President Wilson himself displayed a near-phobic concern about those aliens who "poured the poison of disloyalty into the very arteries of our national life," but refused to sign the measure because it included a literacy test provision. Congress, however, passed it over his veto. The statute itself was largely consistent with Wilson's view of anti-war dissidents. In his June 14, 1917, Flag Day address, he warned opponents of the war: "For us there is but one choice. We have made it. Woe be to the man or group of men that seeks to stand in our way on this day of high resolution …"[8] States other than New York enacted measures similar to its 1902 anti-anarchy statute.

In 1903, for example, Wisconsin and New Jersey enacted identical statutes, the same year that Congress wheeled into action. But alien radicals were not always dissuaded from entry into the United States by multiple anti-radical measures. Many Russian immigrants, for one, flocked to the United States after the failure of 1905 Russian Revolution against the Czar. Freed from traditional community restraints and the conservative authority of their rabbis, they often carried Marxist texts in their trunks and would become active in American labor's struggle for the eight-hour day.

The legal profession shared the ultra-nationalist and anti-alien sentiments of pre-war American society. The president of its major professional society, the American Bar Association, would argue that newcomer and citizen alike, "are enjoying the privileges and protections afforded by residence here, [and] should be taught in no uncertain way that they have no right to place America and American institutions second to any other nation ... on earth."

Reflecting this antagonism to radical aliens, the Court upheld the 1903 immigration statute in a case of the following year, *Turner v. Williams* (1904). It would affirm the deportation order of John Turner, an English alien anarchist, notwithstanding the efforts of legendary defense counsel, Clarence Darrow and Edgar Lee Masters. The literature in Turner's possession upon being arrested indicated an intent to speak with Johan Most on the subject of the Haymarket "legal murder of 1887." Turner's defense had argued that the government violated the First Amendment, but the Immigration Board of Special Inquiry judged him "to be an alien anarchist" and ordered deportation, and the Court would find that Congress clearly had the power to exclude anarchists.[9] Judge Learned Hand sustained this view in yet another case, one involving a philosophical anarchist. "One is as much an anarchist," he contended, "whether one adopts as means rant and gunpowder as rational persuasion and the inner light."[10]

The evils of anarchism were hardly alone in inciting public apprehension. Most Americans indiscriminately lumped socialists with anarchists and saw a symbiotic relationship between them, notwithstanding the fact that Socialist Party candidates would run for municipal and state office and sought only moderate reform measures rather than revolution; and even though Socialists, like all putative followers of Karl Marx—including the communists who appeared on the scene over a decade later—did not espouse bombings and terrorist tactics. Socialists, to enlarge on this salient distinction, argued that the true Marxist did not assassinate and believed that social problems could not be solved by individual acts of terror. Though not rejecting violence, they repudiated terror as a viable tactic of revolution. However, to repeat, this difference was entirely too fine-spun for the great majority of Americans, who equated Socialists with anarchists and with the Industrial Workers of the World (IWW). IWW members, the so-called Wobblies, differed from the anarchists in that their activities occurred primarily in remote venues—the wheat fields, copper mines, logging areas, and textile mills—far from the larger cities where anarchists and socialists found lodgings and where the highly publicized anarchist bombings would take place. An organization of unskilled, disenfranchised, and degraded migrant workers, among the most derelict elements in the Western communities, had been founded in Chicago in June 1905, and its Preamble read in part: "The working class and the employing class have nothing in common .... Between these two classes a struggle must go on until the workers of the world organize as a class, take possession of the earth and machinery of production and abolish the wage system."[11] Toward the goal of organizing the unorganized into "One Big Union," the IWW approved any militant direct action—strikes, slowdowns, sabotage—that seemed tactically appropriate. Unlike the Socialist Party and its program of "political action," IWW weapons were strikes and industrial sabotage; that is "direct action" toward the end of abolishing capitalism and the wage system. Its members considered patriotism an "idiotic and perverted" idea, and their 1916 convention deplored the European conflict and declared IWW members were "determined opponents of all ... patriotism and the militarism preached by our enemy, the capitalist class."

A genuinely radical organization, the IWW militancy aroused local vigilantes, agents provocateurs, and federal and state officials long before American declaration of war. Because of their success in strikes and in organizing workers, and because they opposed any American involvement in the overseas conflict, the IWW came to be considered a danger to the nation itself. It was unsurprising, then, that in September 1917, federal agents, with President Wilson's approval, raided IWW headquarters in Chicago and other cities, frequently without search warrants, and seized tons of evidence that would be used to prosecute over a hundred top IWW leaders on sedition and espionage charges. Robert Murray described what would be the popular national reaction to the IWW anti-war position: "Not bothering to separate fiction from truth, the American public now shrieked at the I.W.W. Patriotic societies called them 'traitors' and 'agents of Germany.'"[12]

Accordingly, the Wobblies joined socialists and bomb-throwing anarchists in the popular imagination, all considered synonymous and equally menacing. In this indistinct amalgam, they embodied the "enemy" and the "outsiders" and stereotyped as immoral and evil, in contrast to the "good" citizen who fought for the just cause. Under statutes in 1903 and 1906, for example, an alien's attachment or alleged attachment to the IWW—not even membership!—was sufficient pretext for denial of citizenship, for deportation, and for exclusion. Witness, for instance, the cases of *Guiney v. Bonham* (1919), *United States ex rel. Diamond v. Uhl* (1920), *United States ex rel. Rakics v. Uhl* (1920). To be expected, citizens and aliens alike, if Wobblies were forced to kneel and kiss the flag before being driven out of strike-bound cities in Pennsylvania and West Virginia. IWW and Socialist Party meetings were regularly broken up, their halls closed in numerous municipalities, and their literature burned in street bonfires (e.g., Cincinnati); and both state and federal actions resulted in mass arrests and the conviction of ninety-seven of its leading officers, all such actions helping to transform the IWW into a weak, defensive organization by 1917.[13] By then, the Wilson cabinet had determined to destroy it, mobilizing the Army as well as the Justice Department in this campaign. Harry Scheiber tells us "that almost all districts reporting high incidences of prosecutions" in federal district and state courts; and they were those in which the Wobblies were active.[14] In short, the Wobblies had become a prime target of that "ruthless brutality" that Wilson, as noted earlier, had worriedly predicted upon being interviewed.

A similar threat to conservative and patriotic values was posed by the Non-Partisan League, a powerful Midwestern organization of agrarian socialists. Opposed to the war, its leaders, Arthur Townley of North Dakota and Joseph Gilbert of Minnesota, were accused of having declared: "We were stampeded into this war by newspaper rot to pull England's chestnuts out of the fire for her. I tell you, if they conscripted wealth like they have conscripted men, this war would not last over 48 hours."[15] Not surprisingly vigilantes across the Midwestern states attacked League partisans and broke up League meetings, and the organization's leaders and members were indicted and convicted.

Until 1919, the Supreme Court did not directly address First Amendment issues emerging out of such arrests and convictions or out of the federal and state governmental actions. It is hardly surprising—for a number of reasons. First, the justices understood their function as deciding only "cases and controversies" and not debate legal abstractions. Second, until the post-war years, the First Amendment was thought to offer only limited protections, following an established legal canon found in William Blackstone's influential Commentaries on the Laws of England of 1770; namely, the common law right of free speech and press was a right within the limitation of "laying no previous restraint upon publications," but not "freedom from censure for criminal manner" upon publication. It meant that the government could not only prevent speech or press but could also punish after the fact if what was expressed was considered dangerous or offensive. Third, the Latin maxim, *silent leges inter arma*—in war, the laws are silent—contributed to the mix, and the belief that radical ideas heard and discussed in wartime was simply unacceptable to the three branches of government and to the public. Before World War I, little commentary on the meaning of free speech could be found. Until then doctrinal exegesis of case law simply codified existing common law and afforded protection only against prior government censorship of expression.

Lacking strongly held convictions about protections guaranteed by the First Amendment, judicial departure from the tradition did not commence for nearly a decade after the wartime years. Federal courts and the executive branch at times admittedly did wrestle with the issues of protected speech and press when the Sedition Act of 1798 was being enforced and again in the antebellum years, when abolitionist printed matter was prohibited from the mails. But until the post-war years, Harvard law school professor Zechariah Chaffee accurately observed that "nobody knew what the First Amendment did or did not protect." Speech and press were generally considered private matters at that time, Paul Murphy observed; that is, they involved interpersonal relations and not government-to-citizen relations. However, these freedoms would become ex officio public policy questions in wartime, with the assaults on socialists, pacifists, and alien radicals, and reached the High Court in the form of wartime convictions under federal and state anti-sedition laws; and only then were a scattered few dissenting judges and justices who felt obliged to try establishing viable standards for free expression issues coming before them.[16] The great majority considered themselves as arms of the state, to reiterate, and hence the results were predictable. They affirmed convictions—on grounds defendants were hindering or conspiring to hinder the draft law, oppose the "capitalist classes," and preach the forcible destruction of the established order.[17]

Intolerance toward dissenters before World War I, or in August 1914, when war broke out in Europe or, for that matter in April 1917, when the United States entered the conflict, characterized the nation and the political branches. Woodrow Wilson immediately recognized that it would simply intensify existing patriotic rhetoric and encourage calls for the suppression of anti-war sentiments. Fully aware that war could desensitize Americans in regard to fundamental rights, he famously predicted, speaking to his friend Frank Cobb of the New York World on April 1, 1917, a week before the congressional declaration of war, "[o]nce lead this people into war, and they'll forget there ever was such a thing as tolerance. To fight you must be brutal and ruthless, and the spirit of ruthless brutality will enter into the very fiber of our national life, infecting Congress, the courts, the policeman on the beat, the man in the street."[18] Conformity would be the norm, he expected, and the non-conformist would have to pay the penalty. He thought that free speech and the right of assemble would go: "a nation couldn't put its strength into a war and keep its head level; it had never been done."[19]

Although very aware of the consequences of war, Wilson did not throw the great moral force of the presidency into any effort to quiet public fears of the internal enemy. At times, to be sure, he sought to restrain wartime excesses.[20] And he sympathized with the plight of those who were victims of mob actions, writing in 1918: "I have very great passion for the principle that we must respect opinion even when it is hostile."[21] Wilson was inconsistent, however, believing the speeches and writings of left-wing Socialists (not moderate and centrist Socialists who were aligned with Wilson on the war issue) who opposed America's participation in the war to be "almost treasonable." Making no distinction between talk and action, he found dissenters and critics of the war identical to spies and saboteurs. Two of his immediate predecessors joined him. Indeed, both Theodore Roosevelt and the normally cautious William Howard Taft would go further in the severity of their response. They criticized the administration for its, feeble counter-espionage efforts, and urged that spies and traitors be apprehended and shot.

Presidential rhetoric would contribute significantly to the popular animosities directed against pacifists (commonly known as "slackers"), "Wobblies," German–Americans, Irish–Americans, indeed all hyphenated Americans, and socialists. Attuned to presidential and popular sentiments, Congress enacted a new Alien Act in October 1918 that enlarged upon the body of immigration laws dating from 1903 to 1917 and reflected the deeply engrained anti-immigrant sentiment. Directed specifically at anarchists seeking to enter the United States, it and reflecting historic anti-immigrant sentiments, it provided for the deportation of those already in residence, it went to the extreme length of finding any alien deportable "who, at any time after entering the United States, is found to have been at the time of entry, or to have become thereafter," a member of any anarchist organization. The measure would in effect criminalize "disloyal" anarchists, under the assumption that they were dangerous—to the nation and the war effort. It would also take deportation proceedings out of the hands of aggressively overreaching sheriffs in western communities and bring it under the federal government. A sign of the popularity deportation may be seen in the anti-alien sentiments that crowded the pages of the nation's press. Or in the tidal wave of petitions calling for deportation or imprisonment of aliens that bombarded the offices of State governors, such as that of New York's Alfred E. Smith, the petitioners being apparently unaware that immigration policy was under federal jurisdiction.

The President's plea "to enact such laws" as would have "creatures of passion, disloyalty and anarchy ... crushed out," was warmly received by a Congress that shared the nation's fearful concern for disloyalty. The actual declaration of war in April 1917 saw a qualitative leap in the nation's xenophobia and ultra-nationalism that eased the way for passage of the Espionage Act, a measure Wilson had proposed and was partly responsible for ramming through Congress in June 19, 1917.[22] An amalgam of seventeen bills prepared in the Justice Department, the statute's Title I, Section 3 read: "Whoever, when the United States is at war, shall wilfully [sic] cause or attempt to cause insubordination, disloyalty, mutiny or refusal of duty in the military or naval forces of the United States, or shall wilfully obstruct the recruiting or enlistment service of the United States, to the injury of the United States, shall be punished by a fine of $10,000, or imprisonment for not more than twenty years, or both" for each separate offense. By implication, consequently, it would be criminal to declare that conscription was unconstitutional or find that war was contrary to the teachings of Christ. Individuals, organizations, and publications were prosecuted on the grounds of "intent" to persuade disloyalty. In fact, indictments were lodged against nearly 2,000 people, though only 877 were actually convicted, many of whom received harsh sentences: thirty sentenced to twenty-year prison terms and seventy to ten-year terms. Under Title XII of the measure, materials "advocating or urging insurrection, or forcible resistance to any law of the United States" were banned from the mails that gave the Postmaster General complete discretion to determine all mailable matter and which power, it will shortly be seen, he used extensively and enthusiastically. Nor were radical publications alone proscribed. Those of the National Civil Liberties Bureau (forerunner of the American Civil Liberties Union) were also denied second-class mailing privileges, and the Bureau itself would become the object of a Justice Department investigation.

Wilson then pressed Attorney General Gregory to implement the statute, though he did not require encouragement. Indeed, he believed some aspects of the measure unsatisfactory in that it failed to reach casual or impulsive "individual disloyal utterances." The White House agreed and requested Montana Senator Thomas Walsh to tighten the earlier act. Modeled after Montana's criminal syndicalism law, his 1918 amendment to the Espionage Act, the so-called Sedition Act, was equally harsh and repressive. It extended the government's power to proscribe seditious speech and press, regardless of whether such statements had direct unlawful consequences.[23]

The Espionage Act applied to anyone who should obstruct the sale of United States bonds, "willfully utter, print, write, or publish any disloyal, profane, scurrilous, or abusive language about the form of government of the United States, or the Constitution ... or the flag ... or the uniform of the Army or Navy ... or bring about the form of government ... or the Constitution ... into contempt ...." It was not necessary, therefore, for the government to prove that the language was false; only that it was "disloyal, scurrilous, profane or abusive." Not only persons but also things—the Constitution, the flag, the uniform of the army and navy—could be considered seditious. Not actual, tangible evils produced by utterance, but the tendency of such utterance to produce the evils, could be presented as a proof of the event. Nor were the statutory penalties trivial. The measure also made it illegal to give "disloyal advice" regarding the sale of Liberty Bonds, advocate "any curtailment of production" of materials necessary for the "prosecution of the war," or "favor[ing] the cause of any country with which the United States was at war." Nor was it necessary to commit an overt act. As Walter Gellhorn states: "[m]ere advocacy alone which is likely to incite is the essence of the crime."[24] Considering the 1918 Sedition Act and its severe penalties, it seems only natural to affirm David Cole's harsh assessment, in writing about sedition measures generally: they crossed the line from non-citizen to citizen—"both 'hyphenated' naturalized citizens... and native-born pacifists, socialists, and critics of conscription."[25]

International affairs deeply influenced the domestic scene. The high drama of the Russian Revolution almost immediately competed for attention with news from the Western front. The Bolsheviks not only concluded a separate peace with Germany in March 1918 (the Brest–Litovsk Treaty) but also immediately advanced the idea of worldwide proletarian revolution. Because the early Bolsheviks believed that their survival in Russia depended on alliance with revolutions elsewhere, Moscow in March 1919 organized the Third International, the Comintern, as the world-wide revolutionary spearhead and for a time it seemed to have considerable success.[26] Post-war Germany was racked by revolutionary sentiment; Hungary went over to revolutionary government; Polish and Italian conditions were promising for a socialist future. At home, America's socialists were re-energized by events out of Moscow, and Party membership jumped by a third between the summer 1918 and the following year. The results were predictable. Fantasies of revolution and invasion filled the movie screens and the press and seeded the shrill chauvinism of wartime America. The spectacular events in 1917 in Petrograd, and the alarming events following upon it stimulated the already apprehensive popular imagination. Popular fears of Russian secret agents infiltrating "all of great cities ... insidiously spreading the propaganda of terrorism and revolution" appeared in *Everybody's Business* of 1919. American moviegoers in 1920, in *The Penalty*, viewed 10,000 armed foreign workers, ready to fire on the police and take over San Francisco at the Kremlin's call for world revolution.

Considering the qualitative jump in ultra-nationalist sentiments triggered by war and revolution, it could be anticipated that governmental statutes and actions would not only powerfully reinforce public opinion but also influence state lawmakers and confer legitimacy on their own measures. Wrapping themselves in Old Glory, they were driven to a wartime repression unknown in previous eras—with one exception, the actions of Lincoln and his officials during the Civil War. As Robert Murray has calculated, at least 1,400 persons were arrested under state sedition, criminal syndicalist, and Red Flag measures around World War I, of whom over 300 eventually received prison terms.[27] Their imprisonment often did not get notice outside the local community and resulted from actions of those communities and state officials who sought to maintain Anglo-Saxon verities.

Thirty-five similar state measures were enacted proscribing opposition to the war or specifically targeting the IWW and syndicalist groups. The latter, having relatively few adherents, proposed to bring industry and government under the control of labor unions—by means of direct action, such as the general strike and sabotage. Minnesota, for one, spurred by IWW labor actions against companies in the Mesabi range, passed a criminal syndicalism bill that received a sixty-one-to-one approval by the State legislature. Idaho, long besieged by violent mining and lumber labor struggles led by the Western Federation of Miners and the IWW, approved anti-sabotage and anti-criminal syndicalism statutes. Montana and South Dakota passed similar statutes during wartime. Other states also testified to the temper of the times. The 1917 Iowa Sedition Act, a model for other states, prohibited attempts to incite insurrection or sedition. The State governor issued an edict that "conversation in public places, or trains, or even the telephone should be in the English language." Connecticut's sedition statute punished public advocacy of "any measure, doctrine, proposal or propaganda intended to injuriously affect the [State] government"; or that in Rhode Island which prohibited language intended to incite a "a disregard of the [State's] constitution or laws"; and the May 1919 Massachusetts statute provided a three-year prison term for anyone who "by speech ... or printed document, paper, or pictorial representation advocates, advises, counsels ... the overthrow by force or violence of the government of the commonwealth."

Considering what had become the working popular assumptions, Americans inevitably exaggerated the number of domestic radicals and, as could be expected, applauded the efforts of government agencies fighting the Red Menace. Foremost among these agencies was the Bureau of Investigation (BI) and its newly organized special anti-radical General Intelligence Division (GID) as well as the Justice Department itself. But other government agencies also remained very active in saving America from the Reds. The State Department, for one, watched over both homegrown radicals and German–Americans and monitored their travel. It denied passports to communists after the 1917 Bolshevik Revolution, and after the United States "became aware of the scope and changes of the worldwide revolutionary movement and the attendant purpose to overthrow all existing governments, including our own."[28] Army and navy intelligence agents also continued their surveillance of suspects.

The Post Office Department, guided by its ever-vigilant Postmaster General, Albert Burleson, whose understanding of the Espionage Act, Title XII, its "Use of Mails" section, authorized him to bar or censor publications requiring second-class mailing privileges when they violated the terms of the statute. Then, too, such publications should not "be conveyed in the mails or delivered from any post office or by any letter carrier." Burleson believed that the measure empowered him to invoke the ban when an offending issue of a publication "begins to say that this Government got in the war wrong, that it is in it for wrong purposes, or anything that will impugn the motives of the Government for going into the war. They cannot say that this Government is the tool of Wall Street or the munitions-makers .... There can be no campaign against conscription or the Draft law ..." In this spirit, any publication that opposed the war became fair game for suppression. President Wilson advised Burleson to "act with utmost caution." The Postmaster General, however, expressed an insouciant disregard for presidential advice, and Wilson yielded, writing, "Well, go ahead and do your duty."[29] Their relationship is suggested in a presidential memo on a matter concerning newspaper censorship: "I must admit that I haven't been able to read all of the enclosed, but you know that I am willing to trust your judgment after I have once called your attention to a suggestion."[30] Presidential approval was consistent with his contention that Burleson had been "most conservative" in exercising his power of censorship over Socialist publications.[31]

Vested with great discretionary authority, Burleson would incautiously and vigorously implement Title XII, and some seventy-five papers either lost their second-class mailing privileges in 1917, which would be a death-blow to many radical papers, or retained it by agreeing to print no words concerning the war; and of them forty-five, perhaps more, were socialist publications. In actuality, the Post Office interfered with about 100 publications, though the precise number is not known. We do know that though Burleson promised that postal regulations would not be political, the legislation was enforced against socialist, radical, pacifist, labor, liberal, German–American journals, and newspapers. That is, the act was applied most rigorously to small and comparatively unknown publications, those unable to register an effective protest. Solidarity, the organ of the IWW, was banned from the mails, as were issues of the American Socialist, *Pearson's Magazine*, *The Crisis*, the *Truth Seeker*, etc. An issue of *The Nation* magazine was denied mailing because of an article criticizing Samuel Gompers, the AFL leader who supported the war effort. "A Voice in the Wilderness" was refused mailing privileges and when circulated under a different name ("I Cannot Tell a Lie"), its editor was arrested. Two issues of *Four Lights*, a journal edited by women who submitted proofs to lawyers, to make certain that they were within the law, was, however, denied, and one of the numbers was banned even before the Espionage Act had been signed into law. Freeman's Journal and Catholic Register were banned from the mails for printing a statement by Jefferson asserting that Ireland ought to be free. The Jeffersonian, a weekly published by the old Populist leader, Tom Watson, was denied the mails in August 1917 because it allegedly advocated disloyalty and treason.

The issues of two major socialist publications, the *New York Call* and the *Milwaukee Leader*, had repeatedly criticized the war and conscription and were banned from the mails in November 1917 under terms of the Espionage Act. Their editors were required to go into the court and show cause why their publications should not be denied second-class mailing privileges. Counsel for the *Milwaukee Leader* then filed a *writ of mandamus* to annul the Post Office order and restore plaintiff's second-class mailing privilege. The lower courts dismissed their petition. Judge Robb, in the Court of Appeals of District of Columbia in 1919,[32] affirmed what would become a familiar refrain: "For three months at least, applicant's publication has been injecting subtle poison into the public mind 'with intent'" as found by the Postmaster General, "to interfere with the operation or success of the military or naval forces of the United States." Branding it "a hostile or enemy publication," he declared: "we are not disposed ... to extend to it the benefits of this equitable remedy [i.e., the *writ of mandamus*]."

The case did not come up to the High Court until three years after the war, when the tribunal, like the trial court, upheld the Postmaster General. Justice John Clarke speaking for the majority—in *United States ex rel. Milwaukee Social Democratic Publishing Company v. Burleson* (1921)[33]—would cite judicial precedents, the Schenck, Debs, and Abrams decisions, presently to be explored, affirming the Espionage Act's constitutionality. Devoting the bulk of his opinion to the claim that the Postmaster General had thus denied freedom of speech and press, Clarke argued that Burleson's statutory authority allowed revocation of the second-class permit. Any newspaper in violation of the statute should be considered "non-mailable": "This is neither a dangerous nor an arbitrary power." After all, Clarke stated that the Postmaster General was able to quote more than fifty editorial excepts during the first five months of the war declaring "the war was unjustifiable," "a capitalist war," "dishonorable on our part" and found that the draft law was "unconstitutional, arbitrary, and oppressive." Undoubtedly, Clarke declared that these articles conveyed false reports and false statements with the intent of promoting the success of America's enemies and giving them aid and comfort.[34]

Considering the First Amendment's ambiguous usage at the time as well as a political climate sharply critical of all dissent, Burleson seemingly had ample legitimacy for Post Office restrictive actions that were also directed against *The Masses*, specifically the August 1914 issue. Suffering the same restrictive fate as the *Milwaukee Leader*, this lively, confrontational and irreverent "monthly revolutionary journal" was vehemently opposed to the war. Its editors, Max Eastman and John Reed in particular, attacked the Allied cause and then American involvement and editorials against militarism and the draft dotted its pages. In a decision supported by Burleson, the magazine was denied mailing privileges by the New York City Postmaster (Thomas G. Patten) under Title I Section 3 of the newly enacted Espionage Act—because of three offenses: making "false statements with intent to interfere with the operation or success of the military or naval forces ... when the United States is at war"; "causing or seeking to cause insubordination" or "refusal of duty" in the military forces; obstructing "the recruiting or enlistment service of the United States."

The offenses charged to the editors were demonstrated by reference to three objectionable articles, four anti-war cartoons (with such heads as "Making the World Safe for Capitalism," etc.), a poem in praise of Alexander Berkman and Emma Goldman, both prominent radicals then in prison, as well as four textual passages that, taken together, opposed the war as imperialistic, denounced the draft, and upheld conscientious objectors. The printed matter of the August 1917 issue, the government argued, caused, or attempted "to cause insubordination, disloyalty, mutiny or refusal of duty in the military or naval forces." Accordingly the issue was deemed "non-mailable" under terms of the Espionage Act and denied second-class mailing privileges. *The Masses* editors went into federal District Court to request a preliminary injunction that would enjoin the postmaster from excluding the offending issue from the mails.

Learned B. Hand, a "skeptical liberal" as Gerald Gunther aptly termed him, had been appointed to the U.S. District Court for the Southern District by President Taft in 1909. Presiding in the case *Masses Publishing Co. v. Patten* (1917),[35] he would grant the injunction sought by the magazine. It was a daring and controversial decision, considering that *The Masses* was a proclaimed "revolutionary" journal. Hand's action openly opposed the dominant anti-radical political climate, and it helped to establish his reputation as a great American jurist. Not immediately acknowledged, however. Indeed, Gunther observes that he was passed over for promotion to the Circuit Court of Appeals because his opinion was so unpopular at the time.

No radical or Bohemian himself, Hand had upheld the Allied cause and America's entry into the war. But he valued freedom of expression to an extent that made him virtually unique among federal judges in this regard. Dismissive of the poem and cartoons at issue, he would not concede the four passages of text under scrutiny "counsel others to follow these examples ... There is not the least intimation in these words that others are under a duty to follow." Hand acknowledged that the cartoon and text in question might "enervate public feeling at home ... and encourage the success of the enemies of the United States abroad," as the government claimed; but Hand was as dismissive of both cartoons and text. "Could any reasonable man say ...", he asked, "that the language [in *The Masses*' text] directly advocated resistance to the draft?"[36]

Though admitting the possible causal relationship between a speaker's censorious words and illegal actions, Hand was struggling with a thorny distinction, one that would challenge judges and legal scholars for decades to come, namely, how far may speech go in criticizing the government. Criticism, after all, can readily segue into a disposition to resist lawful authority, even when this was not the initial intent. At issue was "balancing"; that is, where the line was to be drawn or, more precisely, how to define seditious speech, speech that incites action. Hand went to great lengths in an effort to distinguish between "agitation, legitimate as such," and "direct incitement to violent resistance"—which was not protected speech—because to do otherwise "is to disregard the tolerance of all methods of political agitation which in normal times is a safeguard of free government"; and while not citing the First Amendment or raising the issue of constitutionality, Hand went on to argue that "[i]f one stops short of urging others that it is their duty or their interest to resist the law, it seems to me one should not be held to have attempted to cause its violation." Applying this standard to the case, he found no direct advocacy of illegal action. Upon considering "the general tenor and animus of the paper as a whole," he readily admitted that it was "subversive to authority and seditious in effect." But dismissing this aspect of the prosecution's Brief, Hand forcefully declared that "[t]he tradition of English-speaking freedom has depended in no small part upon the merely procedural requirement that the state point with exactness to just that conduct which violates the law." This principled and assertion, it should be noted, came from a judge who readily conceded broad powers to Congress in wartime, and believed the Espionage Act to be a necessity.[37] But he was compelled by the need to isolate incitement from vigorous criticism and writes in what Harry Kalven termed a "very great sentence": the distinction between political agitation and incitement "is not a scholarly subterfuge, but a hard-bought acquisition in the fight for freedom."[38]

Applying these criteria to the facts of the case, Hand held that the words themselves had not plainly urged others to follow the resisters' example and the contents of this issue of *The Masses* had not crossed the line into "express advocacy of unlawful conduct." Burleson's action "in so far as it involves the suppression of the free utterance of abuse and criticism of the existing law, or of the policies of the war, is not, in my judgment, supported by the language of the statute." Plaintiff, then, was entitled to the preliminary injunction that had been sought.

The full Circuit Court of Appeals for the Second Circuit concluded in November 1917[39] that "the natural and reasonable effect of the publication" was willfully to obstruct recruiting; and even though we were not convinced that any such intent existed, the tribunal deferred to the government "in a doubtful case."[40] Hand's test—judging words by what they say—would not become the law of the land for a half-century. At the time it was not adopted by the judiciary and not one lower federal court decision to censor a paper or journal during World War I would be reversed.

Notes

1. Oliver Wendell Holmes, "Summary of Events—The Gas-Stokers' Strike," *American Law Review* 7 (1873): 582, 583.
2. Quoted in David Cole, *Enemy Aliens* (New York: The New Press, 2003), 108.
3. New York 4 Penal Code 1881, Section 468, Chapter 371.
4. *The State of New York v. John [Johann] Most* (*People v. Most*, 171 N.Y. 423, 64 N.E. 175 (1902); 128 N.Y. 108, 115, 27 N.E. 970, 972 (1891)).
5. For a prior conviction of Most for unlawful assembly in a speech about the Haymarket Massacre, see *People v. Most*, 128 N.Y. 108, 27 N.E. 970 (1891).
6. 32 Stat. 1213, 1214 (1903). See also Cole, *Enemy Aliens*, 107 and Robert Goldstein, *American Blacklist: The Attorney General's List of Subversive Organizations* (Lawrence, KS: University Press of Kansas, 2008), 2.
7. 39 Stat. 889 (1917); see also Cole, *Enemy Aliens*, 109 and Harry Scheiber, *The Wilson Administration and Civil Liberties, 1917–1921* (Ithaca, NY: Cornell University Press, 1960), 26.

8. *Public Papers of the Presidents of the United States—Woodrow Wilson* (Washington, DC: Government Printing Office, 1961–66), V, 67. [Presidential Papers hereinafter cited as PP]. See also Harriet Peterson and Gilbert Fite, *Opponents of War, 1917–1918* (Madison, WI: University of Wisconsin Press, 1957), 149. See also *Turner v. Williams*, 194 U.S. 279, 292 (1904).
9. *Turner*, 194 U.S. at 279.
10. *Ex parte Caminita*, 291 F. 913, 915 (S.D.N.Y. 1922). In yet another deportation proceeding, *Ex parte Pettine*, 259 F. 733 (D. Mass. 1919), the defendant advocated an anarchism as "understood by Tolstoi, Marx, Ferrer, Zola, Kropotkin and many others"; that is, the court in effect did not distinguish between a philosophical form of anarchism and advocacy of violent actions.
11. Robert Murray, *Red Scare: A Study of National Hysteria, 1919–1920* (New York: McGraw-Hill, 1955), 29–30, n. 3. See also Melvyn Dubofsky, *We Shall Be All: A History of the Industrial Workers of the World* (Chicago, IL: Quadrangle, 1969) and William Preston, *Aliens and Dissenters: Federal Suppression of Radicals, 1903–1933* (Cambridge, MA: Harvard University Press, 1963).
12. Peterson and Fite, *Opponents of War*, 66, 49–64, and passim.; see also Scheiber, *The Wilson Administration*, 48.
13. 261 F. 582 (9th Cir. 1919); 266 F. 34 (2d Cir. 1920); 266 F. 646 (2d Cir. 1920). For the astonishingly long list of those named political prisoners, many of them members of the IWW, convicted for violation of federal and state laws, and who served prison terms of over one year between 1917 and 1924; see Stephen Kohn, *American Political Prisoners: Prosecutions Under the Espionage and Sedition Acts* (Westport, CT: Prager, 1994), 83–176.
14. Scheiber, *The Wilson Administration*, 51.
15. Quoted in Richard Polenberg, *Fighting Faiths: The Abrams Case, The Supreme Court, and Free Speech* (New York: The Viking Press, 1987), 269.
16. For example, see *Haywood v. United States*, 268 F. 795 (7th Cir. 1920); see e.g., William Day, in *Wilson v. New*, 243 U.S. 332, 37 S. Ct. 298, 61 L. Ed. 755 (1917) flatly stated: "no emergency and no consequence, whatever their character, could justify the violation of constitutional rights."
17. For example, *Isenhouer v. United States*, 256 F. 842 (8th Cir. 1919); *Reeder v. United States*, 262 F. 36 (8th Cir. 1919); *Anderson v. United States*, 269 F. 65 (9th Cir. 1920).
18. Ray Stannard Baker and William Dodd (eds), *Public Papers of Woodrow Wilson* (New York: Harper & Brothers, 1925–1927), VIII, 102–3.
19. Quoted in Peterson and Fite, *Opponents of War*, 14.
20. Carl Brent Swisher, "Civil Liberties in Wartime," *Political Science Quarterly* 55 (no. 3) (1940): 321–47.
21. Baker and Dodd (eds), *Public Papers*, V, 67.
22. 40 Stat. 217 (1917); 40 Stat. 553 (1918). Fund for the Republic, *Digest of the Public Record of Communism in the United States* [hereafter cited as Digest] (New York: Fund for the Republic, 1955), 188., 189.
23. 40 Stat. 217, 219 (1917); 40 Stat. 553 (1918). See also Polenberg, *Fighting Faiths*, 3–34; Murray, *Red Scare*, 23; Murphy, *The Meaning of Freedom of Speech: First Amendment Freedoms from Wilson to FDR* (Westport, CT: Greenwood, 1972b), 22; Scheiber, *The Wilson Administration*, 17–26; and Digest, 188.

24. Walter Gellhorn (ed.), *The States and Subversion* (Ithaca, NY: Cornell University Press, 1952), 397.
25. Cole, *Enemy Aliens*, 114.
26. Ernest Volkmann and Blaine Baggett, *Secret Intelligence: The Inside Story of America's Espionage Empire* (New York: Doubleday, 1989), 87. The Comintern (Communist International), founded in London in 1864 under the leadership of Marx and Engels, continued to exist through conflicts, challenges, resignations, and expulsions.
27. Murray, *Red Scare*, 23.
28. Brief, *Aptheker v. Secretary of State*, citing "Refusal of Passports to Communists," State Department Memorandum, May 29, 1956, quoted in Appendix B, 82–4, in Landmark Briefs, vol. 60.
29. PP Wilson, Editorial Notes, 48, 148, n. 3.
30. Quoted in Baker and Dodd, *Public Papers*, VII, 165, n. 1.
31. Quoted in Scheiber, *The Wilson Administration*, 39. See also PP Wilson, Editorial Notes, 49, 420.
32. *United States ex rel. v. Milwaukee Social Democratic Publishing Company v. Burleson*, 258 F. 282 (1919).
33. 255 U.S. 407 (1921).
34. Ibid., 413–5. Both editors were indicted and tried twice for violation of the Espionage Act, but each trial ended in hung juries, the majority favoring conviction.
35. 244 F. 535 (S. D.N.Y.), *rev'd*, 246 F. 24 (2d Cir. 1917), 119.
36. Ibid., 540, 541.
37. Ibid., 542–3.
38. Harry Kalven, *A Worthy Tradition: Freedom of Speech in America* (New York: Harper & Row, 1988), 130. See also David Rabban, *Free Speech in Its Forgotten Years, 1870–1920* (Cambridge, UK: Cambridge University Press, 1997), 265.
39. *Masses Publishing Company v. Patten*, 245 F. 102 (C.C.A. 2d 1917).
40. Ibid.

2

Post-War Harvest: "Traitors to America"

The story of security eclipsing liberty does not end with the statutory provisions of the 1917 and 1918 Espionage and Sedition Acts. For one, there were the many peacetime sedition laws (that failed to pass)—no less than seventy!—introduced in the 1919–1920 congressional session. We will presently learn how state lawmakers and local patriots likewise pressed for post-war anti-subversion statutes, and how self-appointed private monitors continued to contrive possibilities of social revolution. However remote the danger, governmental actions as well as private vigilantism persisted into the post-war years. In short, the wartime syndrome continued, from campaigns for local laws to restrict radicalism, to the efforts of local offshoots of national organizations like the National Security League, the American Defense Society, and the Daughters of the America Revolution (DAR), whose leaders assailed "disloyal" teachers and whose members "took a firm and active stance against all forms of attack ... against our national society." Veterans organizations, such as the American Legion, founded in 1919, held Americanization campaigns. Detroit's Legionnaire post, for example, bragged that it had "one thousand Bolshevik Bouncers" at the end of the war, a boast joined by super patriots and red hunters everywhere. Emphatic popular approval greeted these activities, methods, and measures, since public unease persisted long after the 1917 Armistice. It was easily redirected from Germany to the newly formed Soviet Union and then swept from Moscow to Hungary, Austria, Bulgaria, and Italy, nations in which workers seized factories and revolutionary actions had occurred. The growth of radicalism and revolutionary sentiments touching much of the Europe re-energized America's anti-radical forces—as well as America's radicals and, to reiterate, Socialist Party's membership jumped by a third in the year following mid-summer 1918.

The numerous federal agencies hardly ceased in their surveillance of radical, labor, pacifist, labor unions, and efforts to halt the spreading "disease of evil thinking." The Secret Service, founded in 1865 and the oldest federal investigative agency, was still very effective in apprehending alleged spies and saboteurs. The Bureau of Investigation (BI), forerunner to the General Intelligence Division and Federal Bureau of Investigation (FBI), was a more recent player in the domestic investigative game, though only at the time of World War I. Created by executive fiat in 1908, and operating within the Justice Department, the BI was under J. Edgar Hoover, a twenty-four-year-old Georgetown University Law School graduate and the Bureau's assistant director thirteen years after its founding. He became permanent director on May 9, 1924, and his agency would be the primary governmental force seeking out disloyal aliens and citizens. The Bureau's powers would expand in wartime, as could be expected, with Hoover overseeing its extensive investigatory operations—by means of wiretapping and mail intercepts, seizure of membership and financial records of radical groups, and physical surveillance of radical meetings and leaders. That BI practices received widespread newspaper approval reflected its growing success as a powerful propaganda apparatus, and its capacity to invigorate governmental efforts to shape public opinion.

The anti-radical hysteria that gripped the country would be heightened by a wave of post-war strikes involving over four million workers. They were often IWW-sponsored, such as the Seattle walkout of 35,000 shipyard workers, whom Seattle's mayor, Ole Hanson, accused of wanting "to take possession of our American government to duplicate the anarchy of Russia." The strike produced sensationalist newspaper copy and was joined by a general strike of 60,000 workers in Seattle that further electrified Congress and the nation. Six months later, 365,000 of the nation's steel workers walked out, with a strike of miners following them, and they were described by the *New York Tribune* as "red-soaked in the doctrines of Bolshevism, clamoring for the strike as a means of syndicalizing the coal mines ... and even starting a general revolution in America." The Senate swung into action with the Overman Judiciary Subcommittee hearings to determine if the ranks of labor were infected by Bolsheviks, and its final report fed public fears of labor radicalism, nourished by newspaper bold-type headlines: "Red Peril Here" "Plan Bloody Revolution," and so on. The *Los Angeles Times* response was typical. It argued that the steel and coal strikes "mark two of the offenses of the Bolshevist plotters who are trying to smash the American Republic, destroy the Constitution and set up a Soviet government on the ruins."[1]

J. Edgar Hoover's reaction became paradigmatic for legislators as well as for the police: "[c]ivilization faces its most terrible menace of danger since the barbarian hordes overran Western Europe and opened the Dark Ages." During the coal strike, on November 7, 1919, his agents secretly raided the New York headquarters of the little-known Union of Russian Workers, as mentioned above. Its 4,000 members somehow constituted a serious threat to the nation, and those in the New York region were arrested, in the course of which a large quantity of printed matter was seized. Hoover's response was to urge disbarment of the New York lawyer who made the information public. And *The New York Times* applauded "the alacrity, resolute will, and fruitful intelligent vigor of the Department of Justice in hunting down these enemies of the United States."[2]

Americans uncritically identified Communists and Wobblies, as they had anarchists and syndicalists a decade earlier, and the IWW continued to be the target of extensive assault during peacetime. A District Court judge in one 1920 case critically described "a reign of terror [against] Montana's Wobblies, after employers' hirelings, joined by federal agents and soldiers, 'several times'" raided an IWW hall, "and orderly meetings ... without warrants." There was no disorder save that of the raiders. Mainly uniformed and armed, they overawed, intimidated, and forcibly entered, broke, and destroyed property, searched persons, effects and papers, seized papers and documents, cursed, insulted, beat, dispersed and bayoneted union members by order of the commanding officer.[3]

The extended description is typical of the tempo and strenuousness of anti-Wobbly actions, which jumped qualitatively after the United States had entered the European conflict, owing to Wobbly pacifism and anti-capitalist rhetoric. Arrests, trials, and convictions occurred in Kansas, Washington, Idaho, and Minnesota, among other states, often for mere membership. Witness, for instance, the aforementioned Chicago trial of the IWW leadership initiated by the Attorney General in April 1917. It was one of the four great, mass IWW trials others being in Omaha, Sacramento, and Kansas City—with arrests, indictments, and trials also occurring elsewhere.

The ninety-six defendants in Chicago, the most prominent being William "Big Bill" Haywood, the IWW leader, would be indicted for conspiracy to violate or obstruct twelve U.S. statutes, including

Section 3 of the 1917 Espionage Act. They would be "convicted and sentenced on each of four counts of an indictment for conspiracy to violate, or to obstruct the execution of sundry laws of the United States" (see note 16, Chapter 1). The jury deliberated only fifty-five minutes before bringing in a guilty verdict against all defendants, including some without any substantive evidence against them and two who were not even IWW members. Kenesaw Mountain Landis, presiding judge in the Chicago case, *Haywood et al. v. United States* (1920),[4] would find the jury could reach no other decision. In what was the recurrent judicial theme, he declared: "In times of peace you have legal right to oppose, by free speech, preparations for war. But when once war is declared, that right ceases," and he delivered sentences ranging from one to twenty years in prison. In the *Sacramento* case, mass indictments against the IWW members were also based on their writings and not on any violent actions.[5] All forty-six defendants were found guilty, with twenty-four receiving ten-year sentences and lesser terms for the rest. The press and influential periodicals across the country hailed the convictions and sentences, thereby joining as well as influencing popular opinion.

Shocked by the developments at home and especially overseas, Americans watched fearfully as the Red Menace moved westward across Europe. They knew intuitively and via buzzwords in the daily tabloids that Soviet state organs had been commissioned to promote subversion elsewhere and not simply within the European nations. Patriotic societies and the media, exaggerating the dangers of the Soviet scourge for Americans, feverishly denounced the Bolsheviks, now considered counterparts to the hated Huns. Overheated rumors of a radical conspiracy against the United States, one hatched in Moscow and resonating domestically—and many believed that a Red Revolution could occur at home in the immediate post-war years.

Adding to the hyperbolic mix of press reports and editorials, bomb scares and the actual bombings of the homes of judges, businessmen, even Attorney General Palmer's, intensified public apprehensions. These were further exacerbated by the discovery of a plot to assassinate some thirty-eight governors, judges, cabinet members, and other public officials as well as financial leaders (e.g., John D. Rockefeller and J.P. Morgan); and newspaper columns also shouted descriptions of the Wall Street bombings where a very lethal bomb, planted by "American Anarchist Fighters" (according to a handbill), exploded with devastating impact opposite the House of Morgan on Wall Street. Mail-letter bombings occurred almost simultaneously in eight cities. Blazing one-inch headlines, announcing these events to startled readers, provided ammunition for those who attributed them to the lurking shadow of Bolshevism on American shores.

To be sure, Lenin and his new government did not favor terrorist tactics and the literature found at several bombing sites made it apparent that anarchists were responsible. Moreover, only a handful of anarchists were involved. Nonetheless, descriptions of these bombings contributed to local mob actions directed indiscriminately against all radicals (the ACLU estimated at least fifty instances of vigilantism in 1919), and a surge in national apprehensiveness and clamor for governmental action by a public that readily believed a vast radical conspiracy was in the works. Newspaper readers approvingly learned about the sailor who shot a man three times for refusing to stand when the national anthem was played at a victory loan pageant. They learned that army veterans invaded immigrant social centers, forcing everyone present to sing "The Star Spangled Banner," and they read reports of riots in New York and Cleveland and commended patriots and police who attacked radical May Day marchers—or indeed anyone considered insufficiently patriotic. The American Protective League, for one, ended all socialist meetings in Michigan and Minnesota. In short, extra-legal actions by mobs and pressures for conformity remained the norm in post-war America.

As to be expected, Congress and the White House made their contributions in 1919. The Subcommittee of the Senate Judiciary Committee, for instance, turned from investigating German propaganda to Bolshevik influence in America. The Kremlin, so went one alarmist comment at a Subcommittee hearing, was attempting to unravel America's social fabric by smuggling gold into this country. After hearing such testimony from mostly imaginative anti-Bolshevik witnesses, the Committee concluded that domestic Bolshevism was an immediate danger to the nation. The president also continued his anti-Red campaigning during his fight for ratification of the Treaty of Versailles and the League of Nations. He warned of the "poison ... running in the veins of the world" and the "apostles of Lenin in our midst."[6] Other notable Americans contributed to the paranoid style. Thus the out-sized figure of Theodore Roosevelt, in his last public message of January 1919, declared "there must be no sagging back in the fight for Americanism merely because the war is over .... We have room for but one flag, the American flag, and this excludes the red flag, which symbolizes all wars against liberty and civilization." Portending things to come, the Red Flag remained a major trope and Roosevelt's message continued to echo for later generations of Americans.

So effective and so overwhelming was this depiction of domestic affairs that the strident hearsay reports of a radical conspiracy against the United States seemed entirely credible and reached deep into America's culture and consciousness. Best sellers like George Kibbe Turner's *Red Friday*, Thomas Dixon's *The Red Dawn*, and Booth Tarkington's *Poldekin* offered compelling pictures of communist subversion for ordinary readers. Similarly did a string of alarmist films such as *Bolshevism on Trial*, *Look Out for the Snake*, *Common Property*, and *The Red Virgin* added to popular fears of labor and foreign-born radicals; and conversely, organizations like the National Security League and American Defense Society instilled respect for patriotism and the flag. Attorney General A. Mitchell Palmer in 1920 confirmed the worst anxieties. Politically opportunistic and virulently anti-Communist, he organized raids against radical groups. The New York-based Union of Russian Workers was the primary target of the first drive in November 1919. The larger drives of January 2, 1920 that followed was directed at two tiny anarchist bodies, having a combined membership of thirty-seven, as well as the IWW, the Communist Party, and the Communist Labor Party (the last two being factions followed upon the split of the pro-Bolshevik membership in the Socialist Party). The second single night round up of January 5, 1920, resulted in some 5,000 arrests in thirty-three cities and nearly a thousand convictions came from violation of the Espionage and Sedition Acts. Supposedly dealing with menacing revolution and revolutionaries, the two raids turned up a total arsenal of three pistols. Nonetheless, the President, at times mildly paranoid, strongly supported his Attorney General in what became among the most audacious and repressive governmental operations in the nation's history.

Those arrested in January 1920 were not charged with complicity in the terrorist bombings of 1919, but with being members (or suspected members) of the radical organizations in question or for utterances that allegedly had earlier obstructed wartime recruitment or caused military insubordination. Round-up practices included entering and ransacking homes (without search warrants), pulling people out of their houses and off the streets, confiscating letters and literature, and invading labor union headquarters.[7] Emphasis was placed on guilt by association or on advocacy—for example, the possession of radical literature as prima facie evidence of subversive belief or intent—rather than criminal complicity, not unlike prosecutorial charges in litigation decades later. The entire post-war raiding led to a total of nearly 10,000 taken into custody. Some were revolutionaries; many belonged to one or another organization simply out of a desire for companionship and support from fellow-speaking members, but the fact of membership led to their arrest. Though the majority of detainees (ca. 6,500) were ultimately released, they had been held incommunicado and subject to drumhead trials. Of those convicted, citizens or aliens, many were communists, especially from New York, Illinois and California, and they drew sentences ranging from one to five years. Three thousand aliens would be deported.

In describing the raids, the Attorney General portrayed those picked up as having "sly and crafty eyes ... lopsided faces, sloping brows and misshapen features" which hid "cupidity, cruelty, insanity and crime." In all likelihood, the xenophobic portrait was shared by a great majority of his countrymen, who gave the raids widespread support, especially since they were simultaneous with the wave of strikes in the immediate post-war years. Typical of newspaper reactions to governmental actions, *The Washington Post* asserted: "There is no time to waste on hairsplitting over infringement of liberty." Likewise typical, a small town paper, the *Norwood [MA] Messenger* approvingly headed one editorial, "The Justice of Deportation." Ordinary citizens, reading these reports, were convinced the radical menace to be very large and very dangerous. For them, a "radical" was a term interchangeable with a person engaged in bombing attacks or being a Wobbly or union member, or a Bolshevik, or simply someone in opposition to one's beliefs, whatever these might be; and a "Bolshevik" was not simply one who held to Marxism or Leninism, but a person opposed to your personal convictions, broadly defined. Only a comparatively few Americans would not share Palmer's portrait of the victims of the raids or the raiding itself. Harvard's Zechariah Chafee, for one, has written: the raids were "the greatest executive restriction of personal liberty in the history of this country."[8] Finally, it should be observed, the raiding was done broadly, a departure from individual culpability. Moreover, as David Cole has recognized, such government-legitimized vigilantism would become a recurrent feature of law enforcement in crisis times.

Shortly after the Palmer raids, national attention focused on the "Red Special" the train carrying a number of the alien radicals who had been picked up in the raids. It would speed those from the West Coast and Midwest to Ellis Island for deportation, together with others arrested in the cities of the Northeast. Many of the deportees would file petitions in federal courts that blocked expatriation, though Palmer had already managed to deport 249 radicals in December 1919, mostly Russian anarchists, under the broad authority of the October 1918 Immigration Act. The vessel carrying them sailed to Finland under sealed orders, which further stimulated the already aroused public imagination. Contrary to exaggerated press reports, the passengers were an obscure lot, except for Alexander Berkman and Emma Goldman.

Palmer's Justice Department was hardly the only governmental player in the anti-Red game, and mentioned above were various other federal agencies involved in investigative and anti-radical practices. The State Department, for example, continued its practice of denying passports to Communists and Wobbles. A November 1920 memorandum of the Under Secretary of State recommended that passports be refused to persons who fall within any of the following categories.

(1) Any person who counsels or advocates publicly or privately the overthrow or the bringing about of reforms or changes in organized Governments by force ...
(2) Any person who actively espouses the cause of the Soviet Government either through public expression or by the distribution or dissemination of Bolshevik propaganda.

And a few days later, these recommendations were implemented by the December 1920 State Department instructions declaring that it would refuse passports to a broad array of radicals, among them: "Citizens who are anarchists; citizens who believe in or advocate the overthrow by force or violence of the Government of the United States or of all forms of law; citizens who disbelieve in or are opposed to all organized government ...."[9]

Encouraged and reinforced in these certitudes by the federal government's actions and announcements, and assaulted by panicked headlines about the mail bombs and the actual bombing on Wall Street, a broad array of community ordinances from Los Angeles to Mt. Vernon, New York, served to convict radicals for actions that ranged from distributing handbills to holding outdoor meetings without obtaining permission. These measures were usually consistent with state statutes against sedition, criminal anarchy, or criminal syndicalism. Between 1917 and 1921, about two-thirds of the states, often without a single dissenting vote in their legislative chambers, endorsed such measures. Red Flag Laws were among them, triggered by the color of the Russian flag and the red banners that dotted May Day (May First) parades of militant labor and radical groups. Opposing these symbols of subversion and rebellion, state legislators in thirty-three states had passed "red-flag" measures by 1921, making it a crime to display a Red Flag or banner "distinctive of bolshevism, anarchy, or radical socialism," or any "anti-governmental" sign or symbol showing sympathy toward America's enemies. This wording, in a 1919 Iowa statute, was virtually identical to proscriptive Red Flag measures in Illinois, Indiana, Kansas, Kentucky, New Mexico, New York, North Dakota, and Michigan that passed between 1919 and 1921, the only substantive variation being in time served and fines levied upon conviction.[10] It resulted in hundreds being arrested for simply marching in parades waving such banners.

In one year alone, 1919, no less than twenty state legislatures passed anti-anarchy, anti-sedition, criminal anarchy, criminal sedition, and conspiracy statutes. They made it a crime to advocate, publish, teach, advise, or in any way further any doctrine promoting the use of force to bring about social or political change. Idaho, the first state to have such a statute, served as a model for other states, as had Iowa's 1919 anti-sedition law, punishing attempts to incite insurrection, or to advocate the subversion or destruction of the State or federal governments.

Criminal syndicalism, defined as the use of force and violence to change the political and industrial order, was also the target of state laws. California's 1919 statute, for one, triggered a number of State prosecutions. It punished anyone who advocated "crime, sabotage, [or] unlawful acts of force or violence ... as a means of accomplishing a change in industrial ownership or control." Criminal liability was attached not only to the act of personally advocating violence but also to that of knowingly becoming a member of an organization that advocated, taught, or aided and abetted violence. The statute resulted in 108 arrests by the end of that year, and over 160 by 1924 for violating the statute, including many organizers and active members of the IWW, and convictions were upheld in at least a dozen cases.

California's criminal syndicalism law as well as Nevada's were modeled upon New York's criminal anarchy law of 1902, the date suggestive of the persistence of such proscriptions. The criminal syndicalist laws in other states were patterned on California's or Idaho's, though a number of state legislatures—for example, Colorado, Iowa, and Montana—took the 1917 Espionage Act or the 1918 Sedition Act for inspiration, since these federal measures conferring an aura of legitimacy for state lawmakers. Colorado's statute, for one, prohibited persons to "advocate, teach, incite, propose, aid, abet, encourage, advise" injury to property by force or violence "either as a general principle or in particular instances, as a means of affecting governmental, industrial, social or economic conditions."[11] Montana's 1918 statute was virtually a copy of the 1918 Federal Sedition Act of that year. By 1921, thirty-five states and two territories (Hawaii and Alaska) as well as cities across the nation had enacted criminal syndicalist statutes or proscriptive loyalty oath and Sedition Act, statutes, in responsive to the post-war national fears about anarchism, communism, and a Red conspiracy to overthrow the government.

Robert Murray has estimated that between 1919 and 1920 about 1,400 were imprisoned under one of another state syndicalist or state sedition law and 300 ultimately convicted.[12] Many of those arrested were socialists, their newspapers were closed down, their meetings banned, their local halls across the country ransacked by mobs, and some 1,500 of their locals were destroyed. The IWW members and radicals, generally, were not far behind them in the numbers apprehended. The anarchists may be added to this despised sorry lot of radicals. They were probably guilty of the bombings in urban centers, but numbered a pathetic few in these cities. Of them, William K. Flynn, Chief of the BI, boasted that "there is not an anarchist haunt in this country that is not under Federal or local surveillance," a fact he could also have trumpeted a decade earlier, suggesting the enduring anti-radical concerns of federal officials. Finally, the parties of the left were weak. Socialists had bitterly divided on the war itself, and the moderates controlled the August 1919 Party convention—which produced a schism, as noted above, and the bolt of the anti-war left-wingers who formed the Communist Labor Party in August 1919, and another wing, the Communist Party, in September 1919. All this discord in radical ranks made the danger of social revolution exceedingly remote in 1919, yet the Wilson administration acted as if it was imminent.

State attorneys general, holding to the same belief, were most vigilant in apprehending under state statutes any number of communists, socialists, Wobblies, trade unionists, anarchists, pacifists, or radicals.[13] A stream of state prosecutions followed, with the usual convictions. Montana's 1918 Sedition Statute, for one, produced convictions in three cases. Two were for anti-war speeches, and one, *Ex parte Starr* (1920),[14] for refusal to kiss the American flag (and the defendant received a ten-to-twenty-year sentence). An appellate court upheld conviction based on the allegations that the petitioner had sold Communist Party literature and belonged to an organization "indirectly associated" with the Communist Party. State prosecutions were also upheld by the courts in post-war Michigan, California, New York, New Jersey, and Texas, where prosecutions were successful under the State "Disloyalty Act," though some convictions were reversed.[15] At times, it needs be acknowledged, trial outcomes could be spotty: occasional acquittals and reverses for error or insufficient evidence. Possibly more significant than the results of the trials themselves, however, was the fact of their occurrence, revealing the manifold instances of local anti-radical hysteria sweeping post-war society.

The obscure and the unknown comprised most of those arrested and convicted across the nation. However, there were some notable figures among them. The well-known Socialist Party (and later communist) official, Charles Ruthenberg, would be indicted under the Michigan Criminal Syndicalism Act (and under a federal measure in a federal court proceeding on another occasion, shortly to be described). An early Communist Party leader, Ruthenberg had attended a secret national convention near Bridgman, Michigan, and was one of the sixteen arrested. He would be charged with assembling with the Communist Party to advocate syndicalist doctrine, an indictment that itself reflects the mass confusion existing nationally over radical doctrine: syndicalism and communism being by definition starkly different. On appeal, the court upheld the District Court and found that the state measure was not contrary to the First and Fourteenth Amendments or to the Michigan Constitution.[16]

Illinois' 1919 Sedition Act offers another useful example of State prosecutions. It provided legal grounds for a large raid on January 1, 1920, with several hundred arrested, including thirty-nine largely unknown communists as well as the prominent IWW leader, William D. Haywood, and the radical, Rose Pastor Stokes. Twenty were convicted, in *Stokes et al. v. United States*,[17] for advocating the forceful overthrow of the State government. Stokes herself had affirmed, in a letter published in *The Kansas City Star*, "I am for the people while the government is for the profiteers," and she referred to the United States "as a capitalistic form of government which oppresses the poor and enriches one class at the expense of another." Reason enough to indict her. "Attempt to cause insubordination, disloyalty, mutiny ...," read one count in the indictment; another was obstructing the recruiting and enlistment service of the United States. A ten-year prison term was the predictable outcome. Yet one more Illinois case, *People v. Lloyd* (1922)[18] occurred after eighteen were charged with conspiracy under the 1919 State measure for advocating the overthrow of the government by force and violence. The defendants, the most radical elements in the Socialist Party, had attended the Party's Convention of June 1919, and adopted a platform, program, and an organization for the Communist Labor Party. They also voted to affiliate with the Communist International (Comintern), organized that same year in Moscow, and pledged agreement with its principles. The State introduced evidence, in the form of their speeches and writings showing their belief in "revolutionary industrial unionism"; that is, unionism not merely "to strengthen the status of workers as wage earners, but to gain control of industry"—in essence the definition of syndicalism. The legendary lawyer, Clarence Darrow for the defense, argued for free speech and assailed the prosecution's position, but the jury would bring in a verdict of guilty as charged.

Before leaving the immediate post-war court scene, it warrants mention that perhaps the most notable of anti-radical campaigns on the state level occurred in New York. Neither state nor federal courts were involved. The State's lawmakers, having an enviable popular reputation for being in the forefront of anti-sedition measures, passed six laws directed primarily against the Socialist Party and its adherents. Four of these measures, the so-called "Lusk laws," were named after Clayton R. Lusk, chairman of the Joint Legislative Committee to Investigate Seditious Activities, a newly established anti-radical body reflecting a local campaign grounded in the same hyperbolic anxieties and fears triggering the national Red Scare. Agents of the Committee, acting under the State's Criminal Anarchy Act and accompanied by the State Police, raided radical and alien organizations between June 1919 and February 1920. Some seventy-three "Red Centers," including the offices of the IWW and the Union of Russian Workers were targeted.[19] One raid alone seized 500 suspects (that of November 1919) and tons of their files. The aliens among those arrested were immediately turned over to federal authorities for deportation. Additionally, New York Governor Alfred E. Smith ordered a special session of the grand jury to hear charges against those arrested at the time of the raids as well as afterwards, and sixty-seven were eventually indicted.

In a final turn of the screw, the 1920 State legislative session went to the extreme of denouncing five of their members as socialists: "evil-disposed and pernicious persons" with "wicked and turbulent dispositions," and charged them with advocating the violent overthrow of the State government and circulating the Party manifesto. Prominent leaders of the Socialist Party's left wing they were accused of being "elected on a platform that is absolutely inimical to the best interests of the State of New York and of the United States," and they were expelled from the assembly, an action applauded by *The New York Times* as "an American vote altogether, a patriotic and conservative vote ... clearly and demonstrably a measure of national defense as the vote of Congress in declaring war against Germany. And an immense majority of the American people will approve."[20] To add an ironic codicil, these five legislators were members of the bitterly divided Socialist Party's "right-wing", that is, "the conservative branch that sought to introduce socialism by peaceful, parliamentary means – unlike the left wing" that demanded a revolutionary solution.

There were more than a few federal court decisions that upheld the defendant.[21] However, a good number of them closed with guilty verdicts where a defendant refused to register for the draft, owing to socialist or conscientious objector convictions, or opposed the war or sending troops to France. Most of those indicted and convicted were hardly well-known. They were ordinary Socialist Party members and followers. One obscure Connecticut defendant was convicted in 1920 for asserting Lenin was "the brainiest" or "one of the brainiest" political figures in the world.[22] And another for proclaiming in a "loud voice" that the draft law was unconstitutional.[23] Jacob Bentall, for instance, was a Minnesota socialist who opposed sending men to fight abroad and charged that the Morgans, Carnegies, and Schwabs had caused the war—for which speech he was found guilty and received a five-year prison sentence. Confirming the basis for his conviction, the Attorney General said it was a result of the defendants' continued claims that the war had been caused by big business and financial interests.[24] Conviction, usually under Section 3 of the Espionage Act, resulted when a defendant wrote that obedience to conscription "constituted involuntary servitude." Or when one stated "[t]hat the United States Government in the prosecution of said war was corrupt and controlled by the moneyed interests."[25] Or announced: "A Christian ought not and should not fight," "do not shed your precious blood for your country," for which sentiments the speaker was convicted and received a fifteen-year prison term. Or distributed a pamphlet asserting the horrors of war: "Lo, the price you pay! Lo. The price your children will pay! Lo, the agony, the death, the blood ...."[26] Indictment in this instance was the usual: one count of conspiracy to violate Section 3. In another

Espionage Act case, an Iowa District Court convicted D. H. Wallace, and prescribed a twenty-year prison term.[27]

There were of course the federal prosecutions of well-known socialists and radicals generally, such as Scott Nearing, Max Eastman, and Kate Richards O'Hare. In *United States v. Nearing*,[28] the identical charge in *United States v. Schutte*—"conspiracy to violate" Section 3—was brought against Scott Nearing, a defendant recently dismissed from the University of Pennsylvania for his beliefs. His indictment was coupled with that of the American Socialist Society, which was for distributing Nearing's tract, "The Great Madness." It had alleged that Americans "were tricked and cajoled" into the conflict, which was caused by the intrigue of capitalist "plutocracy." District Court Judge Learned Hand ruled in favor of Nearing, but sustained the third and fourth counts against the American Socialist Society.

Hand also presided over another Espionage Act case, *United States v.* Eastman,[29] in which Max Eastman, a prominent socialist and publisher of *The Masses* was indicted on one count of conspiracy and three counts of obstruction of the enlistment service. The last two counts centered on cartoons in the magazine that, Hand commented, "appear to me innocent under any interpretation." Citing District Court Judge Amidon in *United States v. Schutte*, he concluded: "the utterance of spoken words was not connected in any way with the military forces."

Other anti-war radicals were less fortunate than Nearing and Eastman. The prominent Socialist, Kate Richards O'Hare, was also charged with violating Section 3 of the 1917 Statute for having declared, at a Nonpartisan League meeting: "That any person who enlisted in ... for service in France would be used as fertilizer." In a North Dakota federal court, Judge Wade further noted her article in the *Socialist Review* and publication of an anti-war play and, taking the usual orthodox judicial position, contended: "There is a time of free speech, but this is a time of sacrifice .... The jury verdict was predictable."[30]

Long the target of patriotic groups as well as local police and federal government surveillance, Alexander Berkman and Emma Goldman had been arrested in their anarchist party offices in June 1917, on charges of conspiring "to induce persons not to register" for the draft, and being "principals in a nationwide conspiracy against the Government." That they were active members of the No-Conscription League, which manifesto announced its purpose as "encouraging conscientious objectors to affirm their liberty of conscience ... by refusing to participate in the killing of their fellow men ... [to]resist conscription by every means in our power." Declaring her willingness "to take the consequences of every word I said and am going to say on the stand I am taking. I am not afraid of prison—I have been there often," she closed with an appeal for "a general strike, and then the governing class will have something on its hands." Both Goldman and Berkman, acting in their own defense, had used the proceedings to publicize anarchist views as well as to argue that the Selective Draft Law was unconstitutional. Thus at one mass meeting, Berkman declared that "[c]onscription in a free country means the cemetery of liberty, and if conscription is the cemetery then registration is the undertaker." Again exemplifying the observation that courts generally reflected the political branches of government when necessity dictated, trial court Judge Julius Mayer responded to these incendiary speeches by stating that "free speech does not mean license, nor counseling disobedience to the law."[31] Although the government included no evidence that anyone had been "counseled" or influenced to violate the law, conviction was assured.

The cases of Goldman and Berkman were joined on appeal by that of Louis Kramer and Morris Becker[32] and combined with one from the Federal District Court for Northern Ohio, in which petitioners were Charles Ruthenberg, Alfred Wagenknecht, and Charles Baker; and one from a Minnesota District Court where four plaintiffs had been convicted, and with yet another from the District Court of Southern Georgia. Known collectively as the Selective Draft Law Cases, its defendants all challenged the constitutionality of the May 1917 statute. Ruthenberg and his co-defendants as well as Emma Goldman and Alexander Berkman had been indicted on June 15, 1917 for their anti-war public speeches and magazine articles, and charged under the 1917 Draft Act "that they did unlawfully aid, abet, counsel, command, induce" others to refuse to register. Their overt acts of making speeches in the streets of New York and distributing literature advising draft evasion were sufficient to justify the conspiracy charge and the conviction.

Their conviction was a foregone conclusion, the patriotic jurors taking thirty-nine minutes to find them guilty as charged. Reflecting wide-spread popular sentiment, *The New York Times* found that the conviction of "these chronic fomenters of disturbance for conspiracy ... is a public service."[33] The presiding judge, after sentencing them to two years in prison and a $10,000 fine, recommended deportation after the prison terms had been served. However, Anthony Caminetti, Commissioner of Immigration, did not wait. He removed the defendants from prison and, as mentioned above, deported them; and Goldman's deportation occurred only by the devious method of denaturalizing the citizenship of her husband, Jacob Kersner, upon which her own citizenship depended.

Lower federal court decisions further fueled governmental rulings on immigration. *Colyer et al. v. Skeffington, Commissioner of Immigration*[34] was yet another product of the times. But in this instance the outcome was atypical. Of the thirty-nine arrested in the raids, some twenty were aliens, being admittedly members of the Communist Party. They were to be deported because, as Communists, they advocated the violent overthrow of the government. They petitioned for writs of habeas corpus against the *Commissioner of Immigration*. Contending that they had not been apprized of their right to counsel at the onset of the deportation hearing, as pursuant to official administrative procedure. They had thus been deprived due process. The uncommonly enlightened District Court Judge George Anderson agreed, granted their habeas corpus petition, and forcefully declared:

> I refrain from any extended comment on the lawlessness of these proceedings by our supposedly law-enforcing officials. The documents and acts speak for themselves. It may, however, be fitly observed that a mob is a mob, whether made up of government officials acting under instructions from the Department of Justice, or of criminals, loafers, and the vicious classes.[35]

He went on to describe in stunning detail some of the violations of civil liberties that had occurred and they tell us something of the way radicals were then treated that is not *sui generis*:

> Private rooms were searched in omnibus fashion; trunks, bureaus, suit cases, and boxes broken open, books and papers seized. I doubt whether a single search warrant was obtained or applied for.
>
> > The arrested aliens, in most instances perfectly quiet and harmless working people, many of them not long ago Russian peasants, were handcuffed in pairs, and ... chained together .... For several days the arrested aliens were held practically incommunicado.[36]

In retrospect, it seems unarguable that Socialists, IWW members, and aliens victimized during the Palmer raids were not a threat to the public safety beyond the control of local law-enforcement agencies. But by the time the government raids ended, roughly 4,000 primary radical aliens had been arrested and about 1,000 deported. The perceptions of conspiracy haunting most Americans, and held by a large majority of state and federal judges, made the sedition laws, arrests of radicals, and alien deportations palatable. The public and public officials alike shared Attorney General Palmer's views of native-born and alien radicals, all of whom, according to him, were dangerous viruses spreading what he termed, "the disease of evil thinking." He would later liken the situation to a

> [p]rairie fire, [when] the blaze of revolution was sweeping over every American institution of law and order .... It was eating its way into the homes of the American workman, its sharp tongues of revolutionary heat were licking the altars of the churches, leaping into the belly of the school bell, crawling into the sacred corners of American homes, seeking to replace marriage vows with libertine laws, burning up the foundations of society.[37]

In sharp contrast to these chilling metaphors, Judge Hand wrote to about Justice Holmes with characteristic incisiveness that "the merry sport of Red-baiting goes on, and the pack gives tongue more and more shrilly. ... I own a sense of dismay at the increase in all the symptoms in apparent panic. How far people are getting afraid to rapidly demoralized in all its sense of proportion and toleration."

Hand had been one of the relative few federal court judges troubled by the state and federal political repression and by the severe punitive tactics employed. Ever fearful of emotional demagoguery, he was appalled by the flag-waving "know-nothingism" and "blind distrust of the foreigner, [of] thoughtless attacks on alien workers."[38] Notwithstanding his early decisions, Holmes contributed two articles likewise deploring Red Scare tactics and activities, entitled "Prating Patriots Worse than Reds" and "Red Hysteria."[39] Felix Frankfurter, then a member of a governmental commission on mediation, wrote to Walter Lippman that America was becoming "the most reactionary country in the world."[40] A scattering of those on the federal District Court bench shared their views. Judge George Bourquin, for one, described a "reign of terror" against Montana's "Wobblies," and argued that "[a]liens have Constitutional rights." Judge George Anderson, in *Colyer v Skeffington*,[41] condemned the "spirit" of "intolerance," and its "most alarming manifestation" in the United States. The Fourth, Fifth, Sixth, and Fourteenth Amendments are not limited in their application to citizens, he argued: "They apply generally to all persons within the jurisdiction of the United States." And then he added that there was no evidence that the Communist Party advocated violent overthrow of the government. But such sentiments were anomalies in the judiciary, and the popular anti-radicalism and its widespread legal and extra-legal implementation continued undiminished.

Reference to Justice Holmes warrants a pause in the story of wartime and post-war domestic affairs. Holmes would never give unqualified support to a free speech claim. He and his brother justices lacked both experience and precedents in deciding First Amendment cases that came up for review. Moreover, they considered themselves as part of the governmental order responsible for protecting its stability. Hence, it was to be expected that in all nine cases reaching the Supreme Court in these years the prosecution would be upheld, and the defense's claims that the First Amendment prohibited Congress from criminalizing mere speech were flatly rejected. Nonetheless, the cases remain significant because, 128 years after the Bill of Rights was adopted, they were the first High Court rulings on free speech, and marked the real beginnings of judicial thinking about protected expression. Before that occurred, and until the late 1920s, judicial insensitivity to civil liberties litigation would be the rule, though some Supreme Court justices were aware of the Bill of Rights protection in earlier periods.

To recall one early twentieth-century decision, *Patterson v. Colorado* (1907)[42] that illustrates the Court's view of free speech at the time, Senator Thomas Patterson had been indicted for articles and cartoons critical of that State's Supreme Court appearing in newspapers he owned. He had maintained that under the First Amendment, truth was a defense against the charge of libel. Holmes, however, speaking for the Court, found newspaper criticism of judicial behavior tended to obstruct the administration of justice and hence could be considered unlawful, and consequently, no protection for an editor was afforded by the First Amendment. The basis for his opinion had been provided by Blackstone's Commentaries and the aforementioned doctrine of no prior restraint but no "freedom from censure ... when published," and accordingly even factually accurate criticism of Colorado's judges could be criminally punished. Nor, to remind the reader, did the High Court uphold the free speech rights of the Milwaukee Leader, Emma Goldman, Alexander Berkman, among others. Rather it, as indeed all federal and state courts, openly defended government interests. To deny the government would be a deviance from the norm, as Griffith has contended, "an aberration, which occurs most infrequently; and in very special circumstances."[43]

Regarding the Supreme Court in these years, it was a conservative tribunal, with Melville Weston Fuller as Chief Justice, joined by Justices David Brewer and Horace Peckham to form a right-of-center bloc and that gave tone and tendency to majority opinions. The Court's record in these pre-war and wartime years was understandable. Admittedly, the First Amendment seemingly presented an unqualified mandate to the legislative and judicial branches: "Congress shall make no law abridging the freedom of speech, or the press, ...," but the judiciary, to repeat, is often most responsive to the dominant public opinion as well as precedent. "The first requirement of a sound body of law," as Holmes realistically phrased it, "is that it should correspond with the actual feelings and demands of the community whether right or wrong."

Convictions were often punctuated by the automatic judicial declaration about the importance of "free and fearless discussion of public questions," followed by the conditional, "but" as a New York judge wrote in 1922, while denying it to those "advocating forcible overthrow" by means "abhorrent to the entire spirit of our institutions." Or as a California judge wrote in 1921, the "right of free speech was guaranteed, but it did "not include the right to advocate ... overthrow of government."[44] In short, the judiciary applauded tolerance and free speech in the abstract but, as legal historian Michal Belknap succinctly writes of judges and justices in times of crises, they tended to "go to war." They were both sensitive to criticism that they impeded the nation's war effort and were "highly deferential in their reviews of executive and legislative actions." Christopher May rightly contends that they gave "ritualistic approval" to congressional statutes and the executive's emergency measures. Other students of the law and the Constitution, Arthur S. Miller and Martin Shapiro, to name but two, offer similar observations.

After all, it is not difficult for the judges—or for anyone!—to affirm preferred speech for nonconformists in a tranquil era, but in a society at war or at the brink of war, as Robert McCloskey asserts, the difficulties "are thrice compounded." In times of danger, the reader must ask: should free expression be affirmed, regardless of the "difficulties"? In such times do Justice Hugo Black's words—the First Amendment liberties retain "the high preferred place where they belong in a free society"—continue to carry persuasive weight?

Notes

1. *Los Angeles Times*, November 8, 1919. See also Murphy, *The Meaning of Free Speech: First Amendment Freedoms from Wilson to FDR* (Westport, CT: Greenwood Press, 1972b), 75.
2. *The New York Times*, January 5, 1920.
3. *Ex parte Jackson*, 263 F. 110, 111–112 (D. Mont. 1920).
4. 268 F. 795 (7th Cir. 1920). For what is seemingly a near-endless list of individual members and sympathizers of the IWW who were arrested under various state criminal syndicalism and anti-anarchy statutes, among others, see Stephen Kohn, *American Political Prisoners: Prosecutions under the Espionage and Sedition Acts* (Westport, CT: Prager, 1994), 157 and pp 157–182.
5. *Anderson v. United States* 269 F. 65 (9th Cir. 1920); and *O'Connell v. United States* 253 U.S. 142 (1920). See also: Philip Taft, "The Federal Trials of the IWW," *Labor History* 3 (Winter 1962): 76–9.
6. Quoted in Melvyn Leffler, *The Specter of Communism: The United States and the Origins of the Cold War, 1917–1953* (New York: Hill & Wang, 1994), 15.
7. Robert Goldstein, *Political Repression in Modern America: From 1870 to the Present* (Cambridge, MA: Schenkmen, 1978), 153–61.
8. Zechariah Chafee, *Free Speech in the United States* (Cambridge, MA: Harvard University Press, 1941), 214. See also Theodore Draper, *The Roots of American Communism* (New York: Viking Press, 1957), 204.
9. Passports would be denied to Communist Party members until 1931. Philip Kurland and Gerhard Casper (eds), *Landmark Briefs and Arguments of the Supreme Court of the United States* (Arlington, VA: University Publications of America, 1975), V. 60, 23–4 (hereafter cited as Landmark Briefs).
10. Robert K. Murray, *Red Scare* (Minneapolis, MN: University of Minnesota Press, 1955), 234. For instance, in Massachusetts case *Commonwealth v. Karvonen*, 219 Mass. 30, 106 N.E.556 (1914) the defendant was convicted of violating a 1913 measure that stated: "no red or black flag. ... shall be carried in parade." In *People v. Burman*, 154 Mich. 150, 117 N.W. 589 (1908) (defendants would be convicted for having paraded with a Red Flag. See also, for example, *Bentall v. United States*, 254 F. 194 (Cir. Ct. 8th Cir.) 254 F. 189 (8th Cir Ct.) (1921). Convictions resulted in *United States v. D. H. Wallace* (1917); *United States v. D. T. Blodgett* (1918); *United States v. Frederick Kraft* (1918); *United States v. Reverend Clarence Waldron* (1918); *United States v. Pierce et al.* (1917), *inter alia*, cited by Walter Nelles (compiler and edited), *Espionage Act Cases* (New York: New York Civil Liberties, 1918), 35, 44, 65.
11. Fund for the Republic, *Digest*, 267, 296. See also Woodrow Whitten, "Criminal Syndicalism and the Law in California, 1919–1927," *Transactions of the American Philosophical Society* (March 1969): 65. See also Murphy, *The Meaning of Free Speech*, 49–51. Anti-syndicalist laws were passed in California, Oregon, Oklahoma, Georgia, Minnesota, Michigan, Illinois, Idaho, and so on, and those convicted under them in trial courts took their cases to state appellate courts. In virtually every instance, the appeals courts upheld the trial court decision and the state law under challenge. (e.g., *State v. Dingman*, 37 Id. 265 (1923)); *Berg v. State*, 29 Ok. Cr. Rep. 121. 233 P 497 (1925); *State v. Worker's Socialist Pub. Co. et al.*, 150 Minn. 407 (1921); *State v. Boloff*, 138 Ore. 568, 4 Pac. (2nd), 326 (1931). For a listing of many of these cases, see Margaret Blanshard, "Filling the Void: Speech and Press in State Courts Prior to Gitlow,"

in *The First Amendment Reconsidered*, eds, Bill Chamberlin and Charlene Brown (New York: Longman, 1982), 27, 49, nn. 75–80.
12. Robert K. Murray, *Red Scare*, 234.
13. Chafee, *Free Speech in the United States*, 582–5.
14. *Ex parte Starr*, 263 F. 145 (1920).
15. E.g., People v. Steelik, 187 Cal. 361, 375 (1921). See also *State v. Tachin*, 92 N.J. L. 269 (affirmed *per curiam*, 1919). See also Fund for the Republic, *Digest*, 287, 288; *People v. Gitlow*, 234 N.Y. 132, 151 (1922); *In re Hartman*, 182 Cal. 447 (1920); *Ex parte Campbell*, 674 Cal. App. 300 (1923); *In re Lithuanian Worker' Literature*, 187 N.Y.S. (1921); *People v. Taylor*, 187 Cal. 378 (1921); *State v. Holm*, 139 Minn. 267 (1918).
16. *People v. Ruthenberg*, 229 Mich. 315, 201 (1918); *Ruthenberg v. United States*, 245 U.S. 480 (1918); *United States v. Rose Pastor Stokes*, 264 F. 18, 34 (8th Cir. 1920). See also Chafee, *Free Speech in the United States*, 159, 575–97; and Murphy, *The Meaning of Free Speech*, 80.
17. Nelles, *Espionage Act Cases*, 66.
18. E.g., *People v. Lloyd*, 304 Ill. 23 (1922).
19. Alexander Trachtenburg and Benjamin Glassberg, *The American Labor Yearbook 1921–1922* (New York: 1922), 10, 42. See also Thomas Vadney, "The Politics of Repression: A Case Study of the Red Scare in New York," *New York History* 49 (1968) 56, 60. See also Murphy, *The Meaning of Free Speech*, 47; Polenberg, *Fighting Faiths*, 170–1; Fund for the Republic, *Digest*, 267.
20. *The New York Times*, April 30, 1920, see also ibid., January 8, 1920.
21. 251 F/313 (N.D.N.Y., 1918); *United States v. Schuttte*, 252 F. 212 (Dis. Ct. North Dakota, 1918). See also Nelles, *Espionage Act Cases*, 14.
22. Arthur Miller, *Democratic Dictatorship: The Emergent Constitution of Control* (Westport, CT: Greenwood Press, 1981), 94.
23. 269 U.S. 65 (9th Ct., 1920).
24. *Bentall v. United States*, 254 F. 194 (Cir. Ct. 8th Cir. 1921).
25. Walter Nelles, *Espionage Act Cases*, 65.
26. Ibid., 74.
27. Ibid., 44.
28. *United States v. Nearing* 252 F. 223 (S. D. N. Y. 1918); *Goldman v. United States* 345 U.S. 474 (1918); *Haywood v. United States*, 268 F. 795 (7th Cir. 1920), (*cert. denied*). See also Fund for the Republic, *Digest*, 4.
29. *United States v. Eastman* 252 F. 223 (S.D.N.Y 1918).
30. Nelles, *Espionage Act Case*, 45. See also Harriet Peterson and Gilbert Fite, *Opponents of War, 1917–1918* (Madison, WI: University of Wisconsin Press, 1957), 184.
31. Alexander Berkman, *Anarchism on Trial: Speeches of Alexander Berkman and Emma Goldman before the United States District Court in the City of New York, 1917* (NY, n. d.), 73. *Goldman v. United States*, 245 U.S. 474, 477 (1918). See also Transcript of Record. Supreme Court of the United States, October Term, 1917, No. 702, Emma Goldman and Alexander Berkman, Plaintiffs-in-Error (S.D.N.Y); *Goldman*, 245 U.S. at 474.
32. Ibid.
33. *The New York Times*, January 15, 1918, p. 70.
34. 265 F. 17 (D. Mass. 1920).
35. Ibid., 43.

36. Ibid., 43, 44.
37. Henry Wriston, "Education on the Razor's Edge," *Southwest Law Review* 38 (no. 4), (1953): 309.
38. Hand to M. E. Ravage, December 8, 1919, quoted in Gerald Günther, *Learned Hand: The Man and the Judge* (New York: Alfred A. Knopf, 1994), 357.
39. Holmes, in New York World, January 13, 1920; see also New Republic, XXI (January 28, 1920), 250 and also Murphy, *The Meaning of Free Speech*, 29.
40. Frankfurter to Walter Lippmann, January 13, 1919, quoted in Günther, *Learned Hand*, 355.
41. *Colyer v. Skeffington*, 265 F. 17 (D. Mass. 1920).
42. 205 U.S. 454 (1907), 44.
43. J. A. G. Griffith, *The Politics of the Judiciary* (Manchester, UK: Manchester University Press, 1977), 203.
44. A state judge prototypically ruled in 1921, " the right of free speech was guaranteed," but it did "not include the right to … overthrow the government." *Steelik*, 187 Cal. at 375.

3

Judicial Tolerance of Intolerance

In a surge of litigation after the end of hostilities, nine notable cases touching the freedom of expression would reach the Supreme Court. Before they entered the tribunal's docket, only a few references to freedom of expression appeared in judicial opinions, largely restrictive readings when alluding to the libelous or obscene or to dangerous speech, the last usually that of anarchists. The judicial tilt toward the approval of governmental power and policies could be expected, as has been maintained, given the personal, social, and political convictions of judges; the rampant ultra-nationalism in wartime, and the judicial profiles themselves. As Chief Justice, Edward Douglass White would do little to restrain the "merry sport" that Hand lamented. In fact, during White's twenty-seven years tenure, numerous convictions owing to repressive state and federal measures would be upheld by the High Court. For the most part of White's innate conservatism, respect for inherent government powers and reverence for stare decisis prevailed.[1]

Of White's brother justices, the senior figure on the Court, Justice Joseph McKenna, had been appointed in 1898 by William McKinley, after serving first as a hard-line Republican congressman and then in the Ninth Circuit. Having a simple-minded grasp of legal issues, he readily affirmed that the Espionage Act provisions were "neither excessive nor ambiguous." Nominated to the High Court by Theodore Roosevelt in 1902, Holmes was a legal realist. He believed the law derived not from settled principles and precedents, but from "the felt necessities of the time, the prevalent moral and political theories, intuitions of public policy, avowed or unconscious, even the prejudices which judges share with their fellow men," as he wrote on the first page of The Common Law.[2] Law, it follows, was not founded upon enduring principles of right and justice,[3] but on facts filtered through prejudice, misunderstanding, and ignorance.

Among Holmes' High Court brethren, there was Rufus Day, also a Roosevelt appointee to the tribunal. Shocked over the assassination of his close personal friend, William McKinley, he urged legal measures to curb and punish "those who teach or practice the dreadful tenets of this code of lawlessness and ruin." His biographer, Joseph McLean, assessed him as having "a certain reluctance" about entering the twentieth century, a reluctance shared by Justices Willis Van Devanter and Mahlon Pitney, two President Taft appointees. The former had been a powerful figure in Wyoming politics before sitting on the federal bench and would serve on the New Jersey Supreme Court where his ingrained conservatism would be compatible with that of this quartet. Both McLean and Pitney esteemed the ancestral past; were staunchly tradition bound as befitting this outlook on society; and believed that protected speech, press, and assembly had become secondary considerations when the United States entered the European conflict. Rounding out the tribunal, there was the Kentucky-born James McReynolds. He had been rewarded with the post of Attorney General upon backing Wilson's bid for the presidency in 1912, and then, in a defensive maneuver after McReynolds' abrasive manner alienated many congressmen and administration officials, the President appointed him to the High Court in 1914. Conservative to the very fiber of his being, he had a mean spiritedness possibly unrivaled in the Court's history. He was notably anti-German and anti-Irish and unashamedly anti-Semitic, most pointedly antagonistic to Louis Brandeis.

McReynolds was also hostile toward Justice John Clarke, an antagonism that could be expected since Clarke, appointed to the tribunal in 1916, often joined Brandeis and Holmes. But he would also vote with McReynolds at times and was close to him and President Wilson on the issues involving labor unions, radical agitators, and executive use of prerogative power. As such, according to his biographer, Hoyt Warner, he was typical of progressive reformers in that he shared prejudices "against the unwashed, ill-mannered Socialists and Anarchists."[4] Of radical agitators, he expressed hostility toward "the obnoxious, supercilious 'philosophy' of the 'reds' ... accompanied by the most brutal expressions of the spirit of murder .... Their doctrines are most dangerous and should find no room for culture or spread in this free and enlightened government." Admittedly, these comments came in 1901, when Clarke was a lawyer but his views remained unchanged, according to his biographer, always demonstrating an "instinctive hostility to violent change or extreme dissent in any form. Revolutionary talk, no less than revolutionary acts, was repulsive to him." He would, it follows, share both Wilson's war aims and his hostility toward radicals, whether they were at home or abroad.

At the outset, to reiterate, the White Court was like the preceding Court of Chief Justice Fuller and the succeeding one of William Howard Taft. It barely acknowledged the existence of First Amendment guarantees, such as protected speech. Rather, as observed, the judicial majority displayed antipathy to radicals and unremitting pro-government sympathies, as clearly evident in a number of decisions. Their ruling in the case of Austrian-born Louis Berger illustrates as much. He was one of the founders of the Socialist Party and was an editor of the Socialist *Milwaukee Leader*. Elected to the House of Representatives from the Fifth Wisconsin District (1911–1913), Berger had become the first Socialist lawmaker in Congress. The House, reflecting the national antipathies, by a vote of 319 to 1 refused to seat him in 1919, and Wisconsin governor called a new election, which returned Berger to Congress by an even larger vote, and the House repeated its denial in 1920. The *Milwaukee Leader*'s second-class mail privileges had been rescinded by Burleson, as already noted, and his decision would be upheld when the case reached the Supreme Court, with Brandeis and Holmes dissenting.[5]

In a second case, likewise involving him, Berger had been one of the five arrested following a raid of a Socialist bookstore and an office in Chicago in August 1917 and accused of violating Title I, Section 3 of the Espionage Act by preparing and circulating 15,000 copies of an anti-war, anti-conscription leaflet. The prosecution charged that the handbill caused insubordination and disloyalty in the America's military forces and obstructed "the recruiting and enlistment services of the United States." Indicted for conspiracy by writing and circulating seditious and pro-German literature, Berger denied the charge, his counsel arguing that only the defendant's socialist views were on trial. To no avail, he received a twenty-year prison term. The High Court, however, would reverse on the grounds that District Court Judge Landis had made a number of prejudicial, pre-trial comments about German–American life.[6]

Charles Schenck, General Secretary of the Socialist Party in Philadelphia, and Dr. Elizabeth Baer, among others, would be arrested and indicted for violating the harsh terms of the Espionage Act. When initially listed on the Court calendar as scheduled for January 19, 1919, this case, producing the first Espionage Act conviction to reach the

Supreme Court, prompted little notice, though it would become a highly significant free speech case.[7] The three-count indictment included (1) the preparation and circulation of anti-war, anti-conscription reading matter mailed to draft-eligible men, toward the end of causing insubordination and disloyalty in the armed forces, (2) attempting to use mails for transmission of this reading matter (in violation of Title XII of the Espionage Act), and (3) obstructing recruiting, and enlistments. Offered in evidence was a leaflet, some 15,000 copies of which had been distributed to draftees, asking them, "Do you think it [conscription] has a place in the United States? Do you want to see unlimited power handed over to Wall Street's chosen few?" Judge Thompson of Pennsylvania's Eastern District Court found insufficient evidence of conspiracy and overt acts to connect three of the five defendants with the indictment, and they received a directed verdict of acquittal. However, they were found guilty of three violations of the Espionage Act.

Jeremy Cohen in his careful study of the *Schenck* case describes how petitioners raised three major question: (1) did the Espionage Act "constitutes an abridgment of freedom of speech and the right of petition in contravention of the First Amendment to the Constitution"; (2) were their clients "lawfully guilty of conspiracy under all the evidence"; and (3) "whether or not papers seized under a search warrant were lawfully used as evidence against them under the constitutional provision against unlawful search [Fourth Amendment]."[8] As to the First Amendment, defense Brief admitted, it did not protect the person who, by refusing military service, violated the draft law, but it did mean that a person "can say that the Draft Law is wrong and ought to be repealed." The Brief asked: "How can the citizen find out whether war is just or unjust unless there is a free and full discussion?"[9] "The fair test" of protected speech, defense argued, "is whether an expression is made with sincere purpose to communicate honest opinion or belief, or whether it masks a primary intent or incite to forbidden action, or whether it does, in fact, incite to forbidden action."[10] Applying this test, defense argued, would exonerate petitioners, who did not seek to incite to action, but rather urged readers "to go to Socialist Party headquarters and sign a petition to repeal the Conscription Act."

Countering these arguments, the thirty-six-page Brief of the prosecution defended the indictments of Schenck and Baer under the Espionage Act for obstructing the draft and rejected the contention that the Espionage Act was an implied attack on the First Amendment. The statute "did not prohibit speech," it claimed, "and the defendants were not charged with legitimate political agitation for the repeal of the draft law," but with speech used to commit a "crime"; namely to "willfully obstruct the recruiting or enlistment service of the United States" in a time of war. Congress "has a constitutional right to prohibit a person from attempting during the war to induce violations of statute providing for military service."[11] The prosecutors went on to rebut defense claims that the government lacked evidence connecting *Schenck* to the conspiracy, asserting in their Brief that petitioner ordered 15,000 circulars, directed their distribution, as witnesses had testified, that his files included the names of many draftees to whom they were mailed, and that "he was an active, in fact the most active participant in the conspiracy."

Though characterizing the behavior of the lower federal judiciary as "hysterical," Holmes spoke for a unanimous tribunal in 1919 when upholding conviction, the first of the three decisions to do so for what was deemed to be anti-war speech.[12] Neither he nor Justice Brandeis believed at the time that the Court should proscribe governmental actions. The First Amendment, as a check upon legislative abuse of expression, was barely mentioned, and consequently, the *Schenck* decision lacked the elements of a great case, Walter Berns has concluded in that it avoided "fundamental principles of the Constitution." In fact, Holmes went on to find that some words were outside the compass of the First Amendment; that is, words, such as those in a handbill that tended to have "all the effect of force." Words in this category inherently become the act itself. They had a "bad tendency"; that is, it could lead to socially injurious acts and could be proscribed.[13] For Holmes, the handbill, then, became an act rather than words and not protected speech. It was punishable under the Espionage Act. Some words, accordingly, were not to be protected, and Holmes introduced the well-remembered clear and present danger test "as a guide to determine what speech was not protected by the Amendment."[14] Applying his test for the first time, Holmes argued: "The character of every act depends upon the circumstances in which it is done," and "whether the words used are used in such circumstances and are of such a nature as to create a clear and present danger that they will bring about the substantive evils that Congress has a right to prevent."[15] Holmes accordingly formulated a test for governmental actions infringing on speech. The tendency to incite, in Holmes's view, would become the judicial basis for sustaining conviction. Such speech could be prohibited if it had "a natural tendency to produce the forbidden consequences";[16] and Holmes concluded that "the tendency and intent" of Schenck's leaflet was to induce the draftee to oppose his induction, which characterized a "present danger" that became a sufficient legal criterion for conviction.

For the time being, however, the clear and present danger test joined the bad tendency test in being restrictive doctrines to be applied to speech and shortly to leaflets and newspaper articles as well. They were also, Thomas Emerson convincingly finds, "excessively vague" doctrines. Does "clear," as Geoffrey Stone and Lee Bollinger ask, mean ninety-nine percent "probable"? Does "present" mean immediate, or within a day, or a year? Not being self-defining doctrines, they would plunge judges "into consideration of a mass of historical, political, economic, psychological, and social facts" requiring "both evaluation and prophecy of a sort no court is competent to give"; and, most importantly, the inherent ambiguity of the danger test allowed "the state to cut off expression as soon as it comes close to being effective."[17] Of the danger doctrine, David Rabban rightly concludes, it placed restrictions on the rights of the individual; and, moreover "proved to be a continuing constraint on emerging First Amendment theory."[18] It then becomes just an "intent and bad tendency" test, observes Rodney Smolla, a formula that permitted imposition of penalties for speech on mere vague and shadowy proof of danger.[19]

Writing to Pollock later that year, Holmes dismissively noted plaintiffs' First Amendment claims: "There was a lot of jaw about free speech, which I dealt with somewhat summarily in an earlier case," referring to *Schenck*.[20] But he also observes, in another letter, that "[the] federal judges seem to me (again between ourselves) to have got hysterical about the war."[21] And these "federal judges," it should hastily be added, would largely avoid wrestling with free speech thinking until a later date. That is, and it needs emphasis, the First Amendment was treated as ordinary police power until after World War I and not an important judicial aspect of *Schenck*, as Holmes's letters to Frederick Pollock and Herbert Croly reveal. His opinion was plain and simple: obstruction of the draft was punishable under the Espionage Act, and petitioners were convicted not for voicing their opinions but for violating the congressional statute, which Holmes had a judicial obligation to uphold. Admittedly, the actions of petitioners were a form of speech, but Holmes emphasized only the statutory violation: "obstructing the recruiting and enlistment service of the United States." Congress was justified in preventing certain acts, whether they were accomplished "by persuasion" or "by force"—even if he was not convinced, as letters to Laski and Croly convey, that the speech presented a real danger requiring prosecution under the Espionage Act. Holmes thereby would set the scope of free speech rights in a social context. The emergency of war confronting the Court would prompt him to make short shrift of the argument that the First Amendment gave speech, in the form of a street-corner talk or an anti-conscription handbill in absolute protection.

In another statement that has passed into the lexicon of America's legal mythology, Holmes resorted to the famous analogy: "the most stringent protection of free speech would not protect a man in falsely shouting fire in a theater and causing a panic."[22] It is a clever analogy, but a questionable one for two obvious reasons: (1) no evidence was provided that Charles Schenck had influenced a single American and, as John Roche astutely concluded, "he [Holmes] was, if anything, shouting 'Fire!' in an empty theater"; and (2), "shouting fire" is not the equivalent of distributing a leaflet criticizing administration policy. But a simplistic and stunningly persuasive metaphor, especially useful for the popular consumption, this image of fire and its consequences has thwarted time's erosion.

Since the defendants in *Schenck* were convicted of conspiracy under the Espionage Act, it would be useful to elaborate further on the law of conspiracy at this point, if only to avoid confusing it with its warped popular usage, say, the public's perception of America's socialists or communists (or, later, terrorists) as part of a worldwide "conspiracy" threatening the nation. To define this doctrine in narrowly conventional legal terms, conspiracy is simply entering into an agreement to perform an unlawful act or an unlawful act by unlawful means.[23] This unlawful act, according to contemporary statutes, required in addition to an agreement to commit a crime, "some overt act" that could be "noncriminal and relatively minor … if it is in furtherance of the conspiracy."[24] The overt act of one partner, moreover, may be the act of all without any new agreement specifically directed to that act.[25] Once having joined in an illegal plan, the Court added a year later, the conspirator cannot escape responsibility for what happens.[26] Neither purpose nor means need be criminal, it should be emphasized. Even without the evidence of crime, individuals could be indicted, tried, and convicted of conspiracy, although they do not know each other. In fact, no evidence of any meeting or communication among the alleged conspirators need be presented, according to F.B. Sayre, and "no express proof of conspiracy, such as proof that the parties actually met and laid their heads together … and then and there actually agreed to carry out a common purpose." Under the law of conspiracy, prosecutors could convict one defendant for the illegality of another; that is, each defendant can be found responsible for the acts and words of the other codefendants—and also for the acts and words of co-conspirators who are not indicted, who even may be unknown to the grand jury considering the case.[27]

Government lawyers have insisted that conspiracy laws help to stop crimes before they endanger lives or property. On learning of a criminal act being planned, by an individual or a group of individuals, "[y]ou nip it in the bud," as an Assistant U.S. Attorney stated in 1971. But Justice Robert Jackson twenty-three years earlier effectively eviscerated conspiracy law: "[t]he modern crime of conspiracy is so vague that it almost defies definition." As he strongly phrased it when concurring in *Krulewitch v. United States* (1949):[28] the "looseness and flexibility of the doctrine present inherent dangers … The order of proof of so sprawling a charge … the loose application of rules of evidence." Amplifying his deeply troubling feelings about the conspiracy charge, he wrote, "conspiracy comes down to us wrapped in vague but unpleasant connotations. It sounds historical undertones of treachery, secret plotting, and violence on a scale that menaces social stability and the security of the state itself." He cautioned, however, "[i]ts history exemplifies the 'tendency of a principle to expand itself to the limit of its logic,'" and it has evolved into such an "elastic, sprawling, and pervasive offense … that it almost defies definition." Learned Hand, going further, bluntly contended that the possibilities inherent in the conspiracy doctrine, made it "the darling of the modern prosecutor's nursery."[29] Finally, Justice Felix Frankfurter, dissenting in *Nye & Nissen v. United States* (1949), sharply commented on the "atmospheric emanations of guilt" that flow from the conspiracy charge, which make it a uniquely oppressive legal weapon when used against political minorities. Moreover, he insisted, "the concept of conspiracy is not an invitation to circumvent the safeguards in the prosecution of a crime … by making it a device to establish guilt … by association."[30]

Considering its sweeping and endlessly confusing definition, when the conspiracy law was applied to political speech, it has had a potentially chilling effect. For the purposes of this study, it warrants note that the draft and Espionage statutes had conspiracy sections; and IWW members and followers as well as prominent anti-war figures were convicted of conspiracy to interfere with the draft law or overthrow the government.[31] It was easy to intimidate the public and prejudice juries in the post-World War I period, as it would be in the Fifties and Sixties, when the doctrine was placed in Section 3 of the 1940 Alien Registration Act (the Smith Act).

Holmes's 1919 holding in *Frohwerk v. United States*[32] provides a further illustration of his opinions about the right of critics and dissenters to condemn a war. His rulings, Lucas Powe convincingly sums up, "are thus hollow rhetoric," since they all but limited discussions of war policy to those who supported the war.[33] The case itself resulted from a violation of the 1917 Espionage Act, and the convictions of Carl Gleeser and Jacob Frohwerk, publisher and editorial writer, respectively, of the *Missouri Staats Zeitung*. This German-language newspaper had published a series of thirteen anti-war articles in 1917 for which the defendants were indicted on thirteen counts, each count citing one of the articles and all the counts grounded in the language of conspiracy. One of the articles that Holmes would cite declared it "a monumental and inexcusable mistake to send our soldiers to France," and followed the standard anti-war litany by attributing the decision to "the great trusts."

Defense counsel for *Frohwerk* filed a demurrer as well as a motion to dismiss (in the United States District Court for the Western District of Missouri), both denied by trial judge Frank Youmans. A subpoena *duces tecum* for two witnesses was likewise denied. The lengthy and diffuse defense Brief (admitting "brevity was impossible") went through each count of the indictment, and one by one repudiated each of them: for example, count one was unconstitutional, a violation of the First Amendment.[34]

The prosecution team contended that Jacob Frohwerk's efforts to induce violation of the 1917 Selective Service Draft Law, though done through others, did not eliminate his liability. The defendant intended to obstruct recruitment and enlistment. It was sufficient argument for the District Court jurors, since governmental pressures in tandem with prevailing political climate functioning as an instrument of it, were almost irresistible. Little surprise then that the jury would find Frohwerk guilty (on all but one count, of violating the Espionage Act and he received a ten-year sentence). Even Alfred Bettman, one of the lead attorneys for the prosecution, in a letter to Zechariah Chafee, surprisingly admitted that Frohwerk's articles "seemed to me … to fall within the protection of the constitutional guarantees of free speech and press," and Frohwerk was "one of the clearest examples of the political prisoner."[35]

In a High Court opinion easy to write considering the *Schenck* precedent of a week earlier, Holmes upheld conviction. Though admitting these articles were "not much" different from that sent by Schenck, he conceded that, unlike Schenck, much of what Frohwerk had printed was entirely legal in itself, even in wartime. However, the "overt acts" amounted to conspiracy—for the "common purpose" of "intent" to obstruct recruiting. "[C]onspiracy is the crime," and one "may be convicted of conspiracy to obstruct recruiting by words of persuasion."

Repeating his contentions in *Schenck*, Holmes argued that no proof of success in carrying out the conspiracy was required: only the intent to do so. Similarly in *Frohwerk*, he would define and judge intent not by the actual purpose of the accused but by the "tendency" of words in the printed articles; that is, the bad tendency standard, which could be more broadly restrictive in application than the clear and present danger test. In effect, the possibility that, however remote, something illegal might occur as a result of the speech or article was sufficient to uphold conviction.

Holmes did acknowledge: "We do not lose our right to condemn either measures of men because the country is at war" but, Powe concluded, Frohwerk—even more than Schenck or Debs—contradicted this statement.[36] Furthermore, Holmes in his next sentence admitted that the defendant did not appear to have made "any special effort to reach men who were subjected to the draft." But the First Amendment "cannot have been, and obviously was not, intended to give immunity for every possible use of language," a statement that likewise seemed to contradict the assertion immediately above.

Comparable judicial thinking was evident in the last of the early Espionage Act cases, one decided on the same day as *Frohwerk*—namely, *Debs v. United States*.[37] Eugene V. Debs, the nation's most prominent labor leader and the grand old man of American radicalism, had been indicted in District Court of the Northern District of Ohio on ten counts of violating Section 3 of the 1917 Espionage Act. He was ultimately found guilty on three counts of violating the Espionage Act. The pivotal third count centered on his two-hour address—the closing event of the State Socialist Party convention on June 16, 1918. Unlike Schenck, whose leaflet was directed to a specific group, Debs's speech was delivered to a general audience in a public park in Canton, Ohio and, moreover, included fewer words of incitement.

The defense Brief before the Supreme Court, listing the prejudicial errors at the trial, argued that the District Court erred in refusing to direct a verdict of acquittal on every count because there was no evidence that petitioner urging "unlawful conduct on the part of others." The government's rebuttal directly addressed defense contentions. No infringement of the First Amendment was involved in conviction of the defendant, it contended, and the "constitutional guaranty of free speech does not grant immunity for deliberate obstruction of the process of raising army ..."[38]

That Debs had only attacked war in general terms—in the Canton, Ohio, speech and in his own closing remarks to the jury—seemingly should have given the High Court pause. After all, nothing that he stated was directed to America's soldiers or sailors, or could be fairly understood as incitement to resist the draft or attempt to cause insubordination. These matters, however, seemingly did not concern the Court. The defendant, Holmes found for a unanimous Court, had "used words tending to obstruct the recruiting service" and he again upheld the Espionage Act and sustained the conviction under its Section 3. The jury, he argued, had been "most carefully instructed" not to find Debs guilty merely because of the defendant's views, but to convict if his words "had as their natural tendency and reasonably probable effect to obstruct the recruiting service" and if he "had the specific *intent* to do so in his mind" [italics added].[39] The equally vague propositions of presumptive intent and "bad tendency" had in effect become cognate for the equally broad clear and present danger doctrine, unlike Judge Hand's opinion in *The Masses* that found speech unlawful only when it directly incited action. In sum, though Holmes had conceded that the main theme of Debs's speech "was socialism, its growth, and a prophecy of its ultimate success," he thought a jury could find "that one purpose of the speech ... was to oppose not only war in general, but this war, and that the opposition was so expressed that its natural and intended effect would be to obstruct recruiting," a sufficient basis for conviction.

Notes

1. Edward Corwin, *The Twilight of the Supreme Court: A History of Our Constitutional Theory* (New Haven, CT: Yale University Press, 1934), 24. See also Robert Highsaw, *Edward Douglass White: Defender of the Conservative Faith* (Baton Rouge, LA: Louisiana State University Press, 1981).
2. Oliver Wendell Holmes, *The Common Law* (Boston, MA: Harvard University Press, 1863), 5.

3. Oliver Wendell Holmes, "Masters and Men," *American Law Review* VII (1873). See also Vegelahn v. Guntner, 167 Mass., 92 (1896), 92, 104.
4. Hoyt Warner, *The Life of Mr. Justice Clarke: A Testament to the Power of Liberal Dissent in America* (Cleveland, OH: Western Reserve University Press, 1959), 100.
5. *Milwaukee Social Democratic Publishing Company v. Burleson*, 255 U.S. 407 (1921); *Schenck v. United States*, 249 U.S. 47 (1919).
6. *Berger v. United States*, 255 U.S. 22 (1921).
7. *Schenck*, 249 U.S. at 47 Transcript. *United States v. Charles Schenck, et al.* Records of the U. S. Dis. Ct., E. Dis. of Pa. See also Paul Murphy, *The Constitution in Crisis Times 1918–1969* (New York: Harper & Row, 1972), 23.
8. Brief of Plaintiffs in Error, see Philip Kurland and Gerhard Casper (eds), *Landmark Briefs and Arguments of the Supreme Court of the United States: Constitutional Law* (Arlington, VA: University Publications of America, 1975), XIX, 991–2. See also Jeremy Cohen, *Congress Shall Make No Law: Oliver Wendell Holmes, the First Amendment, and Judicial Decision Making* (Ames, IA: Iowa State University Press, 1989), 33.
9. Kurland and Casper, *Landmark Briefs and Arguments of the Supreme Court of the United States*, 996.
10. Ibid., 1002; see also Ibid., 1012.
11. O'Brien & Bettman, "Brief for the United States," in Ibid., 1045.
12. *Schenck*, 249 U.S. at 47.
13. Ibid., 51.
14. Walter Berns, *Freedom, Virtue and the First Amendment* (Baton Rouge, LA: Louisiana State University Press, 1957), 69–70. See also Walter Berns, *The First Amendment and the Future of American Democracy* (New York: Basic Books, 1940), 150–151. Holmes' application of the clear and present danger formula would be uneven. Citing it here (in *Schenck*), he emphasizes the bad tendency test as well. In future cases, *Frohwerk* and *Debs*, he relies only on bad tendency; and in *Abrams* and *Schaefer*, he returned exclusively to the danger doctrine, variables mentioned by Glendon Schubert, *Constitutional Politics: The Political Behaviour of Supreme Court Justices and the Constitutional Policies that They Make* (New York: Holt, Rinehart and Winston, 1960), 521. Joined by Brandeis, Holmes would repudiate the bad tendency test by the time he retired in 1932, but a Court majority continued to equate it with the danger test.
15. *Schenck*, 249 U.S. at 42.
16. Ibid., 51. See also David O'Brien, *Congress Shall Make No Law: The First Amendment, Unprotected Expression, and the U.S. Supreme Court* (Lanham, MD: Rowman & Littlefield, 2010), 2–3.
17. Thomas Emerson, *The System of Freedom of Expression* (New York: Random House, 1970), 16. See also David O'Brien, *Congress Shall Make No Law*, 2–3.
18. David Rabban, *Free Speech in Its Forgotten Years, 1870–1920* (Cambridge, UK: Cambridge University Press, 1997), 132–3, 374; Christopher Wolfe, *Rise of Modern Judicial Review* (New York: Basic Books, 1986), 193; and Paul Freund, *The Supreme Court of the United States: Its Business, Purposes and Performance* (Cleveland, OH: World Publishing Co., 1960), 44.
19. Rodney Smolla, *Free Speech in an Open Society* (New York: Alfred A. Knopf, 1992), 99, 100.

20. Holmes to Pollock, April 5, 1919, in *Holmes-Pollock Letters*, ed. Mark de Wolfe Howe (Cambridge, MA: Harvard University Press, 1942), vol. 1, 100.
21. Holmes to Laski, March 16, 1919, in *Holmes-Laski Letters*, ed. Mark de Wolfe Howe (Cambridge, MA: Harvard University Press, 1953), I, 190.
22. *Schenck*, 249 U.S. at 52.
23. *Dennis v. United States*, 341 U.S. 494, 511 (1951). See also *Gitlow v. New York*, 268 U.S. 652, 669 (1925), and *Schneck*, 249 U.S. at 52; and Franklyn Haiman, *Speech and Law in a Free Society* (Chicago, IL: University of Chicago Press, 1981), 269.
24. Rooted in old English law, the legal definition of conspiracy was established in the precedent-setting *Poulterer*'s case of 1611, when the notorious Court of Star Chamber held that mere agreement to commit a crime, whether the crime was executed or not, would be a conspiracy.
25. "Developments in the Law – Criminal Conspiracy," *Harvard Law Review* 72.5 (1959): 920–1008. It discusses provisions of the general federal conspiracy statute (18 U.S.C. § 371). See also F. B. Sayre, "Criminal Conspiracy," *Harvard Law Review* 35 (1922): 393, 413; and Franklyn Haiman, *Speech and Law in a Free Society* (Chicago, IL: University of Chicago Press, 1981), 269, 384; and see also *Schneck*, 249 U.S. at 47.
26. *United States v. Kissel and Harned*, 218 U.S. 601 (1911).
27. *Hyde v. United States*, 225 U.S. 347 (1912).
28. 336 U.S. 440, 449, 453 (1949).
29. *Harrison v. United States*, 7 F.2d 259, 263 (2d Cir. 1925); and Hand endowed the charge of conspiracy with opportunities for great oppression. Confirming as much, Sayre contends that conspiracy was "seized upon because of its very vagueness ... " Sayre, "Criminal Conspiracy," 393.
30. 336 U.S. 613, 622, 626 (1949).
31. Among cases resulting in the convictions of IWW members or local groups associated with it, see *Haywood v. United States*, 268 F. 795 (7th Cir. 1920); *Bryant v. United States*, 257 F. 378 (5th Cir. 1919); *Isenhouer v. United States*, 256 F. 842 (8th Cir. 1919); *Reeder v. United States*, 262 F. 36 (8th Cir. 1919); *Anderson v. United States*, 269 F. 65 (9th Cir. 1920).
32. 249 U.S. 204 (1919).
33. Lucas Powe, *The Warren Court and American Politics* (Cambridge, MA: Harvard University Press, 2000), 72.
34. Brief of Plaintiff, Landmark Briefs, XIX, 54, 69.
35. Bettman to Chafee, October 27, 1919. Quoted in Rabban, *Free Speech in Its Forgotten Years*, 328–9.
36. Lucas Powe, *The Warren Court and American Politics* (Cambridge, MA: Harvard University Press, 2000) 71. See also *Frohwerk*, 249 U.S. at 208.
37. 249 U.S. 211, 214 (1919). See also Frederick Giffen, *Six Who Protested: Radical Opposition to the First World War* (Port Washington, NY: Kennikat Press, 1971), 44–5. Brief of the United States, Landmark Briefs, XIX, 674, 684.
38. *Debs*, 249 U.S. at 214.
39. Ibid., 216.

4

The First Amendment: Crucible Years

The trio of decisions—Schenck, Frohwerk, and Debs—may be understood as exempting wartime measures and activities from First Amendment protections. Eight months after these cases, the Court took up *Abrams v. United States* (1919),[1] with a ruling that offered further evidence of the degree to which the national mood entered judicial chambers. Being a wartime trial, it also played out against a backdrop of Liberty Loan rallies, patriotic parades, bands marching, martial music playing, and spectacles that established the courtroom's atmospherics.[2] Newspapers carried daily listings of American soldiers who were the casualties of war and news items reporting daily battles, as Allied forces were entering their final combat. The "slacker" raids, widely headlined, led to the arrest of 1,500 "draft dodgers," according to Attorney General Thomas Gregory, which only enhanced the hyperbolic nationalism of the time, as did the trials of eighty-three IWW members, including some notable socialists, such as Rose Pastor Stokes. The widely praised Sedition Act and the indictment of John Reed, a celebrated witness to the Bolshevik Revolution, likewise contributed to the fervent patriotic backdrop against which the trial was played out and the jury deliberated.

The case itself was a farrago of sub-Marxist clichés, factually doubtful claims, and sinister fantasy, revealing in blatant form the persistent radical fears in all branches of government. It concerned Jacob Abrams, confessedly an "anarchist-socialist," and four other poverty-stricken young Jewish immigrants, all Russian-born anarchists, socialists, and pacifists, who displayed a passionate sympathy toward the Bolshevik Revolution and the newly minted communist government in Russia, and Wilson was attacked for dispatching armed forces in Siberia in 1918. The defendants were indicted for printing 15,000 copies of two hyperbolic-worded leaflets, one in English and another in Yiddish: the first was entitled "The Hypocrisy of the United States and her Allies" and the second, "Revolutionists Unite for Action." One sentence proclaimed that "there is only one enemy of the workers of the world and that is CAPITALISM." And another proclaimed that "The Russian Revolution cries: Workers of the World Awake! Arise! Put down your enemy and mine." These handbills were distributed to a crowd of marchers in East Harlem, accompanied by Russian songs, and were also thrown out of an open window of a building at Houston and Crosby streets.

Arrested by military police, the five accused were indicted under Section Four, Title One of the Sedition Act 1918 as well as Section Three of the Espionage Act 1917. In what would be the first test of the 1918 measure they were charged with four counts, the first three being conspiracy. The third and fourth counts on which conviction would eventually turn respectively accused the defendants using language "intended to promote and encourage resistance to the United States in said war" and conspiring, "when the United States was at war, ... by utterance, printing and publication, to urge, incite and advocate curtailment of production of things and products ... necessary and essential to the prosecution of the war."[3]

The Abrams case warrants extended comment because it was a pronounced instance of judicial partiality and old tropes marinated in the rich brine of traditional anti-radicalism. The case was highly publicized and very controversial affair, in part because it was tainted by the running commentary of Henry DeLamar Clayton, an anti-alien, anti-Bolshevik, anti-immigrant, and anti-Semitic District Court judge. Called up from Alabama to relieve New York City's crowded court dockets, he was a stranger to ethnic ghettos, such as New York City's, hostile to Bolshevism, and strongly distrusted immigrants—"the cheap pauper labor of Europe." Being an Alabama landowner and by temperament and preference a champion of the agrarian life, Judge Clayton was predictably antagonistic toward Harry Weinberger, an alien, urban dwelling, book-reading chief defense counsel with a distinct Yiddish accent, and a Jew who had made a career of defending anarchists and aliens.[4] "As he peered down at the defendants and their lawyer," Richard Polenberg reasonably stated, "the judge could not help but feel that his most cherished values—patriotism, paternalism, and 100 percent Americanism—were under attack."

Clayton's enmity toward the defendant managed a leap over the barrier of judicial impartiality when announcing that the Court would undertake the interrogatories, which were done in an openly harsh manner. For instance, he twice asked: "Why don't you go back to Russia?"[5] Continually interjected hostile comments about the conduct of the accused, he stated at one point: "... these defendants, by what they have done, conspired to go and incite a revolt; in fact, one of the very papers is signed, 'Revolutionists.'" Upon being sentenced (to terms ranging from three to twenty years), the defendants were subject to Judge Clayton's *ad hominem* summation: "The only thing they know how to raise is hell, and to direct it against the government of the United States. But we are not going to help carry out the plans mapped by the Imperial German Government, and which are being carried out by Lenine and Trotsky."[6] Expanding, he openly acknowledged to Weinberger: "your theory and mine are at war, they can not be reconciled." These exchanges went on, and amply illustrate that the District Court was marching to the tune of the government and a less than sanguine outcome for Abrams and company could be expected.

Weinberger opened the fifty-one page defense Brief by rejecting the prosecutorial claim of evidence that supported the four counts of the indictment. He rebutted the first count by asserting that "there was not a single word in either government's exhibit one or two against the form of government of the United states ..." and insisted, as he would throughout the trial proceedings, that all his clients did was to criticize the government and the right to criticize was the foundation of their democratic society. Regarding the third and fourth counts, he contended: "... in none of the pamphlets [was there] any expressions of sympathy for Germany or its aims. In fact, the whole trend of the evidence is that these Russian anarchists ... only sought to oppose American intervention in Russia and not to help Germany in any way, shape or form."[7] His Petition to the High Court, similar to his earlier trial argument, would assert that both the Espionage and Sedition Acts were unconstitutional. The Framers, he argued, had sought to guarantee "the unbridgeable liberty of discussion as a natural right." Weinberger insisted that speech must be "perfectly unrestrained." Though admitting that overt acts needed restriction and punishment, "[a] speech or article is not an overt act."

The Brief and oral argument of Assistant Attorney General Robert P. Stewart expanded the indictment that the four defendants had intended to hinder war production, to include the charge that they preached a revolutionary overthrow of the government: "Rebellion and revolution are passionately demanded ..." Stewart's Brief and oral argument carried forward this new accusation. By their own testimony, the defendants "intended in their leaflets ... to advocate resistance to, and overthrow ... of government by force." He further argued that they "despised" the US Government and were "devoted adherents of the Soviet government."[8] After elaborating on a refurbished doctrine of seditious libel, Stewart dismissed the defense contention that the Sedition Act was "outside of any power specifically granted to congress by the constitution." After an hour of deliberation the jurors brought in a guilty verdict for Abrams, and two other defendants, imposing a twenty-year prison term.

Weinberger immediately petitioned the Supreme Court, which would hear the case in October 1919, that is, after the war, but hardly after the anti-Red hysteria had subsided. Justice Clarke wrote the majority opinion. Citing precedents, Schenck and Frohwerk, he dismissed the petitioner's First Amendment claims.[9] For him, the only question before the Court was "whether there was some evidence, competent and substantial, before the jury tending to sustain the verdict." Clarke, later, continually referred to these circulars, quoting "inflammatory" passages. The fact of war was critical for him. The leaflets had been distributed "in the greatest port in the land" and "at the supreme crisis of the war" and had amounted to "an attempt to defeat the war plans of the Government ... by bringing upon the country the paralysis of a general strike"; and such a strike would curtail "the production of ordnance and munitions necessary and essential to the prosecution of the war, as was charged in the fourth count." To achieve this end, Clarke argued that the defendants' avowed purpose would be "to throw the country into a state of revolution ..." Their "plan of action which they adopted necessarily involved defeat of the war program of the United States before it could be realized." Hence, Clarke affirmed that there was "much persuasive evidence ... before the jury tending to prove that the defendants were guilty as charged in both the third and fourth counts."[10]

In emphasizing petitioners' intention, Clarke was obliquely or unwittingly referring to the presumptive "intent" rubric earlier employed by Holmes—which had morphed into the "bad tendency" doctrine—in order to uphold conviction: "Men must be held to have intended ... the effects which their acts were likely to produce ..."[11] Speech or publication "which tend to subvert or imperil the government" was punishable, and therefore, the government need to consider not only explicit advocacy of illegal action but also whatever tended to it. Clarke's rationale for proscription of such speech was that "by their very nature,

[it] involve danger to the public peace and to the security of the state." Such danger might not be immediate but

> [t]he state cannot reasonably be required to measure the danger of every such utterance in the nice balance of the jeweler's scale. A single revolutionary spark may kindle a fire that, smoldering for a time, may burst into a sweeping and destructive conflagration. It cannot be said that the state is acting arbitrarily or unreasonably when, in the exercise of its judgment as to the measures necessary to protect the public peace and safety, it seeks to extinguish the spark conflagration.[12]

In sum, although considered the first modern liberal justice, Clarke affirmed the District Court conviction.

Holmes unexpectedly broke with his colleagues and, joined by Brandeis, issued a lengthy dissent that was almost diametrically opposed to the trio of holdings (Schenck, Debs, and Frohwerk) eight months earlier. Becoming the first great statement from the Court on the issue of free speech, his closing remarks forcefully stated: "Only the emergency that makes it [speech] immediately dangerous ... warrants making any exception to the sweeping command, 'Congress shall make no law bridging the freedom of speech.'" This refinement of his danger formula and his emphasis upon the imminence and immediacy of the threat, as reflected in his shift between the Schenck and Abrams opinions, attests to the difficulty that judges then had in balancing individual rights against government interests. Both he and Brandeis had initially acquiesced in Woodrow Wilson's repressive actions. They had joined the Court majority in producing what Harlan Stone would later call "dismal precedents that took the nation half a century to overcome." The danger formula would scarcely be mentioned by the new Court majority, and then indirectly, on two occasions, notwithstanding the flood of free speech cases in the tribunal headed by Chief Justice Hughes. Judicial wavering on the necessary criteria to uphold conviction reflected on the difficulty that courts would have in determining the doctrinal basis for their decisions. It may be found in a quartet of cases following Abrams, each of which made the wartime views of the majority abundantly clear, and each produced a penetrating dissent that contributed the extraordinary reach of the First Amendment today.

In the same Court term as Abrams, argued the same day and decided months later, the tribunal rendered yet one more free speech split decision—in *Schaefer v. United States* of 1920.[13] In *Schaefer*, five defendants, officers in a Philadelphia corporation, of the Philadelphia

Tageblatt Association, were charged with treason for publishing in a German-language newspaper, the *Philadelphia Tageblatt* (and in the *Philadelphia Sonntagsblatt*), fifteen articles that allegedly glorified Germany by criticizing the United States. Although acquitting the five defendants of the treason charge, the jury entered a guilty verdict against them under the "obstructions" and "false statement" provisions of the Espionage Act—over the objections of defense counsel who argued that the statute was "in derogation of the individual's rights, guaranteed to him by the Constitution." (Schaefer and two defendants were also convicted on the conspiracy count.)

Speaking through Justice Joseph McKenna, appointed to the tribunal in 1897 and its senior member, the Court majority upheld the Espionage Act convictions of three of the five appellants, condemning the "strange perversion" of the First Amendment when it was invoked by those who would "debase" the "morale of our armies." The decision followed judicial thinking established in other wartime cases of the time—and Debs, Frohwerk, Abrams, and Schenck would be cited—that also held wartime dissent was dangerous whether or not any overt act followed from the advocacy of dissenting ideas. McKenna found that there could be, "no more powerful and effective instruments of evil than [these] two German newspapers"; and the Court ascribed their articles, editorials, and innuendo, as the jury had, to an "active and sinister purpose."

Rather than invoke the question of whether a clear and present danger existed, McKenna merely made an inquiry into the consequences and the possible effect of the words of the articles (i.e., did they tend to produce harmful consequences?). Emphasizing the words of the statute—"their 'intent' and 'attempt'"—and quoting generously from the Tageblatt, he found them congruent with the bad tendency standard. His conclusion: "The tendency of the articles and their efficacy were enough for offense … .The incidence of its [the Espionage Act] violation might not be immediately seen, evil appearing only in disaster, the result of the disloyalty engendered …"[14] The bad tendency standard now seemingly permitted an even more expansive formula for the suppression of speech than existed in the past. Utterances that might *tend* to have dangerous results in the future could now be prohibited, a test of their potential danger that would intermittently surface in High Court opinions for years to come.

Once again, in *Pierce v. United States* (1920),[15] the last of the leading Espionage Act cases, a Court majority speaking through the conservative Justice Mahlon Pitney invoked the "bad tendency" rule. He upheld the conviction of a quartet of socialists in Albany, New York, who had circulated the four-page anti-war publication, "The Price We Pay," written by Irwin St. John Tucker, a prominent Episcopal clergyman. A radical prototype for that day, the pamphlet declared:

> into your homes the recruiting officers are coming. They will take your sons of military age and impress them into the army ... Guns will be put into their hands; they will be taught not to think, only to obey without questioning ... Then they will be shipped ... to the bloody quagmire of Europe. Black death will be a guest at every American fireside ...[16]

In a typical radical expression, Clinton Pierce and the other defendants had distributed 500 copies of the broadside, going from house to house in Albany, for which act they were arrested and indicted on three counts of conspiracy and violation of the 1917 Espionage Act; that is, they were charged, as the measure stipulated, with "making or conveyance of false reports or false statements with the intent to interfere with the operation or success of either the military or naval forces of the United States or to promote the success of the enemies of the United States."

Judge Ray District Court for the Northern District of New York had expressed the predictable hostility to these "lurid and exaggerated pictures of the horrors of war" and the "many false statements calculated to incite opposition to the war and opposition to the government." Then he ingenuously stated the following: ... "why may not Congress enact a law making it an offense to make and spread broadcast, when a state of war exists, pamphlets containing materially false statements ... intended to interfere with and obstruct ... the raising of armies and military operations of the government ...?" Such pamphlets give aid and comfort to the enemy. This familiar and damning last sentence was following by an emphasis upon "intent" that, if "willfully made ... to interfere with the operation or success of our military or naval forces ... of willfully attempt to cause insubordination, or refusal of duty ..." would be evidence enough for a jury to convict. "[F]ree speech" and "freedom of the press" have their limitations and do not include and protect the making and promulgation of false statements knowingly made with intent to destroy our arms in time of war ... "

They "did not mean the unrestrained right to do and say what one pleased at all times and under all circumstances."[17]

Thus did the District Court, and the High Court ruling that followed, inferentially reveal how the judicial function was "an essential part of the system of government," as J. A. G. Griffith had contended.

Justice Mahlon Pitney had to determine whether the jury's finding was reasonable—whether the actions of the defendants constituted a conspiracy within the meaning of the Espionage Act, and "whether the statements contained in the [publication] had a natural tendency to produce the forbidden consequences." Rejecting defense argument, he upheld the lower court's ruling on four of the six original counts. These included unlawful conspiracy to commit an offense against the United States by "attempting to cause insubordination, disloyalty and refusal of duty" in the armed forces by "publicly circulating ... certain articles printed in ..." "Pay," and false statements in this pamphlet with intent to interfere with the operation and success of American armed forces; attempting "to cause insubordination, disloyalty, mutiny, and refusal of duty ... by means of the publication, circulation, and distribution" of said pamphlet. To "interfere with" military operations need not be a physical act, Pitney argued, but could be by "words, or writings, to cause insubordination, disloyalty, mutiny, or refusal of duty in the military or naval forces of the United States in time of war ..." Pitney's conclusion was foretold, the trial jury decision was upheld.[18] In so doing, Pitney again illustrates how the judiciary underpinned the stability of the governmental system and resisted attempts to change it.

In *Gilbert v. Minnesota* (1920),[19] a State law was at issue, one of many anti-sedition and anti-syndicalism measures that state legislatures across the country had rushed onto their statute books during and after the war. The Minnesota Statute, enacted in the spring 1917—after war had been declared—made it a crime to discourage cooperation in the war effort. The statute would be invoked against Joseph Gilbert, a prominent member of the small-farmer socialist Nonpartisan League who had been arrested for a wartime speech that lacked any hint of the desirability of illegal action. At a public League meeting he had declared the following: "We were stampeded into this war by newspaper rot to pull England's chestnuts out of the fire for her. I tell you, if they conscripted wealth like they have conscripted men, this war would not last over forty-eight hours."[20] Gilbert was tried and convicted of violating the State statute and federal draft law and the judgment affirmed by Minnesota's Supreme Court.

Displaying no patience or tolerance for such ex parte assaults on publicly endorsed policy, Justice McKenna, for the majority, sustained the State's measure, the jury verdict, and the one-year sentence imposed on the petitioner. He found the statute to be a legitimate exercise of state police power, owing to the need to maintain civic order, which reaffirms earlier observations that the judicial function was to protect and maintain the governing institutions and the nation's stability. It was unnecessary, McKenna ruled, to determine that anything the defendant said had created a clear and present danger to America's conduct of the war. It was sufficient to show that Gilbert's talk might have incited listeners, reason enough to invoke the police power, the familiar term cited when civic order appeared to be threatened. Gilbert's rhetoric, after all, was "resented by his auditors" and met with "protesting interruptions, also accusations and threats against him, disorder and intimations of violence." Referring to Abrams, Debs, and Schenck, McKenna indignantly noted "the curious spectacle was presented of the Constitution of the United States being invoked to justify the activities of anarchy or of the enemies of the United States ...."[21] McKenna's hostility toward petitioner was not yet exhausted. In an afterthought that summed up much of judicial thinking at this time, he declared: The war "was not declared in aggression, but in defense of our national honor"; and this as well as comparable remarks suggest both how deeply and inescapably the war intruded upon the courtroom and how the Supreme Court and courts generally may be seen as agents of the state.[22] For our purposes, we need only note that a High Court majority, although conceding "that the asserted freedom [of speech] is natural and inherent," went on to the usual qualifier and declared, "but it is not absolute, it is subject to restriction and limitation," and "[i]t would be a travesty on the constitutional privilege [Gilbert] invokes to assign him its protection."

A pause is warranted here for an explanatory postscript. Because the *Gilbert* case involved a state measure—the first free speech case to reach the Supreme Court on appeal—it was uncertain whether the First Amendment, exclusively designed to curb Congress' power to restrict speech, was applicable to a state law, Minnesota's in this instance. To this time, the First Amendment had applied exclusively to the actions of the political branches of the federal government. It had not been established that the First Amendment restricted the states as well via the 1866 Fourteenth Amendment—which declared the following: "[n]o State shall make or enforce any law which shall abridge the privileges or immunities of citizens of the United States; nor shall any State deprive any person of life, liberty, or property, without due process of law ..."

In the course of time, and only by a slow process of maturation, judicial activists would successfully argue that the Framers of the Fourteenth Amendment intended to "incorporate," to "carry over," to "nationalize," or to "federalize" the First Amendment, thereby making it applicable to the states. That the due process clause of the Fourteenth Amendment would apply the First Amendment to the states was not an entirely new idea, being tentatively advanced in *Hurtado v. California* (1884);[23] and in *Twining v. New Jersey* (1908), it had been argued that "some of the personal rights safeguarded by the first eight Amendments against National action be safeguarded against state action" by the due process clause of the Fourteenth Amendment.[24] In *Patterson v. Colorado* (1907), the eloquent dissent of the elder Justice John Marshall Harlan declared the following: "... the privileges of free speech and of a free press, belonging to every citizen of the United States constitute essential parts of every man's liberty, and are protected against violation by that clause in the Fourteenth Amendment forbidding a State to deprive any person of his liberty without due process of law."[25] This proposition would be decisively affirmed by Justice Edward Sanford in *Gitlow v. New York* (1925),[26] but the seeds of change in the Court's understanding of the First and the Fourteenth Amendments had been planted with the dissents in such cases as *Schaeffer* and *Pierce* and, we will shortly learn, would flower five years after *Gilbert* when freedom of speech was invoked against state action. Admittedly, it would remain a most divisive issue confronting the Court in cases originating in state statutes; and it would be anathema to Frankfurter others who emphasized the integrity of the federal system.

Notes

1. *Abrams v. United States*, 250 U.S. 616, 40 S. Ct. 17, 63 L. Ed. 1173 (1919).
2. Richard Polenberg, *Fighting Faiths: The Abrams Case, the Supreme Court, and Free Speech* (New York: Viking Press, 1987), 108.
3. 40 Stat. 553.
4. Quoted in Polenberg, *Fighting Faiths*, 120–1.
5. Ibid., 121.
6. Ibid., 128.
7. Brief of Petitioners, Landmark Briefs, XIX, 801, 808.
8. Brief of the United States, Landmark Briefs, XIX, 860, 866.
9. 250 U.S. at 616, 619.
10. Ibid., see also Polenberg, *Fighting Faiths*, 234 [Clarke opinion].
11. 250 U.S. at 621. See also Landmark Briefs, XIX, 842, 846–87.
12. 250 U.S. at 616.
13. *Schaefer v. United States*, 251 U.S. 468 (1920).
14. Ibid., at 479.
15. *Pierce v. United States*, 252 U.S. 239 (1920).
16. *United States v. Pierce*, 245 F. 878 (N.D.N.Y. 1917).
17. Ibid.
18. *Pierce*, 252 U.S. at 251. See also J. A. G. Griffith, *The Politics of the Judiciary* (Manchester, UK: Manchester University Press, 1977), 213.

19. *Gilbert v. Minnesota*, 254 U.S. 325, 41 S.Ct. 125 (1920).
20. 141 Minn. 254.
21. *Gilbert*, 254 U.S. at 332.
22. Ibid., 333.
23. *Hurtado v. California*, 110 U.S. 516; 4 S. Ct. 111 (1884).
24. *Twining v. New Jersey*, 211 U.S. 78, 99, 29 S.Ct. 14, 53 L.Ed. 97 (1908).
25. *Patterson v. Colorado*, 205 U.S. 454, 465, 27 S.Ct. 556, 51. L.Ed. 879 (1907).
26. *Gitlow v. New York*, 268 U.S. 652, 45 S.Ct. 625, 69 L.Ed. 1138 (1925).

5

Freedom of Expression in Flux: The Twenties

The 1920s, consistent with the previous two decades, saw little decline in heresy hunting. The unfolding drama of the Russian Revolution would continue to nourish the possibility of a secret Bolshevik conspiracy in America, as would other events abroad: revolution in Germany, a communist government installed in Hungary, and profound radical unrest in Poland and Italy. For Americans, a Red scourge was seemingly marching across Europe. Also, to remind the reader, a succession of violent events swept post-war American society: the massive steel strike, IWW-led walkouts, militant miners under the United Mine Workers, as labor abandoned wartime restraints and bloody episodes followed in their wake, viewed by many as evidence of a revolutionary anti-capitalist undercurrent.

A deep social malaise prevailed in the immediate post-war years and in the early twenties, a generally unarticulated recognition that America and the world had profoundly changed, corresponding to an equally widespread inability to comprehend the premises of an emerging social order. A rural society understandably believed itself under siege since formerly insulated value patterns were now being assaulted by the lure of new cultural forms, habits, values, reflected in the radio, movies, automobiles, the heterogeneity arriving with new ethnic groups, erosion of the old-fashioned moral code, the rise of a "looser" personal code, Charles Darwin's fearfully growing visibility in urban classrooms, and open defiance of Prohibition. Reacting against this declining status of traditional values rural America counterattacked, but its occasional victories would be nervous ones, owing to emerging secular values. In the search for villains who had destroyed the familiar comfortable social landscape, the simplest response was to darkly attribute this lost world to foreign radicals and foreign ideas, such as those of evolutionists, secularists, anarchists, and drinkers of "hootch."

The possibility of impending conquest of rural America was an alarming prospect that smoothly meshed with the still-vital wartime anti-radicalism. An abundance of post-war deviations from the traditional culture were more often than not charged to Bolshevik influences, leading to a strident anti-radicalism that continued across the twenties. It was evident in 1920, in the representative words of the American Defense Society, which would "[p]urge the public schools of all teachers who are in sympathy Bolshevism, Socialism, IWWism, Sovietism, or other fundamentally un-American theories .... " "IWWism" refers of course to the Industrial Workers of the World. It had enjoyed a modest resurgence and remained a target of opportunity across the entire decade. Though effectively destroyed as an influential force in the labor movement before World War I, it became a renewed object of State and federal authorities. It was, for instance, involved in new strike activities in California's agricultural districts and among State construction workers, and in 1923, the State obtained an injunction against the IWW, virtually prohibiting its very existence within its borders. By 1924, of the 121 radicals in California's prisons who were serving terms of between one and twenty-eight years (though none were charged or convicted of any crime), all but four were Wobblies. In effect, the crippled condition of the IWW was in inverse proportion to popular fears of its members.

This aroused public apprehension of radicals was manifest in many other states. In 1919, twenty state houses enacted criminal anarchy laws, some passing by unanimous vote. New York State's legislature offers another example of state anti-Red activism. Its Joint Legislative Committee Investigating Seditious Activities filed in April 1920 issued a massive 4,456-page, four-volume report entitled, "Revolutionary Radicalism, Its History, Purpose and Tactics with an Exposition and Discussion of the Steps Being Taken to Curb It." The very title was highly suggestive of popular and lawmaker thinking that, as the report stated, radical movements "are not spontaneous expressions of unrest brought about by critical economic conditions in this country," but resulted from a conspiracy "spread by representatives of European revolutionary bodies." Standing alone, these words were incorporated into the sacred texts of state legislators across the country, as well as of the official and unofficial organizations dedicated to combat radical activism and the secret Red conspiracy.

It could not be expected that press and radio would disabuse fears or quiet popular anxieties about the nation's incendiary deviants, such as those who belonged to the Socialist and Communist parties.

Regarding the former, a bitter doctrinal division in the Socialist Party (SP) had long been simmering. Even before 1914, the Party had been sharply divided between a left and right wing, with the latter, led by Morris Hillquit and Victor Louis Berger, being philosophically closer to a reformist center rather than a revolutionary wing. Its adherents for a time sympathized with Russia's Bolsheviks in 1917, but not with their methods, thought inapplicable to the United States.

When the United States entered the European conflict, discord over this decision led to an irrevocable schism within Socialist Party ranks, which played out less than two years later with the formation of two new radical organizations. For a time, the Socialist Party's left caucus managed to work on an ad hoc basis with the dominant Party elements but, to repeat, it tilted worshipfully toward Moscow. Led in Russia by Leon Trotsky and Nikolai Bukharin, and by John Reed, Charles Ruthenberg, and Louis Fraina in the United States, it scorned the reformist road to socialism and its "right-wing" adherents for being gradualists rather than revolutionaries. The increasingly powerful Foreign Language Federations within America's Socialist Party, mostly comprising East European immigrants, moved toward the uncompromising position of the Bolsheviks after 1917, a rallying to the left that was to be expected. For thousands of poor immigrants, exaltation greeted the revolutionary news out of Petrograd and the newly established USSR. It gave meaning and purpose to their lives, providing them with a sense of being "part of an identifiable mass of human beings with a place and a destiny...."[1] As one Socialist Party position paper declared: The Bolshevik Revolution gave back to us our lost ideals. Russia now inspired a "powerful romantic appeal" which drew Socialists away "from a world of hopeless, cheerless realities in a flood of enthusiasm" and naturally it inspired the newly formed communist parties of 1919 to act "as if the Russian Revolution had been bodily transplanted upon American soil." Its exultant members shared the sense of being at the center of the world at a time when it was possible to change society. With the example of a successful revolution in Russia, it could therefore be anticipated that the Soviet model and policy dictated the model for their own future.

The rift between left-wing and conservative elements in the Socialist Party had grown even wider after the war, especially after Moscow announced the Third International in March 1919, with its avowed aim of worldwide proletarian revolution. Cooperative efforts would deteriorate further as the early enthusiasm for the Russian Revolution had waned for the Socialist rightist and centrist bloc.

Though becoming a minority, this bloc retained leadership and control for the time being, but the impatient Slavic-language Federations would bolt, intent on founding a Communist Party (CP). Another group, opposing both factions and led by New York's Socialists, also deserted the main Party organization in 1919 and proclaimed itself the Communist Labor Party (CLP). Until the late twenties, when the Russian Communist Party adopted its harsh and uncompromising Third Period—and resorted to policies that had a profoundly alienating effect upon many America's Socialists—all three radical bodies managed a positive attitude toward Russia.

Owing to the radical schisms, American communism in the interwar years vented no more than a feeble and ineffectual protest against war or capitalism. A few thousand alien and native-born radicals, remaining faction-ridden, more involved in internal disputes than in revolutionary action, comprised the new organizations. The two embryonic communist parties initially had a combined membership of less than 25,000, and, as noted, were themselves divided in program and ideology. The Communist Labor Party emphasized the necessity of an "American" movement, which prompted the Communist Party to charge that it continued to maintain a symbiotic relationship with the Socialist Party. Thus fiercely divided constituencies emerged in the small Communist organizations, and each was locked into social isolation that rendered them helpless.

Personality cults, eccentric rivalries, character assassinations, and bitter ideological divisions continued to rent its ranks, produced additional schisms and schismatics. Some 2,000 Trotskyites, for instance, rejected the idea of a public party and preaching a revolutionary "immediatism."

In 1928, at Moscow's plenary sessions of the Third International, the notorious Third Period was imposed on the international communist movement. The Kremlin ordered Communists to close ranks, weed out deviants, and establish a tightly knit and strictly disciplined party. Ultra-militancy became the style, accompanied by sectarian politics and revolutionary rhetoric. Pacifists, socialists, liberals, and social democrats were to be considered virtually identical to fascists. Witness, for one, the followers of William Z. Foster—by now a legendary Communist Party organizer of iron and steel workers and a future head of the Party—at odds with another Party faction having the "incorrect" line, and with revolvers at the ready took over control of the official Party organ, the Daily Worker. Continuing to reflexively genuflect toward Moscow, the Communist Party in this Third Period would be transformed into an exclusivist, extremist, and isolated revolutionary body.

The fact of two bitterly divided communist parties and a diminished Socialist Party was a matter of indifference to official Washington. Congress made no distinction among the radical parties. Responding to the easily engineered myth of a radical conspiracy was predictable, it debated about seventy peacetime sedition bills in 1919–1920. In January 1920, Attorney General Palmer sent a letter to the press reporting on the "purpose, history, and character of the Red Radical Movement." Including apocalyptic assertions that it "advocates the destruction of all ownership in property, the destruction of all religion," and so forth, Palmer closed by professing: "My one desire to acquaint people like you with the real menace of evil-thinking which is the foundation of the Red movement."[2] Likewise driven by these fabricated possibilities, Palmer, as noted above, established the GID within the BI, and its Director, J. Edgar Hoover, began accumulating files on radicals, socialists, pacifists, collecting over a half million names in short order. Hoover considered his agents to be soldiers opposing what he called "the mad march of Red fascism" intent on creating a Soviet America.[3] Bureau personnel infiltrated radical ranks and acted as agents provocateurs, and they also now undertook their wholesale raids and deportation proceedings. Bureau activities would be maintained across the entire interwar period. They featured an imperial disregard of legal niceties such as search warrants, and reflected the mindset of an administrator whose crusading zeal against Reds, radicals, and dissenters would never be out of style. Coloring the entire decade, the 1921 trial of two Italian radical aliens, Sacco and Vanzetti, culminating in their execution in 1927, fueled further rural hostility to non-Anglo-Saxon, non-Protestant carriers of an alien ideology, and confirmed alarmist views about radical conspiracy.

Shrill expressions of anti-radicalism were hardly limited to ordinary folk living in farm country. Many who had large incomes and dwelt in urban society likewise held that no dissent was tolerable. Staid upper-middle-class conservatives, reflecting popular opinion, believed that communism and socialism were on the rise. Typical of them, William Howard Taft, in the late twenties, wrote: "I must stay on the court in order to prevent the anti-radical voices." And another former President, that hero of America's nationalists, Theodore Roosevelt, aggressively declared in January 1919: "there must be no sagging back in the fight for Americanism merely because the war is over .... We have room for but one flag, the American flag, and this excludes the red flag, which symbolizes all wars against liberty and civilization."[4] Red hunters, accordingly, had a cross-class constituency. Business groups joined with union labor (e.g., members of the AFL) and middle-class patriotic organizations in ostentatious displays of patriotism.

Their organizations, including the American Legion, Better America Foundation (BAF), the DAR, among others, and their patriotic appeals reached those who had no formal connection to them. Accordingly, a model program set forth by the BAF urged a peacetime sedition act, the elimination of "subversive" materials from schools and libraries, vigilant opposition to all measures that opened the door to Bolshevism (e.g., the eight-hour day, forty-hour-work week, compulsory education, and child labor laws). Another ultra-patriotic organization, the National Security League announced a "secret communist conspiracy," and sponsored a national campaign to "forestall the indoctrination" of aliens "with Bolshevistic principles." Likewise typical, the American Legion which had a million members by 1920, held similar convictions, and conjured up the danger of a sinister conspiracy working to undermine American society. Its fiercely patriotic officials cautioned that "the right of the entire nation to free speech may be endangered by the flagrant abuse of the right by a few." Their organization became the model for other service-oriented bodies devoted to assailing the "reds" and the liberals, and the non-communist "fellow travelers," often liberal Democrats. The DAR was equally active in promoting such ultra-nationalist programs, including oratorical contests characterized by reflexive patriotic tones. Predictably, its President in 1923 would insist that "academic freedom of speech has no place in the school, where the youth of our country are taught and their unformed minds are developed. There are not two sides of loyalty to this country and its flag." And in the same vein, the National Defense Committee issued "The Common Enemy," a pamphlet that warned: "Communism, Bolshevism, Socialism, Liberalism, and Ultra-Pacifism tend to the same ends: 1. the abolition of government, 2. the abolition of patriotism, 3. the abolition of property rights.... " Consequently, significant infringements on the freedom of expression, indeed all civil liberties, could be expected by such representative organizations as well as by local, state, and national governments, and would continue to characterize the decisions of state and federal tribunals.

Supreme Court justices, to restate, were very aware of the ongoing anti-radical infestations in post-war American culture. They retained a deep faith in the government's capacity to decide what ideas were "offensive" or "dangerous," and largely complemented rather than impeded the administration's understanding of the Constitution. Under their new Chief Justice, the former President William Howard Taft, having been appointed in 1921, the justices hardly changed their collective attitudes toward radical immigrants and free speech. Taft himself would not even resign when Herbert Hoover entered the White House suspecting him of "liberal" tendencies: "I must stay on the court in order to prevent the Bolsheviki from getting control." And he believed that "[t]he only hope we have … is for us to stay as long as we can."[5] Taft himself was understandably most comfortable with fellow conservative colleagues, the Four Horsemen, George Sutherland, Pierce Butler, McReynolds, and his good friend, Van Devanter, a quartet that, with their Chief, comprised a predicable Court majority committed to protecting the existing social order against radical agitators. Justices Day and Pitney, as well as Clarke, would leave the tribunal in 1922. Justice Edward T. Sanford who remained, had rendered the majority opinion in *Abrams*, though occasionally demonstrating liberal tendencies. However, only two members of the new Court – Holmes, and the Brandeis – could be consistently relied upon to uphold protected speech in this decade, though, as seen above, it was an exiguous hope in earlier First Amendment cases. Indeed, Holmes had insisted in the Abrams dissent that he "never [saw] any reason to doubt that the question of law" in Debs and Scheck "was rightly decided."

Even after President Calvin Coolidge appointed Harlan Stone to replace McKenna in early 1925, the conservative judicial tide remained unchecked. It was only five years later, when Charles Evans Hughes returned to the tribunal as Chief Justice in 1930, succeeding Taft, that Court majority decisions would qualitatively change. Hughes, as will be presently learned, would write the majority opinion in *Stromberg v. California* (1931), a decisive victory for free speech, as well as in *Near v. Minnesota* (1931) that struck down prior restraints on the press, and *De Jonge v. Oregon* (1931), likewise an affirmation of the First Amendment (the oft-forgotten freedom of assembly in this instance).

The preceding Taft Court majority, to repeat, conformed to the dominant social and legal perceptions of the interwar years which were consistent with popular demands for the suppression of radical dissenters. Judicial responsiveness to public opinion appeared in such decisions as *Gitlow v. People of State of New York* (1925).[6] This case evolved out of the arrest and conviction of Benjamin Gitlow and three others. Gitlow himself was native-born, unlike most radicals arrested in the many state and national red raids. Being the son of Russian–Jewish radical immigrants, he inherited their militant unionism, following them again by enrolling in the Socialist Party at age eighteen. Rising to a position on the executive board of New York State's Socialist Party, he embraced the Bolshevik Revolution, and then disavowed the rightwing socialists who trusted in change via the ballot box; and when the Socialist Party divided in 1919, the twenty-eight-year-old Gitlow signed on to the Party's more militantly radical "Left Wing Section" and eventually became one of the prime movers in the founding of a second Communist Party, the Communist Labor Party, later being nominated as its Vice-President (in 1924, and again in 1928).

Becoming business manager of the official organ of the Left-wing Socialist Party, *The Revolutionary Age*, in 1919, Gitlow was responsible for its circulation and for the writing, printing, sale, mailing of 16,000 copies of the Party's "The Left-Wing Manifesto," a pamphlet reflecting the bitter divisions in socialist ranks at the time. It proclaimed that capitalism was "in process of disintegration and collapse, [that] the class struggle is the heart of Socialism ..., [that] the Russian Revolution was the first act of the proletariat against the war and Imperialism ...," that "mass political strikes and revolutionary mass action" are necessary, that the "old machinery of the state... must be destroyed"; and its conclusion proclaimed "immediate class struggle" and the inevitable proletarian revolution. Not surprisingly, the District Court judge decided upon reading the pamphlet: "[i]t is perfectly plain that the plan and purpose advocated ... in this movement contemplates the overthrow and destruction of the governments of the United States and of all the states... through mass strikes and force and violence."

State police and agents of a New York State legislative committee, the previously mentioned Joint Committee to Investigate Seditious Activities (the Lusk Committee), raided Party headquarters in November 1919 where they picked up Benjamin Gitlow and three others. New York State's Criminal Anarchy Act of 1902, a hitherto unenforced statute triggered by the assassination of President McKinley, was the legal basis for their arrests. The measure, to remind readers, made it a crime to "advocate, advise or teach the duty, necessity or propriety" of forcible overthrow of government; or to "print, publish, or knowingly circulate any book, paper, etc. advocating, advising or teaching the doctrine that organized government should be so overthrown ...." The defendants would be indicted and tried in the Extraordinary Trial

Term of the New York State Supreme Court on two counts of criminal anarchy under the 1902 statute.

Archibald Stevenson, Lusk's chief assistant on the Committee, did not emphasize the "Manifesto," with its call for revolutionary overthrow of government and Gitlow's connection with the document. Rather, at both the preliminary hearing and at the trial, he stressed "the revolutionary socialists of the Left Wing," their subversive character and intent, and the similarities between them and the anarchists. Admitting that the revolutionaries were a small coterie of little danger to society, he, however, warned the jurors of the possibility that their views could "get into the minds of the illiterate massed proletariat in our basic industries and stir them up to hatred against our government." Gitlow and his fellow defendants, Assistant District Attorney John Rorke argued that they did not seek reform or peaceful legal change. Rather their goal was "the destruction, the conquest and the annihilation of the government of the United States."

The nationally known defense lawyer, Clarence Darrow, joined the legal team and his presentation did not dispute the facts offered by the prosecution, but he challenged its argument that the "Manifesto" had urged violent revolution, or that it fell into the category of publications prohibited by the 1902 New York Statute. Broadening the argument, he took up the question of the statute's constitutionality, asserting that it violated the State's constitutional guarantee of protected speech and press, and further, most significant for its legal implications, that his client's conviction violated the Fourteenth Amendment, which prohibited states from depriving persons of life, liberty, and property without due process of law. Trial Judge Bartow Weeks rejected Darrow's Fourteenth Amendment constitutional argument, and instructed the jury "that the law of this state" under which Gitlow had been indicted was "not an invasion of any right of free speech," and the First Amendment was not to be considered by the jurors. After forty-five minutes of deliberation, the jurors convicted Gitlow of "advocating, advising, and teaching" by the writings in the "Manifesto"—and he would receive the maximum sentence, five to ten years in prison (serving five before New York's Governor Alfred Smith pardoned him).

Counsel for Gitlow then appealed the conviction for the crime of criminal anarchy to the State's lower appellate tribunal, the Superior Court of New York County,[7] contending that the "Manifesto" was protected speech and not within the meaning of "anarchy." But the three-judge appellate court reflexively emphasized that Gitlow and his revolutionary socialists took a course opposed to that of the moderate Socialist Party and would advocate overthrow the government by force and violence, thereby upholding the District Court. The defendants then took their case to the State's Court of Appeals, where, as Harold Josephson carefully sets forth, they again encountered the same fearful judicial convictions and the same support for conventional and established interests.[8] Chief Judge Hiscock Crane, writing for the Court's alarmed majority, warned "[t]he world is in crisis. Capitalism, the prevailing system, is in the process of disintegration and collapse. Out of its vitals is developing a new social order, the system of Communist Socialism." The automatic judicial paean to "free and fearless discussion of public question" was followed by the inevitable, "[b]ut … advocacy of the destruction of government itself by means which are abhorrent" will not be tolerated.[9] In both state and federal courts, this formula prevailed. Robotic accolades to protected freedoms under the First Amendment was automatically qualified by finding these guarantees "do not permit attempts to destroy that freedom …," as the appellate court asserted in *Gitlow*. Judge Crane, for one, acknowledged that "[t]he Constitution of the United States places a restraint on the power of the Legislature to punish the publication of matter which is injurious to society according to the standard of the common law"; but, and again the expected "but," the state does not "authorize the publication of articles promoting the commission of murder or the overthrow of the government by force," regardless of how zealous the courts may be in upholding free speech provisions.[10] From such standard judicial thinking, a unanimous appellate panel would inevitably conclude it was "competent for the legislature to enact laws for the preservation of the state and nation."

The seven-to-two majority opinion of the Supreme Court affirmed the New York State Court of Appeals finding that advocacy and incitement was inherent in the petitioners' writings. Justice Sanford, for the majority, assumed that the freedom of speech and press were protected by the First Amendment from abridgment by Congress. But then followed the usual qualifier, the claim that these preferred rights were absolute "was not open to consideration"; and "a State may punish utterances endangering the foundations of organized government and threatening its overthrow by unlawful means."[11] Sanford concluded: "Every presumption is to be indulged in favor of the validity of the statute," he declared, and only a measure thought "arbitrary and unreasonable" by the Court could be considered unconstitutional.

In short, the Court upheld the State measure under which Gitlow was convicted, a law that Walter Birns incisively states, "was incompatible with 'the only meaning of free speech.'"[12]

In the course of his opinion, Sanford produced a couple of worrisome passages from Gitlow's "Left Wing Manifesto" to support his ruling "that utterances of a certain kind may be punished," those that tended to "direct incitement," a conclusion that by implication supported the "imminent danger" formula.[13] He argued – and not even Star Chamber proceedings could improve upon his words – "that a state in the exercise of its police power may punish those who abuse this freedom [of speech and press] by utterances inimical to the public welfare, tending to corrupt public morals, incite to crime, or disturb the public peace, is not open to question." "Tend to," "tending to" and "natural tendency" remind the reader that the "bad tendency" rule Justice Clarke had adumbrated in Abrams was now made explicit.[14]

However oblique, Sanford thereby affirmed a capacious judicial test of "bad tendency." Gitlow's "Manifesto" had no immediate effect, Sanford acknowledged, but it, however, tended to incite "breaches of the peace and ultimate revolution." The Constitution had not required that the state had to wait until the "revolutionary utterances lead to actual disturbances of the public peace or imminent and immediate danger of its own destruction." There was no "present danger" of bad acts in this instance, Sanford acknowledged, but the effect of given utterances cannot be accurately foreseen: "[t]he State cannot reasonably be required to measure the danger from every such utterance in the nice balance of a jeweler's scale. A single revolutionary spark may kindle a fire that, smoldering for a time may burst into a sweeping and destructive conflagration."[15]

Given this possibility, the Court majority found that the State was not "acting arbitrarily or unreasonably when ... it seeks to extinguish the spark without waiting until it has enkindled the flame .... "

Sanford's opinion was a "landmark obiter dictum" in one very significant sense, by recognizing a fundamental constitutional issue was at stake and encouraged an unprecedented examination of the First Amendment and its potential scope. Three years earlier (in *Prudential Insurance Co. v. Cheek*), the Court had concluded that the First Amendment was not binding upon the states. However Brandeis, dissenting in *Gilbert v. Minnesota*, had argued that the First Amendment was "incorporated" into the Fourteenth and the Fourteenth Amendment consequently placed the same restrictions upon the states that the First Amendment had on the federal government. Moreover, the defense Brief in *Gitlow*, entering largely unprecedented constitutional territory, argued that the Court should overturn conviction because it violated the federal guarantee of freedom of speech under the due process clause of the Fourteenth Amendment. Now Sanford, almost in an afterthought, expressed a legal principle not necessary for the case before him and resonating down the decades. He casually announced: "For present purposes, we may and do assume that freedom of speech and of the press – which are protected by the First Amendment from abridgment by Congress – are among the fundamental personal rights and "liberties" protected by the due process clause of the Fourteenth Amendment from impairment by the States."[16] Providing a legal rule that had potentially broad national standards and implications, he in effect nationalized the First Amendment's protected freedoms. Though at best only peripherally related to the case before the Court Sanford, in a radical step of great significance, would make protected speech, press, and assembly applicable to state measures.

Neither these First Amendment gleanings nor the incorporation doctrine, one hastens to add, dominated case law in the post-war decade. Gitlow was one of many arrested and convicted under state espionage and sedition laws. "Big Jim" Larkin, Charles Ruthenberg, William Bross Lloyd, Rose Pastor Stokes were among those who fell under a state's statutory hammer. So did the ninety-one-year old social worker, Anita Whitney, in the case of *Whitney v. California*.[17] Unlike these other defendants, she was native-born and had impeccable family credentials. In fact, she was the daughter of a one-time California state senator and the niece of Stephen Field, the former High Court justice who had been known for his ultra-conservative rulings. "[A] woman of refinement and culture" according to the appellate court record, she would join the California's Communist Labor Party, professing that it would take the route of democratic parliamentarianism. The claim meant nothing to California's public or jurists – not when the CLP endorsed the Wobblies in the class war and when the word "Communist" was in the designated name of the organization itself. California, after all, had been consumed by anti-radical fervor, being one of many states having anti-radical laws on its books as well as having its own little un-American activities committee that searched for alleged Communists behind every bush, and readily found them in their organizational infestations.

As a member of the credentials committee that urged "the value of political action," Anita Whitney argued the case for an electoral strategy when attending the State CLP convention, but was defeated in favor of the more militant program of the national Party. Notwithstanding her moderate reformist stance and overall record, she was arrested and indicted under the State's 1919 Criminal Syndicalism Act, a measure similar to New York's criminal anarchy statute cited in *Gitlow*, making it a felony to organize or knowingly join "any organization, society, ... to advocate, teach or aid and abet criminal syndicalism."

Burdened by State-wide notoriety as a "parlor pink," Whitney became the object of a vigorous and successful prosecution by California's Attorney General at a four-day trial in the Superior Court of Alameda County. He charged that "[s]he agreed to do certain things [sic] for the I.W.W. organization," though no evidence existed that she ever belonged to the IWW or had anything to do with it. Upon being found guilty of aiding and abetting criminal syndicalism,[18] defense appealed to the State's Supreme Court, which refused to hear the case; and then to California District Court of Appeals on the grounds that the prosecution had failed to establish that the California Labor Party advocated criminal syndicalism or that she had sufficient knowledge of any such advocacy.

Of the defense contentions heard by Judge Tyler in the Court of Appeals,[19] only the one claiming the evidence was insufficient to justify that the conviction was deliberated upon. He openly acknowledged, as has been earlier repeatedly observed in other courtrooms, that, "[j]udges are part of the machinery of authority within the State ...," and his opinion confirmed as much.[20] Likewise echoing judges elsewhere, Tyler paid tribute to the First Amendment, but contended as well

> that freedom of speech which is secured by the Constitution does not confer an absolute right to speak, without responsibility, whatever one may choose, or an unrestricted and unbridled license giving immunity to every possible use of language ...; a State in the exercise of its police power may punish those who abuse this freedom by utterances inimical to the public welfare ..., or endanger the foundations of organized government and its overthrow by means is not open to question.[21]

Accordingly, as could have been anticipated in an age when the hoof beats of totalitarian communism could be heard by judges and public alike, the lower court decision was affirmed.

With the High Court taking the case on appeal with another state court case, the Brief of defense counsel (Walter Nelles and Walter Pollak, two skilled civil liberties lawyers) reminded the justices that before trial in the lower court, during the trial, and in motions for a new trial, the petitioner had contended that neither the District Attorney nor the trial court judge specified the accusations against Whitney or allowed the defendant to confront her anonymous accusers. Their Brief protested: "We don't know what this lady is being tried for. Is she being tried for being a member of the IWW aiding, abetting or assisting them; or being a member of the Communist Labor Party, and aiding, abetting and assisting them?" Nor was any act or occasion specified that constituted the offense. Their Brief argued that there was "no evidence that the defendant ever attended a single meeting of the IWW" or "that she ever organized, helped to organize or assembled with the Oakland Communist Labor Party"; and moreover, her "resolution for political action" had been voted down by the CLP.[22] Finally, the defense contended that the State Criminal Syndicalism Act was unconstitutional because of its vagueness, because it violated the due process and equal protection clauses of the Fourteenth Amendment by prohibiting advocacy of the use of violence and, in closing, because it violated the freedom of speech and association.

The prosecution Brief charged that Whitney had been "seen at the I.W.W. headquarters," and being "in entire sympathy with the I.W.W." It then went on to list Wobbly violence, incendiarism, barn burnings, cattle poisoning, crop destruction, irrelevancies doubtfully associating the defendant with these criminal acts and with the "horrors of revolution." By no means exhausting the implied illegalities attached to the defendant, the prosecution quoted at length from the constitution of the Communist Labor Party, with its call, for "the overthrow of capitalist rule," inferentially suggesting Whitney's attachment to this goal.

The Supreme Court unanimously affirmed conviction, Justice Sanford rejecting all defense contentions. He found the case similar to *Gitlow*, but Whitney posed a further question of whether an individual member of an organization was responsible for the program and actions of that organization. His opinion relied on twin grounds: (1) the "tending to" standard, and (2) the statute's presumption-of-constitutionality. As in his *Gitlow* opinion, he found certain kinds of speech – "utterances inimical to the public welfare, ... or endanger the foundations of organized government ..." or that tend "to incite to crime" – may be prohibited.[23] An association advocating forcible action,

Sanford stated "partakes of the nature of a criminal conspiracy," and was more dangerous than "the isolated utterances and acts of individuals." That petitioner objected to the official Party program or that he was referring to a group of less than 10,000 members seemingly did not trouble the Court.[24]

Judicial liberalism had an early triumph later that same year in *Fiske v. Kansas* (1927),[25] when a unanimous Court opinion reversed a conviction under the Kansas criminal syndicalism statute that was similar to state laws at issue in *Gitlow* and *Whitney*.[26] Harold Fiske, a IWW organizer, had been convicted under the State law for seeking to recruit members for the organization and for distributing a pamphlet that advocated "criminal syndicalism," though the only evidence introduced against him was the preamble of the IWW Constitution.

Justice Sanford, speaking for an unanimous Court, rejected the District Court and jury summations, and found, "[n]o substantial inference can ... be drawn from the language of this [IWW] preamble, that the organization taught, advocated or suggested the duty, necessity, propriety, or expediency of crime, criminal syndicalism, sabotage, or other unlawful acts or methods ...." Moreover, there was no "charge or evidence" to convict the defendant, and "[t]hus applied the act is an arbitrary and unreasonable exercise of the police power of the state, unwarrantably infringing the liberty of the defendant in violation of the due process clause of the Fourteenth Amendment."[27]

Though not ruling the State law unconstitutional, Sanford removed any previous doubt that freedom of speech was a liberty within the Fourteenth Amendment, and as Milton Konvitz, among others observe, the Court for the very first time overturned a conviction under state law based on First Amendment grounds. Fiske, therefore, did suggest a softening of judicial views toward radical dissent. In the past, after all, it was tacitly assumed or open affirmed that all IWW activities automatically violated anti-criminal syndicalist state statutes. Although the justices did not mention free speech or free association, their decision represented greater sensitivity toward individual rights.

The outcome in Fiske notwithstanding the Court majority continued to uphold the government in case law and showed little solicitude for those who might challenge the nation's security and sovereignty. Witness, for example, three decisions involving wartime conscientious objector cases that reflected the general judicial mindset. These decisions found the tribunal barring from citizenship a minister who had been a chaplain in the First World War (Douglas MacIntosh), and a religiously conscientious woman (Marie Bland) who served as a nurse in the war, because neither defendant would take an unqualified oath to bear arms. Although the cases did not directly center on the First Amendment and dissent, being test oaths rulings, they were, however, indicative of the dominant judicial conservatism in these years.

In a third oath ruling, *United States v. Schwimmer* (1929),[28] a six-man Court majority denied citizenship to the forty-nine-year old Hungarian-born Rosika Schwimmer, an internationally known linguist, pacifist, and feminist who had come to the United States on a lecture tour and, deciding to remain, had applied for citizenship. Affirming a willingness to comply with the congressional measure requiring an oath to "bear true faith and allegiance to the Constitution," Schwimmer was not allowed to take the oath because, as she testified at the naturalization hearing, she refused to bear arms in wartime, being an uncompromising pacifist with no sense of nationalism, but only a "cosmic consciousness of belonging to the human family." Arguing her case in the Northern District of Illinois federal court, Schwimmer observed that as a woman and being forty-nine years of age, she would not be drafted. But, she hypothesized, in the event she was subjected to conscription, she would seek conscientious objector status and undertake alternative service. The trial judge was unmoved, denying naturalization, but the Circuit Court of Appeals reversed the ruling and, taking cert, a High Court majority of six affirmed the District Court ruling.

Concluding that naturalization required that "one favor and support the government" Justice Pierce Butler, speaking for the majority, cited the 1906 Naturalization Act that conditioned citizenship on declaring under oath that one "will support and defend the Constitution and laws of the United States against all enemies, foreign and domestic ...." In his pledge, Butler affirmed that it was "the duty of citizens by force of arms to defend our government against all enemies whenever necessity arises."[29] Conscientious objectors, and Butler included the petitioner, "are liable to be incapable of the attachment for and devotion to the principles of our Constitution that is required of aliens seeking naturalization."[30]

Two cases decided two years later also reflects the anti-radical prosecutorial impulses of both the government and the courts. Each decision was also punctuated by judicial thinking that lingered from the wartime years. In the first case, *United States v. MacIntosh* (1931),[31] petitioner was Douglas MacIntosh, a Canadian-born Baptist minister and professor of divinity at Yale University Divinity School, who served as a wartime chaplain with Canadian forces in World War I. He was not an absolute pacifist, he insisted, but a selective objector; that is, he would bear arms if he believed that the United States was involved in a just war. In effect, he expressed a readiness to take the oath of allegiance expressly required by the 1906 Naturalization Act, but would qualify its broad requirement to bear arms. Possibly he would be unwilling to fight in a future war that, as a Christian, he regarded as immoral. Justice George Sutherland for the five-man majority bluffly retorted that we are "a Christian people," and must assume that the laws "are not inconsistent with the will of God." He indignantly observed that the petitioner "is unwilling to leave the question of his future military service to the wisdom of Congress where it belongs, and where every native born or admitted citizen is obliged to leave it."[32] Guided by the precedent of *Schwimmer*, Sutherland then reversed the Circuit Court ruling and upheld the District Court denial of citizenship.

Justice Sutherland's opinion in *United States v. Bland* (1931)[33] for the five-man majority was "ruled by the decision just announced" in *MacIntosh*. It also pertained to an application for citizenship. A Canadian-born nurse, Marie Bland, had spent nine months in France, nursing wounded soldiers and assisting in psychiatric work. In her case, she expressed a readiness to take only a qualified form of the oath of allegiance, namely, "as far as my conscience as a Christian will allow." The judicial majority, considering the *MacIntosh* precedent, interpreted the oath as including defense of the United States, which mandated a willingness to bear arms. As a consequence, it rejected Bland's petition for citizenship.

In a Supreme Court decision coming after the Second World War,[34] the tribunal partially amended its position in regard to a willingness to bear arms as an absolute requirement of citizenship. James Louis Girouard, a Seventh-Day Adventist, was prepared to take the oath of allegiance. Unwilling to take up arms, he was willing to serve in a non-combat military capacity. An Ohio county judge in 1933, in avowed defiance of *MacIntosh*, granted him citizenship. Douglas, speaking for the Court majority, found "[t]he test oath is abhorrent to our tradition," and upheld petitioner's naturalization.

Notes

1. Quoted in Harold Josephson, "Political Justice during the Red Scare: The Trials of Benjamin Gitlow," in *American Political Trails*, ed. Michael Belknap (Westport, CT: Greenwood Press, 1981) 143.
2. Quoted in Murray Levin, *Political Hysteria in America* (New York: Basic Books, 1971), 193–5.
3. Quoted in Tim Weiner, *Enemies: A History of the FBI* (New York: Random House, 2012), 23.
4. Quoted in Elting Morison, ed., *The Letters of Theodore Roosevelt* (New York: Cambridge University Press, 1954), VIII 1422.
5. Henry Pringle, *William Howard Taft* (Hamden, CT: Archon Books, 1964), 853–4.
6. 268 U.S. 562 (1925).
7. *People of the State of New York v. Gitlow*, 195 App. Div. 773, 782–3 (1st Dept. 1921).
8. *People v. Gitlow*, 234 N.Y.S. 132, 151 (1922).
9. Ibid., 137.
10. 234 NYS 137 (1932).
11. *Gitlow*, 268 U.S. at 667.
12. Birns, op. cit., 159.
13. Gitlow, 268 U.S. at 669.
14. Ibid., 669–71.
15. Ibid., 669.
16. Ibid., at 666.
17. 274 U.S. 357 (1927). For evidence of the sweeping anti-communist animus in California, see Paul Murphy, *The Meaning of Free Speech: First Amendment Freedoms from Wilson to FDR* (Westport, CT: Greenwood Press, 1972b), 82. See also Harry Abraham, *Freedom and the Court* (New York: Oxford University Press, 1982), 211.
18. Ibid., 449.
19. 1957 Cal. App. *People v. Whitney* (1922), 449, 455.
20. Ibid., 458.
21. Ibid.
22. Landmark Briefs, vol. XXV, 585, 604, 611, 618. "It was not her intention that the Communist Labor Party of California should be an instrument of terrorism or violence and ... not her purpose or that of the Convention to violate any known law." Ibid., Landmark Briefs, 336.
23. *Whitney*, 274 U.S. at 371. See also Klaus Haberle, "From Gitlow to Near Judicial 'Amendment' by Absent-Minded Incrementalism," *Journal of Politics* 34 (no. 2) (1972): 469. Wirenius comments on the gradual judicial shift to a position where the Court ruled in favor of petitioners whose actions were "essentially indistinguishable" from Whitney, such as Stromberg's (*Stromberg v. California* 283 U.S. 359 (1931)); John Wirenius, *First Amendment, First Principles* (New York: Holmes & Meier, 1992), op. it., 54–5. 274 U.S. at 357, 359.
24. Brandeis in dissent argued that "[o]nly in very limited circumstances is it legitimate to suppress speech ... the burden is on the government to establish the clarity, seriousness, and imminence of the danger." 374 U.S. 380.

On Frankfurter's "more moderate 'balancing' position," see Christopher Wolfe, *The Rise of Modern Judicial Review* (New York: Basic Books, 1986), 253.
25. 274 U.S. 380 (1927).
26. Ibid., 382. See also Haberle, "From Gitlow to Near", 469. The Kansas criminal syndicalism statute would prohibit the advocacy of "crime, physical violence, arson, destruction of property, sabotage, or other unlawful acts or methods …."
27. Ibid., 387.
28. 279 U.S. 644 (1929). See also "Paul Murphy, The Supreme Court in…"
29. Ibid.
30. Ibid.
31. 283 U.S. 605 (1931).
32. Ibid., 624.
33. 283 U.S. 636 (1931).
34. In the case of James L. Girouard, a Seventh-Day Adventist, the Court partly amended its position in regard to a willingness to take up arms was an absolute requirement of citizenship. Petitioner was prepared to take the oath of allegiance but unwilling to take up arms, though ready; to serve in a non-combat military capacity. *Girouard v. United States*, 328 U.S. 61 (1946); see also Konvitz, op. cit., 227.

6

The Thirties: Evolving toward the First Amendment

In the ten-year period between *Whitney v. California* of 1927 and *Herndon v. Lowry* of 1937, the Court acted to protect civil rights and liberties in several important cases. This was the tribunal presided over by Taft's successor, Charles Evans Hughes, a clear-headed legal scholar who had resigned in 1916 after serving as Associate Justice and in 1930, at age sixty-eight, returned to the tribunal as Chief Justice after being nominated by Herbert Hoover and remained in this post until July 1941. Unlike the Taft Court decisions, many of those of the Hughes Court overturned convictions of political and social radicals, shoring up precedents that the Warren Court would rely upon. Frankfurter would recall "the mastery and distinction with which he [Hughes] presided," which found the Chief Justice generally prevailing in civil liberties cases coming before Court.[1] From the outset, his tribunal established a liberal record on First Amendment issues. It reverted to the clear and present danger rule on only one occasion, relying instead on prior restraint, constitutional vagueness, due process, and the "bad tendency" test.

In civil liberties decisions, as reflected in such opinions as *Stromberg v California* (1931) and *Near v. Minnesota* (1931), involving a Communist and an anti-Semite, respectively), the eloquent majority opinions delivered by Hughes were premonitory signals of the forthcoming judicial shift toward a more expansive view of freedom of expression. Often allied with him was Owen J. Roberts, President Hoover's choice in 1930 to replace Justice Sanford. Both Roberts and Hughes were sophisticated legalists out of the urban East, possessing views on free speech considerably removed from the Court quartet of conservatives. However, it was difficult for super patriots to make effective charges against justices with their status and prestige. The difficulty was compounded for judicial conservatives by expansion of the role of government in depression-ridden society. One cannot confidently assert that the New Deal was a transformative force in jurisprudence, but surely, we may speculate, the atmospherics accompanying the quantum leap in governmental regulatory power played a role in the courtroom. The outcome would the progressive "incorporation" of First Amendment freedoms, and Paul Murphy argues, it began a "quiet, legal, free speech revolution."

The judicial shift came at a time when a number of states passed Red Flag statutes in the 1930s, startlingly similar to that of Massachusetts in 1913, which read: "No red or black flag, and no banner, ensign or sign having upon it any inscription opposed to organized government … shall be carried in parade." Legislative and public sentiments prompted comparable measures in Arizona (1939), Illinois (1935), Indiana (1933), Pennsylvania (1939), Rhode Island (1938), and South Dakota (1938).

Of the two landmark decisions handed down in the Spring 1931, formally endorsing the congruence of the First and Fourteenth Amendments, one originated in a state Red Flag law. At issue in *Stromberg v. California* (1931)[2] was California's statute making it a crime for "[a]ny person [to display] a red flag, banner, or badge … in any public place" as "a sign, symbol or emblem of opposition to organized government" or "as an invitation or stimulus to anarchistic action" or "as an aid to propaganda that is of a seditious character …." Yetta Stromberg, a nineteen-year-old member of the Young Communist League, was a supervisor at a Communist Party (CP)–sponsored children's summer camp where students, ages six to sixteen, read the usual canonical writings of Marx and Lenin. She made a daily ceremony of raising a small homemade Red Flag, symbolic of the Soviet Union and the CP, as the pledge of allegiance. This practice inspired an attack on her camp by members of the BAF and American Legion who suspected Communist doctrine was being taught. It resulted in the arrest of Stromberg and conviction under the recently exhumed State law and a ten-year jail term. Stromberg sought relief in the California Supreme Court. Denied a hearing, she turned to the Supreme Court, which granted the appeal *in forma pauperis*.

Newly appointed Chief Justice Hughes, writing for seven colleagues, delivered the opinion reflecting his deeply held belief that broad tolerance of dissent was essential to the nation. He acknowledged that the right of free speech is not an absolute, citing *Whitney, Gitlow*, and *Fiske* decisions in this regard and that the government may punish "those who indulge in utterances which incite to violence and crime and threaten the overthrow of organized government by unlawful means." However, he condemned the dragnet action condoned by this 1919 State measure. And then he partially invalidated a key reference in it prohibiting opposition to organized government. The wording was "so vague and indefinite" that it interfered with "the opportunity for free political discussion to the end that government may be responsive to the will of the people and that changes may be obtained by lawful means ... [which] is a fundamental principle of our constitutional system." Such public speech, he eloquently continued, is as follows: "...essential to the security of the Republic .... The maintenance of the opportunity for free political discussion to the end that ... changes may be obtained by lawful means ... [which] is a fundamental principle of our constitutional system."[3] Anything less, such as the statute under consideration, was "repugnant to the guaranty of liberty contained in the Fourteenth Amendment." The "conception of liberty" under its due process clause "embraces the right of free speech." In short, a majority of seven justices now found that display of the flag was a form of speech and thus protected by the First Amendment against inhibiting state action through the due process clause of the Fourteenth Amendment – in what became the first occasion for a Court majority to join both Amendments in a sweeping opinion striking down a State measure.

In *Near v Minnesota* (1931)[4] decided two weeks later, Hughes's influence again prevailed. The First Amendment, it was proclaimed, became "the very foundation of our government," which in effect implied that when a state or federal measure restricted these freedoms, the Court must consider the wisdom of the statute. The statute at issue was an "obscure 1925 State Gag Law providing for 'abatement' as a 'public nuisance' any 'malicious, scandalous and defamatory newspaper, magazine or other periodical." The statute was relied upon by a Minneapolis District Court for the Fourth Judicial District, Hennepin County, Minnesota to enjoin a notorious local anti-Semitic scandal sheet, "The Saturday Press," from further sales or publication. Its publishers, Jay Near and Howard Guilford, in the nine issues of their paper had vilified Minneapolis officials of Jewish background, criticizing their public conduct and doubtful ethics, and the action enjoining publication was upheld by the State Supreme Court. The defendants cited the guarantee of liberty of the press in Minnesota's Constitution as well as in the Fourteenth Amendment. When the trial court overruled them, appeal was taken to the State Supreme Court which held the 1925 statute did not violate the State or federal constitutions and affirmed the lower court. Becoming the sole defendant, Near then appealed to the Supreme

Court on a number of grounds, for example, that the Minnesota law abridged freedom of the press, that it "deprives citizens ... of privileges and immunities guaranteed" by the Fourteenth Amendment because it denied them due process of law and "the right to discuss matters of national concern ...."[5]

Though a landmark decision by the Supreme Court, in that the Chief Justice held the injunction against *The Saturday Press* was a prior restraint in violation of freedom of the press protected by the Fourteenth Amendment, it did not involve American radicals and radicalism. Admittedly, then, the *Near* case is not central to our interests; and it is sufficient to note only that – again citing *Gitlow, Stromberg, Whitney*, and *Fiske* – Hughes speaking for five members of the Court undercut another state statute, and found prior restraints on the press impermissible, much as had *Patterson v. Colorado* over two decades earlier. Incorporating the newly established application of the First Amendment's press clause into the Fourteenth Amendment, Hughes categorically declared: "It is no longer open to doubt that the liberty of the press and of speech is within the liberties safeguarded by the due process clause of the Fourteenth Amendment from invasion by state action."[6] Thus did a Court majority extend the "guaranty of liberty proclaimed in the Fourteenth Amendment" to the First Amendment and its prohibition of restrictive state statutes.

Across the 1930s, as *Stromberg* and *Near* tell us, the new Court appointees provided an increasing judicial momentum toward giving greater protection to free speech and press claims. The Court had revitalized the First Amendment by extending it to the states in *Gitlow* and then in *Near*, decisions dealing, respectively, with speech and press. The expansion of constitutional guarantees for protected expression is likewise apparent in two highly significant victories for free speech. In one, *DeJonge v. Oregon* (1937),[7] the Court unanimously upheld the right of peaceable assembly for the CP, thereby again incorporating a First Amendment provision into the due process clause of the Fourteenth Amendment. At issue in this instance was the State's criminal syndicalism law that, like many such state statutes, had been first enacted in 1919, yet another index to the nation's persisting anti-radicalism. Dirk DeJonge, a CP member, would be convicted under the 1930 statute that declared, in language typical of that of many states: "Any person who, by word of mouth or writing, advocates or teaches the doctrine of criminal syndicalism, or sabotage, or who prints, publishes, edits, issues or knowingly circulates, sells, distributes or publicly displays any books, pamphlets, paper, handbill, poster, document or writings or printed matter in any form whatsoever" advocating criminal syndicalism "shall, upon conviction, be imprisoned up to ten years or fined a maximum of $1,000, or both."

According to the defense Brief, DeJonge was arrested at a time when steamship companies sought "to break the longshoremen's and seamen's strike then in progress," and a meeting had been held to protest police raids on union halls and homes of striking workers. DeJonge, speaking there, protested the actions of Portland's police and urged those present to purchase Communist literature on sale at the meeting hall and to attend a forthcoming assembly of the Party. Sharing the hostility toward "reds" and "radicals" of Portland's conservatives, local police broke up the meeting, confiscated a cache of Communist pamphlets, and arrested DeJonge.[8] Indicted solely on the charge that the CP advocated criminal syndicalism and that DeJonge presiding at and "conducting an assemblage of persons, organization, society and group, to-wit, the Communist Party," held in Portland, Oregon on July 27, 1933. He would be convicted, sentenced to seven years imprisonment, and his conviction upheld by the Oregon Supreme Court.[9]

Citing the state syndicalism acts of California, and elsewhere, state measures upheld by the High Court, the prosecution Brief defended the Oregon statute and further argued that the right of free speech and assembly is not an absolute one: "...a State in the exercise of its police power may punish those who abuse this freedom by utterances ... tending to incite to crime, disturb the public peace, or endanger the foundation of organized government."[10] In fact, in 1931, the Oregon criminal statute had been upheld (in *State v. Beloff*) and the defendant, who had been indicted for helping to organize and being a member of the CP, received a ten-year prison term. The Supreme Court's decision was most notable for two reasons. It was the first time that the tribunal, on First Amendment grounds, overturned a conviction of a Communist defendant who had engaged in vigorous public dissent. And it invalidated a criminal syndicalist law strikingly similar to California's that had been upheld in *Whitney*. Chief Justice Hughes, speaking for the Court, noted that the petitioner had not been indicted for joining the CP or for soliciting members or for distributing its literature, or for teaching or advocating criminal syndicalism, but only for assisting "in the conduct of a public meeting, albeit otherwise lawful," held under CP auspices. The right to assemble peacefully, however, was "a right cognate to those of free speech and free press ...," guaranteed by the First Amendment, and Hughes reminded the State officials that such fundamental rights had to be maintained. Although the meeting was Communist sponsored, it afforded no excuse for state action, for peaceable political action and "peaceable assembly for lawful discussion however unpopular the sponsorship, cannot be made a crime ... [and] cannot be proscribed and is equally fundamental"; and the ruling is applicable to the states via the due process clause of the Fourteenth Amendment.[11]

Extending First Amendment incorporation to public assembly for peaceable political action, the Chief Justice affirmed that those who assist in the conduct of such meetings cannot be branded criminals for that reason, effectually rejecting the identification of an individual member of the organization with the organization itself. Discussion of public issues and seeking a redress of grievances – when done without inciting violence – were of the "essence of liberty" guaranteed by the Fourteenth Amendment.[12] Hughes forcefully affirmed what would become the classic First Amendment position: "the imperative ... need to preserve inviolate the constitutional rights of free speech, free press and free assembly in order to maintain the opportunity for free political discussion, to the end that government may be responsive to the will of the people, and that changes, if desired, may be obtained by peaceful means. Therein lies the security of the Republic, the very foundation of constitutional government."[13]

Herndon v. Lowry (1937)[14] was one more case testifying to the nation's unchanging anti-communist zealotry. A state anti-sedition and anti-insurrection measure would again be at issue in what became the last of the significant free speech decisions in the Thirties. This case, however, was unlike earlier ones in two respects: (1) it was the first authentic confrontation with an actual CP officer as defendant, and (2) it was the only occasion in this decade when the Court resurrected the clear and present danger test and cited it to strike down an ancient state statute, one designed in 1833 to prevent anyone from inciting or attempting to incite a slave insurrection or to circulate written materials toward that end; and it included a death penalty unless the jury recommended otherwise.

Angelo Herndon, the defendant in the case, had joined the CP in Kentucky and had come to Atlanta as a paid Party organizer. Being a Communist, he had traveled there because of actions to which communists customarily gravitated, namely, Fulton County had suspended relief payments and unruly protestors blocked the County courthouse demanding their resumption. The demonstration frightened city and county officials, and the local police, after shadowing several radicals, arrested the nineteen-year-old Herndon. CP periodicals and copies of its newspaper, the *Daily Worker*, as well as a number of books were found in his room or on his person when arrested, although there was no proof that he had distributed any of these materials. But some of the literature that included such phrases as "the proletarian struggle," "the revolutionary theory of Marxism," and "the equal rights for Negroes" were sufficient reason for the Fulton County sheriff to arrest him under the pre-Civil War anti-insurrection law.[15] The measure was now construed to apply "to one … conducting meetings of a local unit of that party, when one of the doctrines of such party … might be said to be the ultimate resort to violence at some indefinite future time against organized government …." The indictment specifically charged Hendon with seeking "to induce others to join in combined resistance to the lawful authority of the state," "making speeches for the purpose of organizing and establishing groups … for the purpose of uniting, combining and conspiring to incite riots … and, by force and violence, overthrowing and defeating the authority of the state."

Herndon was represented by the International Labor Defense, a militant New York City left-wing organization that had defended radicals, communists, and Southern Blacks. Its counsel, Ben Davis, a well-known Black lawyer and Communist, challenged the constitutionality of the State law, an argument immediately dismissed by trial judge Lee Wyatt, as he did when defense counsel attacked the composition of grand and petit juries for systematically excluding Blacks from jury panels. However, the court unsurprisingly did allow prosecutors, and their witnesses, to emphasize the written materials seized in Herndon's apartment. Defense counsel repeatedly objected to racist remarks from witnesses and prosecutors alike and denied that his client's actions in a peaceful relief demonstration constituted an attempt at insurrection. But his incautious closing comments condemning Southern racism, and charging that prosecutorial efforts were "a blot on American civilization," represented an unqualified assault on Southern mores and traditions. It was clearly unwelcome by the jurors. In fact, three of them, so it was reported, turned their backs on Ben Davis when he paced near them during the summation.

The defense called two Emory University faculty to rebut the prosecution emphasis on the dangerous texts found in Herndon's possession, and their exchange with the prosecution warrants brief description because it further conveys the Fulton County courtroom atmosphere, a cultural setting hardly unique to the South. It can be clearly ascertained when one defense witness mentioned the slogan, "equal rights for all," and the prosecution bluntly asked: do you "understand that to mean the right of a colored boy to marry your daughter?" It was a query, we may believe, expressing jurors' anxieties about interracial marriage that carried profoundly troubling implications for white Southerners and Southern culture, and which they understood to be a CP slogan. It was a shrewd prosecutorial ploy, one irrelevant to the indictment itself. Playing on the same tactical string, the prosecution emphasized Communist intent to undermine deeply rooted Southern economic and social traditions that not only put Herndon on trial, Charles Martin rightfully contends, but also "the beliefs and teachings of the Communist Party."[16] The prosecution admittedly did advance a legal argument; namely, that Gitlow was controlling and that sufficient evidence existed to conclude that the defendant's utterances had a "dangerous tendency" toward subversion of the State. But it was the prosecution's racist accents that hung over the courtroom and the three-day trial and that would carry the day for the prosecution. The guilty verdict was entirely foreseen, although the jury was divided, as several held out for the death penalty but finally settled on eighteen- to-twenty-year prison term for attempting to incite insurrection.

The Georgia Supreme Court having rejected all defense arguments, the plaintiff appealed to the High Court and Owen D. Roberts would deliver a 5-4 ruling that reversed conviction. Surprisingly, in this first of only two instances, the Hughes Court reaffirmed, somewhat ambiguously, the clear-and-present danger standard in upholding free speech claims against repressive state law. On careful examination of the literature that had been in Herndon's possession, Roberts found only evidence of recruiting members to the Party and some textual passages with specific Party goals, for example, "vote Communist for Unemployment and Social Insurance ... Emergency relief for the poor farmers ... Equal rights for the Negroes ..." None of this written matter, Roberts concluded, "is criminal on its face"; and without further evidence, Herndon's meetings and literature only amounted to an "ultimate ideal" and could not be held as incitement to insurrection or any immediate threat to the State. None suggested advocacy of "forcible subversion of governmental authority"; or that petitioner advocated, "by speech or written words, at meetings or elsewhere, any doctrine or action implying such forcible subversion." The evidence cited "falls short of an attempt to bring about insurrection either immediately or in a reasonable time but amounts merely to a statement of ultimate ideals."[17]

Citing *DeJonge v. Oregon*, Roberts emphatically affirmed that "[t]he power of the state to abridge freedom of speech and of assembly is the exception rather than the rule .... The judgment of the legislature is not unfettered. The limitation upon individual liberty must have appropriate relation to the safety of the state." [18] He also went on to contend that the standard of guilt under the statute was unconstitutionally vague, with its test of danger – "at any time" – being sufficient to condemn it. There simply was "[n]o reasonably ascertainable standard of guilt ..." The measure could result in conviction "if the jury thought the petitioner reasonably might foretell that those he persuaded to join the party might, at some time in the indefinite future, resort to forcible resistance to government." And Roberts closed with a rhetorical flourish: "So vague and indeterminate are the boundaries thus set to the freedom of speech and assembly that the law necessarily violates the guaranties of liberty embodied in the Fourteenth Amendment."[19]

To summarize, the Court now struck down the Georgia's anti-insurrection law for unduly infringing on free speech and in the process struck down all comparable statutes in other states, thereby substantially advancing the cause of protected speech and press. By its decision, the emerging five-member liberal bloc of justices (Hughes, Roberts, Brandeis, Cardozo, and Stone) demonstrated great boldness for that time by stiffening the judiciary's back to current trends and by ignoring the *ad hominem* anti-communist arguments of both prosecution and public. Although a narrow holding, the Court's opinion directly warned the states that the days of shotgun indictments under broad anti-sedition statutes were numbered.[20] This majority overview would prevail over the next fifteen years; even advocacy of forcible opposition to government could not be prohibited.

Charles Evans Hughes, who was appointed as Chief Justice in 1930, remained at this post until 1940 and wrote most of the civil liberties decisions not authored by Justice Roberts. He presided over a divided tribunal in his later years, but by skillful mediation, was usually able to lessen personal discord and find a majority. Harlan Stone, his successor in 1941, could not quiet deeply divisive legal viewpoints in his five years at the Court's helm. His views were similar to those of Benjamin Cardozo, who occupied Holmes' seat in 1932, and was himself replaced in 1939 by Felix Frankfurter, a justice who would have great influence on the Court in the Forties and Fifties, and would contend that if Congress acted reasonably, the Court must defer to the legislative will. This conviction was frequently joined to the belief that his role and function was that of impartial arbiter when clashing interests were at stake. Further, he openly sought to "balance the interests" and tirelessly advocated "a candid and informed weighing of the competing interests ..."[21] In effect, Frankfurter would affirm an ad hoc balancing of freedom of expression and alleged threats to national security – when First Amendment legal issues were before the tribunal.[22] And he pointedly argued that "[n]ot every type of speech occupies the same position on the scale of values"; and the "judicial function is to balance" the principle of free speech against the needs of society.[23] Moreover, as noted earlier, the judicial "balancers" usually voted to uphold lower court convictions of defendants who invoke the First or Fifth Amendment.[24] They did so emphatically in crisis times when freedom of expression for radicals was most unpopular and hence would most likely be vulnerable to legislative and prosecutorial zeal. That courts rarely found for the plaintiff, Mark Silverstein concluded, made their balancing formula appear a sham.[25] (For Judge Learned Hand on balancing, see *supra*, p. 29.)

Harlan would usually join Frankfurter to affirm: "Where First Amendment rights are asserted ... resolution of the issue always involves a balancing by the courts of the competing private and public interests at stake in the particular circumstances shown"; and Justice Jackson eloquent voice was also largely predictable when personal freedoms were at stake.[26] The outcome of their ad hoc weighing approach to freedom of expression, it is apparent, was erosion of the integrity of the First Amendment.

Justice Hugh Black came to the Court two years before Frankfurter, and they would become fierce and lasting antagonists on the tribunal. A Southern poor white out of rural Harlan, Alabama, Black was the youngest of eight children whose father had been a Confederate veteran, then successively farmer and county storekeeper. With only a scant income, the family sent out Hugh Black to pick cotton and then work as a typesetter for a weekly newspaper. As he reminded listeners, "it is a long journey from the frontier farm house in the hills of Clay County, Alabama, to the United States Supreme Court" – to which he was appointed by President Roosevelt after serving as a militantly liberal New Deal Senator. Upon taking a seat on the tribunal, he rejected unfettered judicial deference to the legislature and gradually came to affirm special protection and observed that: [T]he First Amendment was written in the form of a command so unequivocal, and so pervasive in its expression and implications that it is impossible to deny that those who drafted it intended to mark off an inviolable area and dedicate it to the liberties there enumerated."[27] Although cautious at first, he would come around to a "preferred" position on free speech and argued for its absolute protection, "without any 'if' or 'but'" or "whereas," often invoking the founding fathers.[28]

Frankfurter argued that "preferred freedom" was a "mischievous phrase" and assailed its doctrinal implications. But Black never wavered, and even before 1950, when his free speech convictions became fully fixed and evident, they collided with the beliefs of his more restrained colleague. "I understand that it is rather old-fashioned and shows a slight naivete to say that 'no law' means 'no law,'" he confessed; but "[i]t is my belief that there are 'absolutes' in the Bill of Rights, and that they were put there on purpose by men who knew what words meant ..."[29] This literal and uncompromising view of the First Amendment inevitably led Black, and shortly thereafter by Douglas, to oppose the judicial proposition of weighing competing interests of protected speech and national security, as well as the clear and present danger and bad tendency doctrines. Accordingly, both justices became determined to favor those who would be imposed upon by congressional investigating committees, inquisitive state Attorneys General, repressive state or executive measures curtailing protected freedoms.

William O. Douglas, Black's counterpart, had been appointed by Roosevelt in April 1937. Being the son of an impoverished Presbyterian minister in Minnesota, he knew a life that included hard labor among Chicano and Wobblies in the wheat fields. After working in various bureaucracies of official Washington, he became head of the Securities and Exchange Commission during the New Deal days and shaped it into a skilled and feared investigative agency that searched out financial wrongdoing before Roosevelt nominated him to succeed Brandeis. The youngest man ever appointed to the Supreme Court, Douglas would serve for thirty-six years and handed out hundreds of opinions, although frequently deferring to Black as the unacknowledged leader of the Court's liberal wing. Like Black, he came to favor the preferred position for First Amendment guarantees in the "penumbra" of the Bill of Rights. Although less rigidly absolutist than Black, for Douglas, the law was a social instrument designed to achieve useful purposes, and he would reject Frankfurter's view of the Court as a monastic institution.

Frank Murphy deserves special mention in this survey of the liberal Court cohort. Frankfurter dismissively commented on his moral fervor and found that Murphy always voted with his heart, an appraisal not far off the mark. Murphy had fervently defended civil liberties as Michigan governor and then Attorney General, before becoming an early Roosevelt appointee, replacing the conservative Justice Butler. On the tribunal, he continued to display a passionate devotion to the rights of minorities and the poor in cases involving them. He also demonstrated a militant and unyielding regard for individual rights and preferred speech. In fact, in thirty-two non-unanimous decisions, Murphy "cast only one vote against the claims of freedom."[30] Wiley Rutledge, who earlier served briefly on the appellate bench, became the seventh Roosevelt appointee and rounded out the Court's activist bloc. It was joined by the moderate democrat and former solicitor general Stanley Reed, who replaced George Sutherland. This liberal bloc took exception to the view of the judicial function as deferential, and consequentially the tribunal at times splintered into irascible factionalism. It likewise took exception to the government's attitude toward aliens which was hardening in the late 1930s, partly in response to the growing crises abroad.

Finally, this same cohort took its cue from Harlan Stone. In his famous Footnote Four in the 1938 *Carolene Products* case, Justice Stone attempted to formulate a new guiding principle of law that stated in part: "statutes directed at particular ... national ... or racial minorities were to be subjected to a more exacting judicial scrutiny ... than ... most other types of legislation" and should call for a "more searching judicial inquiry" than customarily required.[31] Stone's footnote, for example, became the criterion for an exacting scrutiny of a number of city ordinances, such as one in Los Angeles invoked to convict defendants who distributed handbills supporting republicans in the Spanish civil war. The Court, guided by Stone's footnote, found this measure, as well as those in Milwaukee and Worcester, infringed on fundamental rights and struck them down – to the dismay of strong judicial supporters of "balancing."

A number of cases reaching the High Court revolved around deportation proceedings. Admittedly, they do not present issues of free speech and assembly but warrant passing mention because, as with the Herndon case, they marked the onset of the High Court's involvement with modern communism as well as with the older, more broadly defined America's radical and dissenting tradition. Officials in the immigration and passport–visa divisions had long selectively subjected foreign nationals to detention and deportation. The practice goes back to 1798 and the Alien Enemy Act (still on the books) and held by immigrant officials who perceived themselves to be principled opponents of those who held attitudes or ideologies potentially threatening the nation.

That such views of the bureaucracy were at times hardly compatible with the beliefs of a Court majority may be seen in *Schneiderman v. United States* (1943).[32] The defendant, William Schneiderman, born in Russia in 1905, had come to the United States as a child in 1907 or 1908 and was naturalized under the 1906 Naturalization Act. In 1924, at age eighteen, he filed for citizenship that would be granted in 1927. Already a charter member of the Young Workers League (which became the Communist League), he would join the Workers Party (the predecessor to the CP) in 1924 or early 1925 and eventually become a high-ranking CP official in California. Government efforts to revoke Schneiderman's certificate of citizenship began a dozen years later, on the ground it had been "illegally procured," the wording of the 1906 law and the main charge in the proceedings against him.[33] In the five years preceding naturalization, prosecutors argued that Schneiderman "was a member of the organization whose principles were opposed to the principles of the Constitution of the United States ...." In short, prosecutors asserted that the defendant was an active CP member when naturalized, and they sought revocation of his citizenship, it having been obtained by "fraud" in 1927. The District Court agreed and ordered denaturalization.

The Supreme Court took certiorari and Murphy, after carefully examining the documentary evidence (e.g., the 1848 Communist Manifesto, and the 1938 Communist Party Constitution) introduced by the government in support of its position, found it compatible with constitutional principles.[34] Waving away this evidence "in respect to force and violence" as "susceptible of an interpretation more rhetorical than literal," he contended that there was no "'clear, unequivocal and convincing' evidence which does not leave the issue in doubt...." Such evidence was essential, for otherwise "the security of our naturalized citizens might depend in considerable degree upon the political temper of majority thought and the stresses of the times." This valued right of American citizenship, Murphy asserted, should not be stripped from a person a dozen years after it had been granted "without the clearest sort of justification and proof," and concluded: "[w]e do not think the government has carried its burden of proof ... even under its own test."

In the second part of his opinion, Justice Murphy grappled with defense contentions that the plaintiff did not engage in force and violence. The plaintiff's behavior, he declared, had been "law abiding in all respects." Continuing, he unhesitatingly stated: "there is nothing in the record indicating that he [the plaintiff] was ever connected with any overt illegal or violent action or with any disturbance of any sort."[35] In a flat declarative assertion, he took a position heretical to most Americans and argued that petitioner's CP membership did not in itself establish his opposition to constitutional principles. Moreover, Murphy did so with a rhetorical flourish that found radical political dissent was protected by the First Amendment, and "a court in a denaturalization proceeding ... is not justified in canceling a certificate of citizenship by imputing the reprehensible interpretation [of the Communist Party program] to a member in the absence of overt acts indicating that such was his interpretation."[36]

The persistent opposition to radical aliens is perhaps best illustrated in the government's efforts to deport Harry Bridges, an Australian-born labor leader who had entered the United States in 1920, led the major maritime workers' strike on the Pacific coast of 1934 and became the head of the International Longshoremen's and Warehousemen's Union two years later. In 1937, he captained a successful drive to take the Union out of the conservative American Federation of Labor (AFL) and into the more militant Congress of Industrial Organizations (CIO). His efforts brought him both prominent and powerful enemies – the AFL, shipping and business companies, and (according to Justice Frank Murphy) "those whose interests coincided directly or indirectly with the 'vicious and inhumane practices toward longshoremen.'"

Political trials preceded and followed judicial trials and appeals of the embattled Bridges. Texas Congressman Martin Dies made his own special contribution. The House Special Committee on Un-American Activities that he chaired took a growing interest in Bridges, and in January 1939, the Committee investigated him in connection with "aliens engaged in un-American activities." Bridges would be named a Communist at a 1940 Committee meeting of the House, and its Annual Report of no less than nine years later mentioned Committee efforts in bringing him to trial as one of its accomplishments.[37] House Committee on the Judiciary followed suit as did the Upper House and Senator Styles Bridges before the Senate Committee on Interior and Insular Affairs. There were as well the shrill and bristling voices outside state and federal agencies. Officials in the AFL and Portland's Police

Department charged Bridges with being a CP member and should be deported. The American Legion's national commander added to the growing drumbeat for deportation as did San Francisco business leaders and nativist organizations. The Immigration and Naturalization Service (INS) Seattle office claimed in an affidavit that he was a member of the CP.

It was such clamorous voices and political realities that initially compelled the federal government to act and spurred Frances Perkins, the Secretary of Labor to bring deportation proceedings against him.[38] She ordered a deportation hearing in 1938 (the INS was enfolded within the Department of Labor until 1940), with Dean James Landis, a highly respected authority on administrative law and the government's special hearing examiner. The hearing lasted nearly ten weeks and produced a report of more than 7,700 pages; and Landis, not finding the government's witnesses credible, concluded that the evidence presented failed to sustain the CP membership or affiliation charges leveled against Bridges. Perkins then dismissed the proceedings which in turn produced a second equally long deportation hearing that also cleared him.

Since there was no double jeopardy bar to multiple deportation proceedings, Bridges would become the target of continuous efforts at deportation over sixteen years (1934–1950) on the ground of alleged membership in the CP. In the years between 1934 and 1955, the Justice Department convened yet one more deportation hearing against Bridges, Congress passed two measures directing his deportation, and a third statute passed by the House specifically named Bridges as the deportation target, clearly a bill of attainder and hence most likely found unconstitutional were a case deriving from it to reach the federal courts. In regard, the courts, criminal or civil conspiracy indictments against Bridges led to seven lower and appellate court decisions, and no less than three High Court case that revealed both the unflagging government effort to deport him and the equally unflagging anti-communism of public officials.[39]

The first attempted deportation, as observed, would be dismissed by the Secretary of Labor before reaching the courts. Another federal government effort came in 1941 and would become *Bridges v. California* (1941).[40] The first really significant case involving freedom of expression decided in this decade, it spoke to the readiness of the Court majority to discourage deportation of communists, alleged and otherwise.

Although resting on libel and contempt of court charges rather than on First Amendment grounds, there are two cogent reasons for giving the Black's majority ruling consideration. First, it involved the issue of free speech protections for plaintiff, as defense counsel argued. And second, elaborated upon above, there was a related judicial contretemps, highlighting perhaps the most meaningful judicial division of the next two decades, between Justices Black and Frankfurter. Black's opinion rejected the contention that the First Amendment "speak[s] equivocally" and came close to what would become his later unbendingly explicit position on the First Amendment; namely, that speech was absolutely immune from government restriction.[41] Seizing the trope of clear and present danger, Black maintained that, as a "working principle ... the substantive evil must be extremely serious and the degree of imminence extremely high" before speech can be punished.[42] Moreover, quoting *Schneider v. State* (1939),[43] he affirmed that "'freedom of speech and of the press secured by the First Amendment against abridgment by the United States is similarly secured to all persons by the Fourteenth Amendment against abridgment by a state.'" Black's opinion, Robert McCloskey has concluded, comes close to saying, though somewhat obliquely, "that speech is absolutely immune from governmental interferences."[44] Black now placed the burden of proof for any statutory restriction upon the government that, Mark Silverstein persuades, "was the single most important step" in his First Amendment jurisprudence, for it elevated the Amendment to the preferred position in the hierarchy of constitutional doctrine.[45] McCloskey, accordingly, has rightly argued, it made Bridges "[a] prototypal case" anticipating "the personal and doctrinal clashes between the judges."[46] It provided the dress rehearsal, for the judicial discord that follows over the next two decades.

As described earlier, the INS, upon thoroughly investigating the original allegation of CP membership and deportation in 1934 and 1935, could not find even "a shred of evidence" warranting his exclusion and the effort was officially closed. But the campaign to deport Bridges continued. Jurisdiction over the INS, having shifted to the Justice Department, its counsel invoked the recently passed Alien Registration Act (the Smith Act) of 1940 as the statutory basis for Bridges' deportability. The measure contained a section amending deportation law so that an alien who had been "a member of or affiliated with an organization" advocating or teaching forceful overthrow of the government was deportable. In effect, authorizing deportation retrospectively for past Party membership, this provision was applied to Bridges, a warrant for his arrest was issued in 1941, followed by a hearing before a new special examiner (Judge Charles Sears); and although the government offered no evidence not presented earlier, sufficient grounds for deportation were now found. Bridges was accused of being a Communist, the charge based largely on his public comments and publications. The Attorney General, "without holding a hearing or listening to argument," according to Justice Murphy, reinstated deportation. Bridges then petitioned for a writ of habeas corpus to the District Court, which was denied, and the High Court granted certiorari.

Justice Douglas for five colleagues (in *Bridges v. Wixon* (1945)[47]) considered it necessary to resolve the twin statutory bases for deportability, namely, membership and "affiliation." Bridges' association with various Communist groups, he stated, "seemed to indicate no more than cooperative measures to attain objections which were wholly legitimate." As to his utterances and writings, they reflected a militant advocacy "of the causes of trade unionism" – "wholly lawful activities" – and he did not teach or advocate, or advise "the subversive conduct condemned by the statute." Moreover, plaintiff had been denied an opportunity to confront his accusers. As a result, the Court concluded, Bridges had not been given a fair hearing on the issue of membership, a contention petitioner's counsel had considered pivotal to his case. Nor was the Attorney General's accusation of "a close cooperation with the Communists and Communist organizations" sufficient to establish "an 'affiliation' within the meaning of the statute." Douglas brushed off the evidence for CP "affiliation" as weak and inadequate. The testimony offered by the two major government witnesses in the deportation proceedings, he argued, was unsworn and hearsay, and other testimony was "speculative," conjectural," and "unreliable."[48] Justice Frank Murphy, a consistently strong supporter of labor, agreed with Douglas, but wanted a more forceful indictment of the government. His concurrence did not dodge or duck. It eloquently opened:

> The record in this case will stand forever as a monument to man's intolerance of man. Seldom if ever in the history of this nation has there been such a concentrated and relentless crusade to deport an individual because he dared to exercise the freedom that belongs to him as a human being and that is guaranteed to him by the Constitution ...[49]

Unlike the Bridges opinions, which received continuous media publicity and headlines in the nation's press, there were any number of cases of anarchists, IWW members, and communists denaturalized and deported as a result of multiple lower federal court decisions. It became a convincing demonstration of how often judges were not neutral parties but sought to implement distinct personal and policy preferences through their decisions. Deportation of IWW members remained especially prominent in the post-war years into the 1920s.[50] Alien radicals charged with advocacy of violent overthrow, CP membership, Party activities, etc., were deported or had petitions for naturalization denied, which again demonstrates the unremittingly harsh anti-radicalism existing in administrative hearings and immigrant courts on local and state levels that continued into the Thirties.[49]

The Schneiderman and Bridges cases had arrived at the Court in wartime, when the Constitution largely went into hibernation (e.g., see *In re Yamashita* (1946)). And at a time when hostilities created strange bedfellows, namely, the United States allied with the Soviet Union to defeat Germany. It resulted in the temporarily quieting of the national animus toward communism at home as well as abroad. J. Edgar Hoover, however, remained very active, compiling his secret "Security Index" in 1943, a list of those to be detained in the name of national security. It is surprising in a way, since at no time did the intensity of Bureau activities and popular anti-communism correspond to domestic realities. The Party, after all, even at its height in the mid-Thirties, was relatively insignificant in both numbers and influence. At the outset of the depression, Party membership stood at 8,000, rising to 12,000 in 1932 and, after a vigorous recruiting drive, to 84,000 in 1934. A decade earlier, the Workers (Communist) Party, running William Z. Foster for President, polled 36,386 votes out of the total of 29,091,417 in that election year. Four years later, the Workers Party received 48,770 out of a total of 36,811,717 votes for its presidential candidate. In 1932, Foster received 102,991 votes for President, with a national vote total standing at 39,751,438, and this was the Party's high water mark in presidential campaigns. In 1936, the Party's presidential ticket headed by Earl Browder totaled 80,159 out of 45,647,117. In the election year of 1940, Browder received 48,579 votes out of a total vote cast of 49,820,312. (And to jump ahead, the Party's presidential candidate in 1952, Vincent Hallinan, received 140,138 votes out of the total 61,637,951.)

Even at its height, then, the Party was in actuality little more than one of a number of powerless radical sects, one of those which "acquired the characteristics ...," Christopher Lasch observed, of "sectarianism, marginality, and alienation from American life." Indeed, Harvey Klehr and John Jones rightly contend, the CP "in virtually every industrial nation in the world" was "far larger and far more powerful" than in the United States. Its leadership everywhere invariably adhered to the Soviet "party line," as dictated by the Comintern (Communist International) sitting in Moscow. Hence, as noted earlier, when the Comintern ordered the so-called Third Period (1928–1935), in which Stalin proclaimed revolutionary ideals and perceived depression as prelude to the defeat of capitalism – and America's communists dutifully agreed (*supra*, p. 72, unrevised). CP members and leaders then demonstrated unremitting hostility to Roosevelt's New Deal, charging in 1934, for example, "that it was at the expense of the toilers ... [and] a program of fascization and the most intense preparations for imperialist war." And when in August 1935 Stalin softened the Comintern's revolutionary edicts and announced a "popular front" at the Seventh Congress of the Comintern it produced a political and tactical reversal for communists worldwide. For America's Party leadership, it follows, loyalty to the USSR remained the litmus test of one's bona fide credentials.

The revised Popular Front position resulted from a new awareness of priorities, namely, the conviction that European Fascism posed a greater imminent threat to the USSR than did the capitalist powers. The realities were apparent to all who wished to see. Italy's Mussolini became Il Duce in 1922, and his armed forces invaded Ethiopia in 1935. Hitler took office as Chancellor in 1933, destroying German democracy and all radical parties shortly thereafter, and his forces marched into the territory of Saar by 1935 and then into Austria. Having miscalculated the extent of the threat to his homeland, Stalin then sought a collective alliance of anti-Fascist powers – which initiated political and tactical reversals of policy for Communist parties worldwide.

For communists everywhere, loyalty to the Soviet Union remained the critical test of true radicalism and since Moscow now promoted collective security, so officially did its American members. Between 1935 and 1939, accordingly, Party leaders reversed course. They now embraced a rapprochement with the President, and his New Deal programs were vigorously supported. Seeking collaboration on issues with liberals and radicals of every persuasion, they enshrined Jefferson and Lincoln in the pantheon of American heroes. The policy shift led to a jump in the Party's stock, influence, legitimacy, and membership, which rose to about 55,000 in 1938 and 100,000 in 1939. However, the continuing purges in the Soviet Union, beginning with the secret Kirov trial of sixty-seven suspects, followed by further kangaroo court proceedings two years later, began to alienate many liberals and independent radicals. They watched with growing cynicism, disillusionment, and despair as many of the most prominent of the old Bolsheviks, the heroes of Revolutionary Russia, stood in the dock, uttered their confessions and were then executed. But America's communists suffered in silence or wore blinders to the facts of repression in Russia. They remained loyal to the glorious Soviet motherland, defending the Kremlin, dismissing the charges of Stalinist brutality.

A great ideological shock came to them in August 1939, when the Russo-German Non-Aggression Pact was announced. It also produced another dramatic reversal of Communist policies. "A marvel of invertebrate flexibility," in Earl Latham's apt phrase, the Party immediately dismantled its Popular Front organizations, retreating into an isolationist platform, and engaged in an effort to keep the United States from intervening in the European conflict. Moscow's purges had tarnished the Soviet image for some Party members, the Pact completed the denigration for many more. It hit like a bombshell in CP ranks, destroying the Popular Front that had the defense of democratic values and the struggle against Nazism as its emphases. The hard-core Communist leadership once again cynically subordinated consistent policy to Soviet needs and maneuvers. The official Party "line" was reinvented, and the Communist newspaper, *Daily Worker*, began to denounce England and France, then at war with Germany, as instigating the "Second Imperialist War." But the change of policy cost the Party dearly in credibility and membership, erasing most of the gains made during the depression, generating a qualitative jump in desertions of rank-and-file membership. After June 22, 1941, and the German invasion of Russia, the Comintern ordered yet another policy shift. Reinventing the Popular Front years, America's communists offered unwavering support for the administration, tacked from slogans like Roosevelt the "imperialist warmonger" to Roosevelt the folk hero, and to "communism is twentieth-century Americanism." In May 1944, the euphoria and zeal for US–USSR wartime unity was such that the CP actually abolished itself and became the Communist Political Association.

Even at its height of popularity in the late Thirties, it bears repeating, the Party had been relatively insignificant in numbers and utterly so in political influence. Most of its members may have retained allegiance to the USSR even after the purges, but arguably this was evidence of self-deception and stupidity rather than treason or conspiracy. The contrasting popular national view that equated liberals and communists, and a feckless identification of both with spies and traitors hardly wavered. The strident anti-communism, a recurrent phenomenon of the post-World War I decade, flared up again in the Roosevelt years. Not at first, however. The depression after the crash, it should be conceded, temporarily quieted conservative protest and anti-radical oratory. Yet after a few years of relative apolitical calm, the heresy hunters reappeared in full force, joining the old revanchist conservatives and segueing into a revived and admonitory anti-communism. "That man in the White House" became the problem for the GOP, and his policies would morph into a new incarnation of the Red Menace. New Deal measures mobilized those who in reaction would oppose labor militancy and social welfare legislation. Shrill rhetorical condemnation of the welfare state and pleas for less government could be heard in Congress. Because administration measures were equated with a planned or socialist or communist society, the Party itself, regardless of its diminutive size and featherweight influence, remained a convenient point of attack. It continued, as in the past, to be a massive conspiratorial threat to fundamental American values, such as the free market ideology and free enterprise, as well as to the usual bromide of national security.

The President himself was hardly immune to such conservative outcries and anti-radical pressures. In defense, a series of anti-communist practices emanated from the White House. At first, the Red-hunting campaign was largely indirect because the focus of Roosevelt's initial interest was pro-German domestic activities. Seeking "general intelligence information," the President summoned J. Edgar Hoover, now Director of the FBI (the BI having been so renamed in 1935), to the Oval Office in August 1936; and the Bureau, with Roosevelt's stamp of approval began to shift from law enforcement to investigation of left-of-center labor leaders in the coal, shipping, steel, newspaper, and garment industries, as well as possible "subversives" and "subversive activities" in schools and the federal government. FBI investigations would lead to the collection of massive files of derogatory political and personal information about dissidents of every stripe and their organizations.

Turning to Capitol Hill, congressional hearings and reports on the activities of both alien and native-born radicals were daily events. The House Committee on Immigration and Naturalization, for one, held four hearings in 1935 and one in 1937, the last yielding a report entitled: "Terminate Temporary Stay of, and to Deport, Certain Aliens Found to Be Promoting and Disseminating Certain Propaganda from Foreign Sources."

No less vigilant in preventing radical contamination of the United States, the House Committee on the Judiciary, fifteen years after hearings held in 1919 and after the Espionage and Sedition Acts, were on the books convened investigations on "Sedition, Syndicalism, Sabotage, and Anarchy" and on measures to prohibit "Overthrow of the Government." The obsessive concern with radicals and radicalism prompted Committee members to contemplate yet one more round of hearings in 1939 on another measure making it a "Crime to Promote the Overthrow of Government," the 1940 Smith Act being the outcome. Infatuation with anti-communism continued to motivate Committee members, and they would hold hearings in 1952 "about Communist infiltration of the United Nations." Testimony on anti-radicalism also pervaded hearings of the Committee on Post Office and Civil Service in 1939, as witnesses testified to the need for two measures, one that would "Require Identification of Communist-front Organizations" to appear on mailable matter and another on a proposed bill in 1950, "To Protect the National Security of the United States by Permitting the Summary Suspension of government officials and employees in the interests of national security."

Finally, there was the most prominent of anti-radical congressional committees, the House Committee on Un-American Activities (HUAC). It surfaced in embryonic form in April 1930, when New York Representative Hamilton Fish campaigned for and then headed a House Committee, the Special Committee to Investigate Communist Activities in the United States that would begin with the New York State Communist Party after it charged police brutality. His proposal to relieve the nation's unemployment problem by deporting "every single alien Communist" marked the political mindset of all Committee members. The Committee announced that there were between 500,000 and 600,000 Communists in the United States, a wildly exaggerated claim since dues-paying Party members at the time, numbered about 12,000. Such pronouncements would hardly be unusual. Fish's ad hoc Committee eventually issued 1000-plus page reports in 1930 on "Communist activities" in New York City public schools, "Communist-led strikes" in North Carolina, "Communist activities" in Michigan localities, "Communist-led street demonstrations" in Pacific coast cities, and "the predominance of Negroes, Jews and aliens" involved in communist activities in Birmingham, Alabama, etc.

Such investigations foreshadowed those of the McCormack–Dickstein Committee of 1934–1935 on "a wide range of Communist activities in the United States," where witnesses from patriotic organizations, labor unions, the Chamber of Commerce, the government, etc., offered proposals for anti-Communist legislation. The temper of these hearings may be encapsulated in the testimony of Walter Steele, representing a number of civic and fraternal societies: the "Communist movement in the United States is a declaration of war on our Government and our people by a foreign government."

The McCormick–Dickstein Committee evolved into the newly formed seven-member HUAC, established by Congress in 1938. Chaired by Texas Congressman Martin Dies, the Committee, likewise known at this time as the Dies Committee, its members would be drawn from the ultraconservative wing of House congressional Republicans. Their *cri de coeur*, joined by many on Capitol Hill: Communists were taking over the country! To further elaborate upon the Committee mindset, the Louisiana Democrat, F. Edward Hebert spoke to this great fear at one Subcommittee hearing, darkly referring to: "a disease … spreading on the body politic or on the body human, it behooves us as intelligent human beings to do something to retard it … If you want to live in the way you were brought up in freedom, and believe in free speech, you must know that freedom can destroy freedom."[51] Specifically, Committee members were charged under its charter to investigate: "… the extent, character, and objects of un-American propaganda activities in the United States, [and] the diffusion within the United States of subversive and un-American propaganda that is instigated from foreign countries or of a domestic origin and attacks the principle of the form of government as guaranteed by our Constitution …."[52] Included in the definition of un-American, according to Frank Donner, was "absolute social and racial equality; the destruction of private property …."[53] Being in relentless pursuit of communists, it follows that the Committee members ideologically complemented the FBI, both having the same quarry for decades. In fact, a number of them and their staff had close ties with the Bureau, some former Bureau agents became HUAC employees, and J. Parnell Thomas, a future

HUAC chairman, acknowledged in 1948: "The closest relationship exists between this committee and the FBI ... I think there is a good understanding between us. It is something, however, that we cannot talk about too much."[54] Thomas would admit to "very fine cooperation from the FBI."[55]

It was soon apparent that HUAC would become a major forum for an assault on government workers who had communist or left-of-center leanings, a practice implemented to embarrass the White House. Focusing on what would be a prime Committee target, Martin Dies, in October 1941, announced that 1,124 federal employees including "a large number" in "policy-making positions" were allegedly members of subversive organizations and advocated forcible overthrow of the government. This scarcely veiled attack on the Roosevelt administration became grist for the media mills, as would many future Committee reports. This was also true even after four years later, when the Committee received permanent standing. The "Reds-in-Government" issue was a constant Committee theme. In February 1943, Dies would make newspaper headlines with a two-hour speech on the floor of the House specifically naming thirty-nine "suspect" federal workers whom he accused of being "irresponsible, unrepresentative, crackpot, radical bureaucrats" and "affiliates of Communist front organizations ..." and demanding their dismissal. His recommendations to the congressional Appropriations Committee included taking "vigorous and public steps" to eliminate them from public employment.

Any number of hearings of the Special Committee on Un-American Activities, now popularly known as the Dies Committee, had the obvious intent of embarrassing the White House. Committee hearings were often riddled by the underlying accusation that the administration is riddled with Soviet agents! The Democrats are the party of treason! Some Democratic candidates for political office, the Committee contended, those endorsed by the CP, had "Communistic affiliations." Eleanor Roosevelt, declared the Committee, was "one of the most valuable assets ... the Communist Party possess[es]," and that several cabinet members had "radical associates." One 1946 Committee "Investigation of Un-American Propaganda Activities," for instance, charged that radio scripts of the Office of Price Administration were communist propaganda, with one witness testifying that its propaganda policies were instructed by the People's Commissariat of Internal Affairs (NKVD) (Soviet secret police) in Moscow. In another instance of efforts to taint the administration, the Committee listened to testimony about alleged communist infiltration of the Federal Theatre and Federal Writers Projects, two major New Deal groups under the umbrella of the Works Projects Administration. In 1943, it published the names, positions, and salaries of 563 federal workers who allegedly were members of the American League for Peace and Democracy, considered a "Communist Front" organization. It also repeatedly held hearings on the State Department in 1940 and 1941, to confirm its charge that administration officials facilitated Soviet espionage.[55] In this regard, finally, an "Interim Report on Hearings regarding Communist Espionage in the United States Government" on August 27, 1948, announced its intent was "to permit American public opinion ... an ... opportunity to render a continuing verdict in all its public officials and to evaluate the merit of many in private life who either openly associate with and assist disloyal groups to covertly operate as members or fellow travelers of such organizations."[56] In point of fact, a prime Committee purpose was to investigate, undertaken with maximum publicity in mind, the executive branch and its numerous agencies.

Significantly, HUAC's most important practices represented a departure from the putative function of legislative committees generally, namely, to engage in investigations indispensable to the drafting of statutes and the functioning of Congress. Rather, as Attorney General Clark approvingly declared in February 1948 that the Committee was "bringing into the spotlight of publicity the activities of individuals and groups" and "cleans[ing] our way of life" of those who "cling to alien philosophies." In fact, this intent was openly acknowledged five years earlier, announcing that "discovery and exposure" were its "special functions." Obliquely admitting as much, J. Parnell Thomas, the ranking Republican on the Committee, candidly proclaimed in a 1947 radio address that the "chief function" of HUAC "has always been the exposure of un-American individuals and their un-American activities" in the "conviction that the American public will not tolerate efforts to subvert or destroy the American system of government once such efforts have been pointed out."[57] Toward this end of stigmatizing officeholders as well as radicals and radical activities, the Committee spent more money, called more witnesses, visited more places, issued more subpoenas – in excess of 5,000 – and published over 50,000 pages of hearings and reports more than all other House committees combined.

"Left wingers," to use congressman Dies's imprecise term, understandably became the objects of "fishing expeditions." Initially investigating the German–American Bund, the Committee soon directed its attention exclusively to the CP and toward those employed at schools, trade unions, federal agencies, atomic bomb research facilities, and Hollywood film studios. Regarding the last, movies and movie theatres being the prime source of entertainment in the nation, the nine-day HUAC Hollywood hearings of October 1947 would become gala affairs, with floodlights, cameras, and crowds crushing forward for a glimpse of the glamorous film stars involved. Ayn Rand, for instance, who was one committee witness, listed four films that she insisted contained pro-Communist or pro-Soviet scenes and charged they had been deliberately inserted by communists or their sympathizers. It was to be expected that her testimony, together with that of other "friendly witnesses," would lead to the loss of employment for a considerable number. (Four years later, the Hollywood hearings would be resumed by the HUAC Subcommittee repeating, in the usual shopworn and legitimating tropes, the same charges and with the same results.) To add a codicil: a striking discrepancy between fact and fantasy. Hollywood movie studios employed ca. 30,000 at the peak of their popularity, with the Hollywood branch of the CP numbering 200 to 250. And its members were easily and regularly outvoted by nine-to-one margins in meetings and elections of the governing Screen Actors Guild. The Committee hearings singled out about two dozen screenwriters, actors, directors, and producers, which led to their dismissal and forced the industry itself into blandness.

From the outset, the HUAC hearings sought to compel confessions of political belief and affiliation from witnesses. Indeed, the successful Hollywood hearings themselves produced a standard operating procedure for the future: witnesses who were "friendly" were encouraged to tell all that they knew about Communist infiltration or to name others whom they suspected of being Communists; and they were deified in and out of the Committee. Robert Carr describes how the "friendly witness," such as Louis Budenz, would be "allowed to ramble at length" about the allegedly subversive activities of literally hundreds of organizations and thousands of named individuals.[58] The "unfriendly" or "hostile" witness then would be subpoenaed, confronted by the accusation and would be asked: "Are you now, or have you ever been a member of the Communist Party?" The reply would often be to take refuge in the Fifth Amendment, that is, to invoke the privilege against self-incrimination that would, in the public view, identify the witness as a "Fifth Amendment Communist." The "unfriendly witness" usually was not given notice of the charges against him and could not confront or cross-examine his accusers, usually the ex-communist witnesses. In regard to these rights, HUAC Chairman acidly informed one witness: "The rights you have are the rights given you by this Committee. We will determine what rights you have and what rights you have not got before this Committee."[59]

Under these circumstances, refusal to reveal one's affiliation resulted in a contempt citation (e.g., "the Hollywood Ten") and imprisonment[60]; those who denied communist affiliation were then confronted by informers at their trials and convicted of perjury; and those admitting to pro-communist sympathies were dismissed, blacklisted, and unemployable. These experiences were endured by many called before the HUAC on other occasions. Left-of-center labor unions officials, for example, were predictable Committee targets in the mid-Thirties and Forties, if only because they had supported the Democratic Party. The Committee held hearings, widely publicized by the media, on the charges of communist-dominated union leadership in the United Electrical Workers, the CIO's Food, Tobacco, and Agricultural Workers, and the United Auto Workers, which charges swelled in 1947.

The anti-communist zealotry of the HUAC was such that its listings of communist organizations would swell to five times that of the Attorney General's. The Committee's first volume of proceedings recorded 640 organizations, 483 newspapers, and 280 labor unions as "Communistic." The Boy Scouts, ACLU, Camp Fire Girls, and the Catholic Association for International Peace were among those groups stigmatized as Communist-tainted. The practice of listings became a signature event for the Committee that would continue down the decades. Secretary of the Labor Frances Perkins, Secretary of the Interior Harold Ickes, and other New Dealers, consistent with the Committee's hostility to the administration, were placed on a HUAC list headed by that of Joseph Stalin. Committee reports called for the resignation of these officials: they were "purveyors of class hatred" and "range in political insanity from Socialism to Communism." Other Committee lists reported on the less well known. Among countless hyperbolic assertions having no basis in reality, Martin Dies, in October 1936, asserted that he had the names of 2,000 of the 4,700 Communists in the Chicago area, and two years later he would submit to the Attorney General a list of 1,121 federal workers – not one more or one less! – who were "either communists or affiliates of subversive organizations." And he would shortly thereafter claim that there were "six million Communist and Nazi sympathizers in the United States ...." The Committee itself, in

Appendix IX for instance, settled on a list of the 250,000 names, persons who allegedly were members of "communist-front" organizations.[61] By 1948, it had 300,000 files on "subversive" individuals and organizations and one million names by the following year.

These were wildly exaggerated claims since card-carrying members, as observed, left the Party in droves after the August 1939 Russo-German pact and would not return to Pearl Harbor in December 1941. Moreover, of the half-million government workers less than one hundred were Communists, and most of them were concentrated in the Department of Agriculture, the National Labor Relations Board, and a few in congressional committee staff positions, hardly positions where they had access to vital state secrets that could be passed on to the Soviet Union. But anyone favorably mentioned in the *Daily Worker*, or anyone who publicly criticized the HUAC was likely to find his or her name entered in its files and lists. And they were tainted as communists or fellow travelers, or condemned as "crackpots," radicals, fuzzy internationalists, etc.

Although no congressional committee received greater attention than HUAC, a number of others would be active, both in the Senate and in the states, where the chilling drumbeats emanating out of Moscow could also be heard. Indicating the durability and redundancy of fears about radicalism that punctuated American lives and culture, the Senate Committee on the Judiciary had held hearings in 1919 on "Bolshevik Propaganda" in the United States. Carrying the theme down to 1939 and 1940, this same Committee called witnesses who described the relationship of America's communists with those in the Kremlin. The Committee on Naval Affairs, for its part, was troubled in 1935 about the "'contaminating influences'" of "subversive" literature from Communist organizations, concerned lest it "would incite ... disobedience." Such literature, it argued, had the forcible overthrow of government as its ultimate objective. Four years later, the same Committee again heard witnesses testifying to "Red" literature distributed on Navy premises.[62] Other congressional committees conveyed the same vestigial anti-radicalism. In 1953, the Committee on Appropriation listened to witnesses from the State Department describe lapses in its loyalty and security program. Three years earlier, the Senate Foreign Relations Committee had pursued the same topic, now inflamed by Senator Joseph McCarthy's destructive accusations that "something was radically wrong" in the State Department. The Committee on Labor and Public Welfare submitted no less than three

The Thirties

reports in the 1951–1953 years on communist-dominated unions, with witnesses demonstrating how the views of certain specified unions did not deviate from the CP positions.

Nevada's Senator McCarran, who chaired the Senate Judiciary Committee, headed a subcommittee on internal security in 1950 that had a "very satisfactory" relationship with the FBI and engaged in some spectacular investigations, a few of which "stole the limelight" from the HUAC. Indeed, Paul Murphy concludes that it "overshadowed the House Committee both in the range of subjects with which the members concerned themselves and in the passion for publicity surrounding its activities."[63] Senator Joe McCarthy became chair of the Committee on Government Operations, and it probed subversion in churches, academic communities, and federal agencies.

The Senate's Internal Security Subcommittee (SISS) on Investigations of the Committee on Government Operations rivaled both the FBI and the HUAC in its dogged pursuit of communists. As a "friendly" witness would later testify, the SISS performed "a valuable service in furnishing the public with evaluated information concerning the work of apologists and agents of the Soviet Union who have not – or cannot be proven to have – broken existing laws." The very titles and descriptions of SISS investigative reports reveal the great sweep of its hearings: "Investigations of Career Officers in the Foreign Service"; "Subversive Organizations; Communism Tactics in Controlling Youth Organizations, such as the American Youth for Democracy, and the literature, leaders, programs and objectives discussed"; "Subversive Infiltration of Radio, Television, the Newspaper Industry"; "Passport Policy"; "subversive control of five unions"; "espionage by Soviet-bloc diplomats"; "communist teachers"; "Security–United Nations"; "State Department Information Programs"; and "political background of U.S. employees at the UN."[64] One final committee report, coming after ten days of questioning of thirty-three witnesses, concluded that "there had been no safeguard ... against employment by the United Nations of American citizens ... disloyal to their country." Additional SISS reports likewise indicate its many hearings and broad investigative character: "Security – Government Printing Office, on alleged espionage at the GPO"; "Communist Infiltration in the Army"; "Communist Party Hearings – Western Pennsylvania"; "Communist Domination of Union Officials in Vital Defense Industry"; "Subversive Influence in Certain Labor Organizations"; "Subversive Control of Various Unions"; "Strategy and Tactics of World Communism"; and "Influence in the Educational Process." One report, "Communist influence at The New York Times," derived from a hearing headed by Mississippi's Senator James Eastland, a rabid anti-communist who, perhaps incidentally, had been the target of exposes in that newspaper.[65]

The narrative of congressional hearings and investigations as well as federal statutes was paralleled by those in the state houses across the country. Identical in form and substance to those described in the post-war decade, they continued to flow out of state houses. Maryland's legislators, for one, amended the State constitution to bar any one from their august body who belonged to an organization advocating the forcible overthrow of the government, an amendment overwhelmingly approved by voters in 1948. Washington State lawmakers soldiered along with the same systemic anti-communism. Indeed they arguably trumped Maryland's. For they expanded an "anti-subversive" clause in an appropriations statute to require those receiving welfare funds, as well as all State employees, to swear to disbelief in or support of the "overthrow of the United States government by force or by any illegal or unconstitutional means." Two lawmakers, Albert Canwell and Sydney Stevens, successfully pressed a measure authorizing a "Joint Legislative Fact-Finding Committee on Un-American Activities" in 1945. It used lists of "Communist Front" groups – compiled by the U.S. Attorney General, the HUAC, and the California's Un-American Activities Committee – to hold hearings on alleged CP members and organizations in the State.[66] These hearings featured testimony from such professional anti-communist witnesses as Louis Budenz and used rumors and suspicions in interrogating those suspected of being communists or "fellow-travelers."

Swept by a similar wave of phobic anti-communism, California's evangelical Red-hunting assemblyman and the then Senator, Jack Tenney, a one-time reporter and State legislator, had been awakened by the 1934 West Coast Waterfront Strike to the fact of "Red Harry" Bridges and the threat of communism. He headed the State's legislature's Fact-Finding Committee on Un-American Activities (and its Subcommittee to Control Communism, Subversive Activities, and Sabotage); and from 1941 to 1949, he investigated communist influence in California's unions, schools, textbooks, and alleged communist "front" organizations.[67] It considered any person "who supports the program of the Communist Party as part of the program of world revolution laid down by the Comintern in Moscow is a Stalinist"; and "every communist in the United States is a potential traitor, saboteur and espionage agent of Soviet Russia." The Subcommittee *a fortiori* listed 200 State organizations whose officials and members possibly fell into this suspect category and held hearings to expose them. Similar to HUAC hearings, "friendly" witnesses were treated with deference and allowed to go on at length, whereas "unfriendly" ones were considered criminals, even traitors, and their testimony was challenged and interrupted at every turn.[68] The investigations produced a number of proposals, one evolving into a loyalty oath. All public employees were required to swear: "I do not advocate nor am I a member of any party or organization, political; or otherwise, that now advocates the overthrow of the Government of the United States or the State of California by force or violence." Tenney's committee also fathered a number of anti-subversion bills, and often in the same language as the oath, such as one requiring it of every candidate in the State primary elections.

State investigations of communists had its offspring in strikingly similar repressive measures, namely, statutes barring state employment to members of organizations allegedly seeking the overthrow of government. By 1941, thirteen states had introduced such punitive statutes. However, a good number of these state statutes had been on the books for many years. From 1917 to 1920, identical or quite similar laws were adopted by twenty states and two territories. Maryland's Ober Act or Subversive Activities Act of 1949 conformed to earlier criminal syndicalism and anti-communist measures in other states and in the federal government and reflected concern about radical influence in the State's educational institutions.[69] Ohio's Criminal Syndicalism Act, for instance, had been enacted in 1919, Oregon's in the same year, and would be twice reenacted and embodied in a new 1937 statute, and California's almost identical measure of 1919 would be found constitutional by the Supreme Court in 1927.[70] The loyalty oath was the usual test of state public employment, followed by discharge of the employee who refused to swear that he was not a member of the CP or an organization aligned with it, with the further ramification that the person allegedly or actually involved in such a group often became the subject of criminal sanctions. The practice, as noted earlier, became a standard procedure on the state level after World War I when measures attainting anarchists, syndicalists, and radicals generally had been implemented, especially in such sensitive areas as public education – with state lawmakers and their little HUACs, remaining consumed by an insatiable anti-radical appetite and fears for an imperiled democratic heritage.

The state anarchy laws mentioned earlier, initiated by New York in 1902, likewise had constancy and sweep before the World War II, as witness Rhode Island's in 1938; or measures in Connecticut and Delaware that combined criminal anarchy and sedition. Criminal syndicalism laws on the statute books since 1919 also continued to remain in place in the 1930s and 1940s and invoked for a number of prosecutions. Oregon, for one, would cite its statute in the 1931 case, *State v. Beloff* (and the defendant involved received a ten-year prison term for helping to organize the CP). Michigan provided the state prototype for the arrest of left-leaning non-citizens. Its 1934 alien-registration statute assisted the federal government in the registration and round-up at the time and explicitly targeted radicals.

Prescriptive state Red Flag laws were long in place, as observed above, but new ones would be added in the Thirties and Forties. Michigan's 1919 measure was also a model of its kind. It had been identified with the IWW, with anarchists from the turn of the century, and with the Bolsheviks after 1917; and the public assumed that anyone displaying the Red Flag in the Twenties and Thirties was a Communist. Likewise replicating the long-standing 1919 statute, the 1949 Kansas measure prohibited any person or organization "to fly, to carry, to exhibit, to display ... any red flag, standard or banner distinctive of bolshevism, anarchy, or radical socialism ...."[71] Illinois also shared in the anti-radical overkill, having a Red Flag law in 1935, as well as a measure six years later that denied a place on the ballot to a member of any organization "engaged in activities or propaganda designed to teach subservience to the political principles and ideals of foreign governments."[72] Lawmakers and judges did not cease and desist when World War II broke out and carried the ideological animus to display the Red Flag during and after the conflict. Nebraska, Montana, and Minnesota, inter alia in the Forties, joined in finding the Red Flag that represented a dangerous and abhorrent enemy, the symbol of those who sought to overthrow the government by force and violence.[73] Rhode Island's measured proscribed the display of any flag or emblem "except the flag of the United States," by implication making it illegal to display black anarchist or red Communist banners.

Judicial and legislative branches in the Thirties joined in deciding that distinctions between radical beliefs were of no consequence. The public likewise made no distinction between anarchism, a political doctrine that embraced the absence of law or a supreme government, and communism that held to a highly regulated form of government.

It was sufficient to recognize that all radical groups were understood to *advocate forcible overthrow of government*. Among sweeping anti-red state laws in the Thirties, Rhode Island typically combined the crimes of sedition, criminal syndicalism, and criminal anarchy, included the standard obligatory reference to prohibiting advocacy of any change, alteration or modification, or to advocacy of forcible overthrow of the form of government.[74] Indiana in 1933, Illinois in 1934, and Colorado in 1935 adopted virtually identical proscriptive wording.

At times, the ambiguous and *ad hominem* state language had specific professions in mind. Teachers, for one, being especially vulnerable, would be dismissed because of pacifist liberal or radical sentiments in California, Colorado, South Dakota, and so on in the 1930s. For example, Kristen Lindenmeyer observed, that by 1935 twenty states required teachers to take loyalty oaths, an important mechanism in the sustained effort to eliminate Red influence from their schools.[75] New York State lawmakers were in the forefront of state heresy hunting. They established a Committee headed by Herbert Rapp and Frederick Coudert, the Joint Legislative Committee to Investigate Educational System of State of New York to search out "subversive activities" in the State's schools. It made headlines in the early Forties when reporting that both schools and the Teacher's Union were rife with communists. A further media show occurred with the purge of left-of-center and Communist teachers that inevitably followed, as would the court cases of those appealing their discharge.[76] The need to produce and expose live Communist teachers resulted in a provision added to the State's Civil Service Law that no one should be appointed or continued in employment as superintendent or as a public school teacher who advocated or taught the forcible overthrow of the United States or State governments or who organized or became a member of any such organization having such ends.

These proscriptive state laws focusing on teachers were in some measure influenced by the political branches of the federal government. State legislators, we may believe, were very aware of the announced intent of President Harding's Commissioner of Education – to eliminate "Communism, Bolshevism, and Socialism" from schools, and membership in the major teachers' union. They also surely knew of the 1948 letter that the HUAC sent to eighty-one colleges and high schools demanding lists of textbooks used in various courses (e.g., literature, political, and social sciences). Like their voters, after all, they were influenced by the specious claims of national security. Consistent with the political landscape, the District of Columbia school system prohibited any speaker listed as suspect by HUAC and submitted names of possible nominees to the Committee for clearance. In California, the State legislature passed an ambiguously worded and catch-all measure that forbids teachers to "advocate or teach communism with the intent to indoctrinate any pupil with, or inculcate a preference in the mind of any pupil for communism." Going to a further extreme, the 1949 Indiana Statute declared that it was State policy to "eliminate Communism and Communists and any and all teachings of the same."

State legislative committee investigations of universities and faculty across the country also became a familiar scene, accompanied by a near-intolerable pressure to conform to iconic national symbols and rhetoric, with the predictable penalties if one did not. The Illinois legislature's Broyles Commission, continuing its labors of the Thirties against "foreignisms," urged passage of a "School Code" to permit dismissal of any public school teacher "advocating in his teaching any doctrine to undermine the form of government ... by force and violence"[77]; and it cautioned that "various publications are sent to the students in school are subversive in that they give one side of the theory of government strange to our own." Typical of the constant news items coming out of state assemblies from coast to coast, the Broyles Commission proposed to prohibit any subversive and un-American speaker on University of Illinois campus. It was sparked by the understanding of Illinois lawmakers that "the universities of America have been the breeding ground of a serious of invidious Communist inspired organizations which have sought to instill in the hearts of American youth contempt and hatred ideals to which the people of this great nation have been dedicated." A statement made in 1947 and repeated in 1953 Supplementing this Commission testimony, one lawmaker worrisomely learned "that in the Public Library are complete reference books on the subject of Communism, dealing with the subject at great length and stressing the advantages of the Communist system of government in preference to our type of government."[78]

In short, state legislators that had joined the federal government in the anti-Red chorus in the Twenties hardly ceased before and after the World War II. In its 1949 Report of Joint Fact-Finding Committee on Un-American Activities, for example, Canwell's Washington State Committee concluded that the State "is acrawl with trained and iron-disciplined Communists."[79] The threat of communism at the University of Washington motivated his committee to grill some forty faculty members about their alleged CP connections. As could be expected considering the atmosphere surrounding the State House as well as that in the nation, the University's Board of Regents decided to investigate its own faculty. The 1949 report of the Regents, "Communism and Academic Freedom" disclosed that three faculty members were dismissed and three others were placed on probation, "their continued employment being condition to their signing affidavits that they were not presently members of the Communist Party."[80] Summarizing the effect of such investigations, Robert MacIver understandably concluded that "they have been largely responsible for the spirit of apprehension and the sense of intimidation that, according to a considerable amount of testimony, has invaded the halls of learning."[81]

Private groups, such as the Special Committee of Federation of Citizens' Associations on Eliminating Antipatriotic and Subversive Matter from Public Schools, the National Association of Manufacturers and the American Legion supplemented federal and state legislative actions, and campaigned to sell "the American Way of Life" in school districts, with the Legion urging dismissal of "disloyal teachers," those who taught "subversive" ideas in the classroom or who opposed loyalty oaths.

Returning to the federal scene in the Thirties, anti-radical statutes littered the landscape. Some were not well known to the public, such as the 1939 Emergency Relief Act that prohibited government employment to the members of any organization advocating "or who is a member of an organization that advocates the overthrow of the Government of the United States by force and violence." The 1940 Voorhis Act was one more congressional effort to curb or eliminate the CP or inter alia, any organization "subject to foreign control which engages in political activity," and it was required to register as such. The phrase, "subject to foreign control," was broadly defined in Section One of the statute as directed to any organization whose policies "are determined by or at the suggestion of, or in collaboration with, a foreign government or political subdivision thereof, or an agent, agency, or instrumentality of a foreign government ..."[82]

Section Nine of the Hatch Act 1939 was also responsive to the phobic anti-communism in Congress and the public at large.[83] It prohibited the federal employment "by anyone who was currently a member of any political party or organization that advocated the overthrow of our constitutional form of government," and under these provisions the FBI (as described by Justice Black in the case immediately below) "began a wholesale investigation of federal employees ... [and] thousands were investigated." In fact, the Justice Department Authorization Act of June 1941 included an appropriation of $100,000 to enable the FBI to investigate all federal employees who were "'members of subversive organizations.'"

Turning back a half dozen years, Congress in 1935 began debate on the first federal peacetime sedition statute since 1798, and the measure – the Alien Registration Act – drafted by Representative Howard Smith of Virginia, sailed through Congress in March 1940, only four House members voting against it, while forty-five abstained.[84] The lopsided margin was to be expected, considering its backdrop of seemingly multiple foreign and domestic threats. Modeled on New York's 1902 Criminal Anarchy Act and virtually reenacting the 1917 Espionage Act, the two-decade-plus time span of the 1940 measure as further suggestive of the enduring character of the nation's anti-radical sentiment. Severely restricting the political asylum of allegedly radical aliens in the United States, the statute was hardly limited to noncitizens. Title I (Section 2385) made it a felony for anyone "to knowingly or willfully advocate, abet, advise ... the duty, necessity, desirability, or propriety of overthrowing or destroying any government of the United States by force or violence." Further, it would be unlawful in any way to "impair or influence the loyalty, morals, or discipline of the military or naval forces of the United States," rhetoric strikingly proximate to that of the 1917 Espionage Act. Though directed primarily against the CP, the statute was phrased so broadly, Paul Murphy shrewdly observes, that it would include not only those conspiring to overthrow the government but also those advocating overthrow.[85] Becoming the first federal peacetime espionage measure in 150 years, it applied in times of peace as well as war, and therefore was broader than the 1917 Espionage Act. It was, in fact, the dragnet measure that Attorney General Palmer had unsuccessfully urged legislators to pass in 1920 and signaled that Roosevelt, in unhesitatingly signing the measure, had added his voice to the manic anti-communism of these years.

The registration of aliens in Title One of the 1940 statute was hardly the statute's most consequential aspect. Title Two strengthened the deportation of alien radicals. This Section will be set forth in a timely fashion – when government prosecutors first found it useful in deportation proceedings. Suffice now to observe only that the Smith Act was directed primarily at Communists, although sufficiently broad to include any person advocating or conspiring to advocate overthrow of the government. In addition, a conspiracy provision vague in both content and reach was provided by Section Three, which made it criminal not merely to speak, distribute books, organize a political party, but solely to agree to these activities. As such, the statute offered the government a grab bag of possible prosecutorial strategies. Jerold Auerbach contends that it was the first federal criminal measure to introduce the principle of guilt by association. Surviving many court challenges, shortly to be considered, it remained the law of the land.

A product of domestic anxieties concerning the "Red Menace," the 1940 statute would, like one of ten years later, eventually be used to destroy those attainted. It would ruin their careers and feed the "hysteria," as President Truman termed it.[86] The measure would be first applied to the Socialist Workers Party (SWP), a considerable irony since SWP'ers had unimpeachable anti-communist credentials, being followers of Leon Trotsky, a bitter enemy of the Kremlin. But they dominated two teamster locals and hence were a threat to Dan Tobin's conservative leadership of the teamsters union, then in the AFL. When the locals bolted the AFL and joined the rival CIO, Tobin, who was an ally of the President, complained to the White House about the "radical Trotskyite" CIO teamsters. Shortly thereafter federal marshals raided SWP headquarters in Minneapolis, then a radical labor bastion, especially so among the city's teamsters. Twenty-nine members of this minor Trotskyite sect were arrested, eighteen of whom were convicted. In effect, the case *Dunne v. United States* (1943)[87] originated in a political favor owed by the President to the AFL Teamsters Union rather than as a free-speech case. Those arrested would be charged under the Smith Act with one count of conspiracy – to teach and advocate the violent overthrow of the government. Their conviction would be sustained by the Eighth Circuit Court of Appeals, and the High Court denied certiorari.

In point of fact, there were far fewer wartime prosecutions for the expression of opinions in World War II than during the World War I, the US–USSR wartime alliance and the CP change-of-line providing one reason for the decline. Those few communists who were indicted were usually charged under the 1917 Espionage Act (e.g., *Hartzel v. United States*, (1944)). Then, too, the High Court decisions in the wartime cases tilted toward giving free speech a preferred position. They intimated the onset of a revised standard for review by the Court and provided an opening for judicial activism on behalf of freedom of speech. In 1946, however, a counterweight to the shift in judicial trends appeared in the background. Strains with the Soviet Union had begun to develop in the form of what appeared to be an accelerated program of Soviet expansion in Europe, and for the nation, it was not out of memory that the American Communist Party remained part of a protean Moscow-directed apparatus.

Notes

1. Quoted in Bernard Schwartz, *Inside the Warren Court* (Garden City, NY: Doubleday, 1983), 79.
2. 283 U.S. 359 (1931).
3. Ibid., 359, 369.
4. 283 U.S. 697 (1931).
5. Ibid., attachment: 1930 WL 28681, p. 65. See also in ibid., pp. 47–8, 51, 64. The due process class of the Fourteenth Amendment, cited in the defense Brief, literally defined, meant safeguarding the procedural rights of individuals such as right to confront witnesses, right to a speedy trial, prohibition against self-incrimination. See also Landmark Briefs, vol. 26, 582, 596–7.
6. *Near*, 283 U.S. at 707. For another instance of freedom of the press, secured by the First Amendment against the federal government, also being secured by the Fourteenth against abridgment by the state, see Justice Roberts, in *Schneider v. State*, 308 U.S. 147, 160 (1939).
7. 299 U.S. 353, 357 (1937).
8. *DeJonge v. Oregon*, 152 Or. 315 (1937).
9. Ibid., 357.
10. Ibid., attached: Brief for the United States, 1936 WL 40125, p. 29. In yet another Oregon case, *State v. Boloff*, 138 Or. 568, the defendant was convicted for helping to organize and being a member of the Communist Party in violation of the State's criminal syndicalism statute. Trial judge sentenced him to ten years in prison, and the court candidly acknowledged at a rehearing: "[t]he party program, more than the defendant, is on trial." (at 632).
11. *DeJonge*, 299 U.S. at 365.
12. Ibid., 364.
13. Ibid., 365.
14. 301 U.S. 242 (1937). See two other Georgia cases. In one, *Carr v. State*, 176 Ga. 55 (1932), the defendants were convicted for distributing revolutionary papers that advocated the overthrow of capitalism; and convictions for a similar reason in *Dalton v. State* (176 Ga. 645 (1933)).
15. *Herndon*, 301 U.S. at 258, 252.
16. Charles Martin, "The Angelo Herndon Case and Southern Justice," in *American Political Trials* ed. Michal R. Belknap (Westport, CT: Greenwood Press, 1994), 184, 189.
17. *Herndon*, 301 U.S. at 255.
18. Ibid., 258.
19. Ibid., 250.
20. Ibid., 259.
21. Among those exploring Frankfurter's insistence upon judicial discretion, Silverstein offers a meticulous account. Mark Silverstein, *Constitutional Faiths: Felix Frankfurter, Hugo Black and the Process of Judicial Decision Making* (Ithaca, NY: Cornell University Press, 1984), 171. For one instance

of "striking the balance" by Frankfurter, see *Sweezy v. New Hampshire*, 354 U.S. 234 (1957). See Harlan's opinion in *Braden v. United States*, 365 U.S. 431 (1961), discussed below, as a classic instance of balancing. See also *Beauharnais v. Illinois*, 343 U.S. 250 (1952); and Silverstein, *Constitutional Faiths*, 144, 191, 193, 199–204. Likewise cogent and insightful on the subject, there is Wallace Mendelson, *Justices Black and Frankfurter: Conflict in the Court* (Chicago, IL: University of Chicago Press, 2nd ed., 1966), 19; and Melvin Urofsky, *Division and Discord: The Supreme Court under Stone and Vinson, 1941–1953* (Columbia, SC: University of South Carolina Press, 1997), 168–71.

22. For a thoughtful assessment of Justice Frankfurter, see Mendelson, *Justices Black and Frankfurter*, 124–31.
23. Silverstein, *Constitutional Faiths*, 44, 191. See also Jeremy Cohen, *Congress Shall Make No Law. Oliver Wendell Holmes the First Amendment, and Judicial Decision-Making* (Ames, IA: State University Press of Iowa, 1989), 70, 79, for example, Frankfurter's opinion in *Dennis v. United States*, 341 U.S. 494, 524–6, 544 (1951)
24. Silverstein, *Constitutional Faiths*.
25. Ibid., 200.
26. Samuel Krislov, *The Supreme Court and Political Freedom* (New York: Free Press, 1968), 117.
27. *Beauharnais*, 343 U.S. at 250.
28. Edmund Cahn, "Justice Black and the First Amendment: A Public Interview," *New York University Law Review* 36 (1962): 573.
29. Quoted in Silverstein, *Constitutional Faiths*, 177.
30. Ibid., 184. See also John Roche, "Utopian Pilgrimage of Mr. Justice Murphy," *Vanderbilt Law Review* 10 (1957): 369. For an invaluable elaboration of Justice Murphy's views, see Harry Kalven, A Worthy Tradition: Freedom of Speech in America (New York: Harper & Row, 1988), 429.
31. *United States v. Carolene Products Co.*, 304 U.S. 144 (1938), 152, n. 4. See also G. Edward White, *The Constitution and the New Deal* (Cambridge, MA: Harvard University Press, 2000), 120–31; and Urofsky, *Division and Discord*, 11; and see William Ross, *The Chief Justiceship of Charles Evans Hughes, 1930–1941* (Columbia, SC: University of South Carolina Press, 2007), 192–3; and *Schneider v. State*, 308 U.S. 147 (1939).
32. 320 U.S. 119 (1943).
33. Ibid., 121–2; *United States v. Schneiderman*, 33 F. Supp. 510 (N.D. Cal. 1940); *aff'd* 119 F.2d 500 (9th Cir. 1941). The Nationality Act of 1940, renewed denaturalization proceedings against him, but deportation would succeed a dozen years later only by resort to the ancient 1798 Alien Act – on the grounds that "petitioner had concealed his Communist affiliation" and "Party membership per se precluded true faith and allegiance to the United States," a definition of citizenship found in the 1940 statute.
34. Ibid., 129.
35. Ibid., 126.
36. Ibid., 119.
37. Special Committee on Un-American Activities, 75th Cong., 3rd Sess. Investigation of Un-American Propaganda in the United States. Hearing, Vol. 4, 713 pp. 1938. See also Committee on Un-American Activities, 81st Cong., 2nd Sess. Annual Report on Un-American Activities for the Year 1949.

H. Rep 1950. IV 75 ppd. This report summarizes the Committee's investigations in 1949 and "mentions favorably the Committee's role in the ... trial of Harry Bridges ..."
38. The background to this case is given a scrupulously detailed analysis in Stanley Kutler, *American Inquisition. Justice and Injustice in the Cold War* (New York: Hill & Wang, 1982), 126–19; and in C. P. Larrowe, "Did the Old Left Get Due Process? The Case of Harry Bridges," *California Law Review* 60 (1972): 39–83.
39. E.g., *United States v. Bridges*, 90 F. Supp. 973 (N.D. Cal. 1950); *United States v. Bridges*, 133 F. Supp. 638 (N.D. Cal. 1955); *Bridges v. United States*, 199 F.2d 811 (9th Cir. 1951); *Bridges v. United States*, 184 F.2d 881 (9th Cir. 1950); *Bridges v. Wixon*, 144 F.2d 927 (9th Cir. 1944), rev'd, 326 U.S. 135 (1945); *United States v. Bridges*, 133 F. Supp. 638 (N.D. Cal. 1955); *United States v. Bridges*, 93 F. Supp. 989 (N.D. Cal. 1950); *Ex parte Bridges*, 49 F. Supp. 292 (N.D. Cal. 1943). For a solid, utterly persuasive account of this complex case, see Stanley Kutler, *The American Inquisition. Justice and Injustice in the Cold War* (New York: Hill & Wang, 1982), 118–51.
40. 314 U.S. 252 (1941).
41. Ibid., 263.
42. Ibid. Tinsley Yarborough argues that "[t]he fundamentally absolutist thrust of this passage is unmistakable ...": "any limitation on the freedom granted by the First Amendment" could not be constitutionally imposed by government. Tinsley E. Yarbrough, *Mr. Justice Black and His Critics* (Durham, NC: Duke University Press, 1988), 161.
43. Ibid. See also *Schneider*, 308 U.S. at 160.
44. Robert McCloskey, *The Modern Supreme Court* (Cambridge, MA: Harvard University Press, 1972), 16.
45. Quoted in Silverstein, *Constitutional Faiths*, 180, 185–6.
46. McCloskey, *The Modern Supreme*, 18, 20.
47. 326 U.S. 135 (1945) see fn. 35. The Supreme Court, in a five-to-four post-war decision, eventually sustained the government (*Bridges v. United States*, 346 U.S. 209). For details, see David Cole, *Enemy Aliens* (New York: The New Press, 2003), 134–5. See also Murphy, *The Constitution in Crisis Times, 1918–1969* (New York: Harper & Row, 1972), 232; and Fund for the Republic, *Digest of the Public Record*, l54–61.
48. *Bridges*, 326 U.S. at 157.
49. Fund for the Republic, *Digest of the Public Record*, 241–314, 250, 257, 266, 289, 307.
50. See, for instance, *Branch v. Cahill*, 88 F.2d 545 (9th Cir. 1938), upholding the deportation of Campbell Branch, an English alien who was the managing editor of the West Coast CP newspaper. Or, *In re Hanoff*, 39 F. Supp. 46, 69 (N.D. Cal. 1941), which ordered Elmer Hanoff, a Party activist, deported to the Soviet Union. Ibid., 164–6.
51. Quoted in Robert Carr, *The House Committee on Un-American Activities* (Ithaca, NY: Cornell University Press, 1952), 85.
52. 78 Cong. Rec. 4934 (March 20, 1934). See also Carr, *The House Committee on Un-American Activities*, 13–5.
53. Quoted in Frank Donner, *The Un-Americans* (New York: Ballantine Books, 1961), 21.

54. Quoted in Kenneth O'Reilly, *Hoover and the Un-Americans* (Philadelphia, PA: Temple University Press, 1983), 50.
55. Quoted in Robert J. Goldstein, *Political Repression in Modern America* (Cambridge, MA: Schenkman Publishing Group, 1978), 307. See also quoted in Donner, *The Un-Americans*, 274.
56. Carr, *The House Committee on Un-American Activities*, 279–80.
57. Ibid., 280; see also Donner, *The Un-Americans*, 64; and quoted in Robert J. Goldstein, *Political Repression in Modern America* (Cambridge, MA: Schenkman Publishing Group, 1978), 345.
58. Ibid., 290.
59. Quoted in Ibid., 295.
60. Screenwriter John Howard Lawson, in one typical instance, was cited for contempt, for refusal to tell the HUAC whether he had been a member of the Communist Party, resulting in trial and conviction. *Lawson v. United States*, 176 F.2d 49 (D.C. Cir. 1949).
61. "Appendix IX" may be found in, Fund for the Republic, *Digest of the Public Record*, 54.
62. Fund for the Republic, *Digest of the Public Record*, 521.
63. Murphy, *The Constitution in Crisis Times, 1918–1969*, 293.
64. Fund for the Republic, *Digest of the Public Record*, 523. For further details on the SISS, see David Caute, *The Great Fear: The Anti-Communist Party Purge under Truman and Eisenhower* (New York: Simon & Schuster, 1978), 105.
65. Ralph Brown, *Loyalty and Security Employment Tests in the United States* (New Haven, CT: Yale University Press, 1958), 147.
66. *Digest of the Public Record*, 650–1. See also Vern Countryman, "Washington: The Carswell Committee," in *The States and Subversion* ed. Walter Gellhorn (Ithaca, NY: Cornell University Press, 1952), 285; Caute, *The Great Fear*, 77–8.
67. Fund for the Republic, *Digest of the Public Record*, 296, 304, 671–3. See also Edward Barrett, Jr., "California. Regulation and Investigation of Subversive Activities," in *The States and Subversion* ed. Walter Gellhorn (Ithaca, NY: Cornell University Press, 1952), 7–36; Caute, *The Great Fear*, 77–8.
68. Caute, 29.
69. Fund for the Republic, *Digest of the Public Record*, 274. A number of states passed measures almost identical to Maryland's Ober Act, such as Mississippi in 1950 (Fund for the Republic, *Digest of the Public Record*, 149).
70. 274 U.S. 357 (1927).
71. Fund for the Republic, *Digest of the Public Record*, 274.
72. Ibid., 309.
73. Robert Mowitz, "Michigan: State and Local Attack in Subversion," in *The States and Subversion* ed. Walter Gellhorn (Ithaca, NY: Cornell University Press, 1952), 190, 426–7. See also Fund for the Republic, *Digest of the Public Record*, 309.
74. Fund for the Republic, *Digest of the Public Record*, 286, 313.
75. Kristen Lindenmeyer, *The Greatest Generation Grows Up* (Chicago, IL: Ivan Dee, 2005), 119. See also Caute, *The Great Fear*, 78–9, 408.
76. Lawrence Chamberlain, "New York: A Generation of Legislative Alarm," in *The States and Subversion* ed. Walter Gellhorn (Ithaca, NY: Cornell University Press, 1952), 244–71, 280. See also Caute, *The Great Fear*, 431; Brown, *Loyalty and Security*, 105. See also *Daniman v. Board of Education of*

New York, 306 N.Y. 532 (1954). Teachers in New York City public school and public colleges had been dismissed under Section 903 of the New York City charter. They were denied reinstatement on grounds that they had claimed the privilege against self-incrimination when asked about their Communist Party affiliations. See also Subcommittee on Internal Security of Committee on the Judiciary, January 1953, on Communist influence in New York City schools that concluded "there are yet many hundreds of teachers who are communists" and have great influence.

77. E. Houston Harsha, "Illinois: The Broyles Commission," in *The States and Subversion* ed. Walter Gellhorn (Ithaca, NY: Cornell University Press, 1952), 59. See also Caute, *The Great Fear*, 79–80.
78. Harsha, "Illinois: The Broyles Commission," 64.
79. Fund for the Republic, *Digest of the Public Record*, 686.
80. Ibid., 685.
81. Quoted in Robert MacIver, *Academic Freedom in Our Time* (New York: Gordian Press, 1955), 49.
82. Committee on the Judiciary, 76th Cong., 3d Sess. Requiring the Registration of Certain Organizations. H. Rep. 2582, June 17, 1940. The statute, the Voorhis Act of 1940, required subversive organizations to register with the Attorney General.
83. 53 Stat. 1148 (1939).
84. 54 Stat. 670 (1940).
85. Murphy, *The Constitution in Crisis Times*, 217.
86. Scott Martelle, *The Fear Within: Spies, Commies, and American Democracy on Trial* (New Brunswick, NJ: Rutgers University Press, 2011), 7.
87. *Dunne v. United States*, 138 F.2d 137 (8th Cir. 1943), *cert. denied* 320 U.S. 790 (1943).

7

Stare Decisis: Old Responses to New Crises

Franklin Roosevelt died of a massive stroke in April 1945, and Harry Truman, his Vice President, entered the Oval Office. From the new administration came exaggerated assessments of Soviet military adventurism after World War II. By March 1947, the Truman Doctrine was in place, sold by the President to the public "by emphasizing … Communism vs. democracy" as the "major theme." It pledged $400,000 in economic and military aid to Greece and Turkey, then seemingly threatened by the spread of communism; and broadening the canvas, Truman promised "to support free peoples who are resisting attempted subjugation" everywhere. He did so against a background of seemingly urgent overseas threats and crises. The Soviet Union had emerged as a great military power after hostilities ended, and its policies seemed an intimidating challenge to the democracies, a challenge reinforced by what was believed to be a Sino-Soviet threat posed by the relentless advance of Mao Zedong and Red China's armies against the U.S. ally, Chiang Kai-shek, who had been the recipient of over three billion dollars from Washington. It was followed by his swift and stunning defeat. Within a month, Truman's National Security Council defined the American purpose as "to block further Communist expansion in Asia." In South East Asia as well, where the Viet Minh had begun their struggle against the French in Vietnam, with the State Department convinced that Moscow was casting a long shadow cast over Indochina. These developments shaped what would be the greatest crisis of the early Cold War.

For the moment, the European scene dominated administration thinking, since the Kremlin was driving for hegemony in Eastern Europe. It was purging all anti-communist leaders in Hungary and capping its steel-like grip in Czechoslovakia with the coup of February 1948 that overturned democratic rule and installed a pliant government.

Moscow's response to the establishment of NATO in mid-summer 1948, and to Western initiatives in Germany, was to blockade ground traffic into Berlin. Rather than withdraw from the city, which would possibly have resulted in a re-election defeat for Truman, the President responded unequivocally: "We are going to stay, period." And the airlift of supplies into the city's Western zones was underway by July 1948, followed by the highly publicized order sending sixty B-29s, "atomic bombers," to forward airbases in England. While behind closed doors, Secretary of State Dean Acheson warned of conditions in Greece and the Balkans, and "a highly possible Soviet break through might open three continents to Soviet penetration."

Domestically, this succession of events ramped up a two-fold reaction. They intensified fears of subversion and prompted a response to what was perceived as a dark, unsettling challenge for Americans. Considering themselves destined by history to meet and overcome any and all communist threats to their morally beneficent purposes, their longstanding anti-radical apprehensions were revitalized by the new President. He had earlier stirred the anti-communist pot with a campaign speech on March 18, 1948, St. Patrick's Day, in New York. "The issue," Truman had declared, was "as old as recorded history. It is tyranny against freedom." He went on to charge that "communism denied the very existence of God. 'This threat to our liberty and to our faith must be faced by each one of us.'"[1] Continuing to trumpet the growing menace to the United States in moralistic terms, the President reduced it to a "modern tyranny led by small group who have abandoned their faith in God." Only a relative handful of Americans, we may believe, rejected this normative belief that a God-fearing nation was in a struggle against godless communism. Six months later, in Boston, he added to the toxic brew by bluntly stating: "I want you to get this straight now. I hate communism." Elaborating in January 1949, in his inaugural address, Truman declared that communism glorified violence and postulated the inevitability of bloody class warfare.

In that same year, further national shockwaves were felt across the country when the media reported an atomic bomb had been successfully tested by the Russians, a profoundly upsetting development that was attributable to spies in the United States (e.g., Judith Coplan, the Rosenbergs) who had passed on America's most vital defense secrets to Soviet agents. At the same time, shocking news came out of Europe and Asia, heightening that virile fraternity of ideas and attitudes about the Red Menace. Chiang Kai-shek's demoralized, battered, poorly led forces had fled to Taiwan (Formosa); and it produced the two-fold hyperbolic assertion: Republicans charged former New Dealers in the administration (e.g., Alger Hiss) had "lost" China; and China would become a "Slavic Manchukuo," that is, a Soviet pawn. To compound the deeply unnerving news, there was the onset of war in Korea in June 1950 coupled with Chinese intervention five months later, further evidence for Americans that international communism was a single entity aiming at both territorial aggression and internal subversion.

More to the point of this recital of domestic and international developments, Americans became most susceptible to panic fears. These were promoted by seemingly trivial messages about Red aggression ranging from movies, comic books, television trifles to Truman proposing "an anticommunist program at home to match the anticommunist program abroad."[2] The outcome would be a reprise of the practices developed during the first Red Scare, including a revival of anti-alien, anti-radical impulses, directed primarily toward radicals who came out of Eastern Europe, and a jump in the targeting of liberal-left political groups. Unlike earlier years, the citizen–non-citizen line would now be crossed, and liberal Democrats as well as communists and radical dissenters generally came under attack.

Truman considered himself a liberal in good standing. He had long fumed over the toxic GOP charge that federal agencies were a hot bed of communist. HUAC Chairman J. Parnell Thomas, of New Jersey, expressed the political sentiments, and all Committee members of Thomas asserted in June 1940 that "the surest way to removing the fifth column from our shores is to remove the New Deal from the seat of government." Their Senate counterparts sitting in the Internal Security Committee (SISC) and in the special investigating subcommittee of the Committee on Government Operations (headed by Joseph McCarthy) publicized the Kremlin's American network and its influence in the White House. The November 1946 election swept a Republican majority into Congress and stimulated renewed efforts to investigate every aspect of the "creeping socialism" of Roosevelt's administration. Election results from 1938 to 1946 fathered further astringent views about the White House, repeated GOP efforts to dislodge subversives from their venues along the Potomac, and impassioned rhetoric casting Soviet–American relations in exaggerated, morally embroidered terms.

Administration-friendly political organizations and the Oval Office itself responded by drawing up the wagons. Truman himself reportedly told a Federal Communications Commission member that he created the temporary Commission on Employee Loyalty "to take the ball away from [HUAC chair] Parnell Thomas." Also, acting defensively, the NAACP, for one, began compiling a dossier of communists in its organization. Both Walter Reuther, head of the United Auto Workers and the CIO embraced the anti-communism of William Green and George Meany, conservative-inclined officials in their old rival, the American Federation of Labor AFL. The ACLU tilted toward the center, if primarily to shield itself from soft-on-communism charges; and as early as February 1940, the need for protective coloration prompted it to purge its very board of directors. The same defensive trend marked many liberal Democrats and the Americans for Democratic Action, their main organizational voice.

The Supreme Court was neither ignorant of nor indifferent to the headlines and national sentiments. Indeed, as Learned Hand pungently wrote: "the Nine Elder Statesmen, have not shown themselves wholly immune to the herd instinct."[3] That members of the bench were a poor substitute for Plato's philosopher kings was earlier evident and reiterated in the late Forties. When Chief Justice Harlan Stone unexpectedly died of a stroke in June 1946, his successor vividly personalized and embodied Hand's observation. Fred Vinson, the fifty-seven-year-old Secretary of the Treasury, Truman's "favorite poker player," and a one-time staunch political ally in Congress was sworn in as Chief Justice. The second of four Truman appointments, he was selected, owing in part to his past mastery of resolving divisions on the bench, but he could never accomplish it, as was obvious in the undiminished flow of split decisions and bitter dissents.

Further changes in membership on the High Court occurred when the cohesive libertarian phalanx was halved by the almost simultaneous deaths in 1949 of Murphy and Rutledge. Once again, the familiar truism prevailed that judges and justices will reflect the policies and goals of administrations that appointed them. One Court opening was given over to Tom Clark, a trusted Truman domestic advisor and the pedestrian Attorney General, desired by the Chief Justice as a colleague who would support his position in free speech cases. Vinson's thinking would be on the mark. Clark would hardly be a defender of freedom of expression, having authorized prosecution of Communist officials and been a prosecutor across his entire pre-judicial career. Sherman Minton, Truman's loyal Senate crony from Indiana, held greater promise for the First Amendment positions of Black and Douglas, having enjoyed a reputation as an uncompromising New Dealer. However, he had grown more conservative during eight years on the Circuit Court, and his seven years on the High Court would disappoint those who hoped for a defender of civil liberties.

If the Supreme Court, as Frankfurter observed before leaving Harvard, was "[t]o a large extent... the reflector of that impalpable but controlling thing, the general drift of public opinion," the tribunal over which Vinson presided was unusually sensitive to popular views on communist and the left-liberals in general.[4] Reflecting the vector sum of the dominant political forces of the time, it could then be expected that this reshaped Court majority would adopt a finding that the Bill of Rights should not straitjacket majoritarian government in its struggle against Un-American Activities. As such, the bloc around the Chief Justice provided further support to the repeated observation that the judiciary considered itself an agent of the state, guardian of its security and stability. Judicial majorities on both the state and federal bench paid verbal fealty to protected expression but had little respect for minority rights when convinced that threats to the nation existed.

Two free speech decisions provide support for this observation and offer as well early evidence of the impact of personnel changes on the Court and its shifting view of the First Amendment. These cases also indicate that the Red Scare in American society had reignited. In *Terminiello v. Chicago* (1949),[5] a divided majority, on a dubious point of procedure, reversed the conviction of Arthur Terminiello, a defrocked Catholic priest and henchman of the notorious right-wing Rev. Gerald L. K. Smith. Three years earlier, before an audience of about 800, the defendant had delivered a racially inflammatory, violent anti-Semitic diatribe that stated Chicago's Corporation Counsel was "libelous, abusive and offensive," using such terms as "scum" and "slimy scum" in describing Jews. Justice Jackson (just back from Nuremburg) thought the speech "followed, with fidelity ... the pattern of European fascist leaders." As the High Court later described it, the speech was given amidst bricks, rocks, and threats by a largely hostile and turbulent crowd that had gathered, "a howling mob" of over a thousand. Consequently, Terminiello was charged with violating a city ordinance prohibiting "any 'breach of the peace'" and convicted, which decision was upheld by an intermediate appellate court and by the Illinois Supreme Court. Defense counsel, in District Court, had moved for a directed verdict of acquittal on the grounds that Terminiello's arrest for his speech contravened the Fourteenth as well as the First Amendments, an argument repeated in the defense appeal to Illinois' Supreme Court: "Petitioner's speech [was] no incitement to violence"; and "[f]ree speech is the one and only issue in this cause."[6]

On Terminiello's appeal, the Supreme Court took *certiorari*, and both prosecution and defense repeated their earlier positions. The petitioner was assisted by an ACLU amicus Brief that claimed the Chicago ordinance was in conflict with the First Amendment. The American Jewish Congress (AJC) also submitted an amicus that, as could be expected, was directly opposed to a finding of protected speech. It argued that the epithets in Terminiello's speech were "alone sufficient to warrant the conviction ..." They were an incitement to the audience and not entitled "to the protection of the First Amendment." Douglas's brief majority opinion, also citing *Chaplinsky*, would directly contravene the AJC position and settled for an emphasis on "freedom and discussion" on which the "vitality of civil and political institutions in our society depends." One of the functions of free speech, he insisted, was "to invite dispute" and that it may best serve its "high purpose when it induces a condition of unrest, creates dissatisfaction... or even stirred people to anger," invites public dispute, or brings about a condition of unrest—tolerable unless it was "shown likely to produce a clear and present danger of a serious substantive evil...." Douglas, it follows, would consider the Chicago ordinance on which conviction was based to be unconstitutional. However, he avoided the issue of constitutionality—"we do not reach that question"—and focused instead on a "preliminary question," an error of the trial judge, which led to the further conclusion that petitioner's speech was constitutionally protected.[7]

In contrast to *Terminiello*, the High Court, in *Feiner v. New York* (1951),[8] a year and a half later, upheld the breach-of-peace conviction of the defendant who called upon blacks to fight for their rights. The facts in both cases were similar, in that each centered on provocative speech in a setting that potentially could incite violence. On March 8, 1948, Irving Feiner, a college student, was standing on a literal soap box at a Syracuse street corner. Speaking in occasionally abusive language on behalf of the presidential bid of former Vice President Henry Wallace, he made derogatory remarks about the Syracuse Mayor and asserted that "President Truman is a bum" and that the "American Legion is a Nazi Gestapo." A crowd of about eighty gathered, blocking pedestrians from passing by and forcing them to walk in the street. Vehicular traffic was also obstructed. One person listening to Feiner threatened immediate violence: "If you don't get that son-of-a-bitch off the box," he warned the two police offices who present, "I will go over and get him off there myself." There were "angry mutterings," "pushing," and "shoving and milling around" in the crowd, the officers stated, whereupon one of them, "stepped in to prevent ... a fight." Feiner was at first "asked" to stop, one of the policemen testified and, when he "kept on talking to the crowd," he was arrested and charged with disorderly conduct under Section 22 of the New York Penal Code, which prohibited incitement of a breach of the peace. On conviction in a special sessions court, Feiner was sentenced to thirty days in jail. Judge Albert Conway of State Court of Appeals upheld conviction, contending it "did not infringe on his [petitioner's] constitutional right of freedom of speech."[9] Again demonstrating that, much like the political branches, judges generally should be seen as arms of the state, he ruled that the defendant's speech was "[a]n imminent danger of a breach of the peace," that there was "no absolute right" of free speech ... [and that] "[t]he preservation of order and the prevention of disturbance are of prime importance to the State."

Conviction was upheld by the High Court, six-to-three, which ruling, as Harry Kalven put it, "can be best understood as a reaction against the Terminiello decision."[10] The majority opinion could be expected to uphold conviction since death had removed Frank Murphy and Wiley Rutledge, two of the most emphatic civil libertarians on the tribunal. Vinson, speaking for the new majority, declared that Feiner's arrest "was the reaction which it [the speech] actually engendered." The lower courts had rightly concluded that petitioner's arrest had been "motivated solely by a proper concern for the preservation of order," he self-delusively declared, and "there was no evidence which could lend color to a claim that the actions of the police were a cover for suppression of petitioner's views and opinions." The arrest did not infringe on plaintiff's First Amendment rights because his speech was tantamount to "incitement to riot." The Chief Justice went on to acknowledge "that the ordinary murmurings and objections of a hostile audience cannot be allowed to silence a speaker," but "[i]t is one thing to say that the police cannot be used as an instrument for suppression of unpopular views, and another to say that, when as here "the speaker passes the bounds of argument and persuasion and undertakes incitement to riot...."[11]

In short, *Terminiello*'s conviction for "lunatic fringe" hate speech, provoking open and immediate mob violence speech, had been overturned whereas that of Irving Feiner, for pinkish and strident adolescent talk, was upheld. The potential rioter who threatened to silence him by force was not arrested but became a judicially protected censor of free speech. Justices Black and Douglas filed angry and passionate dissents in *Feiner*, but they remained voices crying in a political and judicial wilderness. The judicial majority supports the contentions of Robert McCloskey about political trials: "The judges have often agreed upon the main current of public sentiment because they were themselves part of that current, and not because they feared to disagree with it."

Considering the times, the "Red Scare" would reverberate through all three branches of government. The President himself was preaching to the choir when rejuvenating the widespread pre-war consensus that Communists were duplicitous and dangerous, that "they" were everywhere, and that domestic security was imperiled. Americans, as could be expected, would avidly support the presidential perception of world affairs and also understand the international scene in Manichean terms—with the forces of light, symbolized by the United States, engaged in mortal conflict with the forces of darkness. *Mutatis mutandis*, a smooth transition followed from the inter-war anti-Bolshevik perceptions of Americans to the post-war belief that communism remained a worldwide conspiracy. The public remained highly susceptible to those who called for an anti-communist program at home to match the one overseas. Such rhetoric and its accompanying mindset spoke to the understanding that the Cold War was a necessary and unavoidable struggle against a godless, brutally repressive ideology. It was a conflict that would carry over and intensify during the next three decades and stain all aspects of American social and political life.

As to be expected, J. Edgar Hoover continued to insist that Americans must stop communism from "carrying out their diabolical plot to wreck the American way of life." Accordingly Hoover notified Truman early in the new administration that the FBI would "intensify its investigation of the Communist Party and others who would be dangerous in the event of a serious crisis" with the Soviet Union. Robert Goldstein states that Truman fully endorsed most Bureau actions, which were built upon the pre-war (October 2, 1941) directive to the FBI—by Francis Biddle, Roosevelt's Attorney General—authorizing it to investigate allegedly disloyal federal workers. The Bureau would take "steps to list all members of the Communist Party," he told the President who gave him carte blanche to investigate possible Communist subversion, particularly in the federal government.[12] Truman was arguably incautious in giving his unqualified approval, considering Hoover's spacious definition of "subversives," which included communist "satellites," their "fellow-travelers," and their "so-called progressive and phony liberal allies," categories that could conceivably embrace any number of New Dealers. In fact, Eleanor Roosevelt and Adlai Stevenson, respectively, the former President's wife and the Democratic contender for the presidency in 1952, were among the targets of FBI investigations.

Included in a sweeping post-war program, Hoover's drew up plans for mass detention of political suspects and suspension of the writ of *habeas corpus* for those held in detention camps that were to be opened in the time of war, "rebellion," threats of invasion.[13] By 1948, the Bureau was repeating the two-decades old practice of by-passing rights associated with criminal procedures. By 1950, the Bureau had checked on six million citizens, and discretely informed employers of those deemed to be "security risks." Hoover also instructed local FBI officials "not to file" instructions for break-ins—the so-called black-bag jobs—and other illegal actions taken against radical groups. However, some twenty-five records in the New York office alone would mistakenly be retained, and they provide a window into the world of clandestine FBI operations between 1954 and 1973.[14] In one more instance of the Bureau's obsessive behavior, a September 1955 internal memo called for a check on every person who had dropped out of the Communist Party between 1940 and 1955.

According to Communists, Hoover informed Congress that the Bureau estimated Party strength at 54,000 members, itself a highly inflated figure, but then went on to emphasize that card-carrying membership was not a true indicator. "There is," he warned HUAC members, "a potential fifth column of 540,000 people dedicated to this philosophy." In 1947, he had estimated that there was one communist for every 1,814 persons in the United States (neither one more nor one less).[15] The threat was purportedly large and real and required action. Between March 1947 and December 1952, according to Churchill and Vander Wall, the FBI conducted 600,000 security investigations, more than 3,000 per day.[16] These included massive surveillance of persons and organizations, including illegal wiretaps, break-ins, and mail openings. That these investigations would segue into a significant blow to free speech in the rapidly deteriorating post-war climate was a matter of indifference to the FBI and to the great majority of Americans.

"Soft on Communism" had become the GOP's impassioned battle cry against Truman after sixteen years as the minority party in Congress.

Recognizing that essential to victory in 1948, the public had to perceive the White House as determined as conservative Republicans in fighting communism, Truman sought to preempt and thereby neutralize the Republican accusation that the Democrats were the "party of treason," a charge that had plagued Roosevelt's time in the Oval Office. Long predisposed to anti-communist tropes and pronouncements, it would not be difficult for him to adopt the loyalty issue as his own.[17] Accordingly, he approved the intent of his Attorney General to increase deportations of radical aliens, enlarge the Justice Department list of subversive organizations, and publicly endorsed the indictment of communists, all actions that politically served as defensive armor, but starting a process that could not be stopped.

In one more attempt to neutralize attacks upon him, Truman offered a virile anti-communist proposal by establishing the first peacetime federal loyalty–security program. Of seminal importance in reviving the anti-communist hysteria that had gripped the nation for nearly three decades, his Executive Order 9835 of would provide "maximum protection" against the "infiltration of disloyal persons into the ranks" of federal employment by authorizing the Civil Service Commission to establish a network of loyalty review boards on a departmental and general level. These boards would evaluate the loyalty of "every person entering the civilian employment of any department or agency of the Executive branch of the federal government."[18]

The executive order provided a sweeping hiring and dismissal standard: when "on all the evidence, reasonable grounds exist for the belief that the person involved is disloyal to the Government...." Dismissal would follow if the person was a member of or affiliated "with any foreign or domestic organization, association, movement, group or combination of persons, designated by the Attorney General as totalitarian, fascist, communist, or subversive," or had "a policy of advocating or approving the commission of acts of force or violence to deny other persons of their rights under the Constitution... or as seeking to alter the form of government of the United States by unconstitutional means." Even "sympathetic association" with such organizations, etc., fell under the ban of federal employment. In fact, "sympathetic association" was the only new criterion for being "disloyal," the remainder—sabotage, espionage, treason, disclosure of confidential information, etc.,—had long been prohibited under many calcified statutes, which suggests a superfluity of directives only understandable as dictated by political necessity.

To suggest the persistence of the repressive anti-communist political climate and the redundancy of the executive order, only two earlier statutes need to be noted. The Attorney General had already been authorized to act under the repressive 1939 Hatch Act (Section 9A); and the 1940 Smith Act further complemented the governmental practices.[19] Indeed, it was in response to the former statute that the Justice Department had established a list of organizations, the membership that would lead to mandatory dismissal from federal employment; and about twenty-five suspect organizations had been listed by 1943. It should be noted as well that listings of "subversive" organizations had remote precedents dating back to 1903 and continuous secret listings existed after 1940.

Seeking an unrealizable goal, "absolute security," the 1947 Order required the Attorney General to list "the name of each ... organization, association, movement, group" designated by him as suspected. It was "of vital importance," and the Order stated that all employees are of "complete and unswerving loyalty." The accused had the right to appeal, but no right to cross-examine the accuser or even learn the person's identity. Counsel could be provided, but hearing procedures were largely arbitrary, and conventional rules of evidence were usually ignored. However, many of those accused quietly resigned rather than turn to the courts and thereby inflict negative publicity and large expenses for themselves and their families. Truman would add an amended follow-up Executive Order 10241 that provided discharge of federal workers if there was "reasonable doubt" as to their loyalty. And such "doubt" could occur in countless instances: the employee who did fund raising for Henry Wallace; or "maintained ... books on Communism, Socialism, and Marxism" or remained "a strong advocate of the United Nations"; or was "a regular purchaser of the New York Times." By 1951, the appeals of some of those named managed to reach the Supreme Court for adjudication, as we will presently learn, and petitioners would be upheld; but Truman's Loyalty–Security Program as a whole remained intact.

The new Attorney General, J. Howard McGrath, Tom Clark's successor, was a known quantity on domestic security issues. He had testified that "There are today many communists in America. They are everywhere—in factories, offices, butcher stores, on street corners, in private business. And each carries in himself the death; of our society." Such allegations guaranteed that he would eagerly implement the loyalty program. In fact, McGrath would eventually list 275 "subversive" organizations and screen 2,000,000 government employees and applicants for government jobs. Known as the "Attorney General's List," it would be first published in March 1948 and included seventy-eight organizations; and more were subsequently added, totaling 254 by 1953, and ultimately 273 would be set down as "subversive." The named organization had no right to a hearing, or to contest a finding of "subversive," or to have a judicial review of the finding. Membership in any one of the listed groups (or subsidiary groups under different subheadings) met the "reasonable grounds" criterion for dismissal from federal employment. Inclusion of the organization on this official "blacklist," moreover, was equivalent to public obloquy. The group's funds and membership lists would dry up and, more significant, so would dissent from orthodoxy.

To jump ahead, President Eisenhower, as an acolyte at the altar of anti-communism, would continue the trend of his predecessor two years later, issuing Executive Order 10450 "in the interests of national security." Expanding the criteria of Truman's earlier Order, that of April 1953, it would mandate investigations to determine whether the government employee had established or continued "a sympathetic association" with a "seditionist" or advocated "the use of force or violence to overthrow the government of the United States." And the Order went so far as to favor an investigation when the individual refused "on the grounds of constitutional privilege against self-incrimination, to testify before a congressional committee regarding charges of his alleged disloyalty .... "[20] It was, moreover, followed by Post Office and the State Department regulations that made retention of employment in these agencies only when "clearly consistent with the interests of the national security."

Almost unnecessary to add, Congress made its own contributions. Its investigatory committees allegedly uncovered Kremlin-directed organizations to carry on intelligence and espionage activities in the United States. According to a SISC subcommittee report of July 1953, which comprised 1,266 pages of hearings and was revealingly entitled "Interlocking Subversion in Government Departments," Communist espionage groups had successfully infiltrated the government, as a subcommittee of the Senate Internal Security Committee reported in July 1953.[21] In the lower House, the HUAC on March 15 of the same year gave vent to the epiphany that ten years of investigation had found "that the Communist movement in the United States is foreign controlled ...," hardly an unusual conclusion since Committee records continually displayed the claim, similar to that of May 11, 1948, in its "Report on the Communist Party of the United States as an Advocate of Overthrow of Government by Force and Violence."[22] The HUAC, on March 15th of this year, reported that H.852 and its provisions would eventually be incorporated into the 1950 Internal Security Act. It added to the fevered anti-Red clamor explicit in Senator Joseph McCarthy's Wheeling, West Virginia speech that proclaimed the State Department was "thoroughly infested with Communists"; and he, moreover, had a list to prove it: 205 "card-carrying communists." Possibly topping his "Fifth Column" accusation of his speech, nine arrests in what seemingly was a large atomic espionage ring (the *Rosenberg* case) that made newspaper headlines.

In establishing context for the argot of official Washington at mid-century, there was the startling and belated report of August 1953 that the Soviet Union had successfully tested an atomic bomb test in September 1949. It would be followed, perhaps not coincidentally, by accelerated implementation of the aforementioned "security" criteria of President Eisenhower's 1953 Executive Order;[23] and, before that year ended, it would result in some 2,200 federal employees being discharged and another 4,300 resigning to avoid security investigations. Within a year, unrelievedly negative reports were coming out of Korea about American military fortunes, and the localized colonial war in Vietnam was in the process of becoming another Cold War confrontation. These developments produced further shock waves nationally, lending further credence to popular anxieties about communists and communism.

The early Fifties, accordingly, produced a heightened atmosphere of disquiet, suspicion, and paranoia in both the capitol and the nation. The State Department discharged employees, often from high-ranking positions, who had once simply made negative assessments of Chiang Kai-shek's anti-communist government. The Atomic Energy Commission and the Department of Defense were among the administration agencies that instituted "clearance" procedures for employees of contractors with access to "classified" materials. The Department of Health, Education, and Welfare attempted to eliminate old-age benefits for those having a radical past. The Department of the Army investigated the armed forces, and soldiers were discharged for "sympathetic association" with communists, which ranged from shared political beliefs to personal contact with Communist Party members, including one's own parents. Groups that wished to rent private halls were rejected if they appeared in the Attorney General's list. An individual who was "a member of an organization" belonging to such groups or suspected of disloyalty were prohibited from living in federal low-income housing projects under a rider attached to the Guinn Amendment in the 1952 Appropriation Act. A million tenants in such dwellings had to sign loyalty oaths, with evictions for failure to comply. Local housing authorities everywhere sought to prohibit the entry of radical tenants. Also, indicative of the sweep of the anti-Red measures, the Magnuson Act of l950, drafted incidentally by Democrat Senate liberal Warren Magnuson, would authorize the President to take measures to "safeguard against destruction, loss, or injury from … sabotage acts … vessels, harbors …." And Truman's executive order implementing it would delegate to the Coast Guard the responsibility to screen and to prohibit employees believed to be "inimical to the security of the United States" from access to seagoing employment or access to restricted waterfront areas.

To further suggest the comprehensiveness of the congressional anti-communist crusade, federal lawmakers in 1943 amended veterans' laws to authorize forfeiture of benefits to those veterans who "rendered assistance to the enemy" (which would be struck down in suits by two veterans, Communist Party members in 1962).[24] Then there was the Taft–Hartley Act of 1947.[25] Consistent with Truman's Federal Employee Loyalty Program, it included an affidavit provision (Section 9h) requiring that each officer of a labor union seeking the benefits of the 1936 National Labor Relations Act had to file annually—with the National Labor Relations Board (NLRB)—the so-called non-communist affidavits; that is, required to swear "that he is not a member of the Communist Party or affiliated with such party, and that he does not believe in, and is not a member of or supports any organization that believes in or teaches the overthrow of the United States Government by force," words that, David Cole rightly tells us was the legal catch phrase for the Communist Party. Contributing to the superfluity of these measures, a late 1950 statute, the Labor Management Reporting and Disclosure Act of 1959 (Section 504) was strikingly similar to Section 5(a) of the McCarran Act of 1950. In fact, a High Court dissent observed as much, when noting that the 1959 Act made it a crime for a member of the Communist Party to serve as an officer or employee of a labor union simply repeated the disqualification prescribed in the 1950 statute. Shortly to be described, the 1950 Internal Security Act and the Immigration and Naturalization Act of two years later fueled similar episodes in political pathology. There were less dramatic consequences of the Red Scare than legislation, as was painfully apparent in a great number of instances when city parks, streets, and public and private assembly halls were closed to all radical organizations and their spokesmen. Local auditoriums, hotels, school boards, and retailers shut their doors to the politically suspect person or organization. Whatever the form—publicized state or federal statutes or unpublicized actions, legislative investigations or teaching about the "communist menace" in public schools—they were greeted by public approval.

It should come as no surprise that private businesses were established to advise employers on how to avoid the hiring of alleged subversives, and it would become standard practice to check out—to "clear"—entertainers before their names were submitted to sponsors of radio programs. Nor was the equally bleak record of non-governmental professional associations unexpected, the lone exception being the American Library Association. The American Medical Association, for instance, introduced a loyalty oath in 1952. Local or state medical societies could exclude doctors whose loyalty was questioned by super patriots. To remind readers, the sweep of state anti-radical strictures, statutes, investigations extended to educators, and "disclaimer" oaths were proliferated. Those suspected of disloyalty after the war and across the next four decades, as we have learned, even more than doctors remained endangered professionals. Also, those hopeful of practicing law, if under suspicion, could be denied admission to most state bars. The American Bar Association, as noted earlier, recommended in 1951 that lawyers were required to take a loyalty oath for admission to the bar and would disbar lawyers who were members of the Communist Party or advocated Marxism–Leninism.[26] Guided by its Special Committee to Study Communist Tactics, Strategy, and Objectives, it further advised local bar associations expel those who were Communist Party members. Many states and local communities matched the ABA's anti-communist strictures with their own. Over twenty state bar associations require affidavits of loyalty before admission to the bar. California was typical in stating that no one who advocated the forcible overthrow of government shall be certified to practice law. North Dakota's application to practice law asked: "Are you now or have you ever been a member of the Communist Party or any organization seeking to overthrow the government?" Ohio's form was also bluntly simple: "Do you believe in the form of and are you loyal to the Government …?" Alabama, Indiana, Colorado, Kentucky, Oregon, Rhode Island, North Carolina, and Washington as well were among the states requiring a loyalty oath before admission to their state bars.[26] Going further, Attorney General Tom Clark had set the political tone and standards for legal professionals. They have to choose their clients with care, he cautioned, and those who represented Communists should be taken "to the legal woodshed for a definite and well-deserved admonition,"[27] a warning he repeated shortly after being appointed to the High Court.

Whether driven by self-serving political ambitions or genuine convictions, or a combination of both, federal lawmakers were hardly finished with the registration provision or with the loyalty issue. Three years after Truman initiated his program, Congress approved the massive Subversive Activities Control Act (SACA), commonly termed the Internal Security Act or McCarran Act.[27] The third federal peacetime sedition measure, the 1950 statute was a massive fifty-six-page omnibus bill that combined a number of internal security measures; that is, it did not suddenly spring full-blown from the brow of Nevada Senator Pat McCarran, the primary author of the measure. It passed easily, and Truman's brave veto of the statute was overridden in twenty-four hours, with only ten liberal Senators daring to sustain the veto. It is unlikely, however, that they disagreed with the dark vision underlying this so-called McCarran Act. The ominous Preamble repeated the familiar, shop-worn warning:

> [t]he Communist movement in the United States is an organization numbering thousands of adherents, rigidly and ruthlessly disciplined. Awaiting and seeking to advance a moment when the United States may be so far extended by foreign engagements, so divided in counsel, or so far in industrial or financial straits, that overthrow ... by force and violence may seem possible of achievement ...

Pursuant to this grim possibility, Title I of the statute established the five-member Subversive Activities Control Board (SACB) empowered to place a communist or radical in one of two statutory categories, "Communist-action" or "Communist-front" (with a third, "communist infiltrated" to be added later). The "Communist-action" organization was defined as "any organization in the United States ... which is substantially directed, dominated, or controlled by the foreign government or foreign organization controlling the Communist movement" and which "operates primarily to advance the objectives of such world Communist movement." For such an organization, a set of statutory prescriptions was established. They included the requirement that its members should be registered with the Attorney General and list the sources of the financing of their organization, give an account of "all moneys received and expended, including sources of them," reveal the funds that were spent disclose "the names, aliases, and addresses of its officers and members"; "a list of all printing presses or machines owned, controlled, or possessed by any of them." Stigmatized as "subject to foreign control," those organizations were, to repeat the very language of the 1940 Voorhis Act, defined as (1) soliciting or accepting "financial contributions, loans, or support any kind, directly or indirectly, from ... a foreign government or a political subdivision thereof, or agent, agency, or instrumentality of a foreign government ..." or (2) its policies, or any of them, are determined by or at the suggestion of ... a foreign government ....""Communist-front" organizations, a second designated category, were defined "as those substantially directed, dominated, and controlled by a Communist-action organization, and primarily operated for the purpose of giving aid and support to a Communist-action organization, a Communist foreign government, or the world Communist movement." This subsection required that every organization in this "front" category also file a similar registration requirement: a list of the names of all its officers and a complete financial statement, including all contribution. Penalties were specified for the organization that failed to register or to file an annual report and then for its executive officer or one of the members of the organization who failed to register. Those officers and members failing to register were subject to a fine of not more than $10,000 or imprisonment of not more than five years or both for each offense—with "each day of failure to register" constituting a separate offense. Adding a postscript that will shortly be expanded upon, the Subversive Activities Control Board would hold hearings in April 1951 and then ordered registration. Party officials of a "Communist-action" organization, as expected, ignored the directive and refused to register. Registration, it need be recalled, opened the person to the possibility of criminal prosecution under the existing Smith Act provisions (as a known and knowing member of or conspirator in an organization advocating violent overthrow), which made registration a foolhardy action.

Nor were the harsh prescriptions of the McCarran Act exhausted. Aliens who belonged to a registered communist organization were subject to deportation; and naturalized citizens who became members of, or affiliated with, the organization within five years after naturalization were liable to revocation of citizenship. One subsection of the statute placed explicit restriction on the use of the mails by a member of an "action" organization. Other subsections, dealing with radio or television broadcasts, had similarly worded proscriptions. Members in "front" and "action" organizations automatically suffered further disabilities: the right of "employment in a defense facility," the right to hold non-elective federal office or employment, to be employed in a labor union, and to apply for or renew a passport.

It is apparent that many of the McCarran Act provisions were decidedly over broad, inhibiting the exercise of speech and assembly. The very words—"perform any act," "substantially contribute"—were strikingly ambiguous. Moreover, arrest was authorized on suspicion rather than probable cause, with imprisonment based solely on membership, and punishment without the usual procedural guarantees defining a fair trial, such as the right to confront accusers and cross-examine witnesses. The use of nameless, faceless informers, irresponsible surveillance, arbitrary attacks on private convictions, utterances, and associations attributed to those under suspicion would all expand on the existing procedural and substantive anomalies.

Title Two of the McCarran Act, Title II, known also as the Emergency Detention Act, amended immigration and naturalization measures to prohibit entry or encourage deportation of suspected alien subversives. Employing numbingly repetitive hyperbole, it opened with the Hobbesian vision:

> There exists a world Communist movement which… is a world-wide revolutionary movement whose purpose it is, by treachery, deceit, infiltration into other groups…, espionage, sabotage, terrorism… to establish a Communist totalitarian dictatorship in all the countries of the world….
>
> The recent successes of Communist methods in other countries and the nature and control of the world Communist movement itself present a clear and present danger to the security of the United States and the existence of free American institutions….

The sweeping terms of Title II were entirely compatible with this dark vision. It included a provision for "detention of persons who there is reasonable ground to believe will commit or conspire with others to commit espionage or sabotage …." The proviso was dear to the heart of J. Edgar Hoover who as early as July 1946 had proposed: "Detention of Communists in the event of sudden difficulties with Russia." And in 1948, the FBI and the Justice Department co-sponsored a plan for the "detention of dangerous individuals at the time of an emergency." This plan also called for the suspension of the writ of *habeas corpus* and the arrest under one master warrant issued by the Attorney General of all those listed on the FBI's "security index" that Hoover had been compiling since October 1939. Ten years later, in a letter to his agents, Hoover ordered that "no mention must be made in any investigative report relating to ... the Security Index," which contained 19,577 names of "dangerous enemy aliens." During a presidentially proclaimed "Internal Security Emergency," declared in the event of an invasion or a declaration of war or a domestic insurrection, those arrested in the name of "national security" could be held for forty-five days without a judicial hearing and without being allowed a *habeas corpus* petition.[28] Potential detainees included those citizens, considered as being dominated by a Communist foreign government or, more broadly, "Communist front" members who intended to "aid and support ... the world communist movement." In the event of a proclaimed "emergency," "detention centers" would hold those "as to whom there is a reasonable ground to believe ... probably will engage in, or probably will conspire with others to engage in, acts of espionage or sabotage." President Truman, in fact, in late March 1951 asked Congress for an appropriation of $775,000 to finance their construction, as provided by emergency provisions of the statute, a somewhat contradictorily request since he had earlier vetoed the entire measure (Congress overrode him) and would later complain about the "un-American activities" of various loyalty boards. By 1957, six "camps" for emergency detention had been established, and they would be maintained in good working order across the Sixties.

Although its origins may be found in the 1947 Mundt–Nixon bill, when the beginnings of the Cold War spawned a revivified and immensely influential anti-communism, the 1950 McCarran Act came in the midst of a number of critical events, both domestic and foreign: the *Dennis* case appeal, which was front and center in the press; McCarthy's notorious West Virginia address; 300,000 Chinese troops crossing into Korea in November 1950; and American troop casualties mounted alarmingly. In the midst of a growing sense of national distress, there remained the near-universal public sentiment that the communist centurions were at the gates of the republic. After all, that legendary anti-radical fighter, J. Edgar Hoover, had stated: "There is a potential fifth-column of 555,000." And breaking down this estimate, Senator McCarran declared: "according to FBI Director, J. Edgar Hoover, there are 12,000 hard core dangerous communists who could immediately be picked up ... 55,000 members ... and 500,000 additional Americans who are either willing tools or party-line followers."

Two years after the Internal Security Act, Congress added to the anti-radical statutory barrage by passing the Immigration and Nationality Act (the McCarran–Walter Act) that would have a long legal life, not being struck down (by a federal District Court) until 1989. This 1952 measure continued the lengthy line of immigration statutes that began in 1903, when anarchists and IWW members were excluded from the admission to the United States and endlessly repeated in the statutes of 1917, 1918, and 1946, all laws that, in the words of the last-dated measure, prohibited entry to "[a]liens who believe in, advise, advocate, or teach," the forcible overthrow of the government, or belong to organizations that so believed; or "[a]liens who write, publish, or cause to be written or published, or who knowingly circulate, distribute, print, or display... opposition to all organized government...." Title Two of the 1950 Act, as described earlier, and the 1952 measure continued the anti-alien statutory redundancy, with the later Act adding possible non-entry or deportation of aliens.[29] This statute often spelled out draconian treatment for alien radicals, including denial of basic rights that, it was dubiously argued, belonged only to citizens, such as the right to see evidence against them and to confront accusers. It would also lead to deportation of some leading Communist Party officials and trade unionists. It is reminiscent of a constant theme from early in the century, one that William Preston recognized as the "fateful and erroneous identification of alien and radical ... firmly implanted in the public mind."

With the passage of two more years, the Communist Control of Act of August 1954 was dropped into the stew of anti-radical measures.[30] Faithful to the language of a 1953 Pennsylvania statute and employing the usual fustian rhetoric, this 1954 "Act to Outlaw the Communist Party" declared that the CP was "the agency of a hostile foreign power" and that it was "relatively small numerically" mattered not for Americans since its very "existence [was] a clear present and continuing danger to the security of the United States." The statute repeated the predictable normative theme and rhetoric: "the Communist Party ... although purportedly a political party, is in fact an instrumentality of a conspiracy to overthrow ..." Hence, it followed that the Party was to be deprived of "rights, privileges, and immunities attendant upon legal bodies ..." The measure added a third category, "Communist infiltrated," to the two groupings of communist organizations stigmatized under the 1950 statute, "Communist front" and "Communist action."[31]

In describing the ceaseless anti-radical efforts of the political branches of government, it warrants reminder, there were the activities of HUAC and the SISC. And as earlier observed, they were hardly alone among congressional committees in drawing widespread publicity to its investigations. Among them, the Senate's Permanent Subcommittee on Investigations was functioning by 1953, with Senator McCarthy bursting on the national scene—with his sensational allegation of 205 Communists working in the State Department—and thereafter turning the Subcommittee into a one-man publicity stunt, his machismo and crude exploitation of the communist issue catching national attention. McCarthy's later investigations of Communist influence in the Voice of America and the United States Army seemingly was winning the day on a tidal wave of extreme anti-communism. In one typical and widely reported venture, that of April 24, 1953, his Subcommittee called the *New York Post* editor, James Wechsler, to testify about whether, when at age eighteen, he had joined the Young Communist League. It mattered not at all to his pursuers that, also in the public record, Wechsler had left the League and the Communist Party four years later. The tenor of the questioning had the well-worn quality of such hearings, whether on the state or federal level, and warrants an excerpt for this reason, McCarthy asking, "Have you always been critical of the heads of the Un-American Activities Committee? You have always thought they were pretty bad men, have you not?"[32]

The reader may substitute the names, voices, and professions of other equally prominent witnesses and investigators, and also recognize that the inquiries seemingly had one obvious intention and expected outcome; namely, taint witnesses, destroy careers, and garner publicity and approval. The legislative trial, it became apparent, was unimpeded by courtroom rules and due process, or even the evidence required to convict in a court of law. Fueling public sentiment as well, there was a highly visible trial.

Nor can one neglect mention a highly publicized trial in a court of law rather than a legislative chamber, the spectacular trial of Ethel and Julius Rosenberg who had been indicted for committing espionage, namely, giving atomic bomb design data to the Soviet Vice Counsel in New York. It produced public hysteria and provided Americans with further confirmation that a vast underground network of Soviet espionage existed. The Rosenbergs went on trial in March 1951 and were convicted. *Certiorari* being denied by the Supreme Court in 1952, they would be executed in June 1953. The presiding District Court Judge, Irving Kaufman would, when sentencing them to death, refer to "this diabolical conspiracy to destroy a God-fearing nation," which served to further exacerbate the steamy anti-communist atmosphere across the nation.

The near-universal popular approval greeting every effort to expose and proscribe Communists national reaction is all the more striking since the Communist Party had returned to its low point of the early Twenties. Its influence was now principally confined to a few unions— furriers, electrical workers, West Coast Longshoremen—and their leadership. In sharp decline, the Party was staggering from disaster to disaster. By 1950 and the McCarran Act, the Party's situation had rapidly deteriorated especially in the labor movement after the CIO expelled Communist-led unions in 1949. Party tactics, it need be recalled, had shifted from lobbying for the war effort to robotically readopting the hard line issuing from Moscow after 1945 and the U.S.–Soviet tensions had resurfaced. To resume our reflections, successive near-fatal blows to Communist Party fortunes at home as well as abroad had occurred: the 1939 Russo–German Pact, the April 1945 Jacques Duclos letter (in the theoretical organ of the French Communist Party) excoriating Party Chief Earl Browder and containing the dreaded charge of "revisionism" against Party leaders; and over a decade later the February 1956 speech of Russian Premier Nikita Khruschev that denounced Stalin's murderous regime and openly admitted Stalin's many brutal criminal actions. The outcome would be a sting decline in Party membership. It had been 54,147 at the end of 1949—with J. Edgar Hoover placing membership precisely at 54,147. It fell precipitously to 25,000 in early 1953 (with J. Edgar Hoover putting the figure precisely at 24,796), and its major organ, the *Daily Worker*, having a pitiful 14,000 subscribers.[33] By the summer 1958, given the combination of repressive domestic actions and the Khruschev speech, CPUSA membership was ca. 4,000, a figure in astonishing and bold relief against the massive legal and social assault upon it. Of these members, moreover, as Harvey Klehr unequivocally states—and affirmed by most students of the CPUSA—only a "few communists were spies."

But the reality of this pronounced decline in Party membership would be ignored in the panicked national climate about internal subversion. The public saw Communists and Communist espionage agents everywhere, what with the prominent Hiss trials, the Rosenberg convictions, perjury allegations against and deportation hearings of

Harry Bridges, Klaus Fuchs's espionage trial in England, Judith Coplon's spying conviction in New York, the multiple congressional investigations into domestic subversion, the growing number of indictments for contempt of Congress, some resulting in federal court trials—events that in concert further demonized the entire Party, permeated the public culture, and provided sustenance for a distinct pathology of moralism, nativism, and conspiracy theory. The 1952 Republican electoral sweep, in which they captured both political branches of government further promoted the farrago of sinister communist fantasy.

The past is indeed prologue. Paralleling the national scene, every state enacted or reenacted a loyalty program for public employees, the loyalty oaths, Red Squads, Red hunts, state investigations of communism so germane to the Thirties and Forties resurfaced in state and community anti-radical measures as soon as the guns of war fell silent. By the mid-fifties, all the states in one fashion or another had bowed to the winds of paranoia: forty-four of the then forty-eight states had enacted statutes making it a crime to advocate the overthrow of government; thirty-four had anti-anarchy or anti-sedition measures on their books (twenty-four of which were enacted after World War II ended); thirty-two required loyalty oaths only for teachers; twenty-eight had laws prohibiting state or local civil service jobs to communists (serving as janitors, secretaries, garbage collectors, librarians, etc.); and a like number prohibited communists or subversive organizations from the ballot and/or denied communists the right to vote (e.g., Arkansas, California, Georgia, Indiana, Kansas, Wisconsin, Wyoming), in effect outlawing the Communist Party, and two states did so explicitly. An Indiana statute of 1953 would simply exterminate communism. Texas and Michigan in 1950 authorized life imprisonment for anyone writing or speaking subversive words. The State of Washington prohibited a subversive organization to exist within its limits as did New Hampshire in 1951, which would appear improbable, because a FBI report found that only forty-three communists were in the residence; however, its lawmakers authorized the State's Attorney General to expose the state's subversives.[34] Tennessee authorized the death penalty as maximum punishment for unlawful advocacy. Massachusetts in the same year made it a crime to become or remain a Communist Party member. Many of these state measures were simply reruns of earlier statutes, often in exact words, or patterned upon the 1918 Sedition Act, such as Montana's 1947 measure. Connecticut's that made it a crime for any person to distribute disloyal, scurrilous, or abusive matter concerning the form of government of the United States. Confirming the enduring character of the anti-radical national mindset, Michigan's 1908 Constitution, for instance, was amended in 1950 to include anti-subversion articles; and Montana's 1947 sedition statute had been patterned on the federal Sedition Act of 1917. In the early Fifties as well, and as entirely foreseen, further Red Flag laws passed in no less than fifteen states. They prescribed prison terms as punishment for displaying a Red Flag or, as a 1953 Utah law declared, for "any flag or banner with intent to proclaim or engender disloyalty to the government ...."[35]

A number of states set up special police units, which worked covertly and often without respect for prevailing legal restraints. Michigan State Police files between ca. 1950 and 1974 reveal the existence of a "Red" Squad within the State Police Department as well as extensive collusion between State, federal, and private agencies.[36] Engaging in political surveillance, its budget and operations expanding over the decade, it operated in secrecy until 1961 when its director announced its existence on the grounds that the public should be alerted to the danger of agents of the "Soviet Purpose" who were "coming out of their holes," especially those on academic campuses where they masqueraded as professors. The State's "Red Squad" was not atypical. There were separate police units in New York City, Los Angeles, and Detroit, as well as in a number of Ohio cities, which engaged in surveillance of suspected left-wing individuals and groups in local government and businesses. Those in New York, for one, infiltrated Communist Party branches and identified municipal workers who belonged to them.

Efforts similar to the states prevailed in municipalities across the Fifties, with local ordinances prohibiting advocacy of forcible overthrow of the government, or prescribing prison terms for the display of a Red Flag. Some localities attempted to remove "communistic" or "subversive" books from schools and public libraries, producing headlines that reflected and in turn heightened public apprehensions. Urban areas in Alabama and Florida prohibited Communists from being present within their limits.

Thousands of Americans on both county and city levels would also take loyalty oaths, as occurred in Los Angeles. New York required it of all civil defense workers, and city authorities investigated welfare, housing, and transit workers for Communist Party membership or left-wing sympathies. The outcome was a bitter harvest for many. Hundreds would have their loyalty questioned, and a good number would lose their jobs and be blacklisted for suspected association with the Communist Party, without any meaningful opportunity to confront their accusers and know the evidence against them. Ralph Brown estimates that about 500 public employees of state and local governments, excluding teachers, had been discharged for political reasons between 1948 and 1956.[37]

Teachers were especially hard hit. They had remained an easy mark for anti-communist state officials. Loyalty oaths exclusively targeting them were always a very familiar provision of state laws. They became virtually a national epidemic in the Fifties.[38] Nearly three-fourths of the states would pass and enforce measures requiring teachers (and often other civil service employees) to sign disclaimer affidavits from the late Forties into the Fifties. To break down the total of thirty-two states mandating teacher loyalty oaths, twelve demanded teachers were to refrain from advocating a change in the form of government by violent means; fourteen had teacher oaths prohibiting membership in subversive groups, with a few making it part of the certification requirement; and fourteen other states were even more specific in their oaths, requiring teachers swear to refrain from Communist Party membership. Oklahoma's oath, for instance, was typical in ordering dismissal "at any time for teaching disloyalty to the American Constitutional system ...," as was New Jersey's requiring an oath that "teachers ... do not believe in the use of force and violence," and Nebraska's directed "[a]ll teachers to sign a pledge to inculcate in their pupils ... devotion to American policies ... and opposition to all organizations and activities that would destroy our present form of government."

Nor were only teachers affected. College students felt the pressure to conform, especially those who belonged to left-of-center campus organizations in the early Fifties, such as the American Youth for Democracy. A 1951 Texas law denied prospective students permission "to register for attendance" unless they took a loyalty oath; and it was supplemented three years later by a measure requiring a loyalty oath of the author of any textbook pending its adoption. Going to extreme lengths a year later, the State Board of Education required an affidavit of loyalty of authors and publishers of school textbooks as well as teachers and students at state universities. Michigan's 1952 Communist Control Act, for instance, would be invoked to convict an undergraduate who refused to answer questions put to him by members of the Select Committee on Un-American Activities of the State Senate in 1948. Rhode Island in 1950 would deny a scholarship to anyone "associated with any group or organization advocating the overthrow of the government by force or violence ..." "Louisiana lawmakers in 1950" would further the policy of preventing subversive activities by students of public educational institutions.

Educators being a prime object of suspicion for serial witch hunters, it could be anticipated that congressional committees would be involved. The HUAC, for example, visited Albany, New York, Washington, D.C., Milwaukee, Newark, Philadelphia, Dayton, Fort Wayne, and cities in Maryland, California, Michigan, Washington, among the many cities and states, with the classroom often the key component of its hearings. Representative Harold Velde's HUAC Subcommittee, for example, made three visits to Philadelphia between 1952 and 1954 that led to over fifty dismissals of teachers who, refusing to testify, invoked the privilege against self-incrimination, that is, "took the Fifth." Senator Homer Ferguson's Subcommittee of the SISS rolled into New York City and joined the Board of Education in warring against the Teachers' Union and teachers with radical sympathies. Those who were called to hearings were asked about what books they read, what people they knew, which colleagues were communists, and how they felt about Loyalist Spain. Refusing to answer such questions resulted in suspensions for insubordination and discharge for dozens of teachers, with nearly 300 others resigning or retiring. HUAC was not to be denied a role in the hunt for heretics. It came into New York City and held widely reported public hearings for employees at Brooklyn College and City College. Faculty and staff, members upon being sworn in, were subject to the familiar refrain: "Are you a member of the Communist Party?"—a question that had a similar contagious impact to what has been described in the pre-war period. New York's Board of Higher Education also held hearings of suspected subversives, and dismissals received great media attention.

And in New York State itself, spurred in some measure by HUAC investigations, the renewed pursuit of subversives came to legislative fruition with the Feinberg Act that the liberal governor, not immune to legislative and popular pressures, signed in 1949. This statute would be added to the New York State's Civil Service Law as Section 3022, bore a marked resemblance to a measure already in the books (Section 12-a of the State's Civil Service law), and was thus superfluous. But superfluous or not, it would be cited in a number of cases (e.g., *Adler*, cited below) and result in 285 teachers being severed from the school system after 1951, the Board of Education acquiescing to the popular hysteria (one source put the number at ca. 350).

The statute authorized the Board of Regents to compile a list of organizations "which it finds to be subversive in that they advocate, advise, teach, or embrace the doctrine" of violent overthrow of the government. It made membership in a designated subversive organization "prima facie evidence" of disqualification for any kind of public school employment; and it denied a teaching position to any person who belonged to an organization that the Board of Regents found advocating forcible overthrow of the government. Any employee of the State's public schools, one section mandated, "shall be removed for the utterance of any treasonable or seditious word or words or doing of any treasonable or seditious act or acts while holding such position." Redundancy in state and federal statutes, this study suggests, was a sign of the times.

Anti-communism was the motor of state investigators on many college campuses. In Washington State, for example, one State Senator estimated that there were about 150 University of Washington faculty "who are Communists or Communist sympathizers," sufficient reason for the Canwell Committee to hold public hearings on the political beliefs of selected faculty members. Faculty elsewhere—at Harvard, MIT, New York University, Columbia University, etc.—fell victim to anti-radical zealotry, with FBI agents or subcommittees of SISC or HUAC visiting campuses. A typical outcome occurred at Ohio State University, for the school's President summarily fired faculty members who invoked the Fifth Amendment in 1955. At Rutgers University, a handful of faculty members came under suspicion. Moses I. Finley, a well-known classical scholar among them, was dismissed by the Board of Trustees after invoking the privilege against self-incrimination when questioned about past activities. Unprepared to charge that the teaching of ancient Greece was subversive, the Board simply found that invoking the Fifth was "incompatible with the standards required." (Oxford University thought otherwise, and hired Finley, and his scholarly standing was such that he would eventually be knighted.) At Rutgers Law School, Abraham Glasser, a tenured professor who had been "cleared" of charges involving communism in 1941 by the Justice Department when employed there would refusal to answer questions at a HUAC hearing regarding possible communist connections between 1935 and 1941. The Law School faculty unanimously urged a new hearing, but the University denied it and Glasser would be terminated. Numerous other colleges and universities also dismissed other faculty who cited the privilege against self-incrimination when questioned about their radical past. Perhaps the most dramatic and highly publicized incident involving academicians and the loyalty oath occurred at the University when, beginning in 1950, the school's Board of Regents directed all employees sign non-communist oath affidavits. A three-year struggle followed, with over one hundred faculty resigning, being discharged, or simply not reappointed. By June 1953, according to the Harvard Crimson, over one hundred faculty nationally had invoked the Fifth Amendment, and fifty-four would be discharged or suspended, the remainder placed on probation or censured.[39] Robert Hutchins, the former President of the University of Chicago, understandably stated: "The question is not how many teachers have been fired, but how many think they might be, and for what reasons.... The entire teaching profession of the U.S. is now intimidated."[40]

As to be expected, the state investigations of colleges and *ad hominem* attacks on university faculty would not be limited to higher education and would have a contagious effect on public schools across the country, the more so when combined with federal investigations of school teachers on every educational level. Thus, school teachers who refused to cooperate with the SISS or who invoked the Fifth Amendment before the HUAC would be immediately suspended and eventually discharged by their respective school boards. The increasing number of dismissals in these post-war years was understandable. Increasingly valued as a weapon of war in the ideological struggle with the enemy, schools and schoolteachers had a highly regarded functional use. Their classrooms became viewed as an instrument of public policy to be employed for national political objectives, a purpose of first becoming the evident in the mid-late Forties. And in fact, as one of the 1949 bulletin of the Education Policies Commission of the National Education Association (NEA) declared, teachers would be "an instrument of national policy." Proposing one side of the equation, the Commission in that year called for the exclusion of all CP members from employment in the public schools because inherent in Party membership was the inability to think independently and therefore the right to teach. Proposing the other side, the Massachusetts Association of School Superintendents declared: "the fight against Communism calls for all the weapons in the arsenal," including education, which was "a grassroots investment in national security." Both goals were fully endorsed by educators, and the spores of each blew around the schools.

In a brief postscript, it should be observed that teachers and other public employees were hardly alone in being singled out. In the course of Red-Hunting enthusiasm, state authorities swept up not only public workers and civil servants, but also entertainers, educators, and lawyers as well.

Few did not experience the loyalty oath requirement. Enlarging on the extent of this anti-radical animus in the private sector, some major corporations companies also entered the investigative picture. Employees in U.S. Steel, Bethlehem Steel, Lockheed, Goodyear Fire and Rubber Company, and United Electrical Company, even New York City department stores, were purged of those harboring radical sympathies, and usually union militants were included. Indeed, it is estimated that 13,500,000 employees, one fourth of the nation's workforce, was checked for loyalty by private industry management.[41] "Taking the Fifth" when questioned by management was a common occurrence as was refusal to take a company loyalty oath. Not surprisingly, many times an innocent person was caught up in the loyalty fever, perhaps for having once been a member of a proscribed organization or simply for signing a petition supporting an issue or a candidate that the Communist Party also endorsed. In fact, most loyalty investigations focused on an employee's thoughts and associations rather than on actions or incitement to actions.

In this manner, the Cold War joined the three previous decades in being richly productive of headlines about the sensational conspiracy trials described earlier and the continuing menace of domestic subversion. Courtesy of misperceptions, misunderstandings, mutual suspicion, and widespread anxieties were prevalent in contemporary popular culture, with a public jargon being employed that exaggerated the febrile imagination of the majority of Americans and eliminated the possibility of dissent, or indeed thoughtful assessment or critical thinking.

After the 1952 Republican presidential victory and given the limited number of communists, the target population was greatly enlarged. It devolved from spies to security risks; and "pink" janitors, left-wing dentists and doctors, consanguinity to a radical parent. It included liberal Democrats out of the New Deal era employed by the Department of Agriculture, chemists with the Food and Drug Administration. Ohio's Senator Robert Taft found that the "Kremlin's greatest asset" was the "pro-communist group in the State Department," and Indiana Senator Albert Jenner accused General George Marshall, then Secretary of Defense, of being a "front man for traitors." And, to reiterate, shortly after entering the White House, Eisenhower would intensified the loyalty fever, as noted, by issuing Executive Order 10540 of April 1953 that extended and toughened the Truman's loyalty program for federal workers. Not only did it reauthorize the existing Attorney General list of subversive organizations but it also would deny employment in defense industries and federal agencies to persons in "affiliation with or sympathetic association with" communist organization. His Executive Order 10835 followed, which expanded loyalty–security screening regulations for government employees. Another Eisenhower Executive Order authorized both the Customs Bureau and the Post Office to seize so-called "Communist propaganda." In a June 1954 press conference, the President listed his administration's anti-subversive actions, including deportations, denaturalizations, and "the constant surveillance of Communists in this country" on a "twenty-four hours, seven-days a week, fifty-two-weeks-a-year-basis." It would be repeated nearly six months later, in a hoped-for record of achievement that would defensively counter highly publicized Senator McCarthy "soft on communism" charges. In this context, it warrants reiteration that Samuel Stouffer's survey, published in 1954, found fifty-two percent of Americans favored imprisoning all communists and other polls registered higher percentages; and eighty percent of those polled would strip communists of citizenship. Socialists, too, remained objects of repression, with forty-five percent of Americans in another public opinion poll, agreeing to prohibit socialist ownership of newspapers, and forty-plus percent would deny the press a right to criticize the "American form of government."[42]

Nor would the persistence and intensity of the Red Scare greatly diminish ten years later. Though it is premature to describe the continued march of public officials to the anti-communist music of the sixties, it suffices to reiterate that hundreds of state and local statutes relating to "subversives" and national security remained on the books in this decade, with thirty-one states having measures making it a crime to be a member of a subversive group; ten outlawed the Communist Party; nine charged it a crime to be a Party member; seventeen prohibited the Party or its candidates from being on the state ballot; three denied the practice of law to members of subversives groups; and twenty-six specifically barred teaching positions to "subversives."

In summary, the surveillance of radical and suspected radicals and radical groups by government agencies that began systematically during and after the World War I, and increasing in the 1930s owing to the world scene and to bloody struggles to organize industrial unions, intensified, if that were possible, during the post–World War II Cold War years. Stanley Kutler effectively concluded:

> [w]e will never fully tally the incidence of official wrongdoing and attempts at repression … we will never fully explore and comprehend the hundreds of incidents in which persons were investigated and interrogated by federal and state legislative committees. The callous unrestrained deportation of undesirable aliens, the mischievous results of alleged counter-intelligence activities by the FBI and police agencies, the stifling of dissent in professions and unions, the chilling intimidation of critics of official policies, and even the use of extralegal tactics to aid and abet desired political aims.[43]

Notes

1. Quoted in Athan Theoharis, *Spying on Americans: Political Surveillance from Hoover to the Huston Plan* (Philadelphia, PA: Temple University Press, 1978), 55–7. See also Leffler, *The Specter of Communism: The United States and the Origins of the Cold War* (New York: Hill & Wang, 1994), 74.
2. Quoted in David Bennett, *Party of Fear: From the Nativist Movements to the New Right in American History* (Chapel Hill, NC: University of North Carolina Press, 1988), 28. See also Kenneth O'Reilly, *Hoover and the Un-Americans* (Philadelphia, PA: Temple University Press, 1983), 169 and William Savage, *Comic Books and America, 1945–1954* (Norman, OK: University of Oklahoma Press, 1990), 39–73.
3. Quoted in Gerald Günther, *Learned Hand. The Man and the Judge* (New York: Alfred A. Knopf, 1994), 169.
4. Quoted in Wallace Mendelson, *Justices Black and Frankfurter: Conflict in the Court* (Chicago, IL: University of Chicago Press, 2nd ed, 1966), 54.
5. 337 U.S. 1 (1949).
6. Ibid., 3.
7. Ibid., 4.
8. 340 U.S. 315 (1951), *aff'd* by the New York Court of Appeals, 300 N.Y. 391. 91 N.E.26 316 (1950).
9. Quoted in Lucius Barker and Twiley Barker, *Freedoms, Courts, Politics: Studies in Civil Liberties* (Englewood Cliffs, NJ: Prentice-Hall, 1965), 53.
10. Harry Kalven, *A Worthy Tradition* (New York: Harper & Row, 1988).
11. Quoted in Barker and Barker, *Freedoms, Courts, Politics*, 563. *Feiner*, 340 U.S. at 321.
12. Robert Goldstein, *Political Repression in Modern America from 1870 to 1876* (Cambridge, MA: Schenkman Publishing Company, 1978), 293–4.
13. Tim Weiner, *Enemies: A History of the FBI* (New York: Random House, 2012), 160.
14. Rhodri Jeffreys-Jones, *Cloak and Dollar: A History of American Secret Intelligence* (New Haven, CT: Yale University Press, 2002), 168–9, 197–8 and Weiner, *Enemies*, 155, 191.

15. Ernest Volkmann and Blaine Baggett, *Secret Intelligence: The Inside Story of America's Espionage Empire* (New York: Doubleday, 1989), 93.
16. Ward Churchill and Jim Vander Wall, *Agents of Repression: The FBI's Secret War Against the Black Panther Party and the American Indian Movement* (Boston, MA: South End Press, 1988), 35.
17. O'Reilly, *Hoover and the Un-Americans*, 112.
18. 12 F. Reg. 3690, 1935–37 (1947).
19. 53 Stat. 1147 (1939); 54 Stat. 670 (1940); 18 U.S.C. (1952 ed.) § 2385. President Roosevelt's Attorney General, Francis Biddle acted after congressman Martin Dies had sent him a list of 1,121 names of government employees he regarded as "Communists or affiliated with subversive organizations." On investigating, Biddle found only two federal employees and they were discharged. He argued, in a September 1941 letter, that "the sweeping charges of disloyalty in the Federal Service have not been substantiated. The futility and harmful character of a broad personal inquiry have been too amply demonstrated"; and he noted that of 4,579 individuals reported to the FBI for investigation, only thirty-six were discharged from government service. H. Doc. 833. See also Alien Registration Act, 1940. See also 54 Stat. 670 (1940) and Fund for the Republic, *Digest*, 54.
20. 18 F. Reg. 2489 (1953).
21. Senate Internal Security Committee Report, "Interlocking Subversives in Government Departments," of the Subcommittee on Internal Security of the Committee on the Judiciary, 83rd Cong., 1st sess. July 1953, in Fund for the Republic, *Digest*, 540–1.
22. Fund for the Republic, *Digest*, 618, 620.
23. 18 F. Reg. 2489 (1953) and 18 F. Reg. 6583. See also Goldstein, *Political Repression in Modern America*, 278.
24. 317 F.2d (D.C. Cir. 1962); Landmark Briefs, 61, 674–5. The origins of this measure may be found in H. Doc. 852, introduced in March 1948 report of HUAC. See also Subcommittee on Internal Security of the Committee on the Judiciary.
25. 61 Stat. 136 (1947).
26. "Proceedings of the House of Delegates," American Bar Association Journal 37 (1951): 309, 319. See also David Caute, *The Great Fear: The Anti-Communist Purge under Truman and Eisenhower* (New York: Simon & Schuster, 1978), 403 and Michael Linfield, *Freedom under Fire: U.S. Civil Liberties in Times of War* (Boston, MA: South End Press, 1990), 78.
27. 64 Stat. 987 (1950); 50 U.S.C. § 781. For the background and provisions of the statute see *Dennis v. United States*, 341 U.S. 494 (1951) Appendix B, Cong Rec., 83rd Cong., lst Sess. Hearings, 1953–54. Report, July 1953.
28. Tim Weiner, *Enemies: A History of the FBI* (New York: Random House, 2012), 83.
29. 66 Stat. 166, 8 U.S.C. § 1101 (1952). The Immigration and Nationality Act of 1952 (66 Stat. 663 (1952)) is not to be confused with the Internal Security Act, Title II (entitled the Emergency Detention Act). For a succinct commentary on the 1950 Act, see Paul Murphy, *The Constitution in Crisis Times 1918–1969* (New York: Harper & Row, 1972a), 291.
30. Pub. L. No. 83-637, 68 Stat. 775 (1954). This 1954 statute passed the Senate unanimously, but with two negative votes in the House, and it effectively

outlawed the Communist Party. Linfield, *Freedom under Fire*, 82. See also Milton Konvitz, *Expanding Liberties: Freedom's Gains in Postwar America* (New York: Viking Press, 1966), 14 and Donald Morgan, *Congress and the Constitution: A Study of Responsibility* (Cambridge, MA: Harvard University Press, 1966), 246–68.
31. Ibid.
32. Quoted in Linfield, *Freedom under Fire*, 78. See also Stanley Kutler, *The American Inquisition. Justice and Injustice in the Cold War* (New York: Hill & Wang, 1982), 154 and Edwin Bayley, *Joe McCarthy and the Press* (Madison, WI: University of Wisconsin Press, 1981).
33. Walter Gellhorn, *The States and Subversion* (Ithaca, NY: Cornell University Press, 1951), 247–53.
34. Fund for the Republic, *Digest*, 314.
35. Ibid., 336, 446. Until the 1954 Communist Control Act all such state laws were presumably invalid, it should be noted, because the 1950 Internal Security Act, Section 4f, unqualifiedly stated: "Neither the holding of office nor membership in any Communist organization ... shall constitute per se a violation of ... this section or any other criminal statute." Among others making this observation, see Caute, *The Great Fear*, 72.
36. Fund for the Republic, *Digest*, 392–5. See also Robert Mowitz, "Michigan: State and Local Attack on Subversion," in *The States and Subversion* ed. Gellhorn (Ithaca, NY: Cornell University Press, 1951), 202–3.
37. Ralph Brown, *Loyalty and Security; Employment Tests in the United States* (New Haven, CT: Yale University Press, 1958), 488.
38. On state teacher oath laws, see Fund for the Republic, *Digest*, 431–4. See also Linfield, *Freedom under Fire*, 107.
39. Caute, *The Great Fear*, 414.
40. Ibid., 429.
41. Ibid., 370–1.
42. Samuel Stouffer, *Communism, Conformity and Civil Liberties: A Cross-Section of the Nation Speaks Its Mind* (New York: Doubleday, 1955), 43.
43. Kutler, *The American Inquisition*, 244.

8

The Cold War Enters the Courtroom

The pervasive popular and judicial anxieties about communism at home and abroad were reflected in the influential case of *American Communications Association v. Douds* (1950).[1] Although it ignored the First Amendment, Douds did involve the Communist Party, test oaths, and the balancing of rights of communists to carry on lawful political activity versus what Chief Justice Vinson stated, "political strikes [that Congress found] are evils of conduct which cause substantial harm to interstate commerce." In *Douds*, the High Court passed favorably upon the "non-communist affidavit" of Section 9(h) of the Labor Management Relations [Taft–Hartley] Act of 1947. As observed earlier, the statute required every union official to file an affidavit declaring that he was not a member of the CP or any organization that favored the forcible overthrow of the government. If the official refused the oath, the union in question was denied the protection and services of the National Labor Relations Board.

Arguing for appellants were a quartet of notable First Amendment lawyers who claimed that the statute violated some fundamental rights, including the right of union officers to maintain political views of their choice, the right to associate with whatever political organizations that they chose to, and the right of unions to select their officers without interference from the government. The appellate court dismissed their complaint that the required affidavit was unconstitutional, and the Supreme Court took *certiorari* "because of the manifest importance of the constitutional issues involved."

In the High Court, three justices for one reason or another would not participate in the *Douds* decision. Of the remaining six, five believed the Taft–Hartley Act constitutional insofar as it required an oath of non-membership, but only three (Vinson, Reed, and Burton) found it constitutional insofar as it required an oath of non-belief. Speaking for them, the Chief Justice ominously noted that Communists "had infiltrated union organizations not to support and further trade union objectives ... but to make them a device by which commerce and industry might be disrupted when the dictates of political policy required such action." One such disruption would occur with the Communist unionist tactic of the "political strike ... in support of policies of a foreign government," and Congress, under its commerce power, could seek "to prevent political strikes and other kinds of direct action designed to burden and interrupt the free flow of commerce." Vinson then bluntly asserted: "force may be and must be met with force."[2] Moreover, Congress might "reasonably find" that Communists represented "a continuing danger of disruptive political strikes" when in union leadership positions. The lawmakers' purpose in passing the "non-communist" affidavit provision had that consideration in mind; and he insisted that there was no First Amendment issue: "[t]he Government's interest here is not in preventing the dissemination of Communist doctrine or the holding of particular beliefs."[3] He disingenuously minimized the impact of Section 9(h) and found that it did "not unduly infringe freedoms protected by the First Amendment."[4] The oath turned instead on the government's power to regulate commerce rather and was found valid in this context. Martin Shapiro then pointedly concluded that "commerce regulation weighs more heavily than freedom of speech and belief ..."[5]

Rejecting the "straw man" defense accusation of "thought control," Vinson argued that the "sole effect" of the statute was to deny union leadership to someone who believed in the violent overthrow of the government.[6] The First Amendment, Vinson acknowledged, prohibited Congress from passing a law abridging freedom of speech, press, and assembly, but (the automatic judicial "but") there was still no "right to speak on any subject at any time." And the public had the right to protect itself "from evils of conduct," even though the First Amendment rights may be infringed upon in the process.[7] Accordingly the Chief Justice deferred to the "legislative judgment": "Congress, not the courts, is primarily charged with determining the need for restriction upon 'harmful conduct,' even if such deference had a negative effect upon rights of speech, assembly and belief."[8] Judicial restraint governed: "this Court is in no position to substitute its judgment as to the necessity or desirability of the statute for that of Congress." Further, Vinson gave solace by finding that the CP as a political organization remained intact. Only a "relative handful of persons" were affected by the statute, and they remained "free to maintain their affiliations and beliefs subject only to possible loss of positions ...". In so affirming, the Chief Justice could be accused of naivety in assessing both the realities outside the courtroom and the impact of Section 9(h), because the statute was one more weapon in the cumulative legislative arsenal proscribing expressions of dissent.

Turning to the clear and present danger test, the Chief Justice believed that "it is obvious that a rigid test requiring a showing of imminent danger ... is an absurdity." It is "the extent and gravity of the substantive evil [that] must be measured by the 'test,'" that in effect meant the need to balance "two conflicting interests" and to determine which of them "demand the greater protection under the particular circumstances presented." In effect, this interest-weighing approach denied an absolute theory of the First Amendment, but would weigh its protections against the congressional determination that political strikes are evils of conduct causing substantial harm to interstate commerce, and there was no doubt in his mind about which in the balance carried greater weight.[9]

Joining the trio that comprised the Court majority in *Douds*, Frankfurter and Jackson issued concurrences. The former predictably affirmed judicial deference and did not believe that it was "the business of this Court to restrict Congress too narrowly in defining the extent of the nature of remedies." But terms like "illegal" or "unconstitutional" were entirely too vague, and he thought Congress "had cast its net too indiscriminately."[10] Jackson's opinion, following reminders about our history after 1776, concluded: "Our forefathers [considered] the evils of evil thinking more to be endured than the evils of inquest or suppression." Congress, he went on, lacked the power to "proscribe any opinion or belief which was not manifested itself in any overt act." The Court admittedly had a responsibility to bolster legitimate efforts to preserve the nation but thought "that under our system, it is time enough for the law to lay hold of the citizen when he acts illegally, or in some rare circumstances when his thoughts are given illegal utterance. I think we must let his mind alone."[11]

However, following a lengthy, painstakingly careful analysis of the differences between the CP and other political organizations, Jackson explained why Congress had justifiably singled it out for different treatments. Adhering to the widely held thesis that "behind its political party facade the CP is a conspiratorial and revolutionary junta," a "satrap party," a "secret enclave," and "a secret cabal," and, he argued, it "was organized to reach ends and to use methods which are incompatible with our constitutional system," that it sought to seize power by and for a minority rather than acquiring it through the vote of a free electorate. Congress, given this familiar viewpoint, could under the commerce clause, "require labor union officials to disclose their membership in or affiliation with the Communist Party" and validly subject Party members to such sanctions as disqualification from holding labor union office.

Momentarily shifting to the related activities outside the courtroom, J. Edgar Hoover, as chief minister of national security, would affirm Jackson's conclusion that the CP was a criminal conspiracy and continued to ceaselessly investigate "the activities of a fifth column." As early as June 1945, he directed the Bureau to re-examine the possibility of prosecution of CP leadership under the Smith Act. Accordingly, the FBI would collaborate with the Internal Security Section of the Justice Department's Criminal Division in assembling a case against the Party's National Board. Their joint efforts over two years produced a 1,850-page prosecutorial report, setting forth the evidence against the CP and its leadership. In January 1948, Hoover forwarded this massive document to Attorney General Tom Clark, an ever-vigilant guardian of the nation against communist subversion. Not only did it include Party records and the testimony of ex-Party members and informers but also over 600 inflammatory excerpts disinterred from Communist classics: *the Communist Manifesto* of 1840s and Lenin's *State and Revolution*, among others, designed to confirm the "teaching" and "advocating" of revolutionary violence. Since most of the exhumed tracts provided dubious evidence because they antedated World War II, the FBI also turned to the current "teaching" component by investigating Communist educational venues like New York City's Jefferson School; and Bureau agents' vetted syllabi, course descriptions and assigned readings for passages advocating revolutionary violence.

Importuning Justice Department action, Hoover relentlessly prodded Attorney General Tom Clark and John McGohey, the United States Attorney for the Southern District of New York, who would head the prosecution team. The Justice Department wheeled into action in July 1948. It assigned George Kneip, a lawyer from its Criminal Division, to help draw up indictment of the top Party officials. After reading the FBI Brief, Kneip concluded that the Bureau lacked legally admissible evidence demonstrating that the Party was Moscow's cats-paw or that it advocated revolutionary violence.[12] McGohey himself was unsure whether to prosecute under the 1938 Foreign Agents Registration Act or the Voorhis Act of 1940 because the evidence requirement—that leading members of the Party were agents of a foreign power—did not exist. It would be difficult to show that any of the defendants were acting as Soviet agents.

Finally, McGohey selected the 1940 Alien Registration Act (the Smith Act). Only this statute seemed to hold out the possibility of a successful indictment and conviction of leading Party notables, though J. Edgar Hoover himself recognized the difficulty of relying on it since the Communist leadership had not preached revolutionary violence after December 7, 1941, when war began and when the Supreme Court, in the *Schneiderman* decision of 1943,[13] conceded that the CP "desired to achieve its purpose by peaceful and democratic means." The Smith Act, nonetheless, seemed most appropriate by the late Forties, especially Section Two, which was even more stringent than the World War I legislation. Appearing a very good fit, the statute would provide the critical legal basis for the forthcoming indictment of CP leadership. McGohey accordingly concluded that an indictment "should have a conspiracy count," thereby exhuming a doctrine dating back to English Star Chamber of 1611 and the darkest days of Anglo-American law, one elaborated upon earlier and also written into the Smith Act.[14] By custom broadly defined, the meaning and intent of conspiracy included any combination of two or more persons who did "conspire" to advocate unlawful conduct, or commit an unlawful act, or hold some unlawful end. By this definition, conspiracy made for sweeping applicability and was an understandable choice in the government's arsenal of possible legal weapons.

In the usual conspiracy trial, it should be understood, the prosecution sought to demonstrate two things: (1) the existence of a conspiracy and (2) the complicity of individual defendants in the conspiracy. Significantly, nine-tenths of the prosecution's case—in the voluminous trial records of nearly 16,000 pages—would be devoted to proving the first, the existence of a conspiracy, to wit, that the CP was engaged in it and guilty of violating the Smith Act. By contrast, efforts to prove complicity on the part of those accused were perfunctory. McGohey, we may believe, was aware of and shared Justice Jackson's observation in *Krulewitch v. United States* "that the minimum of proof required to establish conspiracy is extremely low …." Under the conspiracy charge, as he understood its legal implications, evidence could be introduced that would effectively damage the defendants but had little to do with advocacy-of-overthrow per se. When, as we will presently learn, the prosecution introduced the classics of communism such as Stalin's *Foundations of Leninism* (1929), Marx and Engels *The Communist Manifesto* (1848), Lenin's *State and Revolution* (1917), and Stalin's *History of the Communist Party of the Soviet Union* (1939); these texts were considered admissible since conspiracy prosecutions can include words and acts of the alleged conspirators before formation of the conspiracy.

The Justice Department forged ahead, seeking an indictment of a dozen members of the Party's Central Committee and McGohey appeared before a special grand jury already sitting in New York City. The jurors, an aside is warranted, most likely were aware of events swirling around them. They were deliberating at a time that the Mundt–Nixon bill was scheduled for hearings before the Senate Judiciary Committee, and it would further ratchet up widespread public fears of America's radicals. Heightened anxieties, we may believe, were reawakened by the news of Soviet aggression in Czechoslovakia; Truman's St. Patrick Day's speech with its roll call of nations under threat; the Berlin Blockade; and the communist forces sweeping across China. McGohey made his presentation to the grand jury against this background. On June 29, 1948, he presented a sealed blanket indictment for twelve principal CP leaders under Section Two of the Smith Act. (The case of one defendant, William Z. Foster, would be severed owing to ill health.) The complaint charged that these officials "unlawfully, willfully, and knowingly did conspire with each other, and with divers other persons ... to organize as the Communist Party ... a society, group and assembly of persons who teach and advocate the overthrow and destruction of the Government of the United States by force and violence ..." In short, the indictment drew upon Section 3 of the Smith Act, a conspiracy toward the end of teaching and advocating overthrow of the government. No overt acts, and no detailed plans for forcible overthrow were set forth. The books that the defendants read, the articles they wrote, the political schools they supported provided sufficient evidence.[15]

Dennis, et al. v. United States (1951),[16] being the most significant post-World War II case involving Communists, warrants special exegetical commentary. At the outset, we need to observe that these dozen defendants, as McGohey rightly found, "run the party. They make the policy and decide what it will do." They had come to the Party by various routes, but for them all, even those born in the inter-war years, events out of Moscow and Petrograd in 1917 had shaped their lives and thought. Communist revolution was the dream and Russia embodied it. For these defendants, therefore, as for all Communists, the Party offered a crusade and also a home—"a living religion," Arthur Schlesinger shrewdly stated—and they always gave knee-jerk assent to Kremlin directives.

Only recently appointed to the District Court bench for the Southern District of New York, Judge Harold Medina would be chosen to preside over what was his first criminal trial; and what would became the longest—nine months in length and a trial record of some five million words—as well as one of the most highly publicized in American legal history. More than merely the disinterested application of the constitutional text, it would also be, as Stanley Kutler rightly asserted: "the most blatant political trial in American history, a trial of the Party's purposes, ideology and organization, as well as its leaders ... and signaled a national commitment to destroy domestic Communism."[17]

Medina had set October l5, 1949, for commencement of pre-trial challenges by the defendants, but before that the defense unsuccessfully appealed to the Second Circuit Court of Appeals in an effort to have him disqualified as biased. It was the first of repeated objections and endless and patently collusive pre-trial defense motions in District Court by the five lead defense counsel (and the accused had eleven lawyers at one time), often punctuated by their loud, angry shouts, and by those of the defendants. They were prelude to what would occur throughout the trial, namely clashes between the five-member defense team and Medina that would dominant the proceedings, as Scott Martelle notes, with personality clashes as well as back-and-forth argument over legal issues and procedures consuming more time than the hearing of actual testimony.[18]

Defense delaying tactics were a constant. They became a portent of things to come throughout the trial. One motion, for example, argued that there was no possibility of a fair trial because of "intimidating conditions" in and out of the courtroom, a reference in part to the presence of 400 police and plainclothesmen ringing the lower Manhattan Foley Square Courthouse that made for a "state of armed siege or intimidation." Another argued that President Truman's assertion—"I have no comments on the statements [of defendants Dennis and Foster] by traitors"—violated defendants due process and fair trial guarantees (e.g., jury impartiality) inherent in the Fifth and Sixth Amendments, and hence, the indictments could not stand.

Defense motions were all rejected by the bench, but their proliferation resulted in Judge Medina becoming bitterly antagonistic to the five defense counsel even before the trial formally opened. Finally exasperated, he put an end to the seemingly endless defense tactics, set trial date on the issues for January 17, 1949, and the trial itself went on for some 115 days, until September 23. Thus, began what reporters called the "Battle of Foley Square," a long, sensational, fiercely contentious trial. Though producing a 16,000-page record, it would have a predictable outcome considering the background: the threatening domestic and overseas concerns, the public's anti-communist perceptions, and the primary targets in the dock.

The prosecution's opening statement emphasized the conspiracy allegation. It stated that the defendants were accused of conspiring to reorganize the CP in 1945, toward the conspiratorial goal of teaching and advocating the duty and necessity of forceful overthrow of the government, a violation of the 1940 Smith Act. No arms caches had been uncovered, no blueprints for blowing up bridges, no militia-type exercises for action in the proposed overthrow, and no revolutionary acts other than teaching and advocating were alleged. To reiterate, in the absence of overt acts, the conspiracy-to-advocate section of the Smith Act became the pivotal charge. The unlawfulness of the defendants' purpose was based solely on what they advocated. Accordingly, the prosecution's evidence for conspiracy, similar to Attorney General's accusations in the 1919 raids again alien radicals, had centered almost entirely on the nature of an organization rather than on any specific conduct or action of the named defendants. In reality, the CP itself was on trial: a disciplined body with an "inflexible ideology," reorganized in July 1945 to achieve the goal "of the dictatorship of the proletariat," which could only be accomplished "by violent and forceful seizure of power ...."

Marxist–Leninist economic and political theories were in the dock, it inevitably followed, and McGohey repeatedly contended, these assumed that socialism "cannot be established by peaceful evolution but, on the contrary, only by violent revolution." The prosecution charge of conspiracy to forcibly overthrow the government, McGohey contended, would be proved "through their [the defendants'] own documents and by witnesses" who would show that the accused had established "leadership training schools" in which the Bolshevik Revolution was studied "as a blueprint for revolution." Marxism, students at these schools learned, was "not merely dogma," but "a guide to action."

This accusation was attested to by the four communist classics that the prosecution introduced. Though available at any large bookstore, they became the major evidence. According to legal conventions, these texts were admissible, because conspiracy prosecutions can include words and acts of the alleged conspirators prior to formation of the conspiracy. They may have been out-of-date, the prosecution admitted, but they offered the primary evidence that the accused were about to translate their message into revolutionary action and, it followed, their substantive message fell under the proscriptions of the Smith Act. Accordingly, the Marxist–Leninist doctrine, set forth in these classics, became proof of the intent of the accused. Other than such evidence, little would be offered to show that the transition to a communist society would require forceful overthrow.

In their opening statements, more than one of the five defense attorneys contended that the First Amendment protected political activity, political assembly, the right of petition, and the expression of opinion; that thoughts and "spoken thoughts" were under attack; that the prosecution's characterization of the Party had been completely misperceived. Its goal was to educate and persuade a majority of Americans that socialism was in their best interest. These opening statements revealed that the counsel for the petitioners had no common strategy and no common plan for rebuttal. Rather they had multiple tactics, with six of the accused insisting upon taking the stand and they attempted to teach political theory and to present a positive image of their Party and its activities. Their lawyers were hesitant about using the courtroom as a propaganda springboard, but the accused were able to set strategy, which meant that their trial would serve as a bully pulpit to preach Marxism, doing so before an unsympathetic judge and jury. Entirely political and unlawyer-like, the tactic colored defendants' arguments, and spliced with sectarian hyperbole and ideological rhetoric it placed their lawyers "in an untenable position," as William O'Brien shrewdly notes. In *medias res*, this discordant defense inadvertently cooperated with the prosecution, in that their rhetorical maneuvers subordinated to the defense First Amendment/free speech argument to one emphasizing the legitimacy of Party doctrines, the easier position for government to undercut.

The prosecution would call to the stand eleven FBI undercover agents who had infiltrated the Communist Party. They testified that at the right moment, during a time of war or depression, the Party would turn to violence, that it would sabotage any American war effort against the

USSR, and it taught its members that they would eventually have to overthrow the government. Most of the witnesses were not critical to the prosecution's case. Louis Budenz was the exception. The government's star witness, he had been a member of the Communist Party's National Committee from 1936 to 1945 and was the managing editor of the *Daily Worker* in the early Forties, and close to the inner circle of top Party leadership. A professional ex-Communist witness, Budenz had first appeared before the House Committee on Un-American Activities, as noted earlier, and had testified that all Communists were "a part of the Russian fifth column." In the District Court, he emphasized the communist texts and doctrines and traced the sweep of the Party's trajectory from the Thirties through the end of World War II when it reconstituted itself. In three days on the stand, he tailored his testimony to the claim that the accused were complicit in the alleged conspiracy "to the overthrow of the Government of the United States."[19]

Budenz's testimony, which caused havoc for the defense, also became the major vehicle by which the government inserted lurid passages from the long-dated Communist tracts into the record. By introducing such evidence, Kevin O'Brien tells us in his valuable dissertation, Budenz made the prosecution's case against the Party itself rather than the eleven individual defendants.[20] Medina would overrule all defense objections to admission of these texts into evidence. Justifiably so, since in a conspiracy trial, to repeat, the conspirators' acts and statements prior to formation of the conspiracy, April 1945 in this instance, were admissible. They were relevant to the intent of the accused. By legal conventions, then, the Court rightly allowed statements into evidence about the Party's intent to return to the pre-war revolutionary line, which, hopefully for the prosecution, would be proof of the aim and purpose of the conspiracy to teach and advocate forcible overthrow.[21] Accordingly, the defense charge that the prosecution was engaged in "a trial of books" appeared justified.[22]

The primary defense arguments rested on contentions that communism did not inherently call for forcible overthrow of the government, that the defendants' "political expressions and activities" were protected by the First Amendment, that they were on trial because of their beliefs. These assertions were met and partially neutralized by Judge Medina in a 15,000-word charge to the jury emphasizing "intent" as the operative standard. In effect, he was applying a bad tendency test and embracing the majority opinion in *Gitlow* that allowed the state to proscribe speech, specifically, to "suppress the threatened danger in its incipiency." The jurors could find the defendants guilty of violating the Smith Act if they "conspired willfully or knowingly ... with the intent that such teaching and advocacy be of a rule or principle of action and by language reasonably and ordinarily calculated to incite persons to such action, all with the intent to cause the overthrow or destruction of the Government ...."[23] The defendants, Medina acknowledged, could be acquitted if they did "no more than pursue peaceful studies" or "advocacy in the realm of ideas." However, no one had an absolute right to speak, write, or publish whatever he wished under all circumstances. Medina bridged the gap between speech and action by arguing that "words may be the instruments by which crimes are committed." Guided by these instructions, the jurors deliberated eight hours before coming to the preordained outcome. Thus ended a criminal trial that had lasted 158 days, consumed 20,000 pages and five million words of testimony.

Since anti-communist rhetoric dominated public discourse, it could be expected that the media would unequivocally support the trial court outcome. Affirming the verdict in a typical editorial, *The New York Times* stated that the defendants had been "convicted of secretly teaching and advocating, on secret orders from Moscow, overthrow of the United States Government and destruction of American democracy by force and violence." The *Los Angeles Times* asserted that, as the verdict confirmed, the Communist Party USA was "a criminal conspiracy against the United States, run by Moscow." Medina himself, lionized by the media, became "a national hero, ... an oracle of patriotic wisdom" and received thousands of fan letters during and after the trial praising him for defending American freedom.[24] All of which was understandable. The nation remained frozen in Cold War animosities, and the atmosphere in the country had made conviction a foregone conclusion.

Upon advice of counsel, the eleven defendants went into the United States Court of Appeals for the Second Circuit, where their case was argued on June 21–22, 1950. Before turning to the appeal, it is important to recognize that the Appellate Court had before it Vinson's decision in *Douds*, decided six weeks earlier, one that would unquestionably shape the outcome in *Dennis*. Of this Court, Chief Judge Hand had been pivotal when *Douds* was heard, and he would also hand down the *Dennis* opinion for the three-judge panel. That his *Douds* opinion would prefigure and inform Chief Justice Vinson's High Court decision in *Dennis* is a further reason for having dwelt at length on *Douds* as well as Hand's appellate court ruling. The decision in each instance was decisively shaped by two factors: first, judicial deference to the political branches of government, affirming their authority to define and deal with the Communist threat; and, second, adherence to the virtually axiomatic judicial rule of *stare decisis*. Hand, for one, could scarcely avoid acknowledging the significance of Vinson's opinion in *Douds* when considering the *Dennis* appeal. He and his two comparatively conservative colleagues, Thomas Swan and Chase, seemingly had no choice but to follow precedent; or, as Hand acknowledged, precedent was "in some ways the most important of all" considerations in shaping his opinion in *Dennis*.

At the risk of overkill, a third factor needs mention, namely, news about national and international affairs. Likewise aware of the international scene, Judge Chase, in a concurrence, observed that "as this [*Dennis* opinion] is being written, Fifth Column activities are aiding the North Koreans in their war against the United Nations." Hand was fully aware of events in Korea after the June 1950 invasion of South Korea. He had "trepidation" about international communism and feared that "any border fray, any diplomatic incident, any difference in the construction of the *modus vivendi*—such as the Berlin Blockade ... might prove a spark to the tinder-box, and lead to war."[25] The prospect of atomic war was such, "we do not understand how one could ask for a more probable danger." In addition, there was the 1949 Berlin Airlift, fears about Red China, and the resultant near-universal anti-communism pervading the media and public opinion. To remind the reader, it is almost risible to contend that the courtroom was insulated from these overseas developments. Hand was a highly respected and deeply humane jurist. He recognized that the "hysteria in this country has now reached such a peak that there are few who would dare to acknowledge any Communist inclinations, if they had them." But the judge who, to this time, had argued that the most effective antidote to communism was free discussion, now asserted that the CP was special, that it was a conspiracy, and that free speech, usually the guideline, "does not apply" to the Party. Hence, the *Dennis* case appellate outcome for him and his two colleagues on the bench would be predetermined.

There is little need to describe the defense and prosecution Briefs in detail, since they were largely a repetition of the arguments set forth in the District Court. The government simply reemphasized that the accused were not conventional political figures but agents of a conspiracy to forcibly seize power. However, O'Brien points out that it offered no evidence of immediate revolution or revolutionary planning by the Communist Party. In opening the appellate proceedings, the second and most significant of two defense Briefs, a 403-page document, contended that the Smith Act was unconstitutional on its face and, further, that Medina's interpretation of the statute nullified the First Amendment's guarantee of freedom of political expression. Only direct incitement to criminal violence could be punished, defense claimed, and not "probability and tendency"; and the High Court's bad tendency doctrine in *Gitlow* was inapplicable to their clients.[26] In their three hours of arguments, defense counsel asked the appellate panel to apply the clear, present, and "imminent" danger formula as first formulated by Holmes and Brandeis in their *Schenck* and *Gitlow* opinions, a test that Medina had not recognized.

The prosecution Brief simply reemphasized that the accused were not conventional political leaders but were agents of a conspiracy to seize power forcefully and establish a communist state. It again contended that the legislature had a right to determine and restrict categories of speech that created a "substantial evil." "Intent" had to be demonstrated rather than a specific act or specific evidence; and "intent" joined "advocacy"— of a projected overt act premised on violence—in being constitutionally unprotected. To advocate, the government continued, was simply prefatory to illegal action, and the Smith Act functioned to frustrate it. Advocacy, namely, "specific utterances," had been made with the "specific intent and purpose of bringing about the apprehended evils."[27]

Disquieting affairs at home and abroad were not alone in shaping Hand's decision. *Stare decisis, to repeat*, arguably *governed and accordingly*, the Court of Appeals outcome in Dennis, as in Douds, trumped other considerations entering into Hand's opinion. It frustrated the possibility of offering a more unqualified endorsement of protected speech had he been so inclined. Hand, to be sure, remained uneasy about curtailment of free speech and, interrupting the prosecution's oral argument, he had wondered aloud whether Jefferson's advocacy of rebellion against "utterly offensive" governments would have been circumscribed by the Smith Act. Later, in a February 1952 letter to his former law clerk, Elliot Richardson, Hand would forcefully dissent "from the whole approach to the problem of Free Speech which the Supreme Court has adopted during the last thirty-five or forty years."[28]

Apparently at the time a deeply divided jurist, Hand was torn between confidence in the integrity of protected expression and his perception of dangers threatening from abroad as well as from the

American Communist Party. He now framed the issue as one of "how long a government" must wait, having discovered a conspiracy to make a revolution, before "the conspiracy became a 'present danger'?" For him, that became "the question ... and the only one ...".[29] Hand's emphasis was on "probability," a "probable danger" test that did more than finesse the Brandeis formula of clear and imminent danger, it represented a real departure. Not proximity, but "probability" and risk, as Rodney Smolla states, became the test—in which the "gravity of the evil" and its "improbability" are assessed by judges and jury "to produce a net risk factor" that is then balanced against the infringement on free speech.[30] And the risk factor, the "gravity" of the evil, was very high in this instance: "a danger of the utmost gravity" existed, and "we had no alternative." Fully aware of Vinson's opinion in *Douds*, with its references to the danger test, emphasis on the "probable" answered the question that the Chief Justice had posed: "how long" to wait. Offering this variation on the formulaic clear and present danger doctrine, Hand's rephrased doctrine would provide Vinson with an answer. Conditions were potentially so dangerous, so "probable," Hand concluded that it was permissible to restrict free speech. In short, his opinion was a far remove from Brandeis' concurrence in *Whitney*, which would legitimately apply the danger test only to extremely imminent "evils." Accordingly, on August 1, 1950, Hand, as Chief Judge on the Second Circuit, announced the panel's unanimous opinion, upholding the District Court conviction of those who had intended forcible overthrow.

Counsel for the eleven defendants then petitioned the High Court for a writ of *certiorari*, and *certiorari* was granted on October 23, 1950. It was a "limited grant," restricting review to whether the Smith Act violated the First Amendment rights of the appellants and whether, being constitutionally vague, it violated the First and Fifth Amendments. In short, the justices, unlike Hand, would not consider "the sufficiency of the evidence" (e.g., the introduction of Marxist–Leninist tracts), or the claim of overt acts, or whether the accused did in fact advocate violent overthrow. However restrictive, their decision would indeed be "a great moment" in High Court history, Harry Kalven observed, though not because the Smith Act was at stake but because it was a "highly visible public event" involving a criminal prosecution of America's top Communists at the height of the nation's Red Scare.[31]

Before turning to High Court deliberations, it is to be reemphasized that the tramp of communist armies could be heard through the paneled walls of the Court. Similar to Hand, Chief Justice Vinson noted, the "inflammable nature of world conditions." The justices could hardly be immunized against the loyalty–security fever. It was in the very air around them. After all, they had refused to grant *certiorari* to what became known as the Hollywood Ten, by itself sufficient evidence that they had to be aware of the activities of congressional committees. The majority opinions were founded on the well-established and near-unanimously held popular view that had turned ca. 5,000 communists into an existential threat, and the truism that the Communist Party, as Vinson would hold, was "an apparatus designed and dedicated to the overthrow of the Government, in the context of world crisis after crisis."

Turning to the case itself and the High Court, both defense Petition and Brief (of 570 pages) to the High Court overlapped and simply rehashed arguments expressed in circuit court and in their Petition for *certiorari*, the many motions to dismiss the indictments, the appeals for a mistrial denied by Judge Medina, his "extreme lack of judicial decorum," the motions for acquittal, and the paucity of evidence. Finally, the Petition argued that trial court invaded defendant's rights under the First Amendment. Appellants' lengthy Brief, like their Petition for *certiorari*, devoted considerable space to discussion of the Smith Act, contending it would "impose political censorship over vast segments of our people," and was prima facie unconstitutional. Section Three of the statute, incorporating the conspiracy doctrine, came under sustained and vociferous attack. The doctrine was "invariably used in periods of reaction to punish unpopular associations," and given its "vagueness," its legitimate application "must be confined only to action."[32] The defense Brief predicted, should the statute upheld, widespread arrests would occur were it upheld. In fact hardly a "speculative" prophecy since the Justice Department acknowledged that were the convictions sustained, it would lead to the indictment and prosecution of 12,000 for violation of the statute.[33]

The prosecution Brief simply opened with a painstakingly detailed narrative of events in the 1930s, including the emergence of the Communist International, the Hitler–Stalin Pact, the Party's change of "line" following the German invasion of Russia, and then the reconstitution of the Communist Party. Party schools, of training its members in revolutionary principles at Party schools, the prosecution offered in evidence lengthy quotes from such texts as "Outline in Fundamentals of Marxism for Class Use or Self Study" and the "Foundations of Leninism." It further argued that First Amendment freedoms "may be restricted to protect vital national interests from serious injury" and affirmed that the Smith Act was constitutional: "a valid exercise of the powers of Congress to preserve democratic government in the United States." Congress has correctly viewed the CP of the United States as "schooled" in techniques of "deception, coercion, coup d'etat, terrorism and assassination."[34] Pulling out all the stops, the prosecution Brief called it "a satrap party ... , a potential fifth column for the Soviet Union," and "communists everywhere ... engage in systematic espionage for the Soviet Union."[35]

Chief Justice Vinson clearly recognized the high visibility of the case, assigning the plurality opinion to himself and speaking for Stanley Reed, Harold Burton, and Sherman Minton, in a 6-to-2 decision, with two justices (Felix Frankfurter and Robert Jackson) concurring and two (Hugo Black and William Douglas) dissenting. Of the five majority opinions that were written, and that totaled nearly 100 pages in length, Vinson's was a brief eighteen pages. Seemingly affected as Hand had been by such "facts" and "factors" as the alleged Red Menace both at home and abroad, his plurality opinion was also similar to Hand's in being devoted mostly to countering the defense argument that the Smith Act "stifles ideas and is contrary to all concepts of ... free speech." To the contrary, the Chief Justice argued. Congress did not intend "to eradicate the free discussion of political theories, to destroy the traditional rights of Americans to discussion and evaluate ideas without fear of governmental sanction ...." Rather it was only "concerned with the very kind of activity in which the evidence showed these petitioners engaged." Going to painstaking lengths to uphold the Smith Act, Vinson argued that it was "directed at advocacy, not discussion." Free speech, the "traditional right of Americans to discuss and evaluate ideas," Vinson ritualistically stated, admittedly was subject to First Amendment protection and constitutionally protected. But (and, to remind the reader, once more of the predictable qualifier) "speech is not an absolute." There was no "right to rebellion" against the government, since the Constitution provided for orderly and peaceful change.[36] The advocacy of plaintiffs could constitute intention and actions that had unlawful goals. The government, it follows, was empowered to protect itself against such advocacy. Designed to offer such protection, the Smith Act was constitutional—"inherently or as construed and applied in the instant case." The purpose of the statute, he flatly declared, was "to protect existing Government ... from change by violence, revolution and terrorism .... It is a proposition that requires little discussion."

As a consequence, it was applicable when the facts, as determined by the Court, indicated an appreciable future probability for the successful overthrow of the government. Accordingly, appellants' claims that the Smith Act violated the First Amendment facts were rejected.

Indeed, "probability for successful overthrow ... the government by force and violence" involved a conspiracy, one already in place: "a highly organized conspiracy with rigidly disciplined members subject to call when the leaders, these petitioners, felt that the time had come for action." His *ipse dixit* simply assumed that a conspiracy existed "to overthrow the government by force and violence" and "is a sufficient evil for Congress to prevent." Unlike Justice Jackson's concurrence emphasizing that *Dennis* was a conspiracy case, Vinson devoted only three sentences to it. He simply assumed the fact of conspiracy and "coupled [it] with ... the touch-and-go nature of our relations with countries with whom petitioners were in the very least ideologically attuned." In so finding, Vinson brushed away the distinction between "a conspiracy to advocate, as distinguished from the advocacy itself." It was for him a distinction without a difference, both fell within the requisite clear and present danger formula.[37]

From this position, the Chief Justice was ineluctably led into a discussion of the formula itself; and of what "that phrase imports" and "what has been meant by its use." It "cannot mean that before the Government may act, it must wait until the putsch is about to be executed, the plan ... laid and the signal ... awaited." If the putsch was indeed imminent then the clear and present danger test could come too late. The reference to "putsch," to interject, alluded of course to the failed Nazi revolt against the government that occurred in a Munich beer hall in 1923, a rather dubious parallel to, say, the imaginative scene of communists, gathered in a beer hall near the White House, plotting to attack it.[38] But not an entirely strained possibility for the Chief Justice and the Court majority (as well as most on the federal bench) who were sold on the claim that the "requisite danger" was "present" and had been proven. The Communist Party, however, anemic in reality, was a serious threat and the "facts" were obvious. And given the "facts," "[w]e reject any principle of governmental helplessness in the face of preparation for revolution, which principle, carried to its logical conclusion, must lead to anarchy."

Vinson recognized a judicial trend, as found in the Holmes–Brandeis opinions in *Gitlow* and *Whitney that*, strictly interpreted, could have reversed conviction of the defendants in *Dennis*. Referring to the Stone Court, he thought that "[t]here is little doubt that subsequent opinions have inclined toward the Holmes-Brandeis rationale."[39] Were these opinions followed, it is likely that the defendants' "advocacy," though clear and serious, could hardly be considered "present." Vinson then rationalized, contending that the Holmes–Brandeis danger formula was a "short-hand phrase"—and not intended to be "crystallized into a rigid rule to be applied inflexibly without regard to the circumstances of each case." After avoiding an explicit disavowal of the danger standard in *Scheck*, he turned to Learned Hand's "probability" "reinterpretation" of "present" danger in *Dennis*. Lavishing praise it, the Chief Justice declared:

> As articulated by Chief Judge Hand, it is as succinct and inclusive as any other we might devise at this time. It takes into consideration those factors which we deem relevant, and related their significance. More we cannot expect from words.

In fact the opinion of Vinson approvingly quoted Hand's appellate opinion in *Dennis* verbatim: "In each case [courts] must ask whether the gravity of the 'evil,' discounted by its improbability, justifies such invasion of free speech as is necessary to avoid the danger." Vinson flatly added, "We adopt this statement of the rule." Both trial and appeals courts had found "that the requisite danger existed" and then "we cannot bind the Government to wait" upon the catalyst.[40] Overt action, the mainstay of criminal law, was thus abandoned as the criterion. Speech, he concluded, could be restricted since a society must be able to protect itself, and "certain kinds of speech are so undesirable as to warrant criminal sanction." As a consequence, Samuel Krislov compellingly argued "that the Hand-Vinson formula so completely blurred the sharp lines of the clear and present danger test as to eliminate it for any purpose, except apologetic acceptance of all legislative action."[41]

Implicit in this test, it need be added, was the judicial obligation to weigh whether "present" or "probable" danger existed. Vinson then proceeds to explicitly adopt the balancing formula: "… the duty of the courts is to determine which of the two conflicting interests demands the greater protection…" This weighing, we have seen, frequently had a pernicious result for defenders of free speech since the judicial outcome usually legitimated government actions and authority. The scales in such cases had been decisively weighted toward national security, a number of scholars have concluded. Balancing arguably becomes a hypocritical, even fraudulent, exercise that was open to a restrictive reading of the First Amendment. It then tipped the scales toward "the gravity of the evil" and unfavorably toward free speech. The contrasting propositions do not occupy the same level of analysis; and, Krislov writes, a fairer balance would be struck "by comparing ... the individual net gain in security against a loss in free expression."[42]

By this decision, the most prestigious legal body in the United States placed what law professor Arthur Sabin termed "the seal of approval" on the anti-communist assault. Failing to protect against the exercise *ultra vires* of governmental power, the Court thus encouraged both federal and state lawmakers to continue their pursuit of radicals, aliens, lower-echelon CP officers or sympathizers, indeed those of every persuasion who harbored persistent un-American sentiments. Juries in state and federal trial courts acted with unusual speed in finding defendants guilty as charged, appellate courts likewise speedily and with few exceptions upheld convictions. Writing of these trials and convictions, Belknap had observed that there was a "kind of grinding monotony ...," about them, "for although there was some variations between individual Smith Act cases, on the whole they were extremely repetitious, both of *Dennis* and of each other."[43] In each instance, when studied against the background of crisis, it becomes apparent that, joining the public and the political branches, "the judiciary tends to go to war."[44]

Notes

1. 339 U.S. 382 (1952). *Douds* was the major case arising out of challenges to the non-communist oath provisions of the 1947 Taft–Hartley Act to reach the Supreme Court. Of a number decided in lower federal courts, see *United States v. Valenti*, 106 F. Supp. 124 (D.N.J. 1952); *In re Neff*, 206 F.2d 149 (3d Cir. 1953).
2. Ibid., 396.
3. Ibid.
4. Ibid. McGohey had alluded to the pre-1941 Party position which adhered to the revolutionary implications of the Third International and Marxist–Leninist theory; that is, the Party, he argued, had abandoned the Communist Political Association and returned to its hard line.
5. Martin Shapiro, *Freedom of Speech: The Supreme Court and Judicial Review* (Englewood Cliffs, NJ: Prentice-Hall, 1966), 80.
6. *Douds*, 339 U.S. at 404.
7. Ibid., 398.
8. Ibid., 406, 396, 400.
9. Ibid., 399, 407.
10. Ibid., 413. See also Harry Kalven, *A Worthy Tradition. Freedom of Speech in America* (New York: Harper & Row, 1988), 331.
11. Ibid., 444.
12. Kevin O'Brien, Dennis v. United States: The Cold War, the Communist Conspiracy and the F.B.I. (Ph.D. dissertation, Cornell University, 1979), 248–9.
13. *Schneiderman v. United States*, 320 U.S. 118 (1943).
14. Scott Martelle, *The Fear within: Spies, Commies, and American Democracy on Trial* (New Brunswick, NJ: Rutgers University Press, 2011), 28.

15. Ibid.
16. *Dennis v. United States*, 341 U.S. 494 (1951).
17. Stanley Kutler, *American Inquisition. Justice and Injustice in the Cold War* (New York: Hill & Wang, 1982), 152.
18. Martelle, *The Fear within*, 59.
19. Ibid., 17, 24. O'Brien, *Dennis v. United States*, 479–95. On the Duclos letter and the shift from Earl Browder and his Communist Political Association back to the CP and a policy of militant radicalism, see Martelle, *The Fear within*, 27–8.
20. O'Brien, Dennis v. United States, 493–5. See also Martelle, *The Fear within*, 127–8.
21. Ibid., 488.
22. Ibid.
23. Ibid., 501.
24. Ibid., 544, 546. See also *Dennis*, 341 U.S. at 511–2.
25. Glendon Schubert, *Constitutional Politics: The Political Behavior of Supreme Court Justices and the Constitutional Policies that They Make* (New York: Holt, Rinehart and Winston, 1960), 54.
26. *Dennis*, 341 U.S. at 494. Attachment: 1950 WL 787403, 32–3, 36, 81, 118.
27. Ibid., attachment: 1950 WL 78653, 274.
28. Likewise aware of the international scene, Judge Chase, in a concurrence, observed that "as this [*Dennis* opinion] is being written, Fifth Column activities are aiding the North Koreans in their war against the United Nations." Quoted in Gerald Gunther, *Learned Hand. The Man and the Judge* (New York: Alfred A. Knopf, 1994), 604–5.
29. *Dennis*, 183 F.2d, 200.
30. Rodney Smolla, *Free Speech in an Open Society* (New York: Alfred A. Knopf, 1992), 109.
31. Kalven, *A Worthy Tradition. Freedom of Speech in America*, 195.
32. Ibid., attachment: Brief of Petitioners, 1950 WL 78740, 31.
33. Ibid., attachment: Brief of Petitioners, 1950 WL 78740, 30. See also Landmark Briefs, 47, pp. 217–8.
34. Ibid., attached: Brief for the United States, 1950 WL 78653, 211,212, 300–2. See also Landmark Briefs, 47, pp. 479, 483–9.
35. Ibid., attached: Brief for the United States, 1950 WL 78653, 293, 297.
36. *Dennis*, 341 U.S. at 508; see also William Wiecek, Liberty Under Law: The Supreme Court in American Life (Baltimore, MD: Johns Hopkins University Press, 1988), 149.
37. *Dennis*, 341 U.S. at 509.
38. Ibid., 510.
39. Ibid., 511.
40. Ibid.
41. Samuel Krislov, *The Supreme Court and Political Freedom* (New York: The Free Press, 1968), 88
42. Ibid., 113.
43. *Dennis*, 341 U.S. at 563. See also Michal Belknap, *Cold War Political Justice: The Smith Act, the Communist Party, and American Civil Liberties* (Westport, CT: Greenwood, 1977), 139, 169.
44. Michal Belknap, "The Supreme Court Goes to War: The Meaning and Implications of the Nazi Saboteur Case," *Military Law Review* 89 (1980): 59.

9

The Fifties: The Left under Assault

By the time of *Dennis* decision, the CP had effectually vanished from America's political and social landscape, though the public and official Washington thought otherwise and the Court majorities legitimated further communist prosecutions. Popular and judicial opinions, it follows, tended to run together, and court decisions often paralleled widespread national preferences and sentiments, strikingly so in times of emergency. According to mythic belief, the judiciary engages in the disinterested application of constitutional scripture to legal disputes, applying an approach without regard for public reaction or political consequences. Courts, however, are never insulated from the media and popular opinion, as earlier emphasized, and judicial majorities in fact often marched in tandem to the current popular tunes.

Having been given the green light to the administration by October 1951, the *Dennis* case outcome triggered plans to prosecute CP leaders that corresponded to the forecast of defense counsel during the trial proceedings. Indeed in mid-June, so-called second-string and third-string state and national Communist leaders were taken into custody by the FBI, followed by successive arrests of state and regional officials, bringing the total to 132. Eventually, in the decade after 1947, 145 Communist members and officers were indicted for violating the Smith Act. Over 105 went to trial in Los Angeles, Honolulu, Baltimore, Seattle, Detroit, Pittsburgh, Philadelphia, St. Louis, Cleveland, Denver, New York, Boston, and Puerto Rico, and 116 of the defendants would be convicted.[1] Two lower court judges offered them an alternative to imprisonment, namely, banishment to the Soviet Union.[2] Moreover, in the six years after *Dennis*, appellate tribunals upheld every Smith Act conviction that came before them, and the High Court twice denied *certiorari* to petitioners.

Justice Department attitudes and practices, to reiterate, spanned the Truman–Eisenhower administrations, and so it followed that there was a remarkably smooth transition from J. Howard McGrath to Herbert Brownell, the new administration's Attorney General. On Capitol Hiss, a similar smooth transition prevailed. The HUAC, now headed by Harold Velde of Indiana and the Senate Internal Security Subcommittee (SISS), chaired by Patrick McCarran, the powerful Senate insider, continued to spearhead the congressional assault. The histrionic Joseph McCarthy, as noted earlier, became Chairman of the Senate Committee on the Judiciary, and he also made accusations resulting in bold-type headlines. The hearings of this trio of committees produced the "unfriendly witness," that egregious ukase attached to one who had recourse to the privilege against self-incrimination, becoming what was known as a "Fifth Amendment Communist" and subject to the contempt of Congress charges and to further public animosity.[3]

HUAC at this time concerned itself with its perennial subject of communist infiltration of the nation's schools as well as with US employees of doubtful loyalty at the United Nations. McCarran's and McCarthy's committees held a number of hearings, fully covered by the media, on subversives at the Fort Monmouth, New Jersey Army Signal Corp headquarters, and in the Army itself. One Subcommittee hearing alarmingly concluded that 30,000–40,000 books written by communists or communist sympathizers were on the shelves at one U.S. Information Centers. McCarran died suddenly in September 1954, but his Subcommittee retained the same tireless pursuit of alleged subversives after Indiana Senator Albert Jenner took over its reins. Equally active, another Senate Subcommittee investigated communist influence in various unions in 1952–1953. Its Chair, Senator James Eastland of Mississippi, held widely reported hearings on New York City teachers and teacher's union in 1956. Newspaper reports, radio programs, and the new age of television provided the necessary glare of publicity to congressional investigators and nurtured further popular anti-communist enthusiasms. Congress also offered up legislation frozen *in medias res*, their phantoms exaggerated, with the 1950 McCarran Act, the 1952 McCarran–Walter Act (the Immigration and Nationality Act) dealing with aliens.

These multiple pressures produced a defensive posture among most Democrat lawmakers as well as White House personnel in both the Truman and Eisenhower administrations and a need to brandish their own anti-Soviet and anti-communist credentials. Few among the lawmakers were unmindful of the defeat of the seven liberal Senate Democrats who had voted against the 1950 McCarran Act and had been savaged by the Republicans as well as by many Democrats. It would be followed by the 1952 McCarran–Walter Act, officially entitled the Immigration and Nationality Act. Reconfirming the deportation section of the 1950 McCarran Act and the power of immigration officials, it was legislation frozen *in medias res*, its phantoms exaggerated. During Truman's time in the White House, it may be recalled, Immigration and Naturalization Service officials initiated a campaign to eliminate the anti-communist infection. They would sustain the widespread xenophobia first manifest by the 1903 and 1917 immigration measures, reconfirmed with the Internal Security Act of 1950 and the Immigration and Nationality Act of two years later. Attorneys General again swung into action, James McGranery in October 1952 had announced a drive to denaturalize communists (e.g., Stanley Nowak, a Michigan labor organizer). Herbert Brownell in the following year revealed an investigation of about 10,000 naturalized citizens suspected of subversive affiliations and of another 12,000 aliens for possible deportation owing to alleged communist affiliations or sympathies. Denaturalization proceedings were initiated against some leading communist officials, such as the judicial proceedings against him will shortly be described. A year after entering the White House, Eisenhower unhesitatingly signed into law the 1954 Expatriation Act that provided for the automatic loss of citizenship of anyone convicted of certain crimes, including violations of the Smith Act; that is, "those who ... conspire to violently overthrow the government, or conspire to so advocate."[4] Since lower federal courts had at this time ruled that mere membership in the CP constituted a violation of the Smith Act, every member who was an alien became potentially subject to repatriation, a possibility not overturned by the High Court for a dozen-plus years (in *Afroyim v. Rusk*, 1967).

J. Edgar Hoover, the FBI's Director of three decades, and his Bureau remained intent upon expanding its targets for the investigation and surveillance. Premier Khruschev's assault on Stalin at the February 1956 Twentieth Party Congress in Moscow—in which he detailed Stalin's many brutal crimes against the old Bolsheviks, the Communist Party, and Soviet national interests—would exorcise the ghost of communism for many of America's true believers. It accelerated the sharp decline of CP influence and membership that had begun much earlier, exposing in terms more promising than ever its increasing irrelevance in the nation's politics and society.

In stunning contrast to the decline in CP membership following Khruschev's speech, J. Edgar Hoover would not be diverted from his obsessive pursuit of communist enemies of the republic and retained his standing as the anti-communist evangelist without peer. In conformity with the two percent unfavorable rating, he received in a 1953 Gallup Poll, the Bureau remained fixated with the Communist Party's influence upon "the masses, [its] ability to create controversy leading to confusion and disunity, penetration of specific channels in American life where public opinion is molded, and espionage and sabotage potential." By now one of the FBI's closely guarded secrets, the Communist Index, with its listings of "top functionaries and key figures," was functioning, and Bureau agents added the designation, "Communist sympathizers," to the existing lists of Party members, leading to further prosecutions by the Justice Department as well as lists of those targeted for detention in the event "of sudden difficulties with Russia." By the mid-Fifties, during the Eisenhower years, the Bureau had amassed 432,000 files on subversives and proposed detention of 230,000 of those named in the event of a national emergency.[5] By 1956, it had gone beyond sporadic intelligence and the dull office work of compiling lists of subversive, and developed the Counter-Intelligence Program (COINTELPRO) designed to "neutralize the effectiveness" of the Party. A unilaterally institutionalized domestic spying program and fully operational in Eisenhower's first term, its goal was revealed in an internal memorandum of August 1956; namely, to "disrupt," "discredit," and "neutralize" the CP and domestic protest organizations.[6] This broad Bureau expansion of anti-radical surveillance—by means of wiretaps, anonymous hate mail, IRS tax audits—would expand at one time into 2,300 separate operations against the CP that were completely secret and outside the criminal process and procedures. But Hoover maintained the continued legitimacy of his target and dismissed the declining Party membership with an attack on "the ignorant and the apologists and appeasers of communism in our country as minimizing the danger of these subversives in our midst."[7]

Although antagonistic to McCarthy and other rabid anti-communists, Eisenhower made his own contributions to the mordant fears of the age. Though barely aware of a significant portion of Bureau activities, COINTELPRO in particular, the White House joined in the campaign to eliminate communists in government. *Argumentum ad horrendum*, his administration's anti-communist campaign was unrelenting. The White House security order of October 1953, it will be recalled, stated: any federal employee who pleaded the Fifth Amendment when asked incriminating questions in federal courtrooms or before congressional investigatory bodies was automatically a security risk and ineligible for work on classified government documents. A codicil may be added as a reminder. Any employee of a state, private organization, or business who "took the Fifth" was publicly branded a "Fifth Amendment Communist" and almost immediately discharged, again suggesting the extent and persistence of the Red Menace theme.

Throughout Eisenhower's eight years in office, loyalty oaths also remained the norm in federal and state employment practices. They were complemented by the "security risk" classification, in which the person being investigated might not be disloyal, but could possibly disclose classified information. Those stigmatized as "disloyal" were being hunted down on every level of the federal bureaucracy and discharged. In the Spring 1953, Attorney General Brownell requested the SACB to order a dozen organizations to register as a "Communist front," one of the three categories established by the McCarran Act.

Congress would also provide further legislative shields against the enemy at or within the gate, expressed by fearful metaphors of the "Trojan Horse" or "Fifth Column." These statutes tell us something more about the reigning demotic opinion of the day and so warrant discussion. They warehoused the ongoing delusional convictions of the public as well as official Washington that the ca. 5,000 communists would lead a revolution or hand over military secrets to Moscow. One such statute, the aforementioned Gwinn proviso attached to the 1952 and 1953 appropriation statutes, prohibited "a member of an organization designated as 'subversive' by the Attorney General" from occupying housing constructed under the 1937 Housing Act. Then there was the aforementioned Communist Control Act of 1954 that would outlaw the CP and that was the last major piece of legislation against Communism. The measure had bipartisan approval, it is significant, being guided through Congress by liberal Democrats.[8] Upon signing the statute, Eisenhower boasted that working together, the White House and the lawmakers would "blot out the Communist conspiracy," an administration outlook not unrelated to the famous charge of his Vice President, Richard Nixon, that sinister ties existed between the Democrats and the Communist Party. The 1954 statute, incidentally, added another category—the "Communist-infiltrated" organization—to the Attorney General's list of membership categories requiring surveillance and registration. Nor did matters end here. One more measure of this year, the 1954 Immunity Act sought to restrict the tendency of witnesses to take the Fifth Amendment when questioned by federal investigatory committees and would unsuccessfully attempt to neutralize the self-incrimination defense. Remaining in the Fifties, Congress also enacted the 1959 Landrum–Griffin Act. It replaced Section 9(h) of the Taft–Hartley Act that, *subsilentio*, had allowed a Communist union official to retain his position by resigning CP membership. This 1959 statute would plug the loophole, by making it a crime for an officer or employee of "any labor organization" to be a member of the Communist Party.[9] To sum up, the political branches remained ideologically compatible. They maintained the identical rhetorical stance and activities, thereby adding to the special argot of dark intimations and murky insinuations that were then special features of American politics and society.

Outside of official circles in this decade, commercial heresy hunters operated companies that compiled lists of the suspected. Red Channels, for one, recorded some 150 names in the entertainment industry, accompanied by a list of suspect associations and organizations to which that person was attached. These "blacklists" expanded to target those who worked in government, education, and the professions. The listings were consulted by potential employers, and dark and murky insinuations made those listed unemployable. Nor did the administration ever discouraged such private compilations or FBI listings.

This background, with its regular anti-radical rituals, served as context for the Fifties and for the maintenance of that "the fog of public excitement [which] obscures the ancient landmarks set up in our Bill of Rights" that Justice Douglas alluded to in his Douds dissent. It was the setting for Eisenhower's selection of Earl Warren to succeed Fred Vinson who had suddenly died of a heart attack in September 1953. The nominee, the former Governor of California, did not have an entirely blameless record, for one, having pursued "Communistic radicals" and signed into law a State loyalty oath for all public employees. But Warren was an old-line Progressive Republican, unlike Fred Vinson who had more often than not tilted toward governmental authority. Though hardly a great common-law judge, it should be acknowledged that Warren met a requirement of the moment; namely, the Court's need for the skill of a statesman to repair the damage done to its prestige under his predecessor.

In his sixteen years as Chief Justice, Warren's leadership eventually produced a revolution in the constitutional law of race relations, criminal justice, and voting rights. Among a number of lasting legal monuments to Warren, we will presently learn, was that which broadened freedom of speech and press. In this regard, his Court would be a far remove from that of Vinson's which usually acted as an arm of the state, whereas Warren in the fullness of time demonstrated a strong disposition in favor of protected rights. It is all the more striking, to repeat, considering the repressive climate and judicial retrenchment on First Amendment protections that accompanied the nation's political shift to the right in these decades. Warren would in fact become, as G. Edward White concluded, "the only, as well as the last, liberal Chief Justice of the 20th century."[10] The tribunal that Warren joined has been described as "the most brilliant and able collection of justices who ever graced the high bench together."[11] He had been appointed Chief Justice at a time when meaningful protection of free expression had virtually collapsed under his predecessor. John Marshall Harlan, then in the Second Circuit Court of Appeals, joined Warren after Robert Jackson died in October 1954. However, Harlan was unlike his namesake, the more illustrious and more liberal grandfather who had been an outspoken dissenter and maverick on the bench. The new appointee had conservative, emotionally restrained judicial instincts, expressed in a penchant for skilled craftsmanship, proficient technical analysis, and balanced and impartial opinions. Committed to judicial restraint, Harlan was often of the same mind as Frankfurter and gave him a reliable fifth vote before Frankfurter retired in 1962.[12]

William Brennan, who came out of an immigrant Irish Catholic working class background and sat on the New Jersey Supreme Court, was another Eisenhower nominee two years later. He was surprising choice, being a Democrat and holding liberal beliefs. Although a former student of Frankfurter's at Harvard, Brennan would be drawn to Warren's personality and would become a solid member of what was evolving into a quartet of liberal activists on the bench much to Frankfurter's unhappiness, especially so when a fifth vote could be lured to the viewpoint of this bloc. However, Brennan rarely expressed an unbending rigidity of opinion. In fact, he had "an instinct for accommodation," as a former law clerk once observed and at times could skillfully win the votes of colleagues to his reading of the Constitution and would play a crucial role in bringing a majority together on centrist grounds. Even with a parade of newly appointed Republican colleagues, Brennan managed to form a majority coalition in some significant civil liberties cases. As demonstrated in his nearly thirty-four years on the High Court and in many of the 1,360 opinions bearing his name, he fiercely opposed government intrusiveness, contended that the Constitution shielded the lowliest and the defenseless against the arbitrary use of governmental power. He championed the underdog and revered the Bill of Rights which, in defending, would gradually shape him into an activist justice who, to repeat, gradually aligned himself with the Court's liberals. A pivotal figure in this bloc, Brennan would be "one of the most important defenders of free speech in the history of the court."[13]

Of the other justices, Eisenhower's next choice was a safer one—Charles Whitaker, a Missouri farm boy and a successful corporation lawyer who, like Harlan, was voted as a moderate conservative. Byron White, elevated to the Court by John Kennedy in 1963, could also be so characterized, though even more sharply right of center in matters of civil liberties where he tended to align with Harlan and Clark (both occasionally joined by Potter Stewart). In fact, his opinions could be uncompromisingly one sided and hostile to those advocating First Amendment protections. Tom Clark, a Truman appointee, his lineage was of the Texas legal and political aristocracy, an inheritance contributing to a legal–cultural perspective manifested in an unyielding political conservatism, especially when it was necessary to balance national security against protected freedoms. Potter Stewart was a "competent technician," in Leonard Levy's assessment, and for him "the technical aspects of a case dominated the greater issues from which he shied."[14]

The Warren Court numbered Douglas and Black as well, mutually supportive judicial activists who had been on the Court together for over thirty years and had served five Chief Justices. At times biting, combative, and irascible, Douglas was an alert defender of the First Amendment's guarantees of freedom of speech, press, and assembly, and reacted to violations with swiftness and passion.[15] This study needed elaborate no further than remind readers of his passionate dissent in *Dennis*, grant of a stay of execution for the Rosenbergs (convicted of espionage for the Soviet Union), efforts to persuade his colleagues to address the constitutionality of the Vietnam War. It brought down public and political wrath upon Douglas, including a movement to impeach him. In fact, on orders of Hoover, the FBI secretly scrutinized his writings, speeches, and activities. Joining him was Hugo Black, the unreconstructed New Dealer who, Wallace Mendelson rightly contends, favored the unlimited use of judicial power to further values that he cherished.[16] For him, the First Amendment was an absolute command, "beyond the reach of this government" and required absolute adherence and implementation. His position had been evolving since the Bridges' case and gradually matured into passionate opposition to the balancing concept that, after all, was incompatible with judicial absolutism. An uncompromising strict construction view of the First Amendment, his decision, was derived from a literal reading of constitutional scripture. Conforming to its textual commands, he declared in a well-known 1962 interview:

> The beginning of the First Amendment is that "Congress shall make no law .... I understand that it is rather old-fashioned and shows a slight naivete to say that 'no law' means no law.... I took an obligation to support and defend the Constitution as I understand it. And being a rather backward country fellow, I understand it to mean what the words say."[17]

Frankfurter and Jackson rounded out the current Warren Court membership. Their views have been discussed earlier at length. Frankfurter, to remind readers, generally deferred to the legislative will and intent, rejected "doctrinaire absolutism," and considered seditious utterances not to be "speech" within the meaning of the First Amendment. In a bitter letter to Justice Harlan, he wrote, "Black and company have gone mad on free speech."[18] Robert Jackson largely agreed, his enmity going back to 1946 when, following the death of Chief Justice Stone, he believed Black frustrated his hope of replacing the fallen Chief.

Courting the new Chief Justice, Frankfurter had sought to influence Warren to his predisposition for judicial restraint. At the outset, it did not appear difficult, because Warren confessedly was still "feeling [his] way." He only moved slowly, it need to be cautioned, toward the position held by the Black–Douglas–Brennan trio, as indicated in first term decisions (*Barsky v. Board* (1954), *Cole v. Young* (1956), *Galvan v. Press* (1954), and *Peters v. Hobby* (1955) in his 1957 second term) discussed below, and all revealing that the Chief Justice and the Court majority could be artful dodgers in the late Fifties, settling cases on procedural or statutory grounds rather than take on a constitutional issue. Warren, however, would eventually join the activist ranks, which led to the growing resentment by Frankfurter, his self-appointed and now spurned mentor, and to open acrimony between them. It became more pronounced after the retirement of Sherman Minton in 1956, who had been a reliable vote for Frankfurter, and who would be replaced by Brennan. Open discord prevailed two years later, in *Trop v. Dulles* (1958), as Warren shifted from the support of the government in loyalty–security cases to what Frankfurter, reverting to his position in *Dennis*, termed the "'hard core liberal' wing of the court," in a June

1957 letter to Learned Hand.[19] Potter Stewart not inaccurately summed up Frankfurter's altered view of Warren. He was, wrote Stewart, "as fickle as a high school girl. I understand ... that, when Earl Warren first came to the Court as Chief Justice, Felix was going around Washington saying. "[t]his is the greatest Chief Justice since John Marshall and maybe greater." And by the time I got here [1958], Felix Frankfurter had very much been disenchanted by the Chief Justice."[20] By now, his amour properly wounded, Frankfurter adopted a patronizing attitude toward the Warren and would assess him "as undisciplined by adequate professional learning ...." But Warren would eventually captain the one High Court in judicial history that moved in advance of the dominant popular opinion of its time.

Pronounced judicial opinions often resulted, but there were as well a roller coaster of rulings, with resort to procedural violations as the grounds for many opinions rather efforts to raise constitutional issues. *Communist Party v. SACB* (1956)[21] was a model of sorts. It was a complex and longstanding case that extended beyond the Fifties now under review. Reappearing multiple times on federal dockets, it attested to the persistent anti-communism of successive administrations. Indeed, the Court did not come to a final decision in the case until 1961, some five years later, which will be elaborated upon presently. But it is timely to briefly set forth its origins and early tortuous path through the courts in the context of the Fifties.

We have had reason previously to describe the 1950 Internal Security (McCarran) Act that provided the government with a new weapon of intimidation, namely, the section on registration. Under it, the recently established SACB would be furnished by the Justice Department with the names of those belonging to organizations that sought "to alter the form of government by unconstitutional means" and designated as "communist action" and "communist front." The Board could then hold hearings and order those subpoenaed to register their organization. In November 1950, Attorney General Howard McGrath, pursuant to Section 13 of the Act, petitioned the Board for a directive requiring the CP to register as a "Communist-action" organization. The Party filed suit in the D.C. District Court to enjoin the Board from proceeding.[22] Denied preliminary relief from the SACB registration order, petitioners filed a second injunctive suit that was also dismissed. Hearings began before a three-member panel of Board members in April 1951 and did not close until July 1952. In support of his petition for registration, the Attorney General had called twenty-two witnesses to give testimony before the Board, nineteen of whom had once been Party members, and nine had joined or rejoined the Party as a result of conferences with the FBI. Of those ex-communists, three of them would admit to having committed perjury in earlier testimony. The Attorney General did not deny the perjury allegations against them, though arguing that the SACB hearing record was sufficient to sustain the registration request, regardless of the testimony of the trio in question. In April 1953, the Board agreed, finding that "petitioner was substantially directed, dominated, and controlled by the Soviet Union, which controls the world Communist movement ... and that [petitioner] operates primarily" to advance the Kremlin's ends. Hence the Board's determination that the CPUSA was obligated to register under the 1950 statute as a "Communist-action" organization and to open its records to government investigators beginning litigation that consumed over a decade.

Counsel for the CP then turned to the D.C. Court of Appeals, and the appellate decision of December 1954 overruled all its objections to the statute and to the Board's registration orders. Petitioner's plea for rehearing was denied, as would be its motion to introduce additional evidence before the Board; and Judge E. Barrett Prettyman for a three-judge bench affirmed the "ultimate finding of the Board." In effect, he endorsed that most familiar refrain, repeated in the government Brief, that is, "that the USSR substantially ... dominated" America's CP and "controls the world communist movement referred to in Section Two of the Act."[23] In its opinion upholding the SACB finding that petitioner represented a "communist-action" organization, the Appellate Court admitted "that this statute will interfere with freedoms of speech and assembly .... The registration and sanctions provisions will create restrictions upon what otherwise might be a wider latitude of expression." But—and what followed was the preordained "but," and then the litany—"the right to free expression ceases at the point where it leads to harm to the government.... That point is 'clear and present danger,'" and then "the right of unrestricted speech gives way ...."

The defense then filed a petition for *certiorari*, arguing that the prosecution's case rested on books that had long antedated the 1950 statute: the Communist Manifesto of 1848, Stalin's Foundations of Leninism and Problems of Leninism, the American editions of the second and third volumes published, respectively in 1924 and 1926. It further contended that Section 2 of the [McCarran] Act, "on its face and as applied, violates the First Amendment"; and if the Board order were allowed to stand, "traditional American liberties, already severely restricted, can scarcely survive." The government Brief, presented by Solicitor General Simon Soboloff, also went over the earlier grounds that informed its response to plaintiff's Petition. It reaffirmed the statute's constitutionality, rejecting defense contentions that the Board registration order countered the Fifth Amendment's prohibition against compulsory self-incrimination or its due process clause.

In Court conferences in March 1956, much as he argued in November 1955, Warren claimed that the statute violated the First Amendment as well as the Fifth. Burton thought that Congress "went overboard .... This is an attempt to abolish the Communist Party." But Minton sharply demurred: "Congress had found what everyone around this table should admit—what the Communist Party is. I'd rather have a little of my liberty chipped away today than have it all taken away tomorrow."[24] Troubled by the "diverse rhetoric" of his colleagues, Frankfurter, as could be predicted, searched for ways to avoid constitutional questions when deciding whether the CP could be forced to register. He seized upon District Court testimony that showed three prosecutorial witnesses had perjured themselves when appearing before the SACB. The case, he successfully argued, should be remanded—to determine whether the Party was actually engaged in subversive activities; and wrote to his judicial brethren on April 2, 1956, "after considerable reflection, and with great reluctance, [I have concluded] that the case must now be disposed of exclusively on [that] ground without reaching the constitutional validity of this act."[25] "The untainted administration of justice is certainly one of the most cherished aspects of our institution," and the Court majority, in a six-to-three ruling, agreed with him.[26]

In short, midway through the judicial story of this case, the High Court majority would again reverse the Court of Appeals and once again remanded the case for a further evidentiary finding. The SACB then held additional meetings, carefully described by Milton Konvitz, that expunged the testimony of the three discredited witnesses and reaffirmed its initial findings in a shortened report.[27] Three years after this second appellate court decision and a tortuous eleven years after the proceedings had been initiated, the case, *Communist Party v. SACB*, reappeared on the High Court's docket in 1961.[28] It is not timely to pursue the details and outcome of the case at this point. That will be undertaken in a later chapter dealing with the Sixties. Suffice now simply to note that Frankfurter for a narrow majority would uphold the registration order and sotto voce, the 1950 statute itself. It should be noted that his opinion was related to the fifteen-year government effort since the 1950 statute to find a "willing volunteer" who would register the CP as a "Communist front" organization. It was an almost impossible task, as would be confirmed by the case of *Albertson v. SACB* in 1965,[29] comments on which are now also deferred.

Even before 1954, a few cases relating to the Fifth Amendment reached the Vinson Court, two of which were *Blau v. United States* (1951) and *Rogers v. United States* (1951).[30] In the first, Patricia Blau had been subpoenaed as a witness before a federal grand jury in Denver. She invoked the privilege against self-incrimination when questioned about the CP of Colorado and her employment in it. Her privilege claim being rejected, she was found guilty of contempt of court and given a one-year prison term. The Appeals Court affirmed conviction, but the High Court reversed, temporarily relenting from its largely pusillanimous past record in challenging state and federal legislative practices. Speaking for a unanimous Court, Justice Black upheld Blau's right to take the Fifth Amendment privilege against self-incrimination before a grand jury and refusal to testify concerning her CP activities. Coerced into admitting the knowledge of such activity, he argued, would promptly subject the individual to prosecution under the criminal felony provision of the Smith Act. Coerced self-incrimination, moreover, also violated the Fifth Amendment. In a related second case, that of her husband, Irving Blau, the High Court reversed the contempt conviction arising out of his refusal to tell the Denver grand jury about the activities and records of the Colorado Communist Party, doing so on the basis of the Court's opinion in the Patricia Blau case.

The Vinson Court arrived at a different and harsher conclusion the following year in *Rogers v. United States* (1951). Jane Rogers, an associate of Blau, was subpoenaed by a federal grand jury in Denver, and under interrogation admitted that she had been the treasurer of the Colorado CP and, therefore, that she had possessed membership lists and records of due payments. No longer treasurer at the time of the inquiry, she refused to give the name of her successor, to whom she had given the Party records, and invoked the privilege against self-incrimination, adding: "I don't feel that I should subject a person or persons to the same thing that I'm going through." Charged with contempt, she was given a four-month jail term by the trial court, a sentence upheld by the Tenth Circuit Court of Appeals and then by the Chief Justice, speaking for the majority, took the procedural route. Having admitted her CP activities, she could not invoke the privilege when asked about Party records. Nor could "refusal to answer ... be justified by a desire to protect others from punishment ...."

The Fifth Amendment was also pivotal to *Ullmann v. United States*,[31] a 1956 case that revolved around the 1954 Immunity Act. Ullmann, invoking the privilege against self-incrimination, refused to answer questions put to him in grand jury proceedings regarding his knowledge of espionage and conspiracy to commit espionage or regarding his membership or that of others in the Communist Party. The District Court upheld the 1954 statute and issued an order directing him to testify. His repeated refusal resulted in a conviction of contempt of court and a jail sentence. Petitioner then attacked the constitutionality of the statute in the Second Circuit Court of Appeals, but this tribunal affirmed the trial court judgment. Justice Frankfurter delivered the Supreme Court's opinion, upholding the statutory requirement that witnesses testify in national security cases.

The federal loyalty program was again in front and center in the early Fifties. The first major challenge to Executive Order 9835, in *Bailey v. Richardson* (1951),[32] centered on Dorothy Bailey, a low-level civil employee of the Federal Security Agency (FSA) who, assigned to draw up training manuals for the Department of Labor, had no access to classified information. She had been the anti-communist leader of her local of the United Public Workers (UPW). But the union itself was included on the Attorney General's list as "Communist-dominated"; and Bailey's prominence in the union local sparked an anonymous accusation by undisclosed FBI informants that she belonged to the Communist Party. In her meeting with the Regional Review Board (of the Civil Service Commission), which heard these charges, Bailey was questioned about her contacts with a number of alleged Communists, her ties to several left-wing groups, including those not on the Attorney General's list, as well as her opinions on a range of domestic, political, and international affairs. Answering all questions of the Board, including an admission that she attended one Communist meeting in Philadelphia in 1932, while a graduate student at Bryn Mawr, Bailey testified as well to holding positions contrary to those of the Communist Party. The Loyalty Review Board chairman admitted, "I have not the slightest knowledge as to who they were," referring to the anonymous accusers and hence could not evaluate the reliability of their testimony. These informants had not testified under oath, and they had not appeared in person or submit affidavits. Nor did the Review Board know the identity of the FBI agents who interviewed them or who relayed the second-hand accusations in a secret report to the Board. No one testified against her and she was never allowed to see the incriminating evidence. Despite the haphazard and highly questionable character of the proceedings—the unsworn, secret evidence, the absence of specific charges, and the testimony submitted by unnamed persons—the Board advised the FSA that "reasonable grounds" existed that she was "disloyal to the United States" and discharge from government service followed.

Upon dismissal, Bailey carried a civil action to the District of Columbia Circuit Court of Appeals for a declaratory judgment of reinstatement. It found that the transcript "consists entirely of evidence in her favor." However, it refused to challenge the government's contention that it would be prejudicial to national security to reveal the identity of appellant's accusers or even specific details of the charges because that might enable her to infer who made them. It denied her claims and held that the right to work for the government was not a right but a privilege, one that could be withdrawn at any time and for any reason. And it rejected the defense contention that the First Amendment prohibited dismissal because of political beliefs. In a brief *per curiam* opinion, Justice Clark not participating, the Supreme Court split (four-to-four), thereby upholding the lower court decision. "[T]he President… may remove from Government service any person of whose loyalty he is not completely convinced." In effect, writes the notable legal scholar, David Cole, it provided yet another instance of persons penalized for their political beliefs and associations by being discharged from their jobs and blacklisted for suspected association with or membership in the Communist Party; and having no regard as to whether they engaged in an any illegal activities and without a chance to confront their accusers.[33]

Before turning to *Joint Anti-Fascist Refugee Committee v. McGrath* (1951),[34] a case of the same year as *Bailey* and one arising out of the Attorney General's proscribed lists of "Communist front" organization, a backward look at the appellate court in *Barsky v. United States* (1948)[35] warrants mention for a number of reasons: (1) Edward Barsky, a New York City physician, was national chairman of JAFRC; (2) the decision was further testimony to the durability of America's anti-radicalism, and the longstanding troubles of another beleaguered left-of-center defendant; (3) Barsky's judicial and administrative travail is a tale for the times, the sage of one man caught up in an intricate legal web; and (4) one aspect involved a challenge to the constitutionality of the HUAC investigatory powers, rather than to the Attorney General and his listings.

Indicative of the unforgiving character of government, Barsky would be subject to three federal court cases extending over a half-dozen years. He had been prominent among those who provided medical help to wounded soldiers on the Loyalist side during the bloody Spanish Civil War. Following his return to medical practice, he became head of the JAFRC, which had been established in 1939 by the Veterans of the Lincoln Brigade, whose members had fought against the Nationalist forces of General Francisco Franco during the conflict in Spain, and which organization now offered medical and financial support for those who fled that country after Franco's victory. The dogged pursuit of the Committee is suggested by the more than seventy volumes of files devoted to it in the FBI archives. The HUAC investigation began with a subpoena of sixteen of its officers, including Dr. Barsky. Legitimately concerned that many Committee contributors had relatives in Spain whose lives could be endangered if their names became public, he refused the HUAC demand to turn over "all books, ledgers, records and papers relating to the receipt and disbursement of money" by the JAFRC, "together with all correspondence and memoranda of communications by any means whatsoever with persons in foreign countries ...." All those subpoenaed appeared at this HUAC hearing, but without the subpoenaed documents. Barsky was bombarded by less-than-credible questions about the organization's purposes and innuendo about his suspected Communist associations. Remaining stoically unwilling to respond, he would be one of the eleven Committee officers then convicted of contempt by a jury in the District of Columbia District Court, receiving a six-month prison term and a fine of $500.

In 1948, Barsky took his contempt-of-Congress case to the D.C. Court of Appeals, precipitating a legal challenge to the constitutionality of HUAC. The three-judge panel hearing the appeal acknowledged that for a congressional committee to inquire into belief and affiliation was an intrusion upon the First Amendment. However, in a clear example of judicial thinking at the time, Judge E. Barrett Prettyman speaking for Judge Bennett Champ Clark declared: "In our view, it would be sheer folly as a matter of governmental policy for an existing government to refrain from inquiry into potential threats to its existence or security until danger was clear and present."[36] The logical conclusion: "Congress had power to make the inquiry." Petitioners then appealed to the High Court, but it denied *certiorari*, and their case ended at this point.

An illuminating footnote followed. Barsky's release from prison resulted in an extension of his troubles rather than the end of them and indicated that the widespread intolerance generated by the Red Scare had penetrated into unexpected venues. Licensed to practice medicine in New York State, and seeking to do so upon obtaining his freedom, he was given a hearing before a three-physician subcommittee of the Department of Education's Medical Committee on Grievances, and subjected to the familiar inquisitional questioning about the Justice Department's listing of his organization. The State's officer reasoned: "I think this committee is entitled to know whether this organization is listed ... as being subversive and Un-American ..." Repeated inquiries along these lines convey the flavor of the astringent methods employed at the then current investigatory hearings. As expected, Barsky was found guilty as charged and received a three-month suspension from the practice of medicine, a decision unanimously upheld by a full Medical Grievance Committee of ten doctors.

The egregious narrative continued. Seeking review of this determination in the Supreme Court for the County of Albany, his case was transferred to the State's Appellate Division, where he argued that the State Board of Regents had no right to suspend his license. But the issue was settled adversely for him, the Albany Court affirming the order of the Board of Regents. The Appellate Court majority held that Barsky's rights "had not been violated or denied." For the record, his conviction was upheld not because of membership in a listed organization but for the contempt of Congress.

Early Warren Court opinions were similar to those of the Vinson Court in a number of cases, including the decision in *Barsky v. United States*. Rather than taking the high road of constitutional confrontation with Congress and the HUAC, it decided upon a middle way, resolving issues on due process grounds. In what was his first domestic security case *Barsky v. Board of Regents* (1954),[37] the Chief Justice voted with Justice Burton, who gave the opinion for the six-man majority. This decision upheld the constitutionality of Section 6514 of the State statute under which Barsky had been punished for failure to produce the JAFRC records when so ordered by the HUAC.

To continue, and in what perhaps could be considered a spurious comment on public health by Burton, given the underlying anticommunist motif tincturing the case, he declared a state "has the broad power to establish and enforce standards of conduct within its borders relative to the health of everyone there." Also, dissembling or at least avoiding the political charge that brought petitioner to the attention of State authorities, Burton simply referred to "the importance of high standards of character and law observance" the State required of its doctors. The three-man subcommittee of professionals who had heard the evidence "was not influenced by the character of the Refugee Committee," Burton naively argued, taking on face the Board of Regents shameless disavowal of concern about whether the JAFRC "was completely philanthropic in character, or whether it was engaged in subversive activities." And a further bromide concluded that its Committee on Discipline had demonstrated "a high degree of unbiased objectivity." From this high ground Burton could readily uphold the decision of New York's highest court and brusquely affirmed that the practice of medicine was a privilege, not a right.[38]

Barsky, as noted, also had a central role in *the aforementioned Joint Anti-Fascist Refugee Committee* case.[39] This case may be traced back to the 1950 Internal Security Act and the loyalty program, with its arbitrary listing of Communist "front" groups by Attorney General McGrath. Without notice or hearing, three organizations—the JAFRC, the International Workers Order (IWO), a fraternal benefit society, and the National Council for American–Soviet Friendship—had been classified as "Communist Front." Counsel for JAFRC argued in its complaint that the JAFRC was "a charitable organization engaged in relief work," raising and dispensing funds "for the relief of anti-Fascist [Spanish] refugees ... and other anti-fascists who fought in the war against Franco," and who now were encamped primarily in Southern France. Counsel for the IWO complainant declared that the organization was in the fraternal insurance business, specializing in low-cost insurance for its members, and government actions had caused many members to resign and potential members refusing to join. All three organizations had been denied licenses to solicit funds and their federal tax exemptions had been revoked. Counsel for the JAFRC argued that petitioners had been deprived of their rights under the First and Fifth Amendments and that they were suffering irreparable damage, and they requested declaratory and injunctive relief. The Justice Department Brief argued that the Attorney General's listing was a "political" act of the President, in pursuit of his constitutional power to protect the nation, and "beyond the control of any other branch of the Government ..." It petitioned for dismissal of the JAFRC complaints, which the D.C. District Court granted.

Petitioners then took their case to the Supreme Court. In a five-to-three opinion (Justice Clark abstaining), their complaints were upheld, but for reasons so discrete that the Court offered no single majority ruling; that is, each of the five justices filed separate opinions. The *per curiam* opinion in *Bailey*, though succinct, intimated what the judicial divisions would be in the JAFRC case. Similar to majority contentions in both *Dennis* and *C.P. v. SACB*, the JAFRC majority opinion, a lengthy one written by Justice Burton, took a narrowly technical view of the case. Admitting that the case "bristled with constitutional issues," he, however, sought to avoid them and would dispose of the case on procedural grounds: the Attorney General's actions were "patently arbitrary."

The majority opinion deserves elaboration because it further enhances our appreciation of the pull of anti-communist fears and influences that moved the judiciary and the administration. The Court, Justice Burton stated, had to determine whether the Attorney General was authorized to include these three organizations "in a list designated by him as Communist and furnished by him to the Loyalty Review Board," which procedure had been established "under authority of the Executive Order [Truman's Executive Order 9835]." He observed that "[t]he designation of these organizations was not preceded by any administrative hearing" before calling them "subversive"; and they "received no notice that they were being listed, had no opportunity to present evidence on their own behalf and were not informed of the evidence on which their designations rest." Creditably recognizing that the designation stigmatized organizations, Burton termed it "defamation" by the government. In fact, he displayed a considerable sensitivity to the negative possible impact of the Attorney General's actions: they would "cripple the functioning and damage the reputation of those organizations." and plaintiffs' arguments have "sufficient charge that such acts violate each complaining organization's common-law right to be free from defamation." However, equivocating, he ingenuously declared: "We cannot impute such an attempt to the Nation's highest law enforcement officer any more than we can to the President." Continuing with what was an inherently contradictory opinion, Burton forcefully stated: the Attorney General's allegations do not state facts from which a reasonable determination can be derived that the organizations are communist and, Burton concluded that his actions were "not within the authority conferred by Executive Order no. 9835 ... [which] never has been carried so far as to permit administrative discretion to run riot." Accordingly, he denied the prosecution contention that the complaint be dismissed and would remand the case back to the District Court, which was instructed to determine whether the complaining organizations were indeed communist.

Notes

1. David Caute, *The Great Fear. The Anti-Communist Purge under Truman and Eisenhower* (New York: Simon & Schuster, 1978), 200–5. *United States v. Foster, et al.*, 79 F. Supp. 422 (S.D.N.Y. 1948).
2. Petitioners in *Dennis v. United States* had been defendants in a number of cases directly before or issuing from *Dennis v. United States* e.g., *United States v. Foster*, 80 F. Supp. 479 (S.D.N.Y. 1948); *United States v. Gates*, 176 F.2d 78 (2d Cir. 1949); *United States v. Hall*, 101 F. Supp. 666 (S.D.N.Y. 1951); *Williamson et al. v. United States*, 184 F.2d 280 (2d Cir. 1950); *Davis v. Impelliteri*, 197 Misc. 162, 94 N.Y.S.2d 159 (1950).
3. The Courts were riddled with cases arising after defendants invoked the privilege when asked about the CP and their knowledge of it. For example, *Alexander v. United States*, 181 F.2d 480 (9th Cir. 1950), which reversed convictions of ten appellants who had invoked the Fifth Amendment before a Los Angeles Grand Jury. Then, too, there is *Kasinowitz v. United States*, 181 F.2d 632 (9th Cir. 1950); *Healey v. United States*, 186 F.2d 164 (9th Cir. 1950); *Doran v. United States*, 181 F.2d 489 (9th Cir. 1950). For two instances, where witnesses before the HUAC invoked the Fifth Amendment, see *Quinn v. United States*, 203 F.2d 20 (D.C. Cir. 1952) and *United States v. Fitzpatrick*, 96 F. Supp. 491 (D. D.C. 1951).
4. Thomas Emerson, *The System of Freedom of Expression* (New York: Random House, 1970), 171.
5. Athan Theoharis, *Spying on Americans: Political Surveillance from Hoover to the Huston Plan* (Philadelphia, PA: Temple University Press, 1978), 48. On the "numerous illegal tactics" of the FBI, see also Michael Linfield, *Freedom Under Fire: U.S. Civil Liberties in Times of War* (Boston, MA: South End Press, 1990),134–6; and Robert J. Goldstein, *Political Repression in Modern America* (Cambridge, MA: Schenkman Publishing Group, 1978), 244.
6. Theoharis, 136. For a further description of COINTELPRO, and its programs that continued into the 1960s, see Frank Donner, Age of Surveillance: *The Aims and Methods of America's Political Intelligence System* (New York: Vintage Books, 1981), 178.
7. Quoted in Goldstein, *Political Repression in Modern America*, 329. See also Peter Steinberg, *The Great "Red Menace": United States Prosecution of American Communists, 1947–1952* (Westport, CT: Greenwood, 1984), 206.
8. 68 Stat. 775 (1954).
9. 73 Stat. 522, 536–7 (1959).
10. G. Edward White, *Earl Warren, A Public Life* (New York: Oxford University Press, 1982), 341–4.

11. Quoted in Bernard Schwartz, *Super Chief: Earl Warren and His Supreme Court, A Judicial Bibliography* (New York: New York University Press, 1983), 49.
12. Ibid., 124–5.
13. David Savage, *Guide to the U.S. Supreme Court* (Washington, DC: Congressional Quarterly, 1997), 10–11. See also Jeffrey Rosen, "We Hardly Know When We See It," in *Reason and Passion. Justice Brennan's Enduring Legacy*, eds E. Joshua Rosenkranz and Bernard Schwartz (New York: W. W. Norton & Co., 1997), 71.
14. "Preciseness, conciseness, and directness were Stewart's strengths. He wrote not for posterity, but only to settle the issue at hand in as constricted a way as he could find." Leonard Levy, *Against the Law: The Nixon Court and Criminal Justice* (New York: Harper & Row, 1974), 41.
15. Rodney Smolla, *Free Speech in an Open Society* (New York: Alfred A. Knopf, 1992), 23. "He rejected Frankfurter's image of the Court as a monastery and disdained what he regarded as the hypocrisy of one whom Douglas knew was anything but 'a political monk.'" (Howard Ball and Phillip Cooper, "Fighting Justices: Hugo L. Black and William O. Douglas and Supreme Court Conflict," *American Journal of Legal History* 38 (1994): 1–37.
16. In his thoughtful, scrupulously written study of Justices Black and Frankfurter, Wallace Mendelson argued that Black was an unreconstructed New Deal idealist who favored unrestrained use of judicial power to further the values he cherished. Complementing his reading of Black, Mark Silverstein held that for him, "the First Amendment was written as a command so unequivocal and so persuasive," it could not be qualified or countermanded. Mark Silverstein, *Constitutional Faiths: Felix Frankfurter, Hugo Black and the Process of Judicial Decision Making* (Ithaca, NY: Cornell University Press, 1984), 200–4.
17. Quoted in Schwartz, *Super Chief*, 59. For Black's opposition to balancing, see *Konigsberg v. State Bar of California*, 366 U.S. 36, 60–80 (1961); *Braden v. United States*, 365 U.S. 431, 441–6 (1961); *Wilkinson v. United States*, 365 U.S. 399, 422–3 (1961); *Uphaus v. Wyman*, 364 U.S. 388, 392–3 (1960); *Barenblatt v. United States*, 360 U.S. 109, 140–4 (1959).
18. Quoted in Schwartz, *Super Chief*, 60.
19. Quoted in White, *Earl Warren, A Public Life*, 181.
20. Schwartz, *Super Chief*, 183.
21. 351 U.S. 115 (1956).
22. *CPUSA v. SACB*, 223 F.2d 531, A second App. Ct. opinion (254 F.2d 314) had the same outcome, as did 102 U.S. App. D.C. 395 (1958), with the same judicial opinions expressed.
23. Ibid., 576.
24. Quoted in Schwartz, *Super Chief*, 113.
25. *SACB*, 351 U.S. at 120–1, 125; see also Schwartz, *Super Chief*, 186.
26. *SACB*, 351 U.S. at 124.
27. Milton Konvitz, *Expanding Liberties: Freedom's Gains in Postwar America* (New York: Viking Press, 1966), 143.

28. 367 U.S. 1 (1961).
29. 382 U.S. 70 (1965).
30. 340 U.S. 332 (1951); 340 U.S. 367 (1951).
31. 350 U.S. 422 (1956).
32. 341 U.S. 918 (1951).
33. David Cole, *Enemy Aliens* (New York: The New Press, 2003), 106. See *Bailey v. Richardson*, 341 U.S 918 (1951). The government's failure to produce the informant or the evidence occurred in another case, *Washington v. McGrath*, 184 F.2d 375 (D.C. Cir. 1950), and had the same outcome.
34. 341 U.S. 123 (1951).
35. 167 F.2d 241 (D.C. Cir. 1948).
36. Ibid., 246. For prior proceedings in the *Barsky* case, see *United States v. Barsky*, 72 F. Supp. 165 (D. D.C. 1947); *United States v. Bryan*, 72 Supp. 58 (D.D.C. 1947). A year later, the same tribunal decided yet another case, a joint appeal that derived from the HUAC Hollywood hearings, namely, that of John Howard Lawson and Dalton Trumbo (*Lawson v. United States*, 176 F.2d 49 (D.C. Cir. 1949). The defendants, both screenwriters, were two of ten Hollywood witnesses who refused to answer questions put to them by the House Subcommittee, including the toxic one: "Are you now or have you ever been a member of the Communist Party?" Their refusal to answer resulted in the near-automatic contempt charge and automatic conviction.
37. 347 U.S. 442 (1954).
38. Ibid., 455.
39. 341 U.S. 123 (1951).

10

The Warren Court: The Cloudy Judicial Landscape

Appointed Chief Justice in 1953, Warren inherited a tribunal only fitfully prepared to support freedom of expression when confronted by measures purporting to combat the communist menace. As *Dennis*, *Douds*, *Adler*, inter alia tell us, the judicial majority had abandoned the field of protected expression. Not that these Court decisions indicate an unqualified story of abdication and surrender. Though a few notable exceptions may be cited before 1963 when Frankfurter retired, they were infrequent. *Blau*, for one, did recognize that a witness could claim the privilege against self-incrimination when questioned about Communist Party membership. The *JAFRC* decision held that an organization could not be stigmatized as "Communist Front" without a hearing. There were other instances when early Warren Court decisions countered the sustained anti-radical fervor of the day, in opinions on state anti-subversion measures for one.

State loyalty oaths for public service jobs remained the prescription for seemingly interminable litigation and lengthy judicial briefs, most affirming the constitutionality of the statutes, at least into the early Fifties. (And thereafter, the Court overturned state loyalty oaths, though not on First Amendment grounds.) *Gerende v. Board of Supervisors of Elections* (1951)[1] was typical. Decided on the same day as *Dennis*, *Gerende* found the Vinson Court reinforcing *Douds* and its conclusion that some oath requirements were not unconstitutional. Justice Clark's per curiam decision affirmed the judgment of Maryland's Court of Appeals and unanimously upheld a loyalty oath provision of the State's Ober Act (1949) mandating that any candidate for municipal office make affidavit "that he is not a person who is engaged 'in one way or another' in the attempt to overthrow the government by force or violence," and that "he is not knowingly a member of an organization engaged in such an attempt." Judicial unanimity may be explained by observing that the Maryland oath was restricted to "knowing" membership, and by "engaged in," words implying immediacy.

One High Court case derived from New York State law, *Adler v. Board of Education of City of New York* (1952),[2] illustrates Douglas' later acerbic claim that his colleagues were also running "with the hounds."[3] Irving Adler and five other teachers had brought suit challenging the right of the New York City's Board of Education to dismiss them for refusal to answer questions at a Board hearing. On appeal to the New York State Supreme Court, at Special Term, plaintiffs would be upheld, the lower court judgment reversed, and Ch. 310 of the 1949 "Laws" (that included the Feinberg Act) declared unconstitutional. Two Sections (12-a and 3022) of the statute, it ruled, violated the due process clause of the Fourteenth Amendment. The State's Attorney General then appealed to the Appellate Division of the State Supreme Court that restored the trial court decision and affirmed the constitutionality of the 1949 "Laws."[4]

Appellate Court Judge Lewis, in reversing the State Supreme Court, found the Feinberg Act constitutional: "the Feinberg Law is neither an unreasonable or arbitrary exercise of the police power" and does not "unwarrantably infringe upon any constitutional right of free speech, assembly or association." Unpacking the incantatory pronouncements familiar to all the nation's courts, he charged that those advocating forcible overthrow of the government, "particularly [members] of the Communist Party," had infiltrated the public schools, "despite the statutes designed to prevent such actions," and that to avert such infiltration "the Board of Regents should be directed to meet the menace by affirmative action." On his dismissal of the complaint, petitioners appealed to the High Court.

Justice Sherman Minton's ruling was consistent with judicial voices everywhere. Delivering the six-man majority opinion in *Adler*, he waved off the First Amendment argument of the petitioners and upheld the constitutionality of the challenged Section 3022. Further, he ruled that a teacher, "works in a sensitive area," where he "shapes the attitude of young minds toward the society in which they live," and the state has a vital interest in protecting "the schools from pollution."[5] Consequently, school authorities have the right to "screen the officials, teachers, and employees as to their fitness to maintain the integrity of the schools." And necessary to any review was "one's associates, past and present, as well as one's conduct," since "from time immemorial, one's reputation has been determined in part by the company he keeps."[6] *Adler* serves as a model to highlight how courts everywhere in that stormy time reflected public and official thinking that the United States was involved in an apocalyptic struggle against an implacable enemy.

Beilan v Board of Public Education (1958)[7] offers another example. Though the Fifth rather than the First Amendment came into play on this occasion, the case also involved a schoolteacher, Herman Beilan who had taught in the Philadelphia public school system for twenty-two years. He was called before a Subcommittee of HUAC on November 18, 1953, and questioned at a publicly televised hearing about alleged subversive activities in 1949 and in earlier years; and he denied ever advocating forcible overthrow of the government and, further, that he was not then a member of the Communist Party. But Beilan refused to answer questions about past membership or activities, invoking the self-incrimination privilege of the Fifth Amendment. He also would not testify about affiliations and activities in certain organizations that were put to him in private interviews by the Superintendant of Schools. His reliance on privilege would be decisive as revealed five days later when the Superintendant gave Beilan an "unsatisfactory" rating because of refusal to testify; that is, because "you invoked the Fifth Amendment" when questioned by the HUAC Subcommittee about "past associations with organizations of doubtful loyalty." After a formal hearing, the Board of Public Education in a fourteen-to-one vote concluded that Beilan's refusal to confirm or refute information and his invocation of privilege was justification for removal under the 1949 Pennsylvania Public School Code (Section 1122); and Beilan, following as adverse judicial ruling, turned to the High Court.

Justice Burton, for the five-man majority, limited his unusually brief opinion to petitioner's refusal to answer the Superintendant's questions; that is, whether, as the prosecution claimed, there was sufficient evidence of such refusal as to fall under the statutory designation of "incompetency" and thereby justify Beilan's dismissal.[8] Framing the inquiry in this way made for an easy decision, the gist of which being that competency to teach was not limited to the classroom, but touched on other factors as well. The public school teacher had obligations of candor toward his superiors and, Burton maintained, the school board's questions were relevant to petitioner's fitness. He closed with the startling judgment that "no inferences at all were drawn from petitioner's refusal to answer."[9]

Revisiting the investigation of college teachers, described earlier in the study, New York City's five municipal colleges included a number of faculties who ran afoul of the Board of Higher Education or congressional investigating committees. By June 1953, fourteen had been terminated for refusal to testify, usually before the SISS. In an expression of the national mood, roughly sixty college teachers of the 122 investigated in New York City were eventually purged. *Slochower v. Board of Higher Education of New York City* (1956)[10] provided the paradigmatic case. Harry Slochower, a tenured Associate Professor at Brooklyn College who had taught there for twenty-seven years, would be summarily dismissed on the grounds that he violated a municipal law, Section 903 of the New York City Charter. This measure required automatic discharge of any public employee who invoked the privilege against self-incrimination to avoid answering questions about beliefs or official conduct. Slochower's dismissal came after "pleading the Fifth" before the SISS, then holding hearings in New York City. The Board of Faculty seized upon his claim of privilege before the SISS, converting it into a conclusive presumption of guilt; and shortly after his hearing before the Senate Committee, he was notified of his suspension "pursuant to the provisions Section 903" of the City Charter. The Supreme Court of New York, Kings County, would uphold his summary dismissal.

Warren in conference, in October 1955, contended that the law in question "placed an unwarranted burden on these people. The premise [of the measure] is that the [self-incrimination] plea is one of guilt, and this is violative of the Constitution." Frankfurter argued that the case could be decided on due process grounds; that is, the New York City law violated due process because it assumed guilt whenever the claim of privilege was invoked. It was a realistic position, considering that the term, "Fifth Amendment Communist," was an epithet influencing tribunals across the country and had become a permanent fixture in the public mind.

Five justices, speaking surprisingly through Clark, who deserted his conservative cohort in this instance, held for the majority that the New York City law was unconstitutional, a deprivation of liberty and property under the due process clause of the Fourteenth Amendment. The measure's "heavy hand" had presumed guilt and resulted in automatic dismissal of any city employee who invoked a "constitutional privilege," namely, the Fifth Amendment, with no consideration given to the subject matter of the questions; and furthermore, Clark argued that these questions were "wholly unrelated to his [Slochower's] college functions." Membership in certain organizations was not a standard for employability—in that the membership might be "innocent," and classifying the innocent and guilty together was arbitrary. Finally, under the Fourteenth Amendment, courtesy of the Fifth Amendment, a person's "constitutional right not to testify" extends to a public employee whose discharge was "patently arbitrary." To assert such a "right may not be considered an admission of or presumption of guilt and may not be so interpreted."[11] Dismissal could only be for cause. In 1957, it followed, a judicial majority was in the process of refurbishing the Fifth and Fourteenth as well as the First Amendment.

Revisiting legal challenges to state laws, *Speiser v. Randall* (1958),[12] originated in yet another punitive measure, a 1953 amendment to California's Constitution that had provided special tax immunity for veterans. The amendment prohibited such tax benefits to any person who advocated violent overthrow of the government or "the support of a foreign government in event of hostilities"; and a loyalty oath to this effect was appended to the property tax form. The petitioners, being two veterans (Lawrence Speiser and Daniel Prince), had applied for the standard veteran's tax exemption and were denied it after refusing to sign the oath. The Court majority, Brennan speaking for seven justices (Warren not participating and Clark dissenting), considered the scheme unconstitutional, because it placed the burden of proof on those who wished to exercise First Amendment rights. The State should have the burden—of showing that the person was disloyal, or in any event that he was a demonstrable security risk.[13] California's practice, in Brennan's words, "can only result in a deterrence of speech which the Constitution set free." In ordinary tax cases, he acknowledged, the Court had regularly upheld procedures requiring taxpayers, when challenged by collectors, to prove the accuracy of their own declarations. In this instance, however, "the transcendent value of speech was involved." For him, the chill placed on First Amendment by the State procedure was a direct inhibition on speech. "[A] discriminatory denial of a tax exemption for engaging in speech is a limitation of free speech."

The outcome in *Wieman v. Updegraff* (1952),[14] was also a judicial surprise in a decade when public employment was made contingent upon taking a loyalty oath. On this occasion, it was the State of Oklahoma that made it a condition of employment and required explicitly for those employed at the Oklahoma Agricultural and Mechanical College. The statute, entirely representative of many state measures stipulated, inter alia, that employment in the public sector required that one was not and had never been a member of "the Communist Party ..., or of any other party, organization, association, or group whatever" listed by the Attorney General as "communist front" or "subversive."[15] The employee also had to pledge not to "advocate directly or indirectly, teach or justify by any means whatsoever, the overthrow of the Government of the United States or of this State, or change the form of Government thereof by force or any unlawful means."

The defendant, one of two Oklahoma taxpayers, brought suit in the District Court of Oklahoma County, attacking the validity of the act on a number of grounds, including violation of the due process clause of the Fourteenth Amendment. The court upheld the statute and found that appellants had "willfully refused to take the oath and by reason thereof the Board of Regents is enjoined from paying them, and their employment is terminated." The defendants then appealed to the highest State court, which justified the statute's purpose—"to make loyalty a qualification to hold public office or be employed by the State"—and denied their petition for a rehearing.

Garner, Adler, and Gerende had been a formidable trio of precedents sustaining the loyalty oath as a vehicle by which alleged "subversives" could be barred from public service. Once again the issue was before the Court. Justice Clark, speaking for his colleagues in *Wieman*, upheld petitioners' claim in what Brennan described as "richly colored and impassioned hyperbole." As the *Speiser* opinion and the emergence of four dissenters in *Garner* indicate, Clark's decision reflected a growing trend on the tribunal to question the wisdom of test oaths. It failed to discuss the State's use of the Attorney General's list or define the words "front" and "subversive" in the Oklahoma statute, or to explain why the ruling differed from *Garner* that Clark had upheld by judicial fiat a year earlier. But he did recognize that the State measure was patently tied to the principle of "guilt by association," a device "stifling the flow of democratic expression ..."[16] Therefore, Clark ruled, "constitutional protection does extend to the public servant whose exclusion pursuant to a statute is patently arbitrary or discriminatory."

Yet another defeat for the government, a state government in this instance, *Sweezy v. New Hampshire* (1957),[17] did not originate in a challenge to the test oath, but it is included here as yet one more instance of governmental intrusion into the educational system driven by fears of communist infection. The case centered on a lecture that Paul Sweezy, a well-known Marxist writer, had given at the University of New Hampshire. When confronted by the State's Attorney General, "a one-man legislative committee," he denied membership in the Communist Party. Sweezy was also questioned about his activities in the short-lived Progressive Party of 1948–49 and the contents of his lecture on socialism. Refusing to answer on the grounds that the questions "infringed upon the inviolability of the right to privacy ...," he was cited for contempt.

The High Court reversed the conviction, Chief Justice Warren writing for three others, with two concurrences. He emphasized "[t]he essentiality of freedom in the community of American universities ... Teachers and students must always remain free to inquire, to study and to evaluate ...."[18] Placing the value of academic speech on a higher "scale of values" than the State's security interests, he held that the Attorney General lacked the authority to ask such questions. Frankfurter in concurrence invoked the balancing theory much as the Court had in *Dennis*, weighing New Hampshire's right to self-protection against the protected speech guaranteed by the First Amendment. The balance, he now affirmed, was struck in favor of the First Amendment and concluded that there would be "grave harm resulting from government intrusion into the intellectual life of a university."[19]

In *Shelton v. Tucker* (1960),[20] the "personal rights" mentioned in *Sweezy* did not carry the same weight though the case also occurred in the field of education. The familiar loyalty oath in Arkansas required every teacher in a State-supported school to file an annual affidavit listing all organizations one belonged to or contributed to in the previous five years. Its purpose was to expose those involved in or sympathetic to the NAACP. In an opinion that continued the process of whittling away at the number and scope of state loyalty oaths, Justice Stewart for the majority struck down the statute as overbroad. It was "pursued by means that broadly stifle fundamental personal liberties," and was "a comprehensive interference with associational freedom."[21]

Notwithstanding *Speiser*, *Wieman*, *Sweezy*, and *Shelton*, Warren's full term did not signal any sharp turn from the general trend of the Vinson Court majority, with its failure to exhibit any principled convictions about infringements upon First Amendment rights. In his first two years, the Chief Justice largely avoided controversial legal questions and was only gradually drawn toward the views of Black and Douglas. The movement toward their position, though fitful, did become apparent even in Warren's first term, in the 1955 companion cases of *Emspak v. United States* and *Quinn v. United States*,[22] which arose out of petitioners' refusal to answer questions before the HUAC concerning Communist Party membership. In these cases, the Warren Court would in some measure reduce the universal scorn attached to "taking the Fifth" and to being a "Fifth Amendment Communist." But no radical turn to the left should be imputed.

Jules Emspak and Thomas Quinn, officers in a communist-line electrical union (the United Electrical Workers), were called before a one-man Subcommittee of the HUAC investigating Communist infiltration of labor unions in defense plants. Emspak had filed a non-communist oath affidavit under the Taft–Hartley Act, and the NLRB general counsel announced that this filing was being referred to the Department of Justice for investigation. Emspak was then subpoenaed by HUAC, appearing before it on December 5, 1949. Of the 239 questions asked, about his past and about other union officials, Emspak declined to answer 68, including 8 concerning his alleged Communist Party membership and activities, and 58 about other persons charged with having Communist affiliations and whether they had ever been union officials. Emspak refused to answer them "primarily" on "First Amendment grounds, supplemented by the Fifth," for which refusal he was indicted and convicted on sixty-eight counts and sentenced to six months imprisonment by the D.C. District Court.

In argument before the Court, the government claimed that Congress may constitutionally inquire "into the communist membership of leaders of a particular union who are believed to have access to significant defense information." In rebuttal, the defense Petition forcefully stated: "Surely the Court cannot ignore the fact that the obtaining of information for legislative purposes ... has become a hollow pretext for the compilation of a vast INDEX EXPURGATORIUS, the systematic destruction of political dissent and the invasions of privacy." The Petition continued:"We have reached the stage where a "clearance" from the Committee is often indispensable to one's livelihood, career and good name. The assertion by Congress of these powers to sit in political judgment must be reviewed by this Court."

The pivotal issue in both *Emspak* and *Quinn* turned upon the procedural question of whether they had clearly asserted the privilege against self-incrimination before the Subcommittee. The prosecutors' Brief maintained that neither petitioner had used the proper combination of words to invoke the privilege. Rather, their Brief contended, petitioners had stated their position in "muffled terms" in an attempt to "obtain the benefit of the privilege without incurring the popular opprobrium which often attaches to its exercise," namely, being labeled "Fifth Amendment Communists."

The Court chose the less direct and courageous procedural route when commenting on petitioner's refusal to answer Subcommittee questions about alleged Party membership on grounds of privilege, decided it would not deal too technically with the form in which a witness invoked the Fifth Amendment, and Warren asserted that a privilege against self-incrimination "cannot be ignored simply because it was not phrased in orthodox manner." Petitioner, he continued, had not been informed whether his silence constituted contempt of Congress. As to the First Amendment, the Chief Justice in conference had proposed that the Court "set aside" the issue, and Black agreed to a decision on the "narrow grounds" that Warren had proposed and urged the majority "to draw a line on the powers of the committee ...". Frankfurter likewise so affirmed, writing to Harlan: "I thought and think it was right to charge these loose-mouthed, loose-mannered and loose-headed men on the Hill with a little more responsibility in the serious business of Congressional investigations."

In *Quinn*, Chief Justice Warren again spoke for the majority in overturning the conviction of a field organizer for the United Electrical Worker who, like Emspak, had refused on "the First and Fifth Amendments" grounds to answer questions about alleged membership in the Communist Party put to him before a session of a HUAC subcommittee. As in *Emspak*, the issue was whether a witness is compelled to answer or is entitled to refuse on the grounds of self-incrimination. Although acknowledging the deeply rooted power to investigate, the Chief Justice recalled that the refusal to answer was firmly established in law—in reaction to England's Star Chamber proceedings—and justifiably included among "the specific individual guarantees of the Bill of Rights, such as the Fifth Amendment's privilege against self-incrimination." The Chief Justice put the matter to rest by succinctly asserting: "In the instant case petitioner was convicted for refusing to answer the Committee's question as to his alleged membership in the Communist Party. Clearly an answer to the question might have tended to incriminate him. Consequently, petitioner was entitled to claim the privilege."[23]

Peters v. Hobby (1955)[24] of the same year revealed Warren to be more equivocal on loyalty–security matters than the *Emspak* and *Quinn* decisions indicated. John Peters, Professor of Medicine at Yale University, was a part-time Special Consultant for the U.S. Public Health Service of the Federal Security Agency, the functions of which Agency had been transferred to the Department of Health, Education and Welfare, headed by Oveta Culp Hobby a consultant on grant applications from medical research institutions; Peters was assigned work that was not considered "sensitive" and did not entail access to classified material. Under Truman's 1947 Executive Order, however, the head of every government department and agency was required "to assure that disloyal civilian officers or employees are not retained in employment ...".

Peters' past, coming under suspicion, case went through an astonishing number of turns and convolutions that revealed something of the persistent political climate in Washington and the nation. It included multiple hearings by the Federal Security Agency's Loyalty Review Board. Following one, the Board determined that "no reasonable grounds existed for belief" that Peters was disloyal. He answered all questions directed to him, and his replies, taken under oath, denied Party membership and candidly testified on the other charges, and he was cleared. At a second and third hearing, he again testified that he was not and had never been a Communist and did not know the basis for charges against him or the sources of these charges. Nor for that matter did the examiners who admitted to being unable to identify the informants against Peters. Be that as it may be, they concluded that "on all the evidence, there is reasonable doubt" as to Peters' loyalty.

Following his termination, Peters brought suit, and the Court granted *certiorari*. Though petitioner's position had not been "sensitive," the Justice Department invoked the iconic "national security" defense of its actions and would vigorously oppose the defense contention that Peters had a constitutional right to confront his accusers. Solicitor General Sobeloff refused to sign on to this effect and would break with the prosecution: the government Brief, he argued, "was inconsistent with basic Anglo-American concepts of justice." The defense team charged that Board actions were unconstitutional because petitioner was denied the opportunity to confront and cross-examine his accusers, arbitrarily branding him disloyal, "without basis in fact, and without a fair procedure and hearing,'" and without a judicial trial. And further, his counsel argued that the charges against him violated the prohibition of bills of attainder and *ex post facto* laws. Finally, it was a defense contention that dismissal solely on the basis of his political opinions violated petitioner's right to freedom of speech.

Chief Justice Warren, who delivered the seven-to-two majority opinion—Justices Reed and Burton dissenting—again took a narrow procedural approach. He found that the Board's Loyalty Review Board initiative in this instance "was plainly beyond its jurisdiction ...". Warren went on to cite *Wieman*, in which the Court had recognized that a "'badge of infamy' attaches to a public employee found disloyal," and indiscriminate charges destroying reputations were "not in the American tradition and should not be encouraged." However, much as had the Vinson Court in *Bailey*, the majority contended only with technical matters and artfully avoided constitutional questions. It would take two years before Warren was prepared to face directly constitutional issues subsumed in internal security cases.

Another notable security case, *Cole v. Young* (1956),[25] closed the 1955–1956 term. Once again relying on the procedural, it evaded the discussion of substantive constitutional issues. Unlike *Bailey* and *Peters*, plaintiff in this instance did not challenge the vagueness of the charges against him or the use of anonymous informants but rather the government's right to discharge on security grounds persons employed in non-sensitive jobs. Kenneth Cole, it need be emphasized, was hardly a risk to national security. He was a New York State food and drug inspector who had worked at tracking down harmful chemicals, insects, and the like, for the Food and Drug Administration, a branch of the Department of Health, Education and Welfare (HEW). Pursuant to Eisenhower's Executive Order 10450 (amending Truman's Executive Order 9835)—which mandated dismissal when a "reasonable doubt existed" of an employee's loyalty—Cole was summarily suspended from his position in November 1953 on charges of "a close association" with alleged communists and "a sympathetic association" with "an allegedly subversive organization" (the Nature Friends of America, which was on the Attorney General's list of "subversive" organizations). On Cole's refusal to answer these charges, the Secretary of HEW, citing the 1950 Internal Security (McCarran) Act, determined that his continued employment was not "clearly consistent with the interests of national security" and discharged him. Similar to the plaintiff in *Bailey v. Richardson* (1950) challenging the federal loyalty program five years earlier, Cole would then appeal to the District Court of the District of Columbia that held for the government and dismissed the complaint, and the Court of Appeals would affirm trial court's decision.

The High Court granted *certiorari* and agreed with petitioner. In an exacting, highly technical legal opinion typical of him, Harlan spoke for six colleagues in finding that Congress, in its Internal Security Act, had not authorized summary discharge of civil service workers in "non-sensitive" positions. Harlan's opinion rested there. Similar to the outcome in *Peters*, that is, it avoided constitutional issues and confined the majority's opinion to a narrow statutory interpretation. The question before the Court, he stated, was to determine whether petitioner's position "would affect the 'national security'" as the term appeared in two executive orders and in the 1950 statute, Public Law 733. Wrestling near-endlessly with these talismanic words, believing their precise definition pivotal to the case, he concluded: "[W]e think ... [national security] was intended to comprehend only those activities ... directly concerned with the protection of the Nation from internal subversion or foreign aggression ..." The term did not apply to "all positions in the Government," only to "sensitive positions," and being a food and drug inspector the petitioner, was not in this category.[26] In view of the "stigma attached to persons dismissed on loyalty grounds," Harlan declared, this Court "will not lightly assume" that the lawmakers intended to abolish usual procedural safeguards on a sweeping non-selective basis. Assessing the opinion, Robert McCloskey, consistent with his customary skepticism, believed that the judicial majority had endowed Congress with questionable "presumptive good intentions."

It is evident that Warren in these years lacked finished convictions regarding protected expression, a judgment confirmed by cases that followed the *Cole* decision. Consider, for one, *Lerner v. Casey* (1958),[27] in which the defendant, Max Lerner, was a New York City subway motorman who had been discharged under the State's Security Risk Act. This statute authorized the State Civil Service Commission to suspend and dismiss any employee who was a member "in any organization or group found ... to be subversive." Its formulaic rhetoric applied to one whose continued employment "would endanger the security or defense of the nation and the state." Such a person would be automatically discharged. Lerner had pleaded the Fifth Amendment privilege against self-incrimination when asked by investigators if he were a member of the Communist Party. His refusal to answer was considered adequate grounds for the conclusion he was of "doubtful trust and reliability," and he would be terminated. "No inference of membership in [the Communist Party] was drawn from [appellant's] refusal to reply to the question asked ...," the State Court of Appeals disingenuously stated: "[A]ppellant was not discharged for invoking the Fifth Amendment; he was discharged for creating a doubt as to his trustworthiness and reliability in refusing to answer the question as to Communist party membership."[28] And in a far-fetched and fanciful contention, the appellate tribunal found that a subway employee's continued employment would endanger national and state security. His suspension and then discharge were upheld. The High Court granted *certiorari* and Harlan, speaking for the same five-man majority that decided *Cole*, in an opinion strikingly similar to *Beilan*, and quite unlike that in *Slochower*, concluded that the State measure allowed dismissal of one considered to be of doubtful loyalty, a classification he did not consider arbitrary. Petitioner had contended that the New York statute deprived him of procedural due process, in that it provided for dismissal without the right to a hearing and opportunity for cross-examination or to challenge evidence on which the discharge had been based. Harlan, however, relied as usual on a technicality that appellant had failed to pursue his rightful administrative remedy and obtain a hearing before the State Civil Service Commission. By refusing to testify and to pursue his rightful remedy, petitioner's claim of denial of procedural due process was rejected. Harlan added that the State's classification of employees as "security risks" was not so arbitrary as to offend due process and to be constitutionally impermissible, not when applied "to one employed in the major artery of New York's transportation system ...."[29] That the petitioner's work was simply to open and close doors on subway cars appeared not to carry any weight with Harlan.

Vitarelli v. Seaton (1959),[30] one of the two federal loyalty security cases decided late in the 1959 term, upheld plaintiff in this instance, but likewise testified to the Warren Court's reluctance to take other than the narrow, technical route when dealing with communists and "security risk" charges. William Vitarelli worked as an Education and Training Specialist in the Department of Interior's Education Department (overseeing a group of South Pacific islands), a position designated as "non-sensitive." An investigation determined that he had registered as a supporter of the left-of-center American Labor Party in 1945, subscribed to the USSR Information Bulletin, and purchased copies of the *Daily Worker* and *The Masses*, a newspaper and a magazine, respectively, that adhered to the Communist Party line. After being suspended, Vitarelli had been served with written accusations that his "sympathetic association" with three named persons alleged to be communists or communist sympathizers had been concealed from the government. No evidence was cited to support the accusations and no witness testified against him, but he would be discharged for security reasons after a hearing that followed procedures similar to those prescribed by the McCarran Act of 1950 and by Executive Order 10450 and regulations of the Interior Department.

At his hearing itself, Vitarelli and the four witnesses who testified in his favor were subjected to a prolonged cross-examination, one going well beyond the activities specified in the charges. Vitarelli was asked about his educational and social beliefs and even whether he was "a religious man." Excerpts from the record, not atypical of such hearings in the Fifties and Sixties, revealed what the Supreme Court majority later described as "a wide-ranging inquisition." To convey its flavor, a brief and revealing except follows, in which the departmental security officer inquired about the defendant's work as a Georgia college teacher:

> Were these activities designed to be put into effect by both the white and colored races? ... What were your feelings at that time concerning race equality? ... How about civil rights? Did that enter into a discussion in your seminar groups? ...
>
> Do I interpret your statement correctly that maybe Negroes and Jews are denied some of their constitutional rights at present?
>
> Mr. Vitarelli: Yes ... I saw it in the South where certain jobs were open to white people and not open to Negroes because they were Negroes ... there was a quota at Columbia College for the medical students. Because they were Jewish, they would permit only so many. I thought that was wrong.

Because of such testimony, as well as his associations and activities, Vitarelli was not considered "reliable or trustworthy," and his continued employment might be "contrary to the best interests of national security." Challenging his discharge as illegal, he filed suit in the United States District Court for the District of Columbia seeking for a declaratory judgment that his discharge was illegal, and for an injunction directing his reinstatement. The Court ruled against him.

Eventually, Vitarelli's case came to the High Court. Once again, the Court majority, speaking through Justice Harlan, was unwilling to expand beyond the narrowly technical specifics or to look behind the proclaimed resort to "national security" and other shopworn linguistic icons. The record, he found, revealed that the procedures leading to petitioner's dismissal on the grounds of national security violated petitioner's due process rights under relevant Department of the Interior regulations. The Secretary of the Interior was entitled to discharge an employee summarily, but since he gratuitously decided to give a reason, and that reason was national security, the Secretary was obligated to conform to the procedural standards he had formulated for dismissal on security grounds. To sum up, dismissal was illegal and petitioner was entitled to reinstatement.

Greene v. McElroy (1959)[31] also involved a government employee, terms like "loyalty" and "security," and specifically the constitutionality of the Department of Defense Industrial Security Program, which affected some 3,000,000 defense plant workers. And in a repeat of *Vitarelli, et al.*, the petitioner would be upheld and constitutional issues would be avoided. Further, similar to *Bailey* and *Peters* as well as *Vitarelli*, the longstanding Red Scare phobias that clouded the American social and political landscape once more surfaced. In this instance, a serious blow was delivered to the usual procedures in the national security system.

William Greene had been an aeronautical engineer and general manager of Engineering and Research Corporation (ERCO), a private company engaged in developing and producing electronic products for the U.S. military. Since these products involved military secrets, all corporate employees required security clearances. In December 1951, the Army–Navy–Air Force Personnel Security Board (PSB) notified Greene it had "decided that access by you to contract work and information [at ERCO] ... would be inimical to the best interests of the United States." The Board's action depriving Greene of his security clearance owed to regulations set forth by the Secretary of Defense and was grounded on alleged communist associations and sympathies. As a consequence of a series of exiguous charges, Greene was dismissed by the corporation, one for which he had worked since 1937, and he was then unable to obtain other employment in his field.

Greene sued for a judgment declaring that the revocation of security clearance was illegal and void. At the PSB hearing, he categorically denied that he had ever been a "Communist" and discussed at length his dislike for "a theory of Government which has for its object the common ownership of property." Witnesses in his behalf included top-level ERCO executives and even some military officers who had worked with him in the past, and they corroborated many of Greene's statements and affirmed his loyalty. The prosecution presented no witnesses at the hearing, and lamely explained the identity of informants and their statements had been kept secret "to insure an unimpeded flow of information ... concerning subversive conduct." It obviously relied on confidential reports, but Greene was not given an opportunity to confront and question those who made these reports or challenge government investigators who recorded their allegations. Moreover, it became apparent that the PSB itself had never questioned the investigators or even seen those whose statements would be the substance of their reports. But the Secretary of the Navy, following many bureaucratic convolutions, concluded that Greene's "continued access to Navy classified security information [was] inconsistent with the best interests of National Security." ERCO corporate officers, after petitioning for a "personal conference" to reconsider the decision and being informed by the Navy that it would "serve no useful purpose," had no choice but to agree to discharge an employee whose "knowledge, experience and executive ability have proven of inestimable value in the past."

In its Brief to the Court, the prosecution would acknowledge that revocation of security clearance caused petitioner to lose his job and "seriously affected" his ability to obtain work in his field. But these results, it concluded, were indirect by-products of necessary governmental action to protect the integrity of secret information and hence not unreasonable, and they did not "constitute deprivations within the meaning of the [Fifth] Amendment." The High Court, however, Warren speaking for a majority of five, undercut the all-too-apparent deficiencies in the government's case. Upon a point-by-point review of petitioner's testimony, he riddled the prosecution. He dismissed most of the hearing's charges against Greene, such as listening to a radio station that played classical music, or that he followed the Communist Party "line," or presented "fellow-traveler" arguments. Turning to matters of greater substance, Warren criticized the 1947 National Security Act that created "an industrial security clearance program under which affected persons may lose their jobs and may be restrained in following their chosen professions on the basis of a determination concerning their fitness for clearance made in proceedings in which they are denied the traditional procedural safeguards of confrontation and cross-examination." Not even the investigative reports and statements of informants were made available to the petitioner, the Chief Justice observed, and went on to insist that there are certain "relatively immutable principles in our jurisprudence," one being the evidence to prove that the government's case must be disclosed to the individual, especially so when the memory of those giving testimony might be faulty or had been "motivated by malice, vindictiveness, intolerance, prejudice, or jealousy." These protections have ancient roots and were formulized in the Sixth Amendment which provided for the right of confrontation of one's accusers. It was not necessary, however, to decide whether the industrial security program infringed upon constitutional rights, Warren concluded, since neither the President nor Congress had explicitly authorized the Secretary of Defense to make an end-run around his Department's Industrial Security Program and "deprive petitioner of his job in which he was not afforded the safeguards of confrontation and cross-examination."

As a codicil to the narrative of aforementioned cases centering on "security risks" and the dismissal of federal workers, it would be helpful to add some statistics. The best estimate of dismissals from 1953 to 1956 is 1,500, with at least 6,000 resignations, David Caute estimates. The latter were by those who recognized that, given their past, there was no hope of overcoming the odds against discharge and quietly resigned. Extending the time frame back to 1946, and covering a ten-year period, an estimated 2,700 were discharged and 12,000 resigned as a result of investigations into subversive activities and associations within the federal civil service.[32]

Returning to another category of anti-communist activities, this study has chronicled deportation of alien radicals from the time of Johann Most, Emma Goldman, and Harry Bridges, as well as the numerous and largely redundant statutes legalizing it: the 1903 measure that excluded anarchists and those advocating forcible overthrow of government; the February 1917 law deporting all aliens who advocated or taught violent overthrow; the 1920 statute that enlarged the deportation net to include persons who violated the Espionage and Sedition measures; the 1950 Subversive Activities Control Act (the McCarran Act, Section 22) that added those "who are members of or affiliated with the Communist Party …" to the list of those who were aliens excluded from entry or deportable, though earlier laws had already implied as much.[33] Proceedings against alleged communist or ex-communist foreign nationals continued in the Fifties. In fact, the Eisenhower administration boasted in 1953 that it had deported forty-two "subversives" during its first eight months in office, suggesting that the radical alien remained a promising target for the Red Hunters.

Deportation served as well as one more index to the ongoing national mood, reminiscent of the earlier decades when xenophobia was the norm and "subversives" and "anarchists" were considered *persona non grata*. Recall, for example, the near-interminable attempts to deport Harry Bridges. There were also the ongoing less publicized deportation proceedings of aliens who were communists or fellow travelers in the Thirties, such as one defendant who belonged to the Workers Party of America; a second who had just been expelled from the Communist Party; a third who sold the *Daily Worker* and "was affiliated with the Party"; a fourth who worked in a bookstore that also sold the newspaper; and the fifth who was director of a school that announced itself as "under the official guidance and leadership of the Communist Party", and the list continued and was expanded in the early Cold War years.[34]

Recurrent anti-radical deportation efforts in the Fifties inevitably produced litigation in federal tribunals. Personnel changes in the High Court resulted in sharp shifts of opinion in deportation proceedings. Justices Murphy and Rutledge who had been in the majority when the decision came down in favor of Bridges in 1945 would be replaced by Justices Sherman Minton and Tom Clark, which left only Justices Black and Douglas favoring petitioners scheduled for deportation—as witness, for example, *Harisiades v. Shaughnessy* (1952),[35] a case involving a resident alien whose deportation had its legal basis in the 1940 Alien Registration Act (the Smith Act). Harisiades was a Greek national who had been in the United States since 1916, joined the Communist Party in 1925 and became a Party organizer, but denied any belief in the use of force and violence. Two other noncitizens whose cases were combined with that of Harisiades had also been Communist Party members and, testifying much as he did, all had ended Party membership at least a dozen years before deportation proceedings commenced. The defendants gave three reasons for challenging their pending deportation: (1) the statute deprived them of liberty without due process of law in violation of the Fifth Amendment; (2) it abridged their freedom of speech and assembly contrary to the First Amendment; (3) and their deportation was a constitutionally prohibited *ex post facto* action, since their past Party membership had terminated before the 1940 Alien Registration Act (the Smith Act) had been enacted.

Justice Jackson for the Court asserted that the question before the bench was whether a resident alien can be legally deported for membership that ended before 1940. He answered in the affirmative. The statute may inflict severe hardship, he ruefully acknowledged, but it did not violate the Fifth Amendment as the defense argued, since the statute was not a deprivation of liberty without due process. Turning to another defense contention, Jackson brusquely rejected the claim that First Amendment rights, and their violation, came into play. Nor was the 1940 statute applied *ex post facto* as defense counsel argued, it was simply a continuation of the previous legislation. The deportability provision, Jackson contended, was within the sovereign power of the every sovereign state. Though recognizing that its application to an alien with long residence "bristles with severities," he believed that "internal dangers" were immediate and menacing and allowed for expulsion. The worldwide communist conspiracy, which relentlessly intruded upon Jackson's judicial consciousness, provided the cause for his conclusion that it was wise for a nation to retain "the power of deportation" of those within its midst.[36] In closing, he deferentially affirmed that the establishment of an "exclusionary immigration policy was for Congress and not the judiciary." The legislature was the venue for correcting "unwise or cruel legislation touching aliens."

The *Harisiades* decision hardly suggested an immediate turn to greater tolerance for free expression, at least not for aliens. Nor did another deportation case, *Galvan v. Press* (1954).[37] Norbert Galvan, a Mexican alien, had been brought to the United States in 1918 at age six, lived in America for thirty-six years, had an American wife to whom he was married for twenty years, and fathered four children, all born in the United States, and a stepson who served in the military forces. He admitted to the Immigration and Naturalization Service (INS) that he had been a member of the Communist Party in 1944 (when it was a legal entity), but decided to leave the Party two years later. Furthermore, he was apparently unaware of its advocacy of violent overthrow of the government. Nonetheless, as a onetime Party member, he was threatened with deportation under the 1950 Internal Security Act. The INS hearing resulted in an order of deportation, the Board of Immigration Appeals rejected his appeal, and the District Court denied his petition for a *writ of habeas corpus*, which decision would be affirmed by the Ninth Circuit.

On *certiorari*, Galvan challenged the evidence as inadequate to sustain deportation under the 1950 measure and attacked the validity of the statute as applied to him, issues that raised questions about the interpretation as well as the constitutionality of the measure. Frankfurter, speaking for the majority, acknowledged the harshness of the deportation order but considered the evidence presented at the administrative hearing adequate to support the charge that petitioner had been a member of the Communist Party. Deferring to Congress as was habitual with him, Frankfurter argued that in light of the fact that the lawmakers had broad powers over immigration, it could not be held that their classification of Section 22 of the McCarran Act was so baseless as to violate due process and hence to be beyond congressional power.

Neither Harisiades nor Galvan were instances of the Red Scare virus infecting deportability practices. Indeed, a near-pathological anti-radicalism had long driven the INS, and denaturalization trials and deportation procedures for radical aliens in the Fifties rivaled those of the post-World War I decades. Two years before the *Galvan* case, for instance, this recurrent animus was manifest in *Carlson v. Landon* (1952).[38] The origins of this case decided on the same day as *Harisiades* and antedated the deportation provisions of the 1950 Internal Security Act. In fact, Frank Carlson, a Polish citizen, was one of the four first arrested under the 1918 Sedition Act prohibiting entry or residency to "aliens who ... advocate, or teach, or who are members of or affiliated with any organization, association, society, or group, that believes in ..." forcible overthrow of the government. Carlson had come to the United States at age seventeen, sold $50,000 in war bonds, donated blood to the Red Cross on seven occasions, and his sons served in World War II. He was arrested (under a warrant charging that he belonged to an organization advocating violent overthrow of the government, namely, the Hamtramck, Michigan section of the Communist Party). Released on bail, Carlson would be rearrested together with three others, after passage of the 1950 statute, Section 22. The four defendants, "active, alien communists," were denied bail by Herman Landon, District Director of the INS, as directed by the Attorney General, owing to the belief that they would be unavailable for the hearings and possible deportation. District Court Judge Ben Harrison would affirm the ruling decision. And testifying to the prevailing national and judicial fears, he added, "I am not going to turn these people loose if they are Communists, any more than I would turn loose a deadly germ in this community." (Sixth Circuit Court of Appeals Judge Stephens reversed his decision but upon rehearing, the District Court judge again denied bail, which the Court of Appeals then upheld.)[39]

Plaintiffs filed petitions for *habeas corpus* alleging that their detention without bail was arbitrary, capricious, and a violation of the due process clause of the Fifth Amendment. They also charged that both Section 20 of the 1917 Immigration Act and its amendment in the Subversive Activities Control Act (1950) were unconstitutional in that the statutes and procedures purported to authorize indefinite detention. The Sixth Circuit Court of Appeals would uphold the defense contention that denial of bail could not rest solely on Communist Party membership and the prosecution appealed to the Supreme Court.

In a five-to-four vote, Justice Reed echoing the sentiments of Harlan and Frankfurter acknowledged the harshness of the outcome. He also conceded that, except for Party membership, petitioners had displayed model behavior during their long stay in the United States, and deportation was "a particularly drastic remedy"; but the 1950 statute had authorized the Attorney General to arrest and to deny bail to all alien Communist deportees. Thus did the Court majority make pre-trial detention possible for any offense that was cited. It found no abuse of discretion in denial of bail and, Kalven concluded, thereby rendered the Eighth Amendment provision on bail "illogical and largely impotent."[40] In effect, the majority condoned indefinite detention of alien radicals solely on the order of a government official if he had reasonable cause to believe their release would endanger national security. It was yet one more decision demonstrating how compulsive anti-communism corrupted aspects of the law.

Denaturalization as well as deportation, would continue into the Fifties. Consider, for example, the similar outcome in *Nowak v. United States* and *Maisenberg v. United States*, two 1958 decisions that also reflected the anti-radical feeding frenzy of the decade.[41] In the first case, the Polish-born petitioner, Stanley Nowak, arrived at Ellis Island in 1913 at age ten, became a citizen in 1938, and served in Michigan's Senate for a decade. Attorney General Francis Biddle sought to set aside Nowak's naturalization under the 1940 Nationality Act on the grounds it had been fraudulently obtained, because petitioner failed to disclose that he had been an active member and officer of the Communist Party, a disclosure revealed by professional informers. Similarly in *Maisenberg*, the government sought to revoke the naturalization of a Russian-born woman who had become a citizen two decades before the suit was brought against her under the 1952 Immigration and Nationality Act. Her naturalization, it was charged, had been obtained by "concealment of a material fact [and] willful misrepresentation"; namely, in the Petition for Naturalization, she had answered falsely to the form's Question 28: "Do you belong to or are you associated with any organization which teaches or advocates anarchy or the overthrow of existing government in this country?" And she had committed perjury by her answer.

Both District and Circuit Courts found for the government in each case. The High Court reversed both tribunals in a *per curiam* opinion. Harlan, speaking for the six-man majority, ruled the government had not proved petitioner was aware that the Party advocated violent revolutionary action for the overthrow of government. He held that the 1940 statute did not make Communist Party membership "a ground for loss of citizenship" and that the government did not meet the "clear, unequivocal and convincing evidence" standard set forth in *Schneiderman*. In summary, the Court once again concluded that members of groups advocating forcible overthrow were not grounds for loss of citizenship. It was a surprising decision, one seemingly in disregard of the provisions of the 1940 Nationality Act that had prohibited citizenship for such persons and, we may believe, contrary to the views of most Americans.

The very fact of multiple loyalty oath and denaturalization decisions makes it obvious that anti-communism remained the motor of all three branches of government. These rulings engendered strict compliance with the provisions of Truman's and Eisenhower's executive orders. *Greene* and *Bailey* were still controlling and broad removal powers of federal employees tainted as communists or communist sympathizers remained largely inviolable. And any federal employee, such as John Peters, who might belong to a listed organization had no way to prove the innocence of his membership. Furthermore, as any number of cases disclose, a government employee could be discharged as a security risk without any hearing at all, and even without knowing the specific charges made against the person. Nor could consistent adherence to the strict requirements of due process be expected of the Court. Protection from the "probability" of radical attack as essential to the nation's stability remained the legal standard of the judicial majority in the mid-Fifties. As such, deferential attitudes continued to prevail when the judiciary was called upon to review administration actions.

Though not mentioned earlier, when litigation resulting from congressional committee hearings was elaborated upon—such as that of Harry Slochower in New York State—there was the case of *Pennsylvania v. Nelson* (1956).[42] Though occurring in the same year as *Slochower*, it is perhaps more relevant to discuss it now since it was prelude to a pronounced shift in the Warren Court majority when dealing with case law on free expression. Indeed, it was, for the time, one of a series of bombshells by the Court. Steve Nelson (A.K.A. Steve Mesarosh) had joined the Lincoln Brigade—to fight in the Loyalist cause in the Spanish Civil War. On returning to the United States, he became an important Communist Party officer, trained in Moscow, then fought in World War II, and, finally, chaired the Western Pennsylvania Communist Party. In August 1950, Nelson was one of the three Communists who landed in jail and charged with sedition under a Pennsylvania anti-subversion law.

Nelson's arrest began a six-year ordeal for him that included being shunted from county jail to State prison, from State jurisdiction to federal court, from guarded hospital room (which an armed man invaded and threatened to kill him) to solitary confinement. The 1919 State measure under which he was charged had initially been designed to deter union organizing, but had been a dead letter since the 1926 prosecution of some steel plant workers at the Jones and Laughlin's Aliquippa facility. The measure was "reminiscent of the Sedition Act of 1798," Chief Justice Warren would later assert, but it was the legal basis for a trial before Judge Harry Montgomery in the Court of Quarter Sessions of Allegheny County and for Nelson's conviction in 1952. The trial prosecutor had been most convincing, having wheeled into court a dolly loaded with the works of Marx, Engels, Lenin, and Stalin as well as magazines, posters, leaflets, and maps of the Soviet Union. Michael Musmanno, a Pennsylvania State judge, likewise supplied evidence. He had led sheriff's deputies to Nelson's office; illegally seized a stack of books, maps, and magazines; and then appeared in court with the printed matter in hand. Defense counsel protested to Judge Montgomery, which would be fruitless considering that he and Musmanno were prominent members of Americans Battling Communism, a Pittsburgh Red-hunting vigilante group that had demanded Nelson's indictment. Astonishingly, Musmanno would become the chief witness for the prosecution. Notwithstanding serious trial errors and questionable departures from a defendant's right of due process, Nelson would be sentenced a prison term of twenty-years and fined $10,000, the conviction upheld by the Superior Court.

The Pennsylvania Supreme Court, in hearing the appeal, cautioned that the extreme unpopularity of the defendant made it "especially incumbent" on his judges to "scrutinize the record with utmost care." It would overturn the decision for a surprising and concussive reason: the supersession of State law by the Smith Act. Since a possible outcome of the case would put many state statutes at risk, a number of *amici curiae* were filed by the State Attorneys General as well as by the Solicitor General of the United States and other interested parties when the State prosecutor carried the case to the High Court. Chief Justice Warren's opinion took the same supersession grounds: "We need not now be concerned" with these alleged infractions of due process, because "Congress has intended to occupy the field of sedition" and "no room has been left to the States to supplement it." In effect, the federal interest in protecting national security was so dominant that congressional action, in the form of the 1940 Smith Act, superseded the 1919 Pennsylvania State sedition statute; that is, consistent with the supremacy clause of the Constitution, all comparable state laws had been preempted. Though clearly avoiding constitutional issues, Warren's narrow ruling was a blockbuster, one that shocked many, in that it partly invalidated or overturned sedition laws in forty-two states.

The uproar that developed with the Court's decision in *Nelson* became even more strident a week later when *Mesarosh v. United States* (1956)[43] was announced. Steve Nelson again made an appearance, being one of the five Pennsylvania Communist Party officials arrested in the nation-wide FBI sweep of June–August 1951 that picked up 126 so-called second-string Communists across the United States and charged them with conspiring to violate the Smith Act. After his trial ended, with a conviction, the Circuit Court considered defense motions for production of the relevant FBI reports of one Matthew Cvetic, an FBI informant, a request that had been denied in District Court. Appellate Court Judge Staley upheld the lower court ruling and also reaffirmed the denial of a defense motion for a mistrial. On inquiring whether the trial court jury had read newspaper accounts of the dubious testimony of Joseph Mazzei, the principal witness before a hearing of the Senate Internal Security Committee, Judge Staley affirmed the trial judge's *voir dire* and ingenuously concluded that the publicity surrounding Mazzei "had not prejudiced the defendants."[44] Seeking a review of the conviction on the grounds that Mazzei had possibly committed perjury, Nelson took this case to the High Court, and a majority reversed conviction and ordered a new trial. "The dignity of the United States government," Warren determined, "will not permit the conviction of any person on tainted testimony." This decision was one of the three (with *Pennsylvania* and *Slochower*) that markedly limited the states' anti-communist statutes and activities.

The *Slochower* decision and Nelson's two victories were premonitory signals. In fact, a near-360 degree swing by the bench occurred on May 6, 1957, owing to the changes in Court personnel. Two challenges to state power, owing to the state court decisions that had denied admission of applicants to the bar because of questionable loyalty, would be reversed.[45] And in the following Court term, the justices decided no less than twelve cases in which legislative investigations of communists and communist activities were under review, and the government was defeated in every instance—though often on technical and procedural grounds, decidedly less dramatic than the alarmist response to these decisions in Congress and the media.

With reference to the state bar cases of May 1957, they are hardly derived from unprecedented actions of the state bar associations. The loyalty oath requirement for admission to the state bar, usually taking the form of a loyalty affidavit on an application blank or of an investigation of the candidate's fitness and character, dating back to the post-World War I period when some lawyers were disbarred on loyalty grounds. Following World War II, some states adopted measures that would specifically disbar attorneys who were believed to advocate forcible overthrow of the government. The ABA itself in 1950 had proposed a test of "loyalty to our form of government" by the anti-communist oath. It adopted similar resolutions over the next two years. As to be expected, the candidate who was denied admission, or the lawyer disbarred because of Communist background, would turn to the federal courts for relief.

Such was the case of Rudolph Schware, in *Schware v. Board of Bar Examiners of New Mexico* (1957),[46] who had been denied permission to practice by the State Board of Bar Examiners. One function of the Board was to determine whether an applicant to the New Mexico bar had the required qualifications, and it was authorized to deny permission to take the bar exam of a candidate lacking a "good moral character." Schware was informed that this was the basis for his denial. The Board called no witnesses and introduced no evidence, and its minutes stated that the denial of the requisite "moral character" resulted from "the use of alias ..., his former connection with subversive organizations, and his record of arrests," all of which had been disclosed on the application form. Schware's formal hearing provided the autobiographical sketch of a archetypal young West Coast radical: two arrests resulting from union activism during the West Coast maritime strikes, membership in "subversive organizations" owing to the impact of the great depression on his family, the resulting interest in socialism, joining the Young Communist League, which segued into Communist Party membership, participating in the effort to recruit men to serve the Loyalist cause during the Spanish Civil War, and the final severance all ties with the CPUSA in 1940 after being disillusioned by the 1939 Nazi-Soviet Non-Aggression Pact. In 1944, he entered the United States army, volunteering for duty in the South Pacific. His letters to his wife, introduced into the record, demonstrated a desire to serve his county and his faith in it. It was all to no avail. Schware petitioned the State Supreme Court, which affirmed the Board's denial, and then turned the Supreme Court, alleging that denial of an opportunity to practice law was contrary to the due process clause of the Fourteenth Amendment.

The Supreme Court took *certiorari* and Justice Black, no longer in last-ditch isolation along with Douglas, spoke for a unanimous Court including, *mirabile dictu*, Justice Burton. Following a detailed examination of Schware's past, Black contended that being a striker during a labor dispute was not evidence of "bad moral character more than twenty years later." Likewise the two arrests in 1934, while participating in a bitter maritime labor dispute, were flicked away by Black as having "very little, if any, probative value in showing that he [Schware] has engaged in any misconduct." Dismissive as well of Schware's arrest for violating the 1917 Neutrality Act, Black contended that it was "not clear" that petitioner violated the statute and, even if he had, it hardly "indicated moral turpitude." And sensitive to national sentiments in the mid-Thirties, Black recalled with forbearance that "[m]any persons in this country actively supported the Spanish Loyalist Government … [M]any idealistic young men volunteered to help causes they believed were right." Finally, Schware's Communist Party membership was in a time of grave national economic crisis, Black recalled, but there is no indication that petitioner "had anything more than a political faith in a political party," or that he had engaged in or advocated overthrow of the government by force and violence.47 In short, the Court ruled that petitioner had been deprived of his rights under the due process clause of the Fourteenth Amendment. It thereby extended to lawyers the teaching privilege granted to civil servants in *Slochower* and *Updegraff*. In those cases, the Court had decided, this privilege could not be arbitrarily prohibited by the state. And in this instance, it could not be denied to another of the "public professions," that being the practice of law.

In the companion case decided that day, *Konigsberg v. State Bar of California* (1957),[48] the plaintiff's record seemed at least as damning. The political derelictions of Raphael Konigsberg were more recent. A graduate of the University of Southern California law school, he had passed the State bar examination with its requirement that he was a person of good moral character and did not advocate violent overthrow of the government. But he had written a series of intemperate editorials in opposition to the Korean War, to Secretary of State John Foster Dulles, and to "the high tribunal [which was] an integral part of the cold war machine." Before the Committee of Bar Examiners in September 1947, he answered all questions asked of him, except the specific one about past or present membership in the Communist Party. Konigberg's defense, he "could hardly be expected at this point for expediency to give up principles that have been upheld by the highest court in the land."

Repeatedly objecting to the Committee's questions about his beliefs and associations, Konigsberg forthrightly asserted that they infringed rights guaranteed to him by the First and Fourteenth Amendments. He argued to no avail. In September 1957, the Committee informed him of its refusal to certify, a decision virtually guaranteed considering the times. Konigsberg had failed to demonstrate the "good moral character" required by the State's Business and Professional Code or prove he had not advocated forcible overthrow of the government. He then sought review in the State Supreme Court, contending that the Committee's action deprived him of his rights under the Fourteenth Amendment, as he had contended at all stages of the proceedings and requested it to review this refusal of certification. His request, being denied, defense counsel petitioned the Supreme Court for review. Konigsberg's Petition argued that no State statute existed "authorizing denial of admission to the bar solely because an applicant declines to answer questions propounded ..." about his political affiliations, though "the entire record" had "overwhelmingly established his loyalty and good moral character." Opposing the defense Petition, the State's counsel was content with quoting the record: petitioner had refused to answer whether or not he had been a member of the Communist Party.

Justice Black, speaking for five colleagues, rejected the contention that "an inference of bad moral character can rationally be drawn" from petitioner's editorials. Carrying his argument further, he staked out a position daring for that day though typical of him. It affirmed that being a Communist Party member at the time "would not support an inference that he [Konigsberg] did not have good moral character." Even if it be assumed that plaintiff was a Communist Party member in 1941, Black reminded the dissenters, "the Communist Party was a recognized political party in the State of California" at the time and those who "joined that party had a right to expect that the State would not penalize them, directly or indirectly, thereafter." Neither Party membership nor the derisive opinions of public officials were adequate grounds for exclusion from legal practice. Nor was refusal to answer questions put to him by the Committee "ipso facto, a basis for excluding an applicant from the Bar ..."[49]

Notes

1. 341 U.S. 56 (1951).
2. 342 U.S. 485 (1952).
3. William O. Douglas, *The Court Years: 1939–1975* (New York: Random House, 1980), 96.
4. *Thompson v. Wallin*, 301 N.Y. 476 (1950).
5. *Adler*, 342 U.S. at 493.
6. Ibid., 493.
7. 357 U.S. 399 (1958). See Harry Kalven, *A Worthy Tradition* (New York: Harper & Row, 1988), 540.
8. Lucas Powe, *The Warren Court and American Politics* (Cambridge, MA: Harvard University Press, 2000), 137–8.
9. *Beilan*, 357 U.S. at 409, 410–11.
10. 350 U.S. 551 (1956).
11. Unexpectedly sensitive to the usage of the Fifth and Fourteenth Amendments, Clark stated: "At the outset we must condemn the practice of imputing a sinister meaning to the exercise of a person's constitutional right under the Fifth Amendment ...." Ibid., 557, 559.
12. 357 U.S. 513 (1958).
13. *Speiser*, 357 U.S. at 518.
14. 344 U.S. 183 (1952).
15. *Wieman*, 344 U.S. at 184–5, n. 1. See also Fund for the Republic, *Digest*, 37.
16. *Wieman v. Updegraff*, 344 U.S. 183 (1952).
17. 354 U.S. 234 (1957).
18. *Sweezy*, 354 U.S. at 250.
19. Ibid., 256.
20. 364 U.S. 479 (1960).
21. Ibid.
22. 349 U.S. 190 (1955); 349 U.S. 155 (1955).
23. *Quinn*, 349 U.S. at 162.
24. 349 U.S. 331 (1955).
25. 351 U.S. 536 (1956).
26. Ibid.
27. 357 U.S. 468 (1958).
28. *Lerner*, 2 N.Y.2d at 372.
29. *Lerner*, 357 U.S. at 473, 479.
30. 359 U.S. 535 (1959).
31. 360 U.S. 474 (1959).
32. David Caute, *The Great Fear: The Anti-Communist Purge Under Truman and Eisenhower* (New York: Simon & Schuster, 1978), 275. See also Ralph Brown, *Loyalty and Security: Employment Tests in the United States* (New Haven, CT: Yale University Press, 1958), 487.
33. Early instances of anarchist deportation cases are: *Lopez v. Howe*, 259 F. 401 (2d Cir. 1919); *Ex parte Pettine*, 259 F. 733 (D. Mass. 1919); *United States v. Parsons*, 22 F. Supp. 149 (S.D. Cal. 1938).
34. Examples of Communist deportation cases in the 1920s are: *United States v. Bilokumsky v. Tod*, 263 U.S. 149 (1923); *United States ex rel. Tisi v. Tod*, 264

U.S. 131 (1924); *United States ex rel. Vajtauer v. Commissioner*, 273 U.S. 103 (1927); and in 1921, the Massachusetts case of *Colyer v. Skeffington*, 265 F. 17 (D. Mass. 1920) (Chapter 2 *supra*). And in the Thirties, among decisions of Communists, Party members or "affiliates," being deported before the first Bridges cases, are: *Murdoch v. Clark*, 53 F.2d 155 (1st Cir. 1931); *Berkman v. Tillinghast*, 58 F.2d 621 (1st Cir. 1932); *Wolck v. Weedin*, 58 F.2d 928 (9th Cir. 1932); *In re Saderquist*, 11 F. Supp. 525 (D. Me. 1935), *aff'd per curiam, Saderquist v. Sonquist* , 83 F.2d 890 (1st Cir. 1936); *Branch v. Cahill*, 88 F.2d 545 (9th Cir. 1937).
35. 342 U.S. 580 (1952).
36. *Harisiades*, 342 U.S. at 590, 594.
37. 347 U.S. 522 (1954).
38. 342 U.S. 524 (1952).
39. *Carlson*, 342 U.S. at 550. See also 186 F.2d 183 (9th Cir.); 186 F.2d 190 (9th Cir.); 187 F. 2d 991 (9th Cir.). Justice Black would quote the lower court concession: "there is nothing here to indicate the Government is fearful that they are going to leave the jurisdiction."
40. Kalven, *A Worthy Tradition*, 416.
41. 356 U.S. 660 (1958); 356 U.S. 670 (1958).
42. 350 U.S. 497 (1956).
43. 352 U.S. 1 (1956).
44. *United States v. Mesarosh*, 116 F. Supp. 345 (W.D. Pa. 1953); see also 223 F.2d 449, 458 (3d Cir. 1955).
45. In the background, there were the many state statutes requiring "good moral character" as the criterion for admission to the bar or remaining member and barring Communists, including Alabama, Kentucky, Ohio, and North Dakota. Inevitable legal challenges followed. Beginning as early as 1921 in Pennsylvania, the petitioner would be denied admission if he or she is an anarchist, syndicalist, communist, or an IWW member: *In re Margolis*, 269 Pa. 206, 112 Atl. 478 (1921). Applicants for the bar in Georgia, Indiana, Idaho, and Oklahoma could not belong to an organization on the Attorney General's list and/or explain if they were. Robert Goldstein, *American Blacklist: The Attorney General's List of Subversive Organizations* (Lawrence, KS: University Press of Kansas, 2008), 80.
46. 353 U.S. 232 (1957).
47. *Schware*, 352 U.S. at 244.
48. 353 U.S. 252 (1957).
49. *Konigsberg*, 353 U.S. at 260, 276. *In re Anastaplo*, 366 U.S. 82 (1961) was yet another bar admissions case, that of Illinois, in which plaintiff refused to answer questions about "possible membership in the Communist Party"; and the Court struck down the State bar admission requirement.

11

Red Monday

Decision day, June 17, 1957, also known as "Red Monday," would unleash immediate anti-Court outcries and fervid denunciations on Capitol Hill, and with good reason. The four rulings of that day were portended by *Jencks v. United States* (1957),[1] which was decided on June 3, less than a month after the state bar association cases of *Schwarz* and *Konigsberg*. Before turning to this decision, notice should be given of the altered Court membership. The reconstituted tribunal, in its first decision of the 1956 term, had been confronted with the cases of *Nelson* discussed earlier, followed by that of Clinton Jencks, and the Court decision in each was an omen of what would shortly follow.

Though born in a conservative "rather religious working class family in Colorado, Springs," Jencks would lead a fifteen-month strike against a small mining company in a dispute over wages and working conditions. Becoming President of a local of the "Communist-dominated" Union of Mine, Mill and Smelter Workers, Jencks was required to file a non-Communist oath—"Affidavit of Non-Communist Union Officer"—under the Taft–Hartley Act, and he was accused of filing an allegedly false one. Jencks swore under oath that he had not been a Party member at the time specified and maintained that the written reports of the FBI informants (Matusow and Ford) to the Bureau would refute their trial testimony. Defense lawyers then moved for "an order directing an inspection of [the FBI] reports" of the two informants about the meetings they described, to examine them for possible discrepancies. The prosecution refused to produce the reports, the trial judge denied the defense motion, and Jencks was convicted of perjury on largely circumstantial evidence. In fact, one of the two informants, Harvey Matusow, who had identified Jencks as a Communist Party member, later recanted, admitting that his statements were fabricated. He had confessed his doubts about testifying to an FBI agent—because "I didn't feel my testimony was honest"—and the agent duly recorded his statement. If true, then the government went to trial aware that its case depended on tainted testimony. Matusow's confession came after he had denounced Jencks to the HUAC and the SISC, and after the Appellate Court upheld the trial judge decision and Jencks's five-year prison term for perjury.

The Court considered the *Jencks* case at no less than five conferences, beginning on October 19, 1956, at which five justices (Warren, Douglas, Black, Harlan, and Brennan) served notice that they were no longer disposed to uncritically accept FBI testimony or uphold punishment for contempt of Congress for those who fell afoul of what HUAC investigators charged were "un-American" activities. Brennan was assigned the seven-to-one opinion. Of the defense request that the original FBI files of the two informants be brought into court—to examine them for possible discrepancies—Brennan contended, with only Clark passionately dissenting, that "[t]he criminal action must be dismissed when the Government on the ground of privilege, elects not to comply with an order to produce ... relevant statements or reports in its possession of Government witnesses touching the subject matter of their testimony at the trial." The prosecution had a right not to reveal the reports, Brennan continued, but "only at the price of letting the defendant go free." If the FBI evidence was relevant, defense had a constitutional right to see it: "justice requires no less."[2] Brennan, Harry Abraham tells us, here spoke eloquently about the historic judicial function "of protecting the rights of the individual against the alleged unlawful acts of government." Quoting a 1930's opinion of Justice Sutherland, Brennan affirmed that the "interest of the United States in a criminal prosecution ... is not that it shall win a case, but that justice shall be done."

The Court's ruling was—for that time!—an audacious refutation of the claim that national security provided wide latitude to the FBI. The decision came at a time when Hoover's popularity and hieratic dictums remained overwhelming. One 1953 Gallup poll recorded a favorable rating of seventy-eight percent, with only two percent unfavorable (and twenty percent expressing no opinion).[3] Popular idolatry of the FBI, when paired with Brennan's opinion, revived public furor, many sharing Justice Clark's impassioned dissent. The fuse had first been ignited by the four prior decisions—of *Cole v. Young, Slochower v. Board of Education, Pennsylvania v. Nelson*. Congress, the press, and the public joined in blatantly proclaiming that the Court protected communists, usurped "states rights," improperly interpreted the Constitution and negatively affected the talismanic standard of national security. It meant all FBI files were now opened to Soviet intelligence agents, a proposition that greatly alarmed J. Edgar Hoover since it could expose Bureau secret files and his ongoing covert war against the Party. In a memo to top administration officials, he claimed that the communists were now "jubilant." Yet the *Jencks* decision meant only that the government could either dismiss the prosecution or provide the reports of those informants that touched "the events and activities as to which they testified at the trial." It asserted one of the oldest and most venerated principles of American law; namely, that in a criminal trial, where the liberty and perhaps the life of the accused is at stake, he is entitled to all evidence that is relevant and essential to his defense.

J. Edgar Hoover, it should be observed, had continued to wage personal wars against perceived enemies of the republic. In 1959, he grimly warned a Subcommittee of the Senate Appropriations Committee that "the international Communist conspiracy is clearly the greatest menace free civilization has ever known." In the following year, he launched a sixteen-year campaign against the Socialist Workers' Party, burglarizing its New York City headquarters ninety-two times. COINTELPRO, discussed above had been initiated three years earlier, characterized by spying, bugs, and break-ins practices.[4] The threat of *Jencks*'s ruling was such, Hoover believed, that the Program had to be reactivated to destroy the Communist Party.[5] It reflected his convictions that the CPUSA remained a very serious threat to national security, though by the Bureau's own admission, the Communist Party numbered ca. 4,400 members in the early Sixties. Indeed, by the mid-sixties, one of every six Party members was an FBI agent.

The popular uproar over the Court's decision was pronounced in Congress as well, and members on both sides of the aisle competed to push through legislation nullifying *Jencks*. In fact, eleven House Bills were introduced the day after Brennan's opinion, all harsh measures designed to overturn the decision or give the Attorney General jurisdiction over inspection of FBI documents, and over seventy anti-civil liberties bills would be introduced during the next year, eventually topping 100, with a number designed to curb the powers of the Court.[6] The anti-communist recidivism of Congressman Howard Smith of Virginia prompted his angry reaction: "I do not recall any case decided by the present Court which the Communists have lost." Indeed as early as January 1955, he led a covey of Southern House members in pressing for House Resolution Three, designed to end the Court's preemptive dilution of federalism (by the *Nelson* ruling) by barring Congress from "occupying the field ... to the exclusion of all State laws on the same subject matter." It would restore to the states the power to prosecute alleged subversives, in effect overruling *Pennsylvania v. Nelson*. The bill eventually was defeated by the narrowest of margins (41–40). In the Upper House, Mississippi's Senator James Eastland, Chair of the Senate Internal Security Committee, dolefully remarked to a like-minded Senator McCarthy: "There is just one pro-communist decision after another from this court ...." He considered the implication of the decision in *Jencks* "even more frightening than the decision itself" and assailed the High Court for "[a]mending the Constitution" at a Senate hearing on Jenner's draft measure.[7]

Another notable anti-Red spear carrier, the Indiana Republican, William Jenner charged that "by a process of attrition and accession, the extreme liberal wing of the Court has become a majority" and introduced an omnibus measure, Senate Resolution 2646 in 1957, "to limit the appellate jurisdiction of the Supreme Court in certain cases," and it, too, would be narrowly defeated in the Senate.[8] Reflecting knee-jerk lawmaker reactions to the decision, his bill would strip the High Court of its appellate function over five categories of cases, each one corresponding to a recent controversial ruling and issue. In short, it would prohibit High Court review of a broad categories of cases relating to the functions of congressional committees (e.g., HUAC and SISC), such as the Federal Loyalty–Security Program; state anti-subversive statutes; acts and regulations of boards of education concerning subversive activities in schools; and state bar admission practices and decisions.[9] One provision of Jenner's bill would limit constitutional interpretation to the highest state courts and the eleven federal appellate courts were authorized to be the final judicial bodies.

Four Supreme Court opinions that were handed down on the same day greatly contributed to the anti-Court outcries. The least publicized and least provocative of these Court decisions, *Service v. Dulles et al.* (1957),[10] originated in the federal Loyalty Program, established by President Truman's 1947 Executive Order 9835, as had the *Bailey, Peters*, and *Cole* cases. Its beginnings dated back a half-dozen years, to December 1951, and concerned John Service. One of the "Old China Hands" at the State Department and a high-level foreign service officer who had taken on various assignments in China for some sixteen years. Secretary of State Dean Acheson, having succumbed to anti-communist political pressures—from the China Lobby, Senator McCarthy, inter-alia—arbitrarily discharged him. Service would receive three successive "clearances" by the State Department, a fourth from its Loyalty Security Board, and a "post-audit" by the Board that concluded: "reasonable grounds do not exist for belief that ... Service is disloyal to the Government of the United States" and that "... he does not constitute a security risk to the State Department." However, given the toxic anti-communism that had invaded all governmental departments and branches, *Service's* his case would be remanded to the Board for reconsideration, and he was examined in the light of Eisenhower's Executive Order 10241. However, the State Department Board again found that the petitioner was not a security risk. In sum, Service had been investigated six times and six times cleared. But after the seventh hearing, the departmental Board concluded that "a reasonable doubt" as to his loyalty existed, and it advised the current Secretary of State John Foster Dulles that Service "should be forthwith removed," and he was immediately discharged as a security risk. "In making this determination," Dulles admitted, "I did not read the testimony taken in the proceedings in Mr. Service's case ...." I did not make any independent determination of my own as to whether on the evidence submitted before those boards there was reasonable doubt as to Mr. Service's loyalty.

Describing the record in this detail is possibly of greater significance than the decision itself, because it is yet one more demonstration of the unrelenting anti-communism of the Cold War years. Regarding the decision itself, the High Court avoided the seemingly intrinsic constitutional issue. Harlan (Whittaker and Brennan not participating) wrote an opinion similar to that of *Cole v. Young* and *Peters v. Hobby*, among others, deciding the case on strict procedural grounds that upheld petitioner's claims. The discharge was illegal, the State Department's own procedures had been violated, and reinstatement was ordered. The decision rested on narrow technical grounds and did not establish any new doctrine. It was primarily Supreme Court watchers who took note of the case and of the temporary restoration of employment of a "security risk."

But a second Court opinion of that same day, June 17, *Watkins v. United States* (1957),[11] aroused the media, producing intense popular and political rancor. A sensational defeat of the government, specifically the HUAC and Congress, it would be restrict the jealously guarded investigatory power of the congressional legislative committee. John Watkins, a former leader of Illinois' local branches of the Farm Equipment Workers (FEW), had been subpoenaed by a Subcommittee of the HUAC, then investigating communist activity in labor unions, and appeared as a witness before it on April 24, 1954. He testified freely about his own activities and associations, but flatly denied the accusations of witnesses and went on to declare:

> I am not now nor have I ever been a card-carrying member of the Communist Party .... I would like to make it clear that for a period of time from approximately 1942 to 1947 I cooperated with the Communist Party and participated in Communist activities to such a degree that some persons may honestly believe that I was a member of the Party.

As the government acknowledged, "[a] more complete and candid statement of his past political associations and activities ... can hardly be imagined." However, while openly admitting his own past activity in assisting the Communist Party, Watkins refused to reveal the names of allegedly or onetime Party members on three grounds: (1) that he was denied due process under the Fifth Amendment, (2) the Committee questions exceeded the Committee's investigative scope, and (3) they failed to meet the test of pertinacity. Regarding the Fifth Amendment, which many invoked when caught in Committee statutory crosshairs, Watkins declared:

> I am not going to plead the Fifth Amendment [and invoke self-incrimination], but I refuse to answer certain questions that I believe are outside the proper scope of your committee's activities ... I will answer any questions which this committee puts to me about myself ... I will not ... answer any questions with respect to others with whom I associated in the past ...[12]

In response to this refusal to testify, the HUAC cited him for contempt and submitted its highly critical report to the House of Representatives, which in turn directed the House Speaker to forward it to the Attorney General for initiation of a criminal prosecution and a seven-count indictment was returned. Waiving his right to a jury trial, Watkins was tried and convicted on all counts, sentenced to a one-year prison term and fined $100,000. An appeal was taken to the Court of Appeals that reversed conviction, but a rehearing en banc reaffirmed it.

Arguing before the Supreme Court that had granted *certiorari*, petitioner's counsel Joseph Rauh repeated the defense arguments set forth in District Court. To call a man before a legislative committee, he contended, and ask him to expose former associates to "public humiliation for acts of the past" when it is not necessary for any legislative purpose, "invades freedom of speech and belief" guaranteed by the First Amendment.[13]

Accepting petitioner's argument, Chief Justice Warren wrote a discursive thirty-five-page opinion for the six-to-one Court majority (Clark dissenting) that reversed conviction on technical grounds, though it raised serious constitutional questions about the scope of congressional investigations. Warren opened with a lengthy survey of HUAC's history and criticized its broad intrusion into the lives and affairs of citizens as well as Congress for granting the Committee a "hunting license." There was "no congressional power to expose for the sake of exposure," as Warren stated: "the Subcommittee had precisely engaged in this practice and that there was no public purpose served in his interview."[14] In fact, the "sole purpose ... was to bring down upon himself [Watkins] and others the violence of public reaction because of their past beliefs, expressions, and associations." Clearly favoring petitioner, he incisively cautioned: "it is the responsibility of Congress ... to insure that compulsory process is used only in furtherance of a legislative purpose," that "instructions to an investigating committee spell out that group's jurisdiction and purpose with sufficient particularity," and that the justices "cannot simply assume ... that every congressional investigation is justified by a public need that overbalances any private right affected." And then, after quoting from the House resolution defining the HUAC authority, Warren bluntly contended:

> [i]t would be difficult to imagine a less explicit authorizing resolution. Who can define the meaning of "un-American"? What is that single, solitary "principle of the form of government as guaranteed by our Constitution?"[15]

"No inquiry is an end in itself," the Chief Justice affirmed. It had to be related to "a legitimate task of Congress." And investigations solely "to 'punish' those investigated are indefensible." Following upon these scarcely veiled hostile comments toward HUAC, the Chief Justice argued that the House of Representatives had exercised "slight or non-existent" control on the Committee. "We are asked to uphold the Committee's actions unless it appears that they were clearly not authorized by the charter," he stated and could scarcely control his indignation. Thus, he continued:

> The Government contends that the public interest at the core of the investigations [by HUAC] is the need by Congress to be informed

of efforts to overthrow the Government by force and violence so that adequate legislative safeguards can be erected. From this core, however, the Committee can radiate outward infinitely to any topic thought to be related in some way to armed insurrection. The outer reaches of this domain are known only by the content of "un-American activities."[16]

The Chief Justice insisted pertinence was essential; that is, plaintiff required "explicit and clear" knowledge "of the subject to which the interrogation is deemed pertinent" so that the relevance of questions to valid legislation on legislative purposes was made clear. "The 'vice of vagueness' must be avoided here ...," he firmly stated: there must be "a jurisdictional concept of pertinency drawn from the nature of a congressional committee's source of authority." Presumably the subject under inquiry was Communist infiltration in the labor movement but, Warren observed, six of the nine witnesses "had no connection with labor at all," and seven of the thirty names asked of the defendant "were completely unconnected with organized labor." And when petitioner objected to the questions on the grounds of lack of pertinency, the Chairman announced that the Subcommittee "was investigating 'subversion and subversive propaganda,'" which, Warren thought, was "a subject as broad and indefinite as the authorizing resolution of the Committee, if not more so." Petitioner's conviction then became "necessarily invalid under the Due Process Clause of the Fifth Amendment." The indictment must fall: a person in jeopardy of statutory punishment must have the scope of the authority of a congressional committee spelled out with unambiguous clarity by the resolution establishing it.[17]

The Chief Justice also took the opportunity to read a spirited essay on the abuse of investigatory power and the relation of it to the First Amendment freedoms which, he insisted "cannot be abridged." Alluding to the Fifth Amendment, he stated with jugular directness: "[w]itnesses cannot be compelled to give evidence against themselves." These heated and forceful assertions demonstrate a readiness to go beyond the procedural gambit that had prevailed in the past, with *Emspak* and *Quinn* of two years earlier among such instances. Warren's view of the investigative process had clearly matured and he had become aware that an investigation "may imperceptibly lead to abridgment of protected freedoms" for the witness. The very "summoning of a witness and compelling him to testify, against his will, about his beliefs, expressions or associations [which] is a measure of governmental interference. And when those forced revelations concern matters that are unorthodox, unpopular, or even hateful to the general public, the reaction in the life of the witness may be disastrous."[18] Nor was the Chief Justice only sensitive to the chilling effect of coerced testimony upon the witness. He recognized that those whom the witness may name are "thereby placed in the same glare of publicity," and "equally subject to public stigma, scorn and obloquy."[19]

Admittedly Warren did not proceed to the seemingly inevitable conclusion that the Committee's "excessively broad charter" was unconstitutional or its investigation was unconstitutional. Of his lengthy opinion, only five pages were devoted to the constitutional question and as a result his ruling took on an abstract quality. Being narrowly framed, the legality of coercive questioning was evaded. The Chief Justice and the Court majority were very aware that a prime function of congressional committees like HUAC, among others, was to reap publicity and keep the anti-Communist pot boiling, but Warren's opinion left in place the very dangers of unrestrained inquisitions that Justice Black among others found impermissible. Indeed, the evasion was flatly announced: it is not our function "to undertake such an examination" of congressional motives, a view that was surely intended to accommodate justices like Frankfurter and Harlan who tilted toward judicial discretion.

Notwithstanding these reservations, it can be argued that *Watkins* formulated, more emphatically than in past decisions, the protections to be accorded witnesses in Congressional investigations. It also intimated that judicial attitudes toward protected rights were in the process of being drastically altered. In fact, all four decisions handed down on June 17, 1957, demonstrate a more pronounced leadership role of the Court than in the past. To illustrate as much, it should be recorded that Warren at one point in his Watkins opinion briefly introduced some forthright and unafraid comments on the balancing doctrine of competing interests:

> We cannot simply assume that every congressional investigation is justified by a public need that overbalances any private rights affected. To do so would be to abdicate the responsibility placed by the Constitution upon the judiciary to insure that Congress does not unjustifiably encroach upon an individual's right of privacy nor abridge his liberty of speech, press, religion or assembly.[20]

Another shock wave came on the same decision day when the Court decided yet another contempt conviction, in *Sweezy v. New Hampshire* (1957),[21] and Justice Clark, as in *Watkins*, was the solitary dissenting voice. The case was the outcome of a sweeping 1951 State statute, the

Subversive Activities Control Act, one similar to many others state measures over the decades. The New Hampshire measure stipulated that "subversive organizations" were to be declared unlawful and ordered dissolved, that "subversive persons" were ineligible for State employment, and that a loyalty program should be instituted to determine who were "subversive." Remaining caught up in the feverish national Red Scare, the State legislature in 1953 passed a "Joint Resolution Relating to the Investigation of Subversive Activities." It authorized New Hampshire's hard-line anti-communist Attorney General, Louis Wyman, to determine whether "subversive persons are presently located" in the State and to recommend legislation on that subject. Toward this end, Wyman subpoenaed Paul Sweezy to a hearing in January 1954 (and a second time in June 1954). A well-known professor at the University of New Hampshire, who called himself a "classical Marxist," had once edited the *Monthly Review*, a Marxist theoretical journal. Sweezy was subject to a barrage of questions by Wyman: did he believe in Communism, or was he a member of the Communist Party, or attend its meetings, or know any Communists in or out of the State, or whether he knew specifically named persons with alleged connections to organizations on the list of the United States Attorney General or cited by the HUAC, or whether he taught or supported the forcible overthrow of the State, or had known or assisted any persons or groups with that intent? Further inquiries followed about Sweezy's career and personal life, his activities and those of others in the Progressive Party, the meetings of the Liberal Club at the University of New Hampshire, and his ostensibly "subversive" lecture at the University. Sweezy, for his part, announced his refusal on First Amendment grounds to answer questions that were not pertinent to the investigation. He stated for the record:

> ... I am prepared to answer certain questions about myself .... I am also prepared to discuss my views relating to the use of force and violence to overthrow constitutional forms of government.
>
> But I shall respectfully decline to answer questions concerning ideas, beliefs, and associations which could not possibly be pertinent to the matter here under inquiry and/or which seem to me to invade the freedoms guaranteed by the First Amendment to the United States Constitution (which, of course, applies equally to the several states).

After an unqualified denial of membership in the Communist Party, Sweezy stated that he never taught violent overthrow of the government, never knowingly associated with communists in the State, "never attended any meetings of the Communist Party ..., never contributed to the Communist Party ..., did not know any person in New Hampshire who was a member of the Communist Party ..., did not advocate or teach, and had never advocated or taught, overthrow of the Government by force or violence ..., not assisted any group which advocated the overthrow of the government by force or violence ..."

He admitted to being a socialist who favored peaceful change and at one time had joined some of the organizations listed by the United States Attorney General. However, he declined to answer certain questions about his belief in communism, the Progressive Party, a University lecture he had given, and whether he knew some of those named by Wyman. At the follow-up hearing, he refused to answer any question concerning opinion or belief—on the grounds that they were not pertinent to the inquiry and violated his First Amendment rights. Held in contempt of the State legislature, Sweezy was indicted and convicted by the trial court, the decision upheld by the State Superior Court; and the State Supreme Court, to which Sweezy then appealed, affirmed the lower Court's order.[22] Sweezy then petitioned the High Court.

New Hampshire's statutes, plaintiff's Brief contended, contravened the "the First Amendment as applicable to state action under the Fourteenth Amendment"—in that the power conferred upon the Attorney General was so "vague and uncertain," it was "impossible to ascertain its meaning ..." Continuing, the Brief argued: "The questions dealt with an area of political expression clearly protected by the First Amendment and hence excluded from the state's power of inquiry." It was "precisely these forbidden areas" that the Attorney General sought to enter. His inquiries would "strip the First Amendment of its force" and leave legislative inquiry "without limitation." Taking an unusual turn, counsel for Sweezy resorted to the "balancing" metaphor, his Brief arguing that the state's interest in obtaining information designed to prevent forcible overthrow was "outweighed [by] the social costs of interfering with freedom of discussion at the University and throughout the state."

Wyman's Brief defended the questions directed to Sweezy as "relevant and pertinent" and basic to State law. Referring to the First Amendment, it disingenuously argued: "nothing in the record ... is manifest of any action by the State of New Hampshire which suppresses, restricts, or otherwise destroys appellant's freedom of speech." Enlarging upon this flimflam, he rejected petitioner's argument that the State statute offended due process or "arbitrary imposed sanctions ... for innocent membership in subversive organizations." To buttress his position, Wyman referred to the HUAC as authority, when observing that some of the organizations with which petitioner was acquainted were described by the Committee as "Communist controlled or manipulated." Insisting upon the "lawful and constitutional investigation of subversive activities," Wyman found it necessary "to [the] essential legislative process," an almost laughable contention since there had been no legislative notice that the statutes on the books needed amendment or replacement.

In oral argument, at the March 8, 1957, Court conference, Warren established the proper legal rationale for HUAC interrogatories by forcefully declaring: "The committee must show why its questions are relevant and why they can get answers in this kind of case. And they do not have the right to expose for the purpose of exposure."[23] It was a statement that would help consign the HUAC to the dustbin of history since, from the time of its inception, the Committee's primary intent had been "exposure"—of allegedly Un-American Activities. In fact, Martin Dies, the moving spirit behind the HUAC's creation, stated as much many years earlier in House debate.[24] Tacking in another direction, Frankfurter, in conference, asserted that "my chief concern here is the special position of educational institutions and teachers .... I can't think of a situation where a teacher should be hauled before a committee to ask, 'What did you lecture on?'" Brennan in a sweeping comment declared the case was "all bad .... The classroom is a sanctuary."

Speaking for the High Court majority, Warren rested reversal of the lower courts on a narrow basis: the State legislature, in authorizing the Attorney General to conduct an investigation of "subversive activity," had not been sufficiently clear about what information it sought of petitioner. In a close scrutiny of the State legislature's authorizing resolution, he asserted that the Attorney General had "been given such a sweeping and uncertain mandate" that he had not been "directed to gather the kind of facts comprised in the subject upon which petitioner was interrogated." At bottom, the Chief Justice was placing the same restrictions on the investigative powers of a state legislative committee that he had on those of Congress in *Watkins*, where the question before the Court concerned the constitutional limits of a legislative inquiry; that is, whether the investigation deprived petitioner of due process of law under the Fourteenth Amendment. Warren again held that plaintiff's procedural rights had been violated, an argument that thereby managed to avoid the need to structure an opinion centering on the First Amendment, possibly because he recognized the Court majority could only be carried on the grounds set forth in *Watkins*. However, he implicitly alluded to it by affirming the "essentiality of freedom" imperative to the university community. He stated:

> To impose any straitjacket upon the intellectual leaders in our colleges and universities would imperil the future of our nation ... Scholarship cannot flourish in an atmosphere of suspicion and distrust. Teachers and students must always remain free to inquire, to study and to evaluate, to gain new maturity and understanding: otherwise our civilization will stagnate and die.[25]

Warren was also deeply troubled by the "sanction emanating from legislative investigations," and not only because it had an "inhibiting effect in the flow of democratic expression" but also because it placed "the stain of the stamp of disloyalty ..." upon "those directly affected and those touched subtly," which was as equally grave as the loss of employment.

Frankfurter's concurrence (with Harlan) was a fierce and eloquent affirmation of academic freedom that rivaled Warren's. It would be, Lucas Powe asserts, "the most powerful First Amendment defense of academic freedom in the United States Reports that exists to this day."[26] And he went on passionately:

> The inviolability of privacy cannot be constitutionally encroached upon on the basis of some meager a countervailing interest of the state as argumentatively founded upon the remote, shadowy threat to the security of New Hampshire allegedly presented in the origins and contributing elements of the Progressive Party and in [Sweezy's] relations to these.[27]

Frankfurter would balance "two contending principles—the right of a citizen to political privacy, as protected by the Fourteenth Amendment, and the right of the State to self-protection." For him, at least in this instance, the outcome was different: "When weighed against the grave harm resulting from governmental intrusion into the intellectual life of a university, such justification for compelling a witness to discuss the contents of his lecture appears grossly inadequate."[28] Accordingly he concluded, "the investigation itself infringed upon the First and Fourteenth Amendment rights to political and academic freedom."[29] In *Sweezy, therefore*, as well as in *Watkins* of that same decision day, the Court sharply curtailed the investigative power of public officials, emphatically so when such power derived from ambiguous legislative authorization.

By the time *Yates v. United States*, the last of the momentous Red Monday decisions was announced, it had become obvious that the Warren Court had gone went down a very risky legal–political road. In charging ahead of the views governing the Taft, Hughes, and Vinson Court majorities, as well as those of the political branches and the public, the tribunal was left vulnerable to the charge that it had imperiled the nation, and it would be much maligned by those who denounced decisions protecting freedom of expression as "judicial activism" by Supreme Court watchers. Accusation and recrimination became the cost of affirming that no expression was so "dangerous" that it could be proscribed. By being a dynamic and initiating force in American governance, the Court unleashed a flood of controversy, in which Warren's rulings and legal skills came under attack, and the media derided the "pro communist decisions." Both scholarly and popular forums assailed the Chief Justice for what *Time* magazine in 1956 critically stated, was "his role in 'steering the law' rather than in being steered by it." In fact, "Impeach Earl Warren" became the battle cry of a number of Republican conservatives and commentators. Thus did the Warren Court, strikingly so with Red Monday and in later years, pay the price for interpreting the words of the Constitution as commanding respect for the rights and differences of others.

Yates [30] was the most elaborate and technical of the four opinions issued on this decision day. Shortly after the convictions in *Dennis* had been sustained, a bloc of fourteen West Coast Communists would be picked up. They were among 145 "second-string" and "third-string" communists arrested around the nation that would lead to 126 indictments and eventually 108 convictions under Section 3 of the Smith Act, and produced more than a dozen appellate-level opinions, all upholding convictions, as well as a number of Supreme Court rulings.[31] California's "second-string" Communists—Oleta O'Connor Yates and her thirteen co-defendants—were indicted in 1951, courtesy of the Smith Act. Considering the rabid anti-communist political climate, these indictments were hardly surprising. The defendants were charged with conspiracy to teach and advocate the duty and necessity of forcible overthrow of the government and organizing the Communist Party toward this end. The conspiracy, stated the indictment, began in 1940 and continued down to 1951, with petitioners "directed to write and publish articles on such teaching and advocacy, conduct schools for the indoctrination of Party members in such ends, recruit new members, especially in key industries"; and they were alleged to have "committed twenty-three overt acts in furtherance of the conspiracy."

Yates's testimony itself was in marked contrast to Party orthodoxy in that she rejected the whole "programmatic sections of the Communist Manifesto" as "inapplicable" to the United States. In a similar deviation from the Party line, she could find "no circumstances" that would cause her to advocate the violent overthrow of the existing form of government. Defendants in trial court testimony had argued that they had "never met altogether as a group" and that the record was devoid of evidence "from which it might even be inferred that any petitioner had a voice in determining whether or when a call for a violent revolution should be announced."[32]

U.S. Attorney Walter Binns relied on paid informants, much as had McGohey during the *Dennis* trial, but avoided doctrinal exegesis and simply repeated the prosecutorial position in *Dennis*, namely, that the Marxist classics provided a blueprint for revolution. District Court Judge William C. Mathes, managed to avoid the rancor that coursed through the courtroom in *Dennis* but assailed defendants' refusal to disclose the names of Party members demanded in cross-examination. Each refusal to respond to a question was ruled a separate charge of contempt of court, subject to a separate penalty. Yates herself was found guilty of four acts of contempt for refusal to answer and was ordered to prison. The six-month trial went on, and Mathes continued to press the issue of names, which would result in eleven additional citations for contempt. The jury found the defendants guilty of teaching and advocating as well as "organizing" the Communist Party in a conspiracy to forcibly overthrow the government, and Mathes then handed down maximum sentences of five years' imprisonment as well as fines of $10,000. Defense lawyers then took the customary appeals route, first to the Ninth Circuit, where the District Court decision was sustained. Every claim raised by the defendants was rejected: the Smith Act was constitutionally appropriate to the prosecution, and "trial court ... followed the applicable principles of Dennis," and the trial itself was "impeccable from the standpoint of fairness."

Reading the appellants' "Petition for Writ of Certiorari" to the Supreme Court and their Briefs, it becomes apparent that defense counsel tactics had sharply altered from those employed in *Dennis*. The conventional lawyerly argument took precedence, such as the position that there was a lack of evidence to justify the conspiracy charge or conviction. The Chief Justice, in conference, argued: "The government has proved only membership in the Communist Party, not overt acts or unlawful conduct"; and that "nothing was shown there to prove advocacy of force and violence."[33] In fact, the only overt acts were attendance at public meetings. And in discussing editorials written for a Party newspaper by one of the defendants, Warren also contended that the word "organizing" was indeterminate and caustically stated: "the editor of a paper by his editorials is not 'organizing.'" In some further biting comments, he maintained that the charge of "advocacy" was insufficient to convict: rather "it is a question of incitement." As expected, Black went further. The Smith Act, he caustically stated, "provides for political trials" that the First Amendment was supposed to prevent. Although the conferees decided not to overrule *Dennis*, considering it conclusive, and found no new issues in *Yates*, they decided to take *certiorari*.

The Court taking *certiorari*, Warren had selected Justice Harlan to write the decision for six justices (Whittaker and Brennan not participating), possibly because this strategy would win the support of justices Burton and Frankfurter. Both had been troubled by the excesses of Senator McCarthy and more generally, the rabid anti-Communist crusade, with Frankfurter also very disturbed by the thinness of evidence the government brought to other Smith Act trials (e.g., the "tainted" evidence in *Nelson's* trial in Pittsburg). Warren's choice of Harlan also guaranteed that the tribunal's opinion would not be confrontational or overrule *Dennis*. The Court's most meticulous craftsman, Harlan's scholarly ruling repeatedly quoted from the earlier decision, though doing so to arrive at a contrary opinion.

Harlan's text, which ran to forty-three pages, scrupulously examined the very long 14,000 pages of the trial record. He first addressed Communist Party history, tackling what he believed to be one of the major issues in the case, namely, the definition of the term "organize," since the indictment of the fourteen codefendants under the Smith Act was on the charge of "organizing" a Party toward the end of conspiracy to overthrow the government. Congress, however, had not exactly defined the meaning of "organize" in the Smith Act and Harlan, finding it had no precise definition in the statute, declared: "we should follow the familiar rule that criminal statutes are to be strictly construed and give to "organize" its narrow meaning, namely, that the word refers only to acts entered into the creation of a new organization, and not to acts thereafter performed in carrying on its activities ...." Since the

Smith Act included a three-year statute of limitations for prosecution, and the indictments had not been filed until 1951, a half-dozen years after the Party's "organizing," Harlan contended that the charges had come too late.

Harlan's reference to the belated filing, it warrants further explanation, had been pivotal to the petitioners' argument (drawn from the ACLU amicus). Their definition of the term "organize" as used in the Smith Act was coterminous with "establish," "found," or "bring into existence," and the Communist Party was organized in 1945 (after the Communist Political Association was disbanded). However, the indictment was only returned in 1951. (The prosecution in rebuttal stated that "organize" connoted a "continuing concept" across the life of the organization, the lower courts accepting this argument.) Herein was the technical basis for Harlan's decision, to be utilized without a need to consider the First Amendment. Accordingly, he declared the "organizing" charge should have never been in the indictment, which made the conviction of these second-string communists fatally defective.[34]

The jury charge in District Court, Harlan further stated, was so broad that it did not accurately represent congressional intent. Counsel for petitioners had claimed as much: Mathes had inexplicably failed to adopt Medina's instructions to the jury in *Dennis*; that is, only advocacy that employed language calculated to incite its hearers to action was criminally liable. And Mathes had, according to Harlan, improperly charged "that advocacy of violent action to be taken at some future time was enough," which was "too remote from concrete action" to acceptable.[35] The distinction between "concrete action" that the Smith Act had proscribed and belief was one lost on the public and on public officials who, we may believe, were startled by Harlan's sober finding that instances of speech by the plaintiffs "that could be thought amounting to "advocacy of action" are so few and far between as to be almost completely overshadowed by the hundreds of instances in the record in which overthrow, if mentioned at all occurs in the course of doctrinal disputation so remote from action as to be almost wholly lacking in probative value."[36]

"Advocacy of action," or "concrete action"—the Smith Act phrase—that is, conscious involvement in a "conspiracy," became the indictable offense and not mere membership in an organization only advocating forceful overthrow. This restrictive reading to the Smith Act also enabled the Court to avoid the necessity of determining whether the statute was constitutional. But it effectually did as much and in so doing it rendered the measure nugatory as a weapon against the Communist Party.

To elaborate, "[A]dvocacy or teaching" required what Kalven termed "a stringent requirement of concreteness."[37] Intent was not sufficient. Vague references to "revolutionary" or "militant" action of an unspecified character were not sufficient. To be illegal, the speech must have urged illegal conduct, which was to be found in the evidence. Harlan's demand for stricter evidentiary criteria revived Hand's argument in the 1917 *The Masses* ruling, Gunther reminds us. Harlan's words were a variation on the "hard," "objective" evidentiary standard required by Hand, and his opinion represented a doctrinal evolution, one paradoxically leading back to 1917.[38]

Harlan's judicious and utterly persuasive shrewd technical argument thus overturned both trial court judgment and that of the Ninth Circuit Court of Appeals, which had sustained convictions of fourteen of the Communist petitioners. It did avoid the obvious question of the Smith Act's constitutionality, to repeat, deciding the case on a narrow ground of statutory construction. As to the Smith Act itself, Lucas Powe rightly observes that Harlan "thought the Smith Act was 'dumb,' and he had rendered it useless."[39] His opinion, however, did so obliquely. It merely reconstructed the judicial interpretation of the statute and thereby took the usual avenue when the Court sought to avoid directly challenging the constitutional validity of a measure.

That the procedural route had been chosen is arguably defensible; or at least understandable, since the Court was speaking in what was a largely anti-judicial national climate and caution was demanded of the justices. Legislative proposals to curb the Court's power, as earlier observed, flooded from Congress. Ever vigilant in the holy war against communism Hoover, Sabin observed, had been incensed by the *Jencks* decision, and bitterly opposed the Red Monday rulings.[40] The nation's newspapers, to repeat, struck a similar note of angry protest against the decisions of that day. It ranged from the Hearst press headline after Watkins, "Communists Score Greatest Victory," to the Cleveland Plain Dealer editorializing, "Well, comrades, you've got what you wanted. The Supreme Court has handed it to you on a platter. Come and get us." The *Chicago Tribune* headlined, "Major Service for Reds," and commented sarcastically: "the boys in the Kremlin may wonder why they need a fifth column in the United States." Adding its voice, Georgia's legislature, for one, demanded that Congress impeach Warren and five associate justices for giving aid and comfort to the Communist enemy as well as for other high crimes and misdemeanors "too numerous to mention."

Accordingly, the Court was swimming against the current when it moved for dismissal of indictments of the West Coast defendants. Indeed, only in *Denver* did the Justice Department seek to re-indict Communists on Smith Act conspiracy charges. It obtained convictions, but these were reversed by the Ninth Circuit Court of Appeals, and then the government finally gave up in this case as well.[41] Thus did the Smith Act become a dead letter, with no new prosecutions brought under the statute since then. *Yates*, to conclude, was of a piece with the other rulings decided on this decision day. Taken together, Semonche contends, they were a "long overdue reaffirmation of the proper relationship of government" to its citizens.[42] But as predicators of the next few years, they were unreliable indicators since the identical quartet of dissenters was unable to muster a fifth vote in a number of cases, many of them related to fee speech and national security.

Notes

1. 353 U.S. 657 (1957).
2. Ibid., 677. One predictable consequence of *Jencks* occurred in January 1958, when the Court of Appeals in Washington, ruled that the government must produce secret reports made to it by its witnesses (one Mary Markward in this instance) (*The New York Times*, January 10, 1958).
3. Frank Donner, *The Age of Surveillance: The Aims and Methods of America's Political Intelligence System* (1981), 80.
4. Robert J. Goldstein, *Political Repression in Modern America* (Cambridge, MA: Schenkman Publishing Group, 1978), 244.
5. Arthur Sabin, *In Calmer Times: The Supreme Court and Red Monday* (Philadelphia, PA: University of Pennsylvania Press, 1999), 1, 6. On COINTELPRO, see also Robert J. Goldstein, *Political Repression in Modern America*, 452–3, 470–1.
6. Seventy bills were introduced in 1957, and eventually over 100, that proposed to curb the High Court's authority or undermine protected speech. David Caute, *The Great Fear. The Anti-Communist Purge under Truman and Eisenhower* (New York, NY: Simon & Schuster, 1978), 157. See also Sabin, *In Calmer Times*, 148; and Paul Murphy, *The Constitution in Crisis Times 1918–1969* (New York: Harper & Row, 1972), 91–2.
7. Quoted in Walter Murphy, *Congress and the Court. A Case Study in the American Political Process* (Chicago, IL: University of Chicago Press, 1962), 89.
8. Congressional Record, 85th Cong., lst Sess., p. 12806.
9. Ibid., see also Murphy, *The Constitution*, 332.
10. 354 U.S. 363 (1957).
11. 354 U.S. 178 (1957).
12. Ibid., 185; see also Bernard Schwartz, *Inside the Warren Court* (Garden City, NY: Doubleday, 1983), 118; On Watkins' refusal "to discuss the political

activities of my past associates." See *Watkins*, 354 U.S. at 185, and Jonathan Casper, *Lawyers Before the Supreme Court: Civil Liberties and Civil Righs* (Urbana, IL: University of Illinois Press, 1972), 25.
13. Disputing the defense contention that the record showed no questions were related to a valid legislative purpose, Solicitor General, J. Lee Rankin disingenuously contended: "The committee was diligently trying to ascertain facts on which it could legislate." *Watkins*, 354 U.S. at 200.
14. *Watkins*, 354 U.S. at 199, 200.
15. Ibid., 202.
16. Ibid., 197.
17. Ibid., 197–8.
18. Ibid., 197.
19. Ibid., 197–8.
20. Ibid., 198.
21. 354 U.S. 234 (1957).
22. Ibid., 250, 251.
23. Schwartz, *Inside the Warren Court*, 118.
24. Robert Carr, *The House Committee on Un-American Activities, 1945–1950* (Ithaca, NY: Cornell University Press, 1952), 15.
25. *Watkins*, 354 U.S. at 252.
26. Lucas Powe, *The Warren Court and American Politics* (Cambridge, MA: Harvard University Press, 2000), 97.
27. *Sweezy*, 354 U.S. 234 at 265.
28. Ibid., 261.
29. Ibid., 265, 267.
30. *Yates v. United States*, 354 U.S. 298 (1957).
31. Stanley Kutler, *The American Inquisition: Justice and Injustice in the Cold War* (New York: Hill & Wang, 1982), 181.
32. *United States v. Yates*. U.S. Dist. Ct. for S. Dist. of California, Central Division, 158 F. Supp. 480 at 485 (1958). See also 1956 WL 89584 Appellate Brief, *Yates v. United States* (1956). On writ of cert. to 9th Cir. Ct. of App.
33. Quoted in Sabin, *In Calmer Times*, 163; and Schwartz, *Inside the Warren Court*, 117. Warren, in conference, expressed anger at the timing of an FBI report: it contributed to an "impregnating atmosphere" in the *Yates* trial. Schwartz, *Super Chief: Earl Warren and His Supreme Court—A Judicial Biography* (New York: New York University Press, 1983), 223.
34. *Yates*, 354 U.S. at 321–2.
35. Ibid., 321–2.
36. Ibid., 325, 327.
37. Harry Kalven, *A Worthy Tradition* (New York: Harper and Row Publishers, 1988), 216.
38. Gerald Gunther, *Learned Hand. The Man and the Judge* (New York: Alfred A. Knopf, 1994), 603.
39. Powe, *The Warren Court and American Politics*, 95.
40. Sabin, *In Calmer Times*, 147, 151. Barry Friendman, ed. *How Public Opinion Has Influenced the Supreme Court and Shaped the Meaning of the Constitution* (New York: Farrer, Straus and Giroux, 2009), 512, 513 n. 165. See also

Alexander Charnes, *Cloak and Gavel: FBI, Wiretaps, Bugs, Informers and the Supreme Court* (Urbana, IL: University of Illinois Press, 1992), 9; Michael Belknap, *The Supreme Court Under Earl Warren, 1953-1969* (Columbia, S.C.: University of South Carolina Press, 2003), 256–257.

41. Kalven, *A Worthy Tradition*, 219. Ultimately, courts of appeals in four different circuits ordered the release of the remaining nine defendants. See Belknap, *The Supreme Court Under Earl Warren, 1953–1969*, 257, and also Powe, *The Warren Court and American Politics*, 95.

42. John E. Semonche, *Keeping the Faith. A Cultural History of the United States Supreme Court* (Lanham, MD: Rowman & Littlefield, 1998), 258.

12

"Exposure Purely for the Sake of Exposure" (Brennan in *Barenblatt*)

No earlier Court had assumed a more evident sensitivity in the field of civil liberties than had the Warren Court with the *Jencks* decision and the four historic opinions that followed on Red Monday. *Yates* in tandem with *Nelson* did indeed produce a decline in successful prosecutions for sedition and curb the threat to outlaw the Communist Party. In addition, in the 1956–57 term, the Court had struck down or restricted aspects of the loyalty–security program, use of faceless informers, passport and travel restrictions, state anti-subversive statutes, and dismissal for invoking privilege. But too much should not be made of what appeared to be a shift in judicial thought and outlook. After all, no court has ever overturned a national sedition statue, such the Smith Act (1940), the McCarran Act (1950), and repressive provisions in Taft–Hartley Act (1947).

Moreover, the marauding practices of the HUAC and SISC continued, as did the security hearings of other congressional committees where the good name and reputation of "the accused" were at stake. Neither did the FBI cease and desist. After Brennan had affirmed that criminal defendants had the right to inspect and use FBI reports, Hoover had dubbed Jencks as tantamount to a "burglary" of Bureau offices, but it did not discourage his relentless pursuit of the Red Menace. He expanded Cointelpro in March 1960 to frustrate communist infiltration of respectable organizations like the Boy Scouts. In October 1963, he reintroduced an order to "to expose, disrupt, misdirect, or otherwise neutralize" suspected individuals and organizations. Perhaps owing to the slimness of the pickings, the Bureau enlarged the focus slightly from Communist Party members to non-communist groups and individuals thought susceptible to communist ideas and programs, such as the Socialist Workers Party, the War Resisters League, Students for a Democratic Society, Student Non-Violent Coordinating Committee, Black Panther Party, and Women's Liberation Movement. This wider spectrum of dissidents was so inclusive that the Bureau targeted no less than 1,100 organizations by the early 1970s. He broadened Bureau investigative practices to include judicial and executive branches as well; he used spies and informants to gain knowledge of the conversations inside and outside the judicial chambers. Further, his "Special Inquiries" on judicial nominees, as Alexander Charnes details it, enabled him to favorably influence successive presidents toward those federal court nominees favored by the Bureau.[1]

Virtually all Americans considered Hoover a God-like figure and they fully supported FBI practices. There was, after all, little public respite from the familiar obsessive belief that all communists should be hunted down and excluded not only from "sensitive" positions, such as government work, defense plant jobs or the classroom but also from most other employment—to the point of barring them from public speaking, revoking their citizenship, putting them in jail, and excluding them from tenancy in public housing. The very popular Medicare Act of 1965 would deny communists medical care by its provision (later invalidated) withholding benefits from any member of an organization ordered to register with the SACB. Legal professionals readily fell into line. The American Bar Association, for example, instituted a practice of asking all applicants for membership whether they belonged to a "subversive" organization. Reacting to *Schware* and *Konigsberg*, and more recently to such decisions as *Nelson* and *Yates*, the 1958 Conference of State Chief Justices censured the Supreme Court for failing to exercise sufficient self-restraint and passed a report approving congressional revision of judicial decisions that it pronounced "unsound."

Neither political branch needed any encouragement. In 1970, Tom Huston, a Nixon advisor, introduced his plan which proposed surreptitious mail opening, electronic surveillance, illegal break-ins, and infiltrations of campus organizations. Congressmen on both sides of the aisle allied with the FBI and the ABA and, as described earlier, drafted further legislative proposals following upon *Yates*. These proposals were to be expected—considering the media and public reaction to fourteen communists being freed, two suspected communists allowed to practice law, a "security risk" employment discharge overturned, state and congressional investigations checkmated. Five measures to reverse the *Yates's* decision definition of the word "organize" were introduced in Congress, one of which was Senator Jenner's, described earlier, that proposed to curb the Court's appellate jurisdiction in specified categories of litigation.[2] Paul Murphy attributed such proposals to a "well-worn pattern" apparent across Supreme Court history. When important decisions are made on public policy, criticism of them often prompted a congressional reaction. They also encouraged a "judicial retreat." It was no rout, however. The Chief Justice and his majority most likely recognized, as both Walter Murphy and C. Herman Pritchett have speculated, that the Court was required to moderate its position after rendering free-speech decisions that ran across the popular grain. Judicial prudence, moreover, required a shift of only two votes to swing the Court from its recent decisions in the field of civil liberties. And Frankfurter and Harlan apparently got the political message. Frankfurter continued to affirm the government's position in most domestic security cases, even while protesting to Justice Brennan that "there isn't a man on the Court who personally disapproves more than I do of the un-American Committees, of all the Smith prosecutions, of the Attorney General's list, etc. etc."[3] Harlan thought anti-Red measures to be "dumb" though he, too, would reverse himself, retreating from his brave decisions of 1956 and 1957. In short, the 1957 decisions were important and lasting, but regardless of them, in fact because of them, the High Court majority at times understandably made a tactical fall-back in the early Sixties, as suggested by such decisions, as *Noto v. United States* (1961) and *Scales v. United States* (1961).[4]

The administration remained as unready as Congress to accept the message of Red Monday. The Justice Department continued to conduct legal proceedings, observed Michal Belknap, and there would be eight prosecutions under the "membership" provision of the Smith Act of 1940, in addition to the "conspiracy to advocate" prosecutions. The first was that of Claude Lightfoot, a forty-five-year-old Black Communist official in Chicago.[5] Hearing the case, District Court judge Samuel Perry remarked, when refusing to reduce bail: "The government needs to produce very little evidence, if any, in order to establish the defendant is guilty of the charge in the indictment"; and Lightfoot *was* found guilty of being a member of the Communist Party, grounded on the time-honored proposition that it advocated forcible overthrow of the government, and he was sentenced to a five years prison term in January 1956.

The cases of *Scales* and *Noto* were two of the eight prosecutions that would *test the constitutionality of the membership clause of the Smith Act,* and each reached the Supreme Court. Similar to Claude

Lightfoot and to Steve Nelson, Junius Scales held an official position in the Communist Party. A cotton textile factory worker, he had who joined the Party in 1946 and would become head of its North and South Carolina branches. After being arrested in November 1954, he would be dragged through trials and retrials for no less than seven years. Federal District Court Judge Philip Sullivan, rejecting a motion for a directed verdict of acquittal, stated: "there was evidence from which a reasonable mind could conclude beyond a reasonable doubt that the defendant knew that the Communist Party advocated the overthrow the Government of the United States by force and violence ...."[6] Counsel for both Noto and Scales had requested FBI documents that the prosecution withheld. In the light of Jencks, Solicitor General J. Lee Rankin regretfully concluded that the convictions of Scales and Lightfoot had to be reversed. Owing to his memorandum, the Court did not take the case.

Scales, however, would be reindicted under the 1940 Smith Act and its clause of "knowing" membership and "knowing the purpose" of the Party's illegal purposes (as Lightfoot had been). Attorney General Brownell was determined to have the clause sustained by the Court. Judge Albert Bryan in District Court reminded jurors that the issue was not whether they agreed or disagreed with the goals of the Communist Party. "You cannot convict the defendant," he cautioned, "merely because he was a member or an officer of the Communist Party, no matter what were the principles and teachings of the Party; for membership alone is not a crime." Notwithstanding this caveat, the jury found Scales guilty, and he was sentenced to six years in prison, the most severe punishment then dealt out under the 1940 Smith Act, and his conviction would be upheld by the Fourth Circuit Court. Chief Judge Parker, relying on *Dennis*, quoted at length from it in disposing of the constitutional challenge to the membership-equals-conviction clause of the Smith Act.

Scales[7] would be restored to the Supreme Court's calendar in February 1958. Petitioner, as he had in the two lower courts, challenged the constitutionality of the membership clause of the 1940 Smith Act. He added a further challenge on evidentiary grounds, namely specific FBI documents that had earlier been requested and that the prosecution now admitted should have been turned over. The decision, written by Harlan for a majority of five, recognized that membership "alone need be doing nothing more than signifying ... assent to its purposes and activities, and providing" only "moral encouragement."[8] Thereby distinguishing the mere member from the conspirator, he argued that membership alone could not be proscribed. The statute punished only the "active, knowing" member of an organization committed to revolutionary actions, the person who knew it was acting illegally and who would personally further its illegal ends.[9] In short, one who had the "specific intent to bring about violence" and "overthrow of the government as speedily as circumstances would permit," fell under the Smith Act's prohibition. But not the one whose joining was "merely an expression of sympathy with the alleged criminal enterprise."[10] Harlan thus drew a clear line between knowing and passive membership, that is, between the active and non-active, the non-conspiratorial. "Knowing" membership should be construed as interpreted by the Smith Act in both *Dennis* and *Yates* decisions, that is, membership that was active, that was "a purposeful form of complicity," in an organization seeking to incite forcible overthrow of the government.

Harlan then had to determine whether Scales "as a Party official," knew of its true nature; and he located the required concreteness and evidence in the testimony of three lower court trial witnesses, comparable testimony that had been lacking in *Yates*.[11] Moreover, the accused had supplied explicit evidence that communists preached violent revolution and had also openly admitted Party membership and knowledge of its character by testifying to his activities in several states and at seven schools. The petitioner was an "active" Party member, not merely "a nominal, passive, inactive or purely technical" member. The jury had been "instructed that in order to convict," it had to make that distinction, one which fully satisfied the requirements of *Yates*—and it correctly inferred that "the doctrine of revolution ... was put forward as a guide to future action."[12] The prosecution, Harlan concluded, had met the evidentiary standards of *Yates*. "Advocacy" in the sense required by the Smith Act, that is, "advocacy of action," Harlan flatly declared, was not constitutionally protected speech and membership, when it was "a purposeful form of complicity in a group engaged in ... forbidden advocacy." In such instances, First Amendment protections were not applicable and could not be invoked.[13]

To summarize, the Court majority had backpedaled from the landmark decisions of June 1957. As a consequence, it fell out that in the twenty-two years of Republican and Democratic administrations, only one person, Junius Scales, would be sent to prison as a result of the Smith Act's membership clause. Moreover, he would paradoxically receive a heavier sentence, that of five years, than any of the defendants convicted under the "leadership clause" of the Smith Act, except for Eugene Dennis, the onetime General Secretary of the Party.

In *Noto*,[14] a companion case to *Scales* and decided on that same day, John Francis Noto, a onetime Communist Party official in Western New York had been arrested for inflammatory speech. Convicted of violating the Smith Act membership clause and sentenced to five years in prison, Noto challenged his conviction on constitutional grounds as well as on the sufficiency of evidence; and the latter argument was the only one Harlan, speaking for the majority, thought necessary to consider, the other claims having been settled in *Scales*.

Egregious words had produced the defendant's arrest, but Harlan found it was not proof of advocacy of future violence. He looked to the evidence. The testimony of one witness, he noted, consisted mostly of "copious excerpts from the 'communist classics' and dealt with abstract matters"; that of a second witness related to meetings and classes in the Buffalo area, and the local Party's insistence on the priority of industrial work; that of a third witness told of the necessity of "receiving solid support from the labor unions." Harlan then concluded that the mere abstract teaching of Communist theory was not identical with "preparing a group for violent action and steeling it to such action."[15] "The criteria for proof" for future membership cases, he argued, "were strict and clear: there must be some substantial direct or circumstantial evidence of a call to violence now or in the future which is both sufficiently strong and sufficiently pervasive to lend color to the otherwise ambiguous theoretical material regarding Communist Party teaching, and to justify the inference that such a call to violence may fairly be imputed to the Party as a whole and not merely to some narrow segment of it."[16] Accordingly he concluded that "[t]he kind of evidence which we found in Scales sufficient to support the jury's verdict of present illegal Party advocacy is lacking here in any adequately substantial degree."[17] In short, the prosecution had only shown that the Party taught merely the "abstract doctrine" of inevitable revolution, but produced little that would corroborate the charge of unlawful incitement to future action by the accused.

Harlan had thus switched sides, joined by his four colleagues in *Scales*; and for a unanimous, Court reversed the conviction of *Noto*. His opinion would make it impossible for the Justice Department to enforce the statute's membership provision against active Communists, however prominent. As such, it had a chilling effect on the future membership clause prosecutions because it would require a call to violence "now or in the future" to convict. The end result, Belknap concluded, was that the membership clause of the Smith Act had joined the wake for conspiracy prosecutions. Noto had left that provision "a spent bullet," and the government (as in the case of Claude Lightfoot) soon abandoned prosecutions under it.[18]

Considering the outcome in *Scales* and in other cases in these years, it becomes apparent that the shift attributed to the Court on "Red Monday," 1957, as critics angrily termed it, was not entirely seismic. Admittedly in eight decisions after 1953, petitioner challenges to state and federal investigatory authority were upheld by the Court. And with June 17, 1957, after a decade of largely unrestrained state and federal legislative activities, a partly reconfigured High Court did impose its first restrictions on the compelled testimony of witnesses. But as evident in the *Noto* and *Scales* decisions, the judicial seesawing back and forth continued. The fluctuations would also be evident in successor cases, dealing with legislative investigations of alleged subversion. And the outcome indicates that the Court majority did not develop First Amendment safeguards against legislative committee investigations that it had seemingly been on the threshold of implementing in *Watkins* and *Sweezy*.

In *Barenblatt v. United States* (1959),[19] HUAC inquiries and the "pertinency" issue were once again under consideration, with Frankfurter and Harlan reversing their earlier direction. They moved to positions favoring the government, which trend would continue in the forthcoming decisions. The *Barenblatt* case itself was one more signifier of the enduring discord on the bench. Lloyd Barenblatt, a one-term psychology instructor at Vassar College, had refused to answer questions during a June 1954 session of the Subcommittee of HUAC that was scrutinizing "Communist Methods of Infiltration (Education)." When asked about his student days at the University of Michigan, he did not invoke the Fifth Amendment but contended that an inquiry into his political beliefs infringed on rights protected by the First Amendment; and further, that he had not been notified of the pertinency of the questions to the subject under investigation. Overruling every point of defense counsel objections, the trial court convicted him of contempt of Congress and sentenced him to a six-month jail term.

The Supreme Court had to grapple with two basic matters in *Barenblatt*: (1) congressional investigatory powers and (2) the pertinency of the questions asked by the accused. *Hardly a secondary consideration*, there was also the First Amendment challenge that the full Court finally confronted after Frankfurter and Harlan had raised it in their *Sweezy* concurrence. Under the *Watkins* precedent, the defense had argued, conviction should be reversed and Chief Justice Warren, in conference, had no doubt that *Watkins* served as the guide. But in Barenblatt, Harlan's five-man majority opinion for a bitterly divided tribunal represented an abandonment of *Watkins* as controlling. The Court was able to do so because Justice Potter Stewart, a recent appointee to the bench, joined Harlan to form a realigned majority of five rebutting the defense charge of abuse of legislative investigatory powers. In this case, the new majority emphasized congressional authority to conduct investigations, which rested "on the right of self-preservation," a right "in the field of communist activity ... [that] is hardy debatable." Although the HUAC authorizing resolution when read "in isolation" might be considered vague, as plaintiff had argued, the majority had no doubt "that in pursuance of its legislative concerns in the domain of 'national security' the House has clothed the Un-American Activities Committee with pervasive authority to investigate Communist activities in this country."[20] Moreover, the Committee had been investigating communist infiltration in the field of education since 1938, and there simply was nothing in this "legislative history" to indicate congressional disapproval.

On disposing of the vagueness and pertinency challenges, Harlan turned to the "ultimate question, ... namely, the applicability of the First Amendment." In wrestling with the issue, he did not revert to the Hand–Vinson "probability" gloss on clear and present danger, but to the balancing doctrine. The First Amendment Harlan admitted, "in some circumstances protects an individual from being compelled to disclose his associational relationships," but it "always involves a balancing by the courts of the competing private and public interests at stake in the particular circumstances .... We conclude that the balance between the individual and the governmental interests here at stake must be struck in favor of the latter, and that therefore the provisions of the First Amendment have not been offended."[21] Herein the highly schematic balancing of "competing private and public interests" was revived. The right of freedom of association was weighed against the government's interest in self-preservation, and the latter, "the ultimate value of any society," had priority.[22] In short, the widely endorsed trope that Communist Party tenets included "the ultimate overthrow of the government by force and violence," governed Harlan's decision, as did the rationally groundless fears of America's Communist Party. This familiar raison d'état had long morphed into axiomatic judicial doctrine. So phrased, it becomes appropriate to repeat the melancholy conclusion that the Court is not an impartial institution, that it is hardly neutral and elaborating, that those who presided over federal and state tribunals are not insulated from perceptions of the public as well as the political branches, indeed usually sharing their outlook. As such, A. S. Miller harshly concluded, judicial opinion may be characterized as "officially sanctioned thought control."[23]

Uphaus v. Wyman (1959)[24] likewise discloses (1) the ongoing divisiveness on the Court; (2) resort to the balancing doctrine to uphold state investigatory powers; and (3) the continuing majority retreat from its position announced in *Watkins* and *Sweezy*, decided on the same day as *Barenblatt*, it produced the same five-justice majority of Whitaker, Stewart, Clark, Harlan, and Frankfurter, one that would dominate into the immediate future. Two important questions were before the Court in *Uphaus*. First, whether the compelled production of names and correspondence could so inhibit the petitioner's free speech rights as to violate the First Amendment. Second, whether under the 1956 *Nelson* decision, the federal government had pre-empted the field of subversion and state anti-subversive statutes could not stand. The justices in their deliberations again applied the balancing-of-interests doctrine and again tipped the scales in favor of government interests, the State of New Hampshire in this instance. They heard the State's Attorney General, Louis Wyman, that one-man anti-subversives committee, re-affirm the contempt conviction of Willard Uphaus. Under subpoena, Uphaus had testified to his own activities, but refused to turn over a guest and speaker list of those who, during a two-year period, attended a New Hampshire summer camp operated by World Fellowship, of which he was Executive Director. Held in contempt for his refusal, he was sentenced to jail until he purged himself of this charge. With the case before the Court, Wyman argued that "the public interest in disclosure" must be balanced against the rights of free speech. The State, he declared, had a right to protect itself against violent overthrow; and on this occasion, it was just seeking to learn what was occurring within its borders.

The Court would be badly split over Wyman's demand for disclosure of the camp guest list. Frankfurter, as earlier mentioned, disapproved "of all the un-American Committees, of all the Smith prosecutions, of the Attorney General's list, etc., etc.," but—and the "but" remained omnipresent—deference to the legislature dominated his thinking and investigative abuses were not for the Court to reverse. As senior justice for the majority, Frankfurter assigned the opinion to Clark, who had authored dissenting opinions in *Watkins* and *Sweezy*. The outcome was predictable.

Congress, according to the *Nelson* ruling, had pre-empted the field of state legislation directed against sedition but Clark, for the majority, ruled that neither it nor the multiple federal laws dealing with national security had prohibited the right of states to protect themselves from subversion.[25] New Hampshire clearly had authority to "proceed with prosecutions for sedition against the state itself."[26] Since the State could prosecute for sedition within its bounds, *a fortiori*, it may investigate in this area. Having found that at least nineteen speakers at the camp had Communist connections, Wyman's investigation into "subversive activity" was justified, including the compulsory disclosure of guest lists. Once again, the "public interests" were weighted against the "private ones" and a state's interests in discovering the presence of possible subversives "'overbalance' any right to privacy that may have been of concern."[27] This "interest," he continued, "outweighs individual rights in an associational privacy which, however real in other circumstances … were tenuous at best."[28] And the investigation was warranted "in the interest of self-preservation," which was "the ultimate value for any society."

The conservative Ohioan, Justice Potter Stewart, would become a pivotal figure in cases now coming before the Court, replacing Justice Burton after seasoning on the Sixth Circuit Court of Appeals. He was known for qualities of judicial deference and self-restraint coupled with, Leonard Levy contends, "a constipated understanding of the judicial function in the realm of constitutional law."[29] He lacked Warren's readiness to make bold generalizations, or Douglas' to tackle constitutional issues, or Black's moral earnestness. As to be expected, Stewart found Harlan's and Frankfurter's conservatism very appealing, whereas judicial efforts to curb governmental powers or have the Court serve as a vehicle for social change were repugnant to him. Hence, his opinions would be concise and narrow, averse to upsetting precedent and limited to procedural issues if possible. His swing in two 1961 cases, *Braden v. United States* and *Wilkinson v. United States*,[30] would sustain HUAC subcommittee convictions for contempt.

Carl Braden had been a Southern civil rights activist, long devoted to the cause of racial integration, opposed to the HUAC investigations on the subject, and prominent in a petition drive against the Committee.

"Exposure Purely for the Sake of Exposure"

In the companion case, Frank Wilkinson was also well known for his efforts to abolish the Committee. He had traveled to Atlanta to monitor the July 1958 hearings conducted there by a Subcommittee of the HUAC about alleged Communist infiltration of basic industry and about Party propaganda in the South. Both men who were prime congressional targets and, under subpoena, would be questioned about Communist Party membership and activity. Refusing to answer such inquiries, each claimed that the Committee purpose was to harass and expose them for criticizing it. Each was duly indicted and invoked both the First Amendment as well as the question of "valid legislative purpose," that is, the "pertinency" defense—and each was duly convicted of contempt for refusal to answer HUAC questions about Communist Party membership.

In a five-to-four opinion, Stewart for the Court majority upheld these convictions, rendering the opinion in each instance. A number of issues were before the Court, the first being whether the interrogation had been authorized by Congress. Stewart, *sub silentio*, partly reversed *Watkins, the decision that* had found House Rule XI to be vague. By this Rule Congress, he concluded, had conferred "investigative authority upon the committee [HUAC] and its subcommittee." Consequently, "information as to the extent in which the Communist Party was utilizing legitimate organizations and causes ... [in the South] was surely not constitutionally beyond the reach of the sub committee's inquiry."[31] A second concern centered on "whether the question asked the petitioner [was] pertinent to the subject matter of the investigation." The *Watkins* decision, it will be recalled, had struck down the interrogation on grounds of pertinency and hence as a denial of due process. In contrast, the majority in *Wilkinson* and *Braden* contended that refusal to answer because the questions lacked pertinency was "without foundation."

Confronted by the further question, "did the subcommittee's interrogation violate his [Wilkinson's] First Amendment rights of free association and free speech?" Justice Stewart affirmed that congressional authority was "hardly debatable," "unassailably valid," and "a cornerstone of our decision in Barenblatt."[32] Resting on *Barenblatt*, he argued that interrogations about "the nature of the Communist activity involved" had "overbalanced" First Amendment protections.[33] To sum up, Stewart essentially affirmed that HUAC interrogatories were within the scope of a valid legislative purpose under an explicit authorizing House resolution and did not infringe on the First Amendment. His opinion in effect returned an almost limitlessly roving inquisitorial power to the Committee.

The Court was clearly vacillating on First Amendment issues in the late Fifties and early Sixties. Three months after *Wilkinson*, beginning with *Deutch v. United States* (1961),[34] Stewart switched sides, enlisted in the liberal bloc and turned back toward *Watkins*. Admittedly, the case did not turn on a First Amendment or Smith Act issue, yet it deserves explanation because the Communist Party was the subtext. The plaintiff, Bernard Deutch, a graduate student at Cornell University, gave testimony describing Party activities at the school before a HUAC Subcommittee investigating Communist Party activities in the Albany, New York area. "[A]bout all that happened [at Cornell]," he recalled, "were bull sessions on Marxism and some activities like giving out a leaflet or two. The people I met didn't advocate the overthrowing of the Government by force and violence, and if they had, I shouldn't have allowed it." Deutch testified to having known one Cornell faculty member who was a communist, but had quit the Party. He testified to having had once received from "a personal friend, one not connected with the faculty," a $100 contribution for the Party. He also acknowledged being the only graduate student at Cornell who was a Communist and as "head" (and lone member) of the "graduate group," he attended some meetings where a "maximum of 4 or 5" persons were present. Though declaring that he was no longer a Party member, Deutch volunteered that "[t]o a great extent it is only fair to say I am a Marxist today—I don't deny that." Refusing to name those with whom he had been associated in Party activities at Cornell, he would not reply to five questions asked of him by the Subcommittee. Much as had John Watkins and Willard Uphaus, Deutch refused to testify about others; and he stated:

> Sir, I am perfectly willing to tell you about my own activities, but do you feel I should trade my moral scruples by informing on someone else? I can only say that whereas I do not want to be in contempt of the committee, I do not believe I can answer questions about other people but only about myself .... The magnitude of this is really beyond reason.

Refusal to testify earned Deutch an indictment for contempt of HUAC, the charge coming after he had answered all questions about his own Party membership. Brought to trial in the District Court of the District of Columbia, Deutch was convicted on four of five counts of the indictment, those dealing with his refusal to answer questions about other people.

The Court of Appeals affirmed the conviction and the High Court took *certiorari*, with Justice Stewart speaking for a majority that once again had to wrestle with the conviction of an admitted communist. The Court's majority could have continued to endorse inquiries into education or it could reassess *Barenblatt* and deny the propriety of such investigations. But as Warren did in *Watkins* four years earlier and Harlan chose to do in the 1959 *Barenblatt* decision, Stewart decided the case on the issue of pertinency. Vinson for the Court majority in *Douds* had rejected petitioner's objection to the ambiguity of the statute then under review. In contrast, Stewart opinion set forth a twofold basis for the pertinency of an interrogation. First, the investigatory body had to make "the subject matter... appear with undisputable clarity" to the witness, though in this instance it appeared that petitioner was unaware of how the questions being asked were related to the subject. Second, the prosecutor was obliged at the trial phase to make it clear that the questions asked by the subcommittee were in fact "pertinent to the question under inquiry." However, the government, in both instances, "failed to carry its burdens of proving the pertinence of the questions." Stewart further warned against fighting communists by "a statute which either forbids or requires the doing of an act in terms so vague that men of common intelligence must necessarily guess at its meaning and differ as its application ..."[35]

In addition, Justice Stewart observed that the petitioner, being at Cornell University in Ithaca, New York, was convicted for refusal to answer questions about communists at Albany, the city that on record was the subject of the hearing. Committee questioning, however, was unrelated to the Albany area or to Communist infiltration into the Albany labor movement, which was 165 miles distant from the Cornell campus in Ithaca. But according to Stewart, petitioner knew nothing about Albany area communist activities; and, being "basically a cooperative witness," there was nothing to indicate that, "except for giving the names of others, he would not have freely answered any inquiry the subcommittee wished to pursue respect to these subjects." In reversing the contempt citation, Stewart found, possibly with relief we may speculate, that there was no need for the Court to "reach the large issues stirred by the petitioner's First Amendment claims." Stewart held only that the prosecution had failed to make its case. Perhaps, given the times, adherents of freedom of expression should have been grateful that the Court which now, favoring the plaintiff, had at least partly reverted to *Watkins*.

The *Deutch* case was followed by an unbroken sequence of decisions reversing contempt convictions handed down by federal or state investigation committees when those under subpoena—communists or left-of-center witnesses—refused to testify about past activities or organizational commitments. *Mutatis mutandis*, they recall cases of a decade earlier. One case of Sixties, for instance, originated in hearings by a Subcommittee of HUAC, *Russell v. United States* (1962),[36] on communist influence in the press, particularly at the *New York Times*. Norton Anthony Russell, one of six newsmen who testified, refused to answer "any question not pertinent to the question under inquiry." Indulging in his penchant to seek the procedural basis for an opinion, Justice Stewart, for a five-man majority, ruled that the question of pertinency to be of "crucial importance," that "the unfairness and uncertainty are underscored in all the [six] witness cases before the Court," striking down their convictions for contempt.

Gibson v. Florida State Legislative Investigation Committee (1963)[37] originated in another instance of contempt. Florida's State investigatory committee had been authorized to investigate "vital phases of life in this State." In a clumsy and blatant effort to blunt activities of the NAACP, the committee unsurprisingly sought to force public disclosure of the membership list of a local branch of the Association—in the hope that there were communists among them. Hearsay testimony of two informants claimed that fourteen persons previously identified as communists or members of a "communist front" or affiliated organizations had occasionally attended meetings of this NAACP local in Miami "and/or" belonged to this branch. Refusing to divulge the list requested by the committee, the President of the local Miami branch was adjudged guilty of contempt by a local court and sentenced to six months in jail, a decision upheld by the State Supreme Court.

Justice Arthur Goldberg, having replaced Frankfurter and speaking for a majority of five, reaffirmed the trend to protect a witness appearing before a state legislative investigatory body. Referring to the balancing doctrine, Goldberg declared the Court was "called upon once again to resolve a conflict between individual rights of free speech and association and governmental interest in conducting legislative investigations," and he placed the weight decisively on protected rights. Goldberg concluded that informants' testimony about many of the fourteen NAACP communists to be ambiguous and "indirect." It disclosed "the utter failure to demonstrate the existence of any substantial relationship between the NAACP and subversive or communist activities."[38] Each or all of the fourteen, it appears, attended no more than one or two wholly public meetings of the NAACP, and the testimony itself was "indirect, less than unequivocal, and mostly hearsay."[39] Accordingly, the State could not demonstrate the compelling interest necessary to sustain its right to inquire into NAACP membership lists.

Further, Justice Goldberg argued that mere presence at a public meeting or mere membership may not be considered "infiltration" of the sponsoring organization. Goldberg admitted to a compelling government interest, one deemed necessary, since the direct object of the challenged questions was discovery of Communist Party membership, a matter held pertinent to the subject then under inquiry. In this case, however, alleged Communists—and Goldberg named Uphaus, Wilkinson, Braden, Barenblatt—had not been the witnesses before the Committee, and the object of the challenged State inquiry was not to discover their membership. Finally, the NAACP was a concededly non-subversive and lawful body, and it was impermissible to the demand of disclosure of its membership when such action would seriously inhibit or impair the exercise of constitutional rights. Such wholly legitimate groups must be "protected in their rights of free and private association" guaranteed by the First and Fourteenth Amendments.

Yellin v. United States,[40] a 1963 decision, was the outcome of one more instance of HUAC investigations. The Committee Chairman, Francis Walter, a month before the Subcommittee was appointed, announced "[c]ongressional public meetings ... to expose active Communists ..." They would "give ... the full glare of publicity" to those subpoenaed and "expose active communists ..." This tactic, by now three decades old, was a part of "a new plan for driving Reds out of important industries." In the *Yellin* case, a HUAC Subcommittee was engaged in a fishing expedition about communists in the Gary, Indiana steel industry. It led to Edward Yellin's refusal to testify on the grounds that the Committee was inquiring into areas protected by the First Amendment. He added: "...it kinds of appears to me as if this line of questioning is merely trying to create an impression and expose me for the sake of merely exposing me..." Contempt of Congress was followed by Yellin's conviction in a federal court of the Northern District of Indiana on *four counts* of refusing to answer questions put to him by the Subcommittee. He would be sentenced to four concurrent terms of imprisonment of one-year each. The Court of Appeals affirmed.

Chief Justice Warren's decision for the five-man majority was consistent with the Court's recent trend of reining in the practices of legislative committees investigating subversion. The HUAC, it held, had to follow its own procedures for the protection of witnesses. Otherwise it could not persuade the Court to uphold conviction for contempt because of refusal to answer the questions put to a witness. In effect, focusing on the technical rather than broad constitutional questions, Warren emphasized House Rule IV, which provided for interrogation in executive session if a committee majority believed the public inquiry might possible injury to a witness' reputation; and which procedure defense counsel had requested. The Chief Justice asserted that "it seems clear that the Committee realized its public interrogation of Yellin" would tarnish his name. Petitioner was "at least entitled to have the Committee follow its own rules ...," and Warren added, "his only remedy ... was his refusal to testify."

Similar to *Yellin*, *Gojack v. United States* (1966)[41] nearly three years later, originated in the investigate practices of HUAC, specifically in a Subcommittee hearing to hunt for communists and publicize hypothetical dangers. HUAC chair, Francis Walter, set the tone of what would be forthcoming when being interviewed in a local paper: the hearing would expose John Gojack, President of a local of the United Electrical Workers and other subpoenaed witnesses as "card carrying communists" and that "the rest is up to the community." Gojack himself refused to answer multiple questions about Communist Party membership and challenged the constitutionality of the inquiry. He was indicted and convicted of contempt.

Justice Abraham Fortas for a unanimous Court overturned the contempt conviction. Comparable to the procedural spinoff from Russell, he ruled for petitioner on non-constitutional grounds. The indictment failed to state the "subject under inquiry"; that is, the HUAC did not precisely set forth the subject matter of its investigation. Furthermore, the Court held only that the HUAC Subcommittee lacked a "lawful delegation of authority" to engage in this investigation of Communists; i.e., the Committee had not authorized the investigation and had not delegated it to the Subcommittee. HUAC Rule One of Procedures, Fortas stated, provided that "'[n]o major investigation shall be initiated without approval of a majority of the Committee.' ... [But] [t]here was no resolution, minute, or record of the Committee authorizing the inquiry with which we are concerned"; that is, the Subcommittee had not properly been empowered. In short, taking the familiar narrowly technical route Fortas, in overturning conviction declared, "it is not necessary or would it be appropriate to reach the constitutional questions."[42]

Gojack, as Harry Kalven suggests, may be read as a watering down of *Barenblatt*.[43] Indeed, he observes, since *Wilkinson* and *Braden* in 1961 there had been an unbroken sequence of judicial decisions reversing contempt convictions such as in *Deutch, Russell, Gibson, Yellin, DeGregory*, and now resoundingly so in *Gojack*. However, little reference to the First Amendment may be found. Convictions for contempt centered on procedural points: defects in indictments, lack of pertinency, vice of vagueness, committee failure to respect its established rules, and so forth. Only a judicial minority that concurred would firmly enunciate the Amendment's guarantees. In summarizing to this point in time, three observations need reiteration: the split decisions that reflect on the implacable judicial discord, the disinclination to make larger constitutional questions the fulcrum of the Court's opinions, and the anti-radicalism that still beset the three branches of government and the country at large.

Comparable to earlier years, anti-radical pathology and strategies remained indispensable nourishment for state lawmakers and investigators. Communists may have become an endangered species by the mid-Sixties, but not to the states' and their constituent, where fears of infestation persisted. Eventually a select number of cases arising out of state investigations and legislation would be reviewed by the High Court and, as observed earlier, by a new set of justices sitting on the tribunal. They would be confronted by the question of whether earlier decisions such as *Adler, Nelson*, and *Beilan* and state loyalty oaths themselves remained good law. With exceptions, this new Court majority adhered to the decisions of Red Monday. Accordingly, it departed from the Fifties, though its decisions continued to adhere to procedural or "pertinency" guidelines and avoid impeaching the constitutionality of the statutes under review.

To dredge up further loyalty oath cases after exploring the broad sweep and number of test oaths in the Fifties, one might think, would be a tiresome display of overkill. But succumbing to the temptation is not necessarily repetitious for a few reasons. For one, these cases disclose the continuation of police state practices against alleged subversives and also provide signifiers of the barely receding tidal waves of anti-communism sweeping the nation's state houses. They also reveal something of the evolution of judicial thinking. The affirmative-type oaths (the simple pledge of allegiance to the United States) continued to be upheld by the Court. But by the mid-Sixties, disclaimer-type oaths (the affidavit affirming that said employee was not a communist and did not seek forcible overthrow of government) had begun to fall—more often than not, to repeat, because of the "vice of vagueness" or procedural irregularities rather than the finding that such loyalty oaths were per se unconstitutional. Before then, and recalling the Fifties, school teachers had been the exclusive targets of seventeen states. Two of the seventeen had extraordinary legislative sweep, mandating that teachers "refrain from ... teaching any theory of government or economics or of social relations which is inconsistent with the fundamental principles of patriotism and high ideals of Americanism" and four states prohibited the teaching of communism.[44]

In the 1960s, the bell began to toll for test oaths in 1961 with *Cramp v. Board of Public Instruction* (1961).[45] The case originated when a public school teacher in Orange County, Florida, refused to sign the statutory disclaimer oath: "I have not and will not lend my aid, support, advice, counsel, or influence to the Communist Party." The defendant brought an action in the State circuit court asking for a judgment that would declare the oath unconstitutional, restricting his right of free speech and association. The circuit court held the statute valid and denied the plea for injunctive relief. Petitioner then unsuccessfully appealed to the Florida Supreme Court.

Justice Stewart, speaking for a unanimous Court, would invalidate the oath. Displaying an awareness of political and social conditions outside the courtroom, he contended that it would be "blinking reality not to acknowledge that there are some among us always ready to affix a Communist label upon those whose ideas they violently oppose."[46] But the main thrust of his opinion was that adopted in *Deutch* and *Russell* and would be cited in a number of state loyalty oath opinions that followed upon *Cramp*, namely, the statute was so vague as "to inhibit the exercise of individual freedom affirmatively protected by the Constitution."[47] Though not prepared to flatly declare the oath was per se unconstitutional, the Court in *Cramp*, and in forthcoming decisions, did as much by its *de facto* rulings.

Nostrand v. Little (1962)[48] pertained to a 1955 Washington State oath that had replaced a comparable 1933 statute and that likewise applied to all public employees, a repeat performance indicative of the persistent *ad hominem* appeal of counter subversion measures. The 1955 Washington disclaimer oath was familiar to public employees in virtually every state. It mandated disavowal of aiding and abetting forcible overthrow (and incidentally would be incorporated into a memorandum issued by the President of the University of Washington requiring all University employees to take an oath, that added a flourish to the State measure: "I am not a subversive person"). The State Supreme Court affirmed the 1955 measure and the High Court, taking *certiorari*, issued a *per curiam* decision. Vacating the lower State court decision, it remanded the 1964 case to determine whether a "hearing is afforded at which the employee can explain or defend his refusal to take the oath." Without the required hearing, the oath would be unconstitutional, since it meant one could be arbitrarily discharged.

Both Nostrand and Cramp had been directed to all public employees, as observed. The police power of the State of Washington netted a schoolteacher who objected to taking the oath, and he was discharged. The action had numberless precedents, since schoolteachers, to recall only the 1950s, had been the exclusive statutory targets of seventeen states. Coming down to the mid-Sixties, a number of decisions pertained to state oaths that had been directed exclusively toward teachers; (e.g., *Cramp v. Board of Public Instruction*. 368 U. S.) and the justices would rule along lines similar to *Cramp*. In fact, even more clearly than in *Cramp*, the vagueness and overly broad oath arguments provided the basis for upholding petitioners' appeals.

Similar to *Nostrand, Baggett v. Bullitt* (1964)[49] originated in a challenge to the 1955 Washington State oath, and appellants' contention that its language was "unduly vague, uncertain and broad." The District Court had affirmed that the 1955 oath "did not infringe upon any First or Fourteenth Amendment freedoms" and was not unduly vague. The High Court took jurisdiction. Justice White now joined the liberal bloc and spoke for the majority (with Stewart again switching sides). Asserting that criteria for allowable vagueness are more restrictive when First Amendment freedoms are at stake, White caustically asked, what did it mean to those taking the oath that they "must swear … they have not in the unending past ever knowingly lent their 'aid,' or 'support,' or 'advice,' or 'counsel' or 'influence' to the Communist Party. What do those phrases mean? … Indeed, could anyone honestly subscribe to this oath who had ever supported any cause with contemporaneous knowledge that the Communist Party also supported it?"[50] Terms in the oath such as "subversive organization" or "subversive persons," or "sympathetic association with" were entirely too broad. The oath was so ambiguous as to include "guiltless knowing behavior."[51] Cramp was controlling, and the Washington oath suffered "similar infirmities" and could not stand.

The shift in the Court's outlook had become emphatic after Arthur Goldberg replacing the departed Frankfurter established a majority that often deferred to protected rights rather than state power. By 1966, disclaimer as well as affirmative loyalty oaths had begun to fall. This became apparent in *Elfbrandt v. Russell* (1966),[52] possibly the most important state loyalty oath decision. The issue was an Arizona loyalty oath in the State's Communist Control Act of 1961 that was neither vague nor *ex post facto* and that punished only knowing membership. The statute had been whipped up by right-wing State lawmakers, spear-carriers for Arizona's Senator Barry Goldwater. Much like legislators twenty years earlier, they envisaged a vast underground network of Soviet espionage agents and were driven by the need to protect "the safety of the State of Arizona and the fundamental liberties of its citizens from the international Communist conspiracy." Section 2, Title XVI, warrants an extended quote, being the model for lawmakers in all state houses. It proclaimed the tired template for the times:

> The peril inherent in its [Communist Party] operation arises not from its numbers ['relatively small numerically'] but from ... its dedication to the proposition that the present constitutional government of the United States, and the government of the State of Arizona ... ultimately must be brought to ruin by any available means, including resort to force and violence ..."

Consumed by these fears, the legislators required loyalty oaths by public officers and employees. Consumed by fears that the "Communist movement ... numbering thousands of adherents, rigidly and ruthlessly disciplined," sought the "overthrow of the Government of the United states and of the several states," Arizona required a non-communist loyalty affidavit, much like those twenty years earlier.

One of the three petitioners, Barbara Elfbrandt, a Quaker and an elementary school teacher, filed suit for declaratory relief, declaring that "in good conscience" she could not take the disclaimer oath, not knowing what it meant and not being able to obtain a hearing to determine its precise scope. Her Complaint for Declaratory Judgment contended that the State statute violated the First Amendment, "as made applicable to the States by the Fourteenth ...." It was an abridgement of freedom of speech, assembly, and association. The measure also violated the Fifth Amendment's equal protection of the law by compelling a person to be a witness against himself; and deprived petitioner and all others similarly situated, of life, liberty, and property without due process of law. The county's Superior Court denied her Complaint, a judgment upheld by the State's Supreme Court sustaining the oath.

The High Court granted her petition for the *writ of certiorari* and Justice Douglas was assigned the Court's opinion for a five-to-four majority. Abandoning the void-for-vagueness rationales of *Cramp* and *Baggett*, inter alia, he forthrightly struck down the statute as an instance of guilt by association, because the oath could punish not only "knowing" membership but also guiltless membership or actions as well, a throwback to *Yates*. "Those who join a 'subversive' organization but do not share in its unlawful purposes and who do not participate in its unlawful activities," he countered, pose no threat, either as citizens or as public employees.[53] "Mere knowing membership" in the Communist Party could not be penalized, as the State statute had prescribed. "A law which applies to membership without the 'specific intent' to further the illegal aims of the organization infringes unnecessarily on protected freedoms." Entirely too sweeping, it "impose[d], in effect, a conclusive presumption that the member shared the unlawful aims of the organization." In short, a state government could no longer criminally punish for Communist Party membership or prohibit public employment to Party members unless the member personally participated in its illegal activities. When joined to Wieman, Cramp, and Baggett, Elfbrandt indicates how far the Court has moved from the older disingenuous thinking found in *Beilan* and in similar judicial opinions affirming loyalty oaths in the 1950s.

If Elfbrandt meant "the demise of the oath," as Jerold Israel confidently claimed, *Keyishian v. Board of Regents of the University of the State of New York, et al.* (1967)[54] interred it permanently. Yet another loyalty affidavit, one explicitly directed to teachers, it had been dictated by New York State's 1949 Feinberg Act (Section 3022 of the Education Law). This measure, to recall an earlier chapter, had charged the State Board of Regents with promulgating both loyalty oath procedures as well as a list of those organizations that advocated the forcible overthrow of the government. The nearly identical language of the l917 and 1949 measures and the decades-long spacing between them illustrates both the superfluity of the later measure and the decades-long sweep of the Great Fear. Under each statute, repeating the earlier quote, "utterance of any treasonable or seditious word or words" was ground for dismissal from the public school system; and "utterance" was defined expansively: anyone who willfully advocated, advised, or taught forcible overthrow of the government or who printed or published writing to this end.

The current legal challenge to New York State's laws and program in *Keyishian* originated in an action for declaratory and injunctive relief brought against the State University of New York (SUNY) by Harry Keyishian and four other faculty members and one non-faculty employee who refused to sign the certificate that would certify whether or not employees were communists or members of an organization, presently or in the past, advocating forceful overthrow. Each of them was then notified that refusal to comply with a requirement of the University trustees would result in discharge. A three-judge federal panel, in the U.S. Court of Appeals for the Second Circuit, held that the State program was constitutional, and the High Court took *certiorari*.

Justice Brennan, over the biting objections of the same four dissenters in *Elfbrandt*, wrote an opinion that reflected the qualitative change that had overtaken High Court personnel, attitudes, and case law decisions. In the course of expressly striking down the Feinberg Act and the *Adler* decision of the Vinson Court fifteen years earlier, he examined the specific meaning of words, in New York State's education law and in its Civil Service Law. Brennan hammered away at such imprecise words such as "seditious," finding that if they were identical to "criminal anarchy," then the possible scope of "seditious" utterances was virtually without limitation. And in a telling query on the sweep and imprecision of the statute, he asked whether "advocacy" would prohibit the distribution of a text on Marxist doctrines or one on the background of French, American, or Russian revolutions; or whether a university librarian who recommended such materials thereby "advocates" and can be subject to discharge? Or "[d]oes the teacher who carried a copy of the Communist Manifesto on a public street thereby advocate criminal anarchy?" The statute's language in effect "is plainly susceptible of broad and improper application," Brennan held. "It may well prohibit the employment of one who merely advocates the doctrine in the abstract without any attempt to indoctrinate others, or incite others to action in furtherance of unlawful aims."[55]

These statutory ambiguities in effect required a teacher to "guess what a conduct or utterance may lose him his position"—which would make one "steer wider of the unlawful zone." He argued that the "danger of that chilling effect upon the exercise of First Amendment rights must be guarded against," especially in the sensitive area of a classroom.

Consequently, he ruled that the sections of both New York State's Education Law and Civil Service Law under review swept overbroadly into association and were unconstitutional. Accordingly, *Keyishian* overruled *Adler* and eliminated the stigma of Party membership by affirming that such membership did not disqualify one from teaching in the public schools.

Following precedents established by Florida, Washington, New York, and Arizona cases, the Warren Court continued to nullify state loyalty oaths in this 1967 term. On the fifth occasion since 1961 and few months after *Keyishian*—in *Whitehill v. Elkins* (1967)[56]—the Court struck down Maryland's Ober Act. As has been described earlier, the statute's loyalty oath requirement for access to the ballot had been sustained sixteen years earlier by the Vinson Court (in *Gerende*, 1951). The case itself involved Professor Howard Whitehill, a Quaker who taught creative writing at Johns Hopkins University, and would be offered a visiting lectureship at the University of Maryland. Whitehill was unwilling to take a loyalty oath imposed by the University of Maryland Regents and they refused to hire him. His counsel, Sanford Rosen of the ACLU, then asked a special three-judge Federal District Court in Baltimore for a declaratory judgment finding the oath unconstitutional but that tribunal ruled against this suit on the ground that the Supreme Court had approved the same Maryland oath in 1951 (in *Gerende*).

To the consternation of three dissenters (Stewart, Harlan, and White), the Court voided the State oath. Douglas' majority opinion was supported by Justice Thurgood Marshall, the new appointee who had replaced the departed Justice Clark and gave the Court a solid six-vote "liberal" majority when revisiting the Maryland oath in the *Whitehill* case. The statute's Sections 1 and 13 were unconstitutionally vague, Douglas concluded, since they did not distinctly separate "permissible and impermissible" conduct in the area of academic freedom, itself an offshoot of First Amendment rights (citing Brennan's opinion in *Keyishian* that found a teacher loyalty oath was "in the First Amendment field"). He noted statutory ambiguities, such as "engaged in one way or another," a phrase that could include innocent membership—"ignorant of the real aims of the group"—in an organization that advocated forceful overthrow. Supported by judicial precedents in *Elbrandt, Baggett*, and *Keyishian*, Douglas argued that "the oath required must not be so vague and broad as to make men of common intelligence speculate at their peril on its meaning."[57] In summary, the oath lacked [p]recision and clarity. It had an "overbreadth that makes possible oppressive or capricious application," and consequently had a chilling effect upon "conscientious teachers." Although contending that "[t]he continuing surveillance which this type of law places on teachers" is repugnant to academic freedom, the Court in this case, as in the previous four, sidestepped the assertion that loyalty oaths per se were unconstitutional.

Connell v. Higginbotham (1971),[58] for one, explored the constitutionality of various Florida loyalty oaths that had been challenged by a schoolteacher whose continued employment was conditioned on taking the oath. The High Court in a *per curiam* decision affirmed the first section, the routine pledge to support the State and federal Constitution, and struck down the second, the heretofore routine anti-disclaimer pledge, because of the arbitrary character it introduced, namely, prescribing "summary dismissal from public employment without hearing or inquiry required by due process." The Court in short imposed further constraints upon state loyalty oaths, though the limitations were only procedural. (Justice Thurgood Marshall, speaking in concurrence for Douglas and Brennan, would have gone further in curbing loyalty oaths.) And so, it follows, the opinion, similar to the others described above, avoided the major constitutional questions.

At this time as well, the Court also began to strike hard against both federal and state investigatory committees and, in the manner of *Deutch*, tacked toward protection of witnesses before these committees. In one such instance, and in the same term as *Elfbrandt*, the Court—in *DeGregory v. Attorney General of New Hampshire* (1966)[59]—curbed state investigatory powers. Although not centered on teachers and loyalty oaths, it was one more judicial blow to Red Scare activities, joining *Sweezy* as a decisive restraint upon state legislative investigations. It again braked the efforts of Louis Wyman, New Hampshire's hyperactive anti-communist Attorney General. He had relied entirely upon a 1955 report of "'subversive' activities" in the State to justify investigation. The report did mention DeGregory, but connected him to the Communist Party only until 1953, over a decade prior to the current investigation. Summoned to a hearing, he answered questions relating to the post-1957 period, stating he did not engage in subversive activities and lacked knowledge of any current subversion. Though not invoking the privilege against self-incrimination, DeGregory refused to answer a series of robotic and time-worn questions about earlier periods, such as: "Have you ever been a member of the Communist Party?" "When did you join the Communist Party?" And "did you ever attend any Communist Party meeting in New Hampshire wherein any person advocated to ... overthrow, destroy or alter the government of the State of New Hampshire, by force or violence?" Trial court found him guilty of contempt for refusal to answer questions about the earlier period, and sentenced him to one year in jail or until he purged himself of contempt; and the State Supreme Court affirmed.

Speaking for the six-man majority—with Clark unexpectedly joining it as well as Justice Abe Fortas who was now on the bench (replacing Goldberg)—Douglas reversed conviction. He found, with deep satisfaction we may believe, that the New Hampshire Attorney General's inquiry had been based on the 1955 report, which dealt primarily with "world-wide communism" and the federal government rather than with the State; and, moreover, "was historical, not current .... There is no showing whatsoever of present danger of sedition against the State itself, the only area to which the authority of the State extends ..."[60] In an oblique resort to balancing, he concluded: "New Hampshire's interest is too remote and conjectural to override the guarantee of the First Amendment that a person can speak or not, as he chooses, free of all government compulsion." He enlisted two arguments to buttress the tilt placed on the weights. First, the federal government had preempted investigation of communism; and, second, the "staleness" of both the basis for the investigation and its subject matter.[61]

By this opinion, as in nineteen previous decisions in which state or federal legislative investigations would be challenged (including *Watkins, Sweezy, Deutsch, Russell, Gibson, Yellin, and DeGregory*), the Court continued to settle cases on narrow procedural lines, thereby seeking unanimity and avoiding a confrontation with *Barenblatt*. Only one majority opinion, *DeGregory*, even alluded to the First Amendment. Nevertheless, these decisions sharply contrasted to the 1940s, a decade in which the bad tendency test or to the clear and present danger formula remained the standard; and they were in marked contrast to *Dennis* in 1951, when the newly minted Hand/Vinson "probability" revision of this formula provided the guideline. In a real sense, these decisions were surprising, since the belief that subversion lurks everywhere had hardly subsided. But a changed Court majority was now inclining toward the preferred position status of the First Amendment initially proclaimed by Justice Black. Would the tribunal majority consensus prevail when confronting a case originating not in a state investigation but with the HUAC? Would "staleness" of the material and/or of the investigative process remain grounds for overturning conviction? Would the Court continue to balance First Amendment claims against omnipresent security needs? Did Barenblatt in fact represent no more than a temporary deflection from the judicial trend critical of repressive legislation? These questions remained unresolved, the answers uncertain.

Notes

1. Alexander Charnes, *Cloak and Gavel: FBI, Wiretaps, Bugs, Informers and the Supreme Court* (Urbana, IL: University of Illinois Press, 1992), 8.
2. Cong. Rec., 85th Cong., lst Sess., p. 12806; and see *supra*.
3. Letter of *Frankfurter to Brennan*, January 7, 1958, quoted in Arthur Sabin, *In Calmer Times: The Supreme Court and Red Monday* (Philadelphia, PA: University of Pennsylvania Press, 1999), 207, n. 127.
4. 367 U.S. 290 (1961); 367 U.S. 203 (1961). See also Barry Friedman, *The Will of the People: How Public Opinion Has Influenced the Supreme Court and Shaped the Meaning of the Constitution* (New York: Farrer, Straus and Giroux, 2009), 515, n. 177, 178.
5. *United States v. Lightfoot*, 228 F.2d 561 (7th Cir. 1956).
6. *Scales*, 367 U.S., 203.
7. Ibid. Ironically Scales, who had been shaken out of his faith by the revelations of Stalin's terror and left the Party, was found guilty and went to prison, Noto, who never left, would have his conviction overturned.
8. Michal Belknap, *Cold War Political Justice: Smith Act, the Communist Party Act and American Civil Liberties* (Westport, CT: Greenwood, 1977), 272.
9. Ibid., 220.
10. Ibid.
11. Ibid., 228; see also Harry Kalven, *A Worthy Tradition* (New York: Harper and Row, 1988), 226–7.
12. Ibid., 232–3.
13. Ibid., 229–30, 232.
14. *Noto*, 367 U.S. at 290.
15. Ibid., 299.
16. Ibid., 298.
17. Ibid. For a critical commentary on what Harlan considered "sufficient evidence of illegal advocacy" in *Scales*, see Kalven, *A Worthy Tradition*, 225.
18. Belknap, *Cold War Political Justice*, 272. See also *Lightfoot*, 229 F. 2d, 561 (7th Cir. 1956). *Lightwood v. United States*, 355.U.S.2; 78 Sup. Ct. 10 (1057) (reversed Dis. Ct.).
19. 360 U.S. 109 (1959).
20. Ibid., 118, 126.
21. Ibid., 127, 129, 134.
22. Ibid., 134.
23. Arthur Miller, *Politics, Democracy and the Supreme Court: Essays on the Frontier of Constitutional Theory* (Westport, CT: Greenwood, 1985), 125.
24. *Uphaus v. Wyman*, 360 U.S. 72 (1959).
25. Ibid., 78.

26. For background on this case, see Willard Uphaus, *Commitment* (New York: McGraw-Hill Book Co., 1963).
27. Kalven, *A Worthy Tradition*. See also Michael Belknap, *Cold War Political Justice: The Smith Act, The Communist Party and American Civil Liberties* (Westport, CT: Greenwood Press, 1977), 262.
28. Ibid., 101.
29. Leonard Levy, *Against the Law: The Nixon Court and Criminal Justice* (New York: Harper & Row, 1974), 40. See also Miller, *Politics Democracy and the Supreme Court*, 9; and U.S. Senate Committee on the Judiciary, Internal Security and Subversion: Principal State Laws and Cases, Appendix A, Tables 1–36, pp. 439–51; *Yale Law Journal* 97 (77?), 750, 757).
30. 365 U.S. 431 (1961); 365 U.S. 399 (1961).
31. Ibid., 435. See also Robert McCloskey, *The Modern Supreme Court* (Cambridge, MA: Harvard University Press, 1972), 225.
32. Ibid., 410.
33. Ibid., 413.
34. 367 U.S. 456 (1961).
35. Ibid., 469–70.
36. 369 U.S. 749 (1962).
37. 372 U.S. 539 (1963).
38. Ibid., 554.
39. Ibid., 555. See also Kalven, *A Worthy Tradition*, 518.
40. 374 U.S. 109 (1963).
41. 384 U.S. 702 (1966).
42. Ibid., 706.
43. Kalven, *A Worthy Tradition*, 525.
44. U.S. Senate Committee on the Judiciary: Principal State Laws and Cases, Appendix A, Tables 1–36, pp. 439–51.
45. 368 U.S. 278 (1961).
46. Ibid., 284. See also Kalven, *A Worthy Tradition*, 352.
47. Ibid., 286–7.
48. 368 U.S. 436 (1961).
49. 377 U.S. 360 (1964).
50. Ibid., 369.
51. Ibid., 382–3, 373.
52. 384 U.S. 11 (1966).
53. Ibid., 17.
54. 385 U.S. 589 (1967).
55. Ibid., 606, 608.
56. 389 U.S. 54 (1967); see also Notes and Comments, "Loyalty Oaths," *Yale Law Journal* 77 (no. 4) (1968).
57. Ibid., 59. See also Notes and Comments, "Loyalty Oaths," at 746, 750.
58. 403 U.S. 207 (1971).
59. 383 U.S. 825 (1966).
60. Ibid., 829.
61. Finally, to be emphasized, Harlan's dissent (for Stewart and White) reflected the still dominant views about both communist conspiracy and judicial

deference. Anent the latter, he cited Barenblatt, and what was once the dominant contention that "[o]ur function [is] ... not to pass judgment upon the general wisdom or efficacy of the investigating activities under scrutiny." Ibid., 830. See also the following: *Brandenburg v. Ohio*, 395 U.S. 444, 452 (1969); *Communist Party of Indiana v. Whitcomb*, 414 U.S. 441, 94 S. Ct. 656 (1974); *Russell*, 369 U.S. 749; *Yellin*, 374 U.S. 109; *Gojack*, 384 U.S. at 710 (1966); Kalven, *A Worthy Tradition*, 525, 527. See also *Barenblatt* 360 U.S. 109. Following Court rulings in *Elfbrandt, Keyishian, DeGregory, et al.*, federal courts would strike down state loyalty oaths. In a typical instance, the Tenth Circuit ruled an eighteen-year-old Kansas statute requiring a loyalty oath of public officials unconstitutional (*New York Times*, September 12, 1967).

13

Requiem for Precedents

Court personnel, to remind the reader, had begun to qualitatively change in the early Sixties. The dominant majority of the 1950s would eventually be replaced when Frankfurter departed in 1962, and Arthur Goldberg arrived and was succeeded by Abe Fortas in 1965, and when Thurgood Marshall would take Clark's seat in 1967; and a fresh majority would become known for its landmark free speech decisions. Before the tribunal altered, however, it had to confront the toxic detritus of the 1950 Internal Security (McCarran) Act and the Subversive Activities Control Board that statute mandated. As could be expected, the law continued to be applied to those tainted with the brush of communism.

Section 215 of the 1950 measure made it illegal for the members of communist organizations who had registered, or required to register, to use or to apply for passports or to depart the United States without a passport.[1] Reminiscent of World War I days, passport practices reflected the fearful apparitions of administration officials, the latter creating great difficulties for those applicants suspected of subversive activities and loyalties. These practices had been administered by Ruth B. Shipley, Chief of the Passport Office of the State Department until April 1955, and she had almost complete discretion to grant or reject passports.[2] In the parlous anti-Red decades the single criterion for her decisions would be what she perceived was America's best interests, and militant anti-communism guided her, as witness revocation of passport to Paul Robeson, the legendary Negro singer who held pro-Soviet sympathies; Martin Kamen, a Washington University physicist who, she claimed, had not been completely open in his testimony before the HUAC; the well-known civil liberties lawyer, Leonard Boudin who, to her mind, was either a Party member or, if he had resigned, continued "to act in the furtherance and under the discipline of the Communist Party." New regulations issued by Secretary of State Dean Acheson in 1952 hardly departed from Mrs. Shipley's arbitrary methods. Indeed, he revealed that ninety-five persons, "because of membership in subversive organizations" had been denied passports, and another ninety-five had their passports withdrawn owing to "indicated subversive affiliation or intent." His office would then revoke or refuse to issue passports to Robeson; William E. B. DuBois; Corliss Lamont, a Columbia University lecturer; Dr. Otto Nathan, executor of Albert Einstein's will; playwright Arthur Miller; Linus Pauling, a scientist; Rockwell Kent, an artist; and so on. Robeson challenged the State Department decision, but the suit in federal district court was dismissed, on the grounds that it was not judiciable.

Max Shachtman, chairman of the Independent Socialist League, had also been denied a passport, a startling decision since, being a dedicated Trotskyite, he was on record as virulently opposed to the Communist Party and "irreconcilably anti-Stalinist."[3] But the ISL (like its predecessor, the Workers Party and its youth group, Socialist Youth League) had been thoughtlessly placed on the Attorney General's first list of subversive organizations, reason enough to deny a passport to Shachtman. He then went into federal District Court and asked for a declaratory judgment, which the Court dismissed because it found that the State Department had discretionary political authority, though it acknowledged that the ISL "had no connection with the Communist International and was hostile thereto." Appealing the decision in February 1955, Shachtman's case, *Shachtman v. Dulles*, was heard by a three-judge bench in District of Columbia Court of Appeals. His counsel argued that the denial of a passport had been on "legally insufficient" grounds. The Court cited the Fifth Amendment and found that such denial "causes a deprivation of liberty that a citizen otherwise would have." In a resounding opinion Judge Fahey argued:

> Those who inflict a deprivation of liberty are not the final arbiters of its legality. Due process of law is a judicial question ... Arbitrary action is not due process of law ... *Neither the passport act nor any Executive order should be interpreted as intended to authorize the Secretary of State to deny a passport arbitrarily or without a hearing*.[4]

Likewise affirming freedom of expression, his colleague, Judge Edgerton, upheld Shachtman's petition in an equally resounding concurrence: "The premise that a man is not free to work for the government does not support the conclusion that he is not free to go to Europe ..." The Attorney General's list lacks any "competency to prove the subversive character of the listed associations"; and the Secretary of State cannot "deny a passport arbitrarily without a hearing." The government possibly considered these forceful sentiments a premonitory signal of things to come for it did not appeal. Indeed, it delisted the ISL, fearing that otherwise petitioners would carry their case to the High Court, which might nullify the entire Attorney General's list.

Kent v. Dulles (1958)[5] of two years later was another important passport case. Under the ambiguous wording of the 1926 Passport Act exhumed on this occasion, Secretary of State John Foster Dulles issued regulations prohibiting the granting of passports to members of the Communist Party. Rockwell Kent, a well-known artist wished to visit England and Finland; and his case was combined with that of Walter Briehl, a psychiatrist. The Passport Office denied passport applications to both—on the ground, as it informed Kent, that he "had 'a consistent and prolonged adherence to the Communist Party Line.'" Briehl was charged with being a member of the Los Angeles County Communist Party. Each man was informed that before the passport could be issued, it would be necessary to submit an affidavit as to whether he was or had been a Communist. Both applicants refused, Kent's counsel asserting that it "'is unlawful and that for that reason and as a matter of conscience,' he [Kent] would not supply one." The District Court dismissed the complaints of both petitioners, as did the Court of Appeals, and the combined cases went on appeal to the Supreme Court.

Douglas delivered the five-to-four opinion. On reviewing the history of previous executive efforts at passport control, he found no precedent for such an open-ended authority. Although admitting that a 1952 congressional statute made a passport necessary for foreign travel and left its issuance to the discretion of the Secretary of State, he questioned whether the measure gave "him unbridled discretion to grant or withhold a passport … for any substantive reason he may choose" and concluded that the statute's provisions did not give "the Secretary the kind of authority exercised here." In short, the Court invalidated the State Department's unrestricted discretionary power to prohibit travel, contending that the right to do so was part of the "liberty of which the citizen cannot be deprived without due process of law under the Fifth Amendment."[6] If the right to travel were to be so proscribed, Congress must pass a statute to this effect. In closing, Douglas affirmed:

> We must remember that we are dealing here with citizens who have neither been accused of crimes nor found guilty. They are being denied their freedom of movement solely because of their refusal to be subjected to inquiry into their beliefs and associations.[7]

Following this decision, the State Department no longer cited the 1926 statute as grounds for denial of passports. Rather it turned to Section 6(b) of the 1950 Internal Security Act, which authorized the Secretary of State to deny or revoke a passport to any applicant who was a member of a "Communist organization," defined by the statute as "Communist-action" or "Communist-front," as designated by the Attorney General. Such actions were hardly a new or rash departure from the past since, as described earlier, passports were first denied to radicals after the Bolshevik Revolution, a practice reaffirmed in 1920 and not terminated until 1931. On being resumed with the 1950 Internal Security Act, a half dozen or so passport denial cases came to the High Court, having originated in statutory and executive branch limitations placed upon the right to travel.

Consistent with the 1950 statute, Secretary of State Acheson in 1951 declared that American citizens "who are members of the Communist Party, [or] who engaged in activities which support the Communist movement" or whose actions showed that they were "under the direction, domination, or control" of the Communist Party would be prohibited from travel outside the United States.[8] It was a sentiment approved by virtually all Americans and surely most congressmen. Certainly, it was congruent with the views of HUAC Chairman Francis Walter who in 1956 observed "how by stealth, by concealment, and by misrepresentation, members of the Communist Party and adherents to the Communist conspiracy are able to travel abroad for purposes deliberately detrimental to the United States."[9]

Aptheker and *Flynn v. Secretary of State* (1964)[10] was a significant 1964 passport decision and similar to other cases that had their basis in the 1950 Subversive Activities Control Act. The petitioners, Herbert Aptheker and Elizabeth Gurley Flynn, were, respectively, editor of the Communist Party's theoretical journal, *Political Affairs*, and Chairman of the Communist Party, USA. Native-born citizens, they wished to travel to Europe and elsewhere, and to write, study, lecture abroad, they stated, but their passports had been revoked by the State Department in January 1962, pursuant to Section 6(b) of the 1950 statute. Aptheker and Flynn then requested a hearing of the Board of Passport Appeals, at which time the Board concluded that the State Department had acted properly. They then sought declaratory and injunctive relief in the District of Columbia District Court, arguing that Section 6(b) was unconstitutional, *inter alia*, as "a deprivation without due process of law" of the right to travel abroad in violation of the Fifth Amendment.

Sustaining the constitutionality of the subsection, a three-judge panel concluded that "the enactment ... is a valid exercise of the power of Congress to protect and preserve our Government against the threat posed by the world Communist movement ..."

The petitioners then appealed the decision and the High Court took *certiorari*. In their "Jurisdictional Statement" before the Court, they cited *Kent* to the effect that "[t]he right to travel is a part of the 'liberty' of which the citizen cannot be deprived without due process of law under the Fifth Amendment." The First Amendment was also introduced, defense counsel restating the earlier challenge to Section 6(b), namely, it was invalid since it deprived appellants of the freedom to travel abroad. Their Brief forcefully argued that denial of the right to travel in anticipation of "future misconduct is a form of preventive detention" and is contrary to the presumption of innocence. Citing *Scales, Adler,* and *Wieman*, it contended that Section 6 was a dual violation of due process because (1) individual guilt or disqualification may not be conclusively presumed from the fact of membership in the Communist Party and (2) because "one may not be deprived of liberty or property without a hearing at which they may contest the alleged factual basis for the deprivation."[11] Moreover, the right to travel had been prohibited without even a finding that the detainee had "criminal propensities." And finally, it was "an arbitrary and irrational restraint on personal liberty having no substantial relation to considerations of national security."

Tendered by a formidable array of counsel and advisors, including Archibald Cox, the Solicitor General, the prosecution Brief was a point-by-point refutation of the defense arguments. For one, historically the right of travel has been limited by denials of passports "in the interests of national security" and that the Court has upheld congressional powers to pass measures "designed to protect national security from Communist activity." Other than beating the usual drum of "national security" and the "danger" to it, the Brief maintained that Section 6(b) "did not violate substantive rights protected by the Fifth Amendment" and that it did not prohibit what "any person may think or say, orally or in writing." The 1950 measure had characterized communists as engaged in espionage, sabotage, infiltration, etc., and "no evidence [had been] offered or adduced that the leopard of the world communist movement had changed a single spot in the past thirteen years." Consequently, so it was argued, the statute was a "reasonable regulation of conduct."[12]

Since the petitioners were notable Communist Party officials, the Supreme Court could not evade the issue by declaring Party membership unproven, but had to confront their right to travel abroad. Justice Goldberg, speaking for six justices, agreed that Congress was constitutionally empowered to protect "our Nation's security." However, "the powers of government must be so exercised as not, in attaining a permissible end, unduly to infringe a constitutionally protected freedom."[13] Justice contended that "this Court must recognize the danger of punishing a member of a Communist organization for 'adherence to lawful and constitutionally protected purposes ...'" Were a member of a registered organization to apply for a passport to visit a relative in Ireland or read rare manuscripts in the Bodleian Library at Oxford University or to receive medical treatment abroad, "or for any other wholly innocent purpose," Goldberg hypothesized that the applicant would be unable to do so.[14] The Court majority then concluded that "the substantive evil which Congress sought to control sweeps too widely and too indiscriminately across the liberties guaranteed in the Fifth Amendment." The statutory provision under review was "unconstitutional on its face," because it "too broadly and indiscriminately restricts the right to travel."[15]

The Warren Court majority showed a willingness to rule against the government on issues other than passports. The case, *United States v. Brown*,[16] came to the Court after an en banc ruling of the Ninth Circuit threw out Section 504 of the 1959 Labor Management Reporting and Disclosure (Landrum–Griffin) Act, one of many statutes spawned by the Cold War and Red Hunt. This measure, to recall, had made it a crime for a Communist Party member or a person who had been a member in the past five years to serve as a union official. Petitioner was a working longshoreman, an avowed communist, and a member of the executive board of the International Longshoreman's and Workers Union (ILWU); he had been convicted under Section 504 of the 1959 statute. Confronting the constitutional issue, the Ninth Circuit Court issued a bold ruling that found Section 504 "constitutes an invalid restraint upon the freedom of association prohibited by the First Amendment."

The government upon appeal again suffered defeat in an opinion rendered by Chief Justice Warren who, speaking for a five-man majority, supported both defense counsel argument and the Court of Appeals. Though remaining "reluctant to declare that an Act of Congress violates the Constitution," he argued that this statute illegally legislated against the Communist Party by name, thus it was in effect a Bill of Attainder.[17] It had clearly designated that persons attainted as members of the Communist Party could not hold union office without incurring criminal liability. To summarize, the majority upheld the appellate court and reversed conviction.

In a decision that also involved labor matters, but was grounded on the prohibitions of the Subversive Activities Control (McCarran) Act, the Court displayed a similar readiness to engage in judicial activism and strike down provisions it deemed unconstitutional. Section 5(a) of the Subversive Activities Control Act, it will be recalled, stated that when a "Communist-action" organization had been ordered to register, "it shall be unlawful for any member of the organization" to engage in any employment in any defense facility, regardless of the "quality and degree of that membership." Constitutional adjudication of this proscriptive section occurred in *United States v. Robel* (1967).[18] This 1967 case, similar to *Aptheker* of a year earlier, derived from the McCarran Act, only it was grounded on denial of employment rather than denial of a passport. The defendant, Eugene Robel, had worked for ten years as a machinist at Seattle's Todd Shipyards, designated by the Secretary of Defense as "defense facility"; and, as a consequence of his continuing employment there after August 20, 1962—the date of the designation—a criminal prosecution was initiated against him. He would be indicted for (1) the failure to register under a final SACB order in effect since October 20, 1961 and (2) for having "'unlawfully and willfully'" worked in the shipyards "'with knowledge of the outstanding order against the Party and of the notice of the Secretary's designation.'" Conviction carried a penalty of five years imprisonment and a fine of $10,000. The District Court for the Western District of Washington, Judge William J. Lindberg postponed issuance of an opinion for two years, while "awaiting final decision" on the *Aptheker* and *Brown* cases; and he then ruled that the prosecution offered no proof of "active membership or specific intent" to engage in illegal activity.

The prosecution would carry their case to the Supreme Court, which extended the High Court's opinion in Robel beyond Judge Lindberg's dismissal of the indictment, becoming one more blow to the near-moribund Subversive Activities Control Act. When joined by Brown, Aptheker, and Albertson, Robel seemed to announce that a new day had dawned, a departure from the earlier years when narrow technical grounds in decision-making prevailed. Unlike previous internal security cases, the majority opinion, according to Harry Kalven, was in tone, "self-confident, almost eager in confrontation of the ultimate constitutional issue."[19] In an assured six-to-two opinion (Justice Thurgood Marshall not participating), Warren affirmed petitioner's claim that Section 5(a) of SACA was an unconstitutional abridgment of the First Amendment right of freedom of association—which was a protected right comparable to the right to travel. Turning to the prosecution's national defense argument for exclusion of communists in war industries, the Chief Justice went on to declare in a daring rhetorical thrust: "Implicit in the term 'national defense' is the notion of defending those values and ideals which set this nation apart ... It would indeed be ironic if, in the name of national defense, we would sanction subversion of one of those liberties – the freedom of association – which makes the defense of the Nation worthwhile."[20]

Challenges to the constitutionality of the Subversive Activities Control Act were a constant in the Sixties. Before 1962, when Goldberg replaced the retiring Frankfurter, the judicial bloc of four (Brennan, Warren, Black, and Douglas) was in the minority, and decisions hardly congenial to the constitutional imperatives of the First Amendment at times prevailed. A signal example occurred in 1961 when the Court had to rule on the refusal of a member of the Communist Party to register as belonging to a "Communist-action" organization. Before turning to the outcome, a brief reminder that the background of the case, beginning in 1953, has earlier been set forth.[21] When resurrected in 1961 as *Communist Party v. SACB*,[22] three issues divided the justices: (1) whether the evidence was sufficient to support the registration order; (2) whether the 1950 Act infringed on First Amendment freedoms and; (3) whether, being compulsory, the government's registration requirement violated the self-incrimination privilege of confessedly communist registrants (and thereby made them vulnerable to the criminal sanctions of the Smith Act). For a Court majority, national security remained the talismanic standard across eight years of the judicial proceedings and there would be no wavering. Although less than 5,000 remained Communist Party members, they apparently continued to be an omnipresent threat, so thought the political branches as well as the public and, as argued earlier, the judiciary does not exist in a social vacuum. It follows that the judicial position and the outcome was unsurprising.

Frankfurter's 115-page majority opinion sustaining the McCarran Act's registration provision was among the longest in Court history. Speaking for five justices who likewise bowed to the prevailing winds, Frankfurter avoided the most vexatious question, namely, that of self-incrimination which, would occur when compelling officers or members of a "communist action" organization to register, that to repeat was a likelihood resulting in possible punitive sanctions—such as arrest, criminal charges, and imprisonment under the 1940 Smith Act—all legally possible upon registration. Since no one was compelled to incriminate himself, coercive registration would implicitly violate the Fifth Amendment's privilege against self-incrimination, invoked when refusing to testify. The 1950 McCarran Act, however, required one to come forward to register as a Communist.

Frankfurter, as the study has earlier noted, scrupulously avoided grappling with this issue of coercive registration explicitly antithetical to the constitutionally protected First Amendment right of association. However, by setting the registration order in isolation, unrelated to its compulsory disclosure of Party membership (and possibly punitive actions), he was able to parry claims that the self-incrimination privilege had been violated. By so doing, Frankfurter rendered a flawed analysis, Kalven critically argues, "mixing the statute [SACA] into separate, discrete steps, each of which he either evaluates in isolation or finds justification for not passing on. Thus he never confronted the cumulative impact of the Act."[23] This contention is supportable when observing that Frankfurter rejected petitions' claim that registration conflicted with the self-incrimination provision. He found the defense contention "premature" in that "[w]e cannot know now that the Party's officers will ever claim the privilege," raising a procedural option that avoided the critical issue. In short, by a strained commentary that failed to acknowledge the obvious conflict of laws and, treating registration as simple disclosure he could readily uphold the SACB's renewed registration order for Communist "action" and "front" organizations.

Frankfurter's opinion, shared by the Court majority, remained driven by the understanding that communists belonged to a "world-wide integrated movement" and would use every means "to destroy the government."[24] Since the CPUSA was a "foreign-directed" conspiracy and within the gates, expressed in the Forties and Fifties by the "Trojan Horse," metaphor, and contending, "we cannot say that the danger is chimerical." Hence, the actions of the SACB, undertaken "pursuant to its continuing duty to protect the national welfare," namely, by compulsory disclosure of Communist Party officers, resources, etc., was justified, and communists could be denied "the fair hearing which due process of law requires."

Having dismissed petitioner's claim to privilege, Frankfurter likewise refuted the further argument of a constitutional clash between the First Amendment and the registration requirement. He invoked his favored judicial doctrine of "balancing," one that implied a possible dilution of First Amendment protections. Admitting that coercive disclosure of the names of Party members "may in certain instances infringe constitutionally protected rights of association," he argued that against these rights "must be weighed the value to the public of the ends which the regulation may achieve."[25] The "gravest external dangers," he reminded his colleagues, had to be balanced against the "safeguarding of personal freedom." Rather Frankfurter expressed deference to "the congressional judgment," a conviction shared by justices Clark, Whitaker, Stewart, and Harlan who formed a majority; and it was not to be set aside "because the judgment of judges would ... have chosen other methods."[26] Congress repeatedly found "that agents of communism have devised methods of sabotage and espionage ...." and "[i]t is not for the courts to re-examine the validity of these legislative findings and reject them." By this opinion, the Court majority again signaled that it was a prism reflecting what both the public and official Washington believed at the time.

Ultimately, no one did come forward to register; and the SACB would expire in 1973 for lack of funding, the McCarran Act becoming a dead letter. Twenty years earlier, however, doctrinal and punitive aspects of the government's anti-communist registration campaign had been alive and well. The Attorney General would order twenty-three organizations to register with the SACB after April 1953. The Board dismissed eight cases, and of the fourteen that remained, ten organizations would cease to function and no action resulted. Of the four remaining cases, one became inactive before judicial action could be taken, and the Appellate Court set aside another case owing to insufficient evidence. Two cases eventually reached the High Court—the American Committee for the Protection of the *Foreign Born v. SACB* (1965) and *Veterans of the Abraham Lincoln Brigade v. SACB* (1965)[27]—and the judicial majority threw out the proceedings against both "front" groups in *per curiam* opinions.

The American Committee case came to the tribunal following the Court of Appeals decision upholding the registration order of the Subversive Activities Control Board. The Board's evidence supporting registration, which dated back to the late 1940s, the Court ruled was too dated and "stale" to be admissible. For these reasons, a "decision of the serious constitutional questions raised by the order is neither necessary nor appropriate." The *per curiam* opinion as a result would do no more than remand the order to register back to the SACB, prompting Douglas, Black, and Harlan dissents. Remand was also ordered by the appellate court in the *Veterans of the Abraham Lincoln Brigade* case because the Attorney General John Mitchell had listed the organization without notice or hearing, a procedural violation the Department of Justice had sought to follow since 1953.

A couple of codicils relating to the fate of the registration and the self-incrimination privilege in the Appellate Court are appropriate. They illustrate the government's determination to press ahead against the fast-disappearing Communist Party. In 1962, to cite one instance, at a District Court trial (*Communist Party v. United States*), Judge Alexander Holtzoff presiding, the jury found the defendant (the Communist Party), "a voluntary association," guilty of a failure to comply with the Board order to register, and it was sentenced to a fine of $120,000. In 1963, however, the District of Columbia Court of Appeals squarely met the self-incrimination issue by reversing the conviction for failure to register. The government, the Court concluded, "had the burden of showing that a volunteer [registrant] was available, and that its failure to discharge that burden requires reversal of the conviction." Chief Judge David Bazelon, for a unanimous appellate panel, recognized that unavailability was by reason of the privilege against self-incrimination and that "mere association with the party incriminates" and suffers the criminal liabilities imposed by the Smith Act.[28] The High Court, in June 1964, refused to review and thereby left stand the appellate court decision, constituting a defeat for the government.[29]

Mention of the *Albertson* decision above refers to, *Albertson v. Subversive Activities Control Board* (1965),[30] a case that originating in the administration's continued effort to find a Communist Party member, a "willing volunteer," to register an almost impossible task considering the likely criminal penalties that could be imposed. Indicative of the government's subversive-hunting zealotry, fifteen years after the first attempt to force registration upon the Party, recurrent efforts produced still another indictment by a federal grand jury. William Albertson is yet one more Party official indicted in the now-familiar saga of decisions involving the Communist Party and the registration order. The new ruling received less public and media attention than had *Dennis* or some of the later decisions grounded in the 1950 Subversive Activities Control Act, although the defendant, like so many others, allegedly represented the ongoing threat to national security. As to the case itself, Albertson was one of the two Communist functionaries (with Roscoe Quincy Proctor) arraigned by the government (under two twelve-count indictments, those of December 1, 1961, and February 25, 1965) for failure to register. The District Court would uphold the Attorney General's registration order.

The Albertson legal team opened a Petition for *certiorari* with the following: "[c]ompulsory self-identification ... is a coerced admission of political affiliation that was historically a tool of oppression. By making the admission, the registrant bows to the proposition that government has the right, as an end in itself, to inquire into, determine, and compel the avowal of political affiliation."[31] Appellants, it further stated, were entitled to a hearing, and the SACB order thus denied them due process; and, finally, the registration order constituted a bill of attainder. The arguments were repeated in the defense Brief, which noted that the Party had long sought adjudication of "the privilege issue," contending that the SACA compelled self-incrimination. Headed by the then Solicitor General, Thurgood Marshall, the prosecutorial legal team engaged in an effective point-by-point refutation of petitioners' claims. It also voiced the usual incantatory rhetoric about the "grave danger the Communist movement poses to national security and ... [its] secret and conspiratorial character ...." Their Brief declared that "[c]ontrary to petitioners' contention, the act of registration is not a compelled declaration of political belief."[32] This disingenuous comment was followed by the astonishing one that compulsory registration was not to be "considered an admission of membership."

In an eight-man unanimous opinion (Justice White having recused himself), Justice Brennan would address only one defense challenge, namely, that the registration order violated petitioners' Fifth Amendment privilege against self-incrimination. Petitioners, he contended, need not be required to wait for a criminal trial to assert their constitutional privilege, the "ripeness" contention advanced by Frankfurter in *CP v. SACB* of 1961 and now adopted by the prosecution. The 1950 McCarran Act placed the individual on the horns of an unconstitutional dilemma. By registering, that person would be subject to possible prosecution under the Smith Act and under other anti-subversion measures. Brennan cited *Blau v. United States* and *Quinn v. United States*, where questions put to those testifying on the witness stand were found by the Court to present sufficient threat of prosecution to support the claim of privilege. Similar to Judge McGowan of the Court of Appeals, he decisively intervened to vindicate the claim of privilege. It had been made "in an area permeated with criminal statutes (e.g., the Smith Act and Section 4(a) of the Subversive Activities Control Act), where response to any of the questions on the registration form would possibly involve the petitioners in the admission of a crucial element of a crime."

Although failing to openly declare the "individual membership registration" requirement unconstitutional, Brennan's opinion would in effect arrive at this conclusion. It may be said that he teases out the question of constitutionality by his unqualified declaration that the registration requirement "is inconsistent with the protection of the self-incrimination clause." Brennan it follows did confront the challenge of the Fifth Amendment that had been postponed by Frankfurter and Harlan. Communist Party members, he ruled, may invoke their constitutional privilege and refuse to register with the government.

The 1965 *Albertson* decision administered the *coup de grace* to the registration provision of the Subversive Activities Control Act, sealing its legal fate, but Harry Kalven noted that the "stigmatizing adjudication of Party status" remained unaffected.[33] The ruling became simply the latest in a series of Board cases decided in the federal courts preceding 1965. As early as 1950, as observed earlier, the Court majority upheld Patricia Blau's refusal to answer questions on Fifth Amendment grounds, and her claim to constitutional privilege against coerced confession. And it has been noted, in the year before *Albertson*, there were the *Aptheker* and *Robel* opinions and the registration orders of two Communist-"front" organizations (*American Committee for the Protection of the Foreign Born* and *Veterans of the Abraham Lincoln Brigade*), all decisions running against the government. Moreover, the *Albertson* decision resulted in the dismissal of forty-two other pending cases against alleged Communist Party members for failure to register—on the grounds that compelling them to do so would be self-incrimination in violation of the Fifth Amendment and could then subject them to the criminal penalties of the Smith Act. In summary, these decisions rendered the SACB toothless and it died an unnoted death in June 1973, after its budget line disappeared.

As this study has recorded, decisions after Red Monday, especially those in the mid-1960s, with the appointments of justices Arthur Goldberg, Thurgood Marshall, and Abe Fortas, portended a marked decline in successful prosecutions under both the 1940 Smith Act and the 1950

Internal Security (McCarran) Act, the major pillars of the government's loyalty–security program. In one more ruling, that of January 1968, the Court in *Schneider v. United States*[34] overturned another relic of the Cold War, the 1950 Magnuson Act. It had prohibited waterfront or seagoing employment to any person the Coast Guard considered "inimical to the security of the United States," a proscription resulting in the discharge of nearly 4,000 workers by 1955. This case had its beginning when Herbert Schneider, a marine engineer, was denied a license after admitting that he had once been a member of the Communist Party. Douglas, speaking for an unanimous Court, would find that the government had exceeded its authority by inquiring into the beliefs of seamen before granting them licenses. First Amendment protection of political beliefs and association, he declared, took priority over the assumption that Congress had given the government a hunting license to inquire into political beliefs.

By 1969, Warren's last term, the Court had freed the law of the *Dennis* decision. It also effectively abandoned Whitney and state anti-syndicalist laws by handing down a short unsigned *per curiam* opinion—in a watershed First Amendment decision, *Brandenburg v. Ohio*[35]—that overturned the 1919 Ohio Criminal Syndicalism Act. This 1919 statute, initially directed toward the IWW, was identical or similar to those adopted by twenty states and very much like the California statute of 1927 that had been upheld in the *Whitney* decision of 1927.

Brandenburg warrants brief mention, though it did not involve radicals of the usual stripe, but related to a red-hooded Ku Klux Klan leader speaking at a local Klan rally in rural Ohio. Culminating judicial liberalism in these years, the Brandenburg decision had high-profile status, unlike most of the decisions mentioned immediately above, because of the all-too-obvious extremism of the defendant. Addressing a raptly attentive hooded audience, some of whom carried guns, Clarence Brandenburg promised "revengeance" would be had if "our president, our Congress, our Supreme Court continued to suppress the white, Caucasian race."[36] His speech also included racist commands (e.g., "burying the nigger" and "sending the Jews back to Israel"). Indicted under the State statute, he was convicted for "advocat[ing] ... the duty, necessity, or propriety of crime, sabotage, violence, or unlawful methods of terrorism as a means of accomplishing industrial or political reform." Both the Appellate Court and Ohio's Supreme Court upheld conviction for criminal syndicalism.

In the High Court conference, all the justices agreed that the verdict should be reversed. The Chief Justice selected Justice Fortas to write what would be an unsigned *per curiam* opinion. Becoming a prominent voice affirming freedom of expression when First Amendment issues were at stake, Fortas circulated a draft opinion in April 1969 that, though *sub silentio*, refined the clear and present danger standard to the point of virtually discarding it. A second *per curiam* draft was written by Justice Brennan after Fortas had been forced to resign from the Court. Eliminating all references to clear and present danger as a governing doctrinal standard, Brennan asserted that conviction required incitement to immediate action, defined as a high and imminent probability, thereby vindicating Hand's opinion in *The Masses* of a half-century earlier and undreamed of by Vinson in the *Dennis* opinion. This revised standard was clearly protective of political dissent. "Mere advocacy," as distinct from "incitement to imminent lawless action" became insufficient, and "the contrary teaching of *Whitney v. California*, thoroughly discredited by later decisions," was explicitly overruled.[37] "As we said in *Noto v. U.S* ... the mere abstract teaching of the moral propriety or even moral necessity for a resort to force and violence, is not the same as preparing a group for violent action and steeling it to such action ...."[38]

However, interjecting a thought that may perhaps dampen accolades to the Court by champions of protected expression, Brennan's apparently firm decision on protected speech occurred in 1969, at a time when there was no war or war effort and when the fevered anticommunism had begun to wane. Only time would tell, Lee Bollinger has written, "whether the scope of First Amendment rights articulated in the Brandenburg era reflects the distilled wisdom of historical experience, which makes it more likely to survive in future periods of social upheaval, or whether the Brandenburg era will turn out to be just one more era among many, in which the freedom of speech varies widely and more or less according to the sense of security and tolerance prevailing in the nation at the time."[39]

The *per curiam* opinion effectually restored the requirement of immediacy eliminated in *Dennis*, namely, Vinson's revised probable danger standard. It ratified *Brandeis*' eloquent liberal dissent in *Whitney* and was a requiem for a long line of preceding post–World War I decisions as well. It also meant final rites for the landmark *Dennis* decision of eighteen years past, though the opinion avoided directly overruling it. In summary, the *Brandenburg* decision reflected the Court's steadily growing respect for First Amendment freedoms over an eighty-year period. But the ebb and flow of judicial protection for preferred freedoms always exists; and, as Bollinger has wisely observed the possibility of "exceptional circumstances" arising—when the country feels seriously threatened—could lead to the erosion of protection for free expression.[40] For the time being, however, Warren's conviction that "[t]he Court's essential function is to act as the final arbiter of minority rights," now guided the tribunal. Although there would be lapses with his successor, we will presently learn, the tribunal of Chief Justice Warren had finally established the entire battery of First Amendment rights as its guide and star. Admittedly, its decisions were on complex and narrow grounds and frequently fueled by bitter internecine commentary. However, final taps could be heard for a long list of precedents that upheld conviction for so-called subversive speech and activities.

Earl Warren strategically resigned in June 1968, in the expectation that President Johnson would nominate Justice Fortas to succeed him as Chief Justice. However, the incoming President, Richard Nixon, had displayed a longstanding antagonism to the existing Court majority when a congressman: it "has been wrong and the four-man minority has been right."[41] He was strongly drawn to Warren Burger, a leading conservative and strict constructionist who was Chief Judge of the Court of Appeals for the D.C. Circuit. Rumors of Justice Fortas' financial improprieties and an IRS investigation of them became public knowledge, forcing him to resign his position as Associate Justice, leaving the newly installed Chief Executive with two vacancies.

Although a well-known critic of Warren's jurisprudence, Burger had no specific agenda in regard to the First Amendment. Failing to adopt the Vinson Court majority viewpoints, his tribunal eschewed qualitative changes in case law. Though not expanding the protections afforded by the First Amendment, it preserved the major decisions of the Warren Court. It did not invoke either the Smith or McCarran Acts or the clear and present danger formula. Less activist than its predecessor, it tended to be more deferential toward the political branches. On the other hand, a few decisions of the Burger Court upholding freedom of the press and Communist Party policy statements may be cited. In the *Pentagon Papers* case of 1971, for instance, the Supreme Court, over a dissenting minority including the Chief Justice, rejected the government's claim that further publication of the "Papers" should be enjoined on grounds of national security. For the first time in several years, it should be acknowledged, the Court did rule in favor of a loyalty oath for State employees—it "does not impinge conscience of belief"—when the case of *Cole v. Richardson* (1972), after remand, was returned to the High Court (the District Court having again found the oath unconstitutional).[42] However, in another lingering State loyalty oath case, *Communist Party of Indiana v. Whitcomb* (1974),[43] the Court did in fact follow the late Warren Court precedents rather than resort to the familiar ex parte arguments for upholding a test oath. The decision was noteworthy considering the Burger Court's conservative impulses, and the departure from the bench of the great champions of freedom of expression, Justices Black and Douglas, in 1971 and 1975, respectively.

In contrast to the Warren Court, the opinions of the new judicial majority would be largely dull and unemotional and more pronounced in "underpinning the stability" of governance than it had been in the recent past—in "protecting that system from attack by resisting attempts to change it."[44] Reminiscent of Vinson in *Dennis*, Burger deferred to executive power when claims of national security were asserted. Similar to those in the past, his tribunal was responsive to the social and political context as has been adumbrated in the decades across this study. The influence of political turmoil upon the judiciary resulting from the war in Vietnam need be recalled. Court members again showed themselves as far from impassive and impartial oracles of the law. Thus, to offer one instance, they upheld a severe sentence for a young man who burned his draft card as an expression of anti-war protest.[45] It need to be emphasized, however, that on balance the Burger Court did not strip its predecessor of its formidable legacy in the field of civil liberties and First Amendment law.

Notes

1. Passport Act of 1950. Section 215 of the 1952 Immigration and Nationality Act. 66 Stat. 18, 8 U.S.C. § 1182 "excluded from admission into the United States ... aliens who are anarchists." For details on statutory precedents, see Harold Edgar and Benno Schmidt, "Curtiss-Wright Comes Home: Executive Power and National Security Secrecy," *Harvard Civil Rights-Civil Liberties Law Review* XXI (1981): 376–7.
2. Alan Rogers, "Passports and Politics: The Courts and the Communists, 1957–1965" (unpublished paper in possession of author), 4. See also "Passport Refusals for Political Reasons: Constitutional Issues and Judicial Review," *Yale Law Journal* 61 (1952): 176, an article that provides detailed instances when passports have been denied; and see Shipley to Boudin, February 24, 1955, cited in *Boudin v. Dulles*, 136 F. Supp. 218, 221 (D.D.C. 1955).

3. *New York Times*, June 24, 1955.
4. 225 F.2d 938, 938–41 (1955) (D.C. Cir. 1955). See also Rogers, "Passports and Politics," 1, 8; and Stanley Kutler, *The American Inquisition. Justice and Injustice in the Cold War* (New York: Hill & Wang, 1982), 100.
5. 357 U.S. 116 (1958).
6. Ibid., 125, 130.
7. Ibid., 129.
8. Quoted in Rogers, "Passports and Politics," 4.
9. Quoted in Eric Bentley (ed.), *Thirty Years of Treason: Excerpts from Hearings before the House Committee on Un-American Activities, 1938–1968* (New York: Viking Press, 1971), 728.
10. 378 U.S. 500 (1964).
11. Ibid., attached: Brief of Petitioner, 1963 WL 106011, 9.
12. Ibid., attached: Brief of the United States, 1963 WL 106011, n. p.
13. Ibid., 509.
14. Ibid., 512.
15. Ibid., 514. See also Rogers, "Passports and Politics," 16.
16. *Brown v. United States*, 334 F.2d 488, 495 (9th Cir. 1964); 381 U.S. 437 (1965).
17. Ibid., 458.
18. 389 U.S. 258, 258 (1967).
19. Gerald Gunther, "Reflections on Robel: It's Not What the Court Did but the Way It Did It," *Stanford Law Review* XX (1968): 1141.
20. *Robel*, 389 U.S. at 265, 266.
21. See *supra*.
22. 367 U.S. 1, 53–4, 59 (1961). This decision held that the McCarran Act provision compelling the Communist Party to register as a subversive organization with the SACB violated the Fifth Amendment's privilege clause. The District Court had ruled in favor of the SACB order and defendant's conviction. The District of Columbia Court of Appeals would reverse conviction, though leaving the constitutional issues "'unstirred' … we ventured 'no opinion concerning the Communist Party's duty to submit the data demanded.'" The government then retried appellant and District of Columbia Circuit Court Judge McGowan forcefully concluded: "I think the Government cannot compel people to incriminate themselves, either by testifying or by supplying documentary evidence … " (*Communist Party v. United States*, 384 F.2d 957, 968 (D.C. Cir. 1967)). Concurring, the Senior Circuit Judge Prettyman stated: "The constitutional protection is against compulsory incrimination of oneself … the members cannot be compelled to incriminate themselves … " (ibid., 968). See also *Communist Party v. United States*, 331 F.2d 807 (D.C. Cir. 1963); and *Albertson v. SACB*, 382 U.S. 70 (1965).
23. Harry Kalven, *A Worthy Tradition: Freedom of Speech in America* (New York: Harper & Row, 1988), 274. The statute, Konvitz cogently argued, "is more than a mere registration requirement" (Milton Konvitz, *Expanding Liberties* (New York: Viking Press, 1966), 147). It was of an "incriminating nature [that] seems plain on its face," and "would establish a main ingredient of the crime proscribed in the membership clause of the [Smith] Act as this Court construes it today." See also Konvitz, 141.
24. *SACB*, 367 U.S. at 96.

25. Ibid., 90. The Court majority, however, repeated its shilly shallying to avoid "the serious constitutional question." Critical of Frankfurter, Kalven stated: "he never confronts the cumulative impact of the Act." Kalven, *A Worthy Tradition*, 277.
26. *SACB*, 367 U.S. at 96–7.
27. 380 U.S. 503 (1965); 380 U.S. 513 (1965). Thomas I. Emerson offers a compact and useful summary of cases that arose owing to the order that Communist-"front" organizations were required to register, in *The System of Freedom of Expression* (New York: Random House, 1970), 141–2.
28. *Communist Party*, 331 F.2d at 815.
29. *United States v. Communist Party*, 377 U.S. 968, 84 S. Ct. 1696 (1954).
30. 382 U.S. 70 (1965). The three-judge appellate panel for the District of Columbia in May 1966 would hear the case upon petitioners' convictions in District Court. In its first review of the case, the appellate tribunal had affirmed the Board registration order. Upon a second appellate review, the High Court had decisively intervened, and "vindicate[d] the [self-incrimination] privilege." Judge McGowan of the appellate bench, upon a second review, arrived at the same conclusion as the High Court regarding "the vitality of the Fifth Amendment protections" (as he had affirmed in *Communist Party v. United States*, 384 F.2d 957, 968 (D.C. Cir. 1967), and the Court of Appeals reversed convictions).
31. *Alberston v. United States*, 74. See also 382 U.S. 70. Attachment: 1965 WL 115638.
32. *Albertson v. United States*, 382 U.S. 70 (1965). Attachment: 1965 WL 115638, 9.
33. Kalven, *A Worthy Tradition*, 287.
34. Emerson, *The System of Freedom of Expression*, 36–7, 190–1. *Schneider v. Smith*, Commandant, U.S. Coast Guard. 390 U.S.17; 88 S. Ct. 682 (1968).
35. 395 U.S. 444 (1969).
36. Ibid., 446–7.
37. Ibid., 448–9. On eliminating "all references" to the clear and present danger doctrine, see Bernard Schwartz, *Decision* (New York: Oxford University Press, 1996), 173; and on the "evolution" of the doctrine, see Kalven, *A Worthy Tradition*, 227–8.
38. *Brandenburg*, 395 U.S. at 448.
39. Lee Bollinger, "Epilogue," in *Eternally Vigilant, Free Speech in the Modern Era*, eds Lee Bollinger and Geoffrey Stone (Chicago, IL: University of Chicago Press, 2002), 312–3.
40. Bollinger, "Epilogue," in *Eternally Vigilant, Free Speech in the Modern Era*, 7.
41. Quoted in Keith Whittington, *Political Foundations of Judicial Supremacy: The Presidency, the Supreme Court, Constitutional Leadership in U.S. History* (Princeton, NJ: Princeton University Press, 2007), 222.
42. 405 U.S. 676 (1972). Lucinda Richardson, an employee of Boston State Hospital, challenged the State's loyalty oath statute as unconstitutional, as did a three-judge District Court that held the "overthrow" clause "'fatally vague and unspecific' and therefore a violation of the First Amendment." The High Court implausibly affirmed it. For a sharply critical and compelling commentary, see Kalven, *A Worthy Tradition*, 363–6.

43. 414 U.S. 441, 94 S. Ct. 656, 662 (1974). The case, to briefly linger over it, had originated in a 1969 Indiana loyalty oath that excavated the political detritus of previous decades, being identical to a host of earlier statutes on both federal and state levels. No "existing or newly-organized political party or organization," the measure held, "shall be permitted on or to have the names of its candidates printed on the ballot" until it has filed a loyalty affidavit. After complex legal maneuvering, the appellants turned to the Supreme Court, and Chief Justice Burger assigned the opinion to Justice Brennan who made the usual distinction between advocacy of abstract doctrine and advocacy of action. He rejected the State argument that any group advocating violent overthrow as abstract doctrine "must be regarded as necessarily advocating unlawful action" and hence should be denied a place on the ballot, an argument that had been "thoroughly discredited." The Indiana loyalty oath provision, Brennan concluded, violated the First and Fourteenth Amendments and in effect he announced a First Amendment right to political association.
44. Quoted in Arthur Miller, *Toward Increased Judicial Activism: The Political Role of the Supreme Court* (Westport, CT: Greenwood Press, 1982), 266.
45. *United States v. O'Brien*, 391 U.S. 367 (1968).

Conclusion

It should occasion little surprise that the Burger Court did not suddenly reverse Warren Court decisions, and that it sustained established free speech protections. The Supreme Court usually proceeds at a gradual pace—by chipping away at precedents it finds repugnant rather than any sudden and unqualified reversal of past decisions. To offer an early example, the justices actually began the process of refining or frustrating barely understood or acknowledged First Amendment law in the half-century after World War I ended. Only in the 1920s, however, would they even enter upon any substantial discussion of free speech and press, with decisions of the post-war years that curtailed both. A variety of government impositions upon freedom of expression occurred during and after the World War I. As it is typical in a time of crisis, the longer the emergency period continued, the greater the possibility that existing judicial thought and practices would become a fait accompli; that is, they would be continued in periods of relative tranquility, having their parallel in the unwillingness of executive branch officials to surrender expanded emergency powers once the emergency ended. Although emergency was thought to be transient, the line between emergency and normalcy has been blurred. Accordingly during and after both wars, a multiplicity of emergency-inspired statutes flooded forth from Congress and state houses: loyalty oaths, Red Flag laws, anti-alien and anti-radical statutes, deportation and denaturalization practices, registration orders for communists; and they remained in steady usage across the peacetime (non-"emergency") decades.

These measures and actions of the political branches produced a variety of judicial tactics, often marked by a seemingly insouciant disregard of the First Amendment. They included the avoidance of constitutional inquiry by raising a variety of non-judiciable doctrines: e.g., "ripeness" or "standing," or the ill-defined "political questions." At times procedural priorities or "pertinence" or deference to Congress—the "democratic branch"—would be cited. The tribunals graced by these defenders of judicial circumlocutions were also prone to invoke stare decisis and stasis rather than activism. By these various judicial stratagems, being peremptorily affirmed, the judiciary gave tacit permission to evade the challenges before them or they found the allegedly urgent needs of national security trumped the seminal importance of First Amendment protections. In effect, until the Warren tribunal challenged the political branches on substantive grounds, the judicial majority rarely questioned or struck down congressional or the presidential actions and thereby contributed to what at times would become officially sanctioned thought control.

Cautious judicial encounters with the First Amendment, however, ever so gradually and unevenly evolved into more adventurous, more activist judicial responses that would expand the protection of personal liberties. Thus, the Taft Court at times handed down some quiet decisions on liberty of expression; the Hughes Court expanded this process in guarded opinions that protected free speech from governmental intrusions; Chief Justice Stone's Caroline Products addendum promised greater sensitivity toward preferred personal liberties; and though the tribunal presided over by Chief Justice Harold Vinson would block further expansion of protected freedoms, the groundwork had been laid for the more sweeping decisions of the Warren Court.

At its outset, the tribunal captained by Warren adhered to the usual judicial pattern, departing slowly, almost painfully, from precedents. After a couple of years, it fitfully began to distinguish itself from the half-century of preceding Supreme Courts that had been largely deferential toward willful state and federal lawmakers. A pair of decisions in 1955 (*Empsak v. United States and Quinn v. United States*) recognizing the privilege against self-incrimination were modest harbingers of things to come. *Pennsylvania v. Nelson* of the following year that voided a state sedition law would be another telling augury, and with the four decisions of Red Monday, the Warren Court began to emerge as the champion of individual rights.

Not that the Warren Court had a spotless record in upholding the right of unrestricted expression—as *Barenblatt v. United States* of 1959, and three 1961 decisions (*Communist Party v. SACB, Braden,* and *Wilkinson*) tell us. However, one can maintain that the tribunal, after the mid-Fifties, entered what was perhaps its most creative and

Conclusion

confrontational period in our constitutional history respecting the First Amendment. The momentum stalling, the process continued at a glacial pace in the mid-Sixties when a judicial shift in Court personnel accompanied a shift in judicial opinion, a shift primarily on non-constitutional grounds became pronounced. It corresponded to a modest decline in the paranoia and passions generated by fears of subversion from homegrown anarchists and syndicalists, or communists who bent the knee to Stalin's Russia. Only then did the Court majority come close to the bold doctrinal belief in the freedom of expression that Black and Douglas vainly brought to the Court for almost four decades. Only then did the Court become a powerful force for the protection of fundamental rights and demonstrate a readiness, argues William Nelson, to take "responsibility for transforming America's ideology into reality." The exceptions regardless, Warren's last years as Chief Justice, to sum up, marked a time of triumph for First Amendment rights.

America's courts in theory are not supposed to react in conformity to the political branches when presented with a gusher of sober reports of danger to the system of governance. In theory, its members were expected to act with credible restraint and engage in the disinterested application of the constitutional text even during the times of emergency. But that they were hardly immunized from the social concerns of their day, that they had always been affected by stormy weather, is no cause for surprise.[1] Supporting this conclusion, evidence litters the twentieth century that in climacteric times both federal and state judiciary were not only aware of events outside their courtrooms, but also they were unable to distinguish between criminal conduct and dissident political expression—between the few who resort to violence and the many who criticize the government and work for peaceful change in its practices. It may be seen in the Court's response to the challenge posed by the danger of anarchism in the 1900s, by that of communism after the 1920s, by the social turbulence accompanying the Vietnam War, or by the threat of terrorism after 2001. As a consequence, Owen Gross has understandably concluded, "The First Amendment has not fared well in times of great actual or perceived peril."[2]

This judicial response, as we have repeatedly emphasized, reveals that members of the courts are not impartial and disinterested arbiters, but part of the governmental order and, therefore, function to maintain and protect it. Their rulings accordingly tended to affirm the hegemonic culture and hence social control, especially when confronted by cases involving radical critics of government. Enfolded within this observation has been the insistent contention that free expression is tolerated by the three branches of government only when important interests of state are not jeopardized.[3] The other side of the coin is that most of those wearing judicial robes had in fact always revealed themselves to be political actors, sensitive to sociopolitical considerations, seldom lagging far behind or forging far ahead of consensual thinking. Very aware of both society's internal tensions and the reactive popular consensus, their decisions were in some measure sculpted by these considerations.

Rulings in case law involving it, as adumbrated in this study, were rarely unanimous and usually sharply discordant. Indeed, divisiveness burrowed deep into the tribunal. There was always a cohort that displayed a readiness to tilt the scales from deference to the political branches and from affirmation of anti-subversive statutes and activities. This minority of judicial activists would affirm protected freedoms, question the never-ending claims of national security, and deliver philippics against "balancing" contrapuntal priorities. But they were invariably frustrated by a majority who weighted the scales in favor of the government's alleged security needs rather than in favor of individual rights.

Clashing personalities figured in this decision-making mix. For over a half-century, dark clouds of discord swirled around the *Black/Douglas v. Frankfurter* and *Warren v. Frankfurter* antagonisms that first stormily gathered in the Forties. Brennan came closest to reconciling the judicial divisions, though having only limited success. Frankfurter, for example, could not heal, being too centrist, too cautious, and too ready to mount a defense of state or federal legislative priorities. Nor could Harlan, for his legal thinking typically produced the nine-page opinion in *Yates* prioritizing procedural and semantic nuances. Vinson and Clark, *inter alia*, were too poisoned at the well of state interests to undertake this healing function. Nor could Whittaker or Burton restore judicial unanimity, since their opinions were invariably more bland and lackluster than Minton's. And among activists and defenders of protected speech and assembly, the efforts of Murphy, Black, and Douglas to limit the scope of government and the phobic impulse of national security were too extreme for their judicial brothers.

In seeking to explain why intransigent protection of the First Amendment freedoms was only supported by a small Praetorian guard, the fact of context, this study has repeatedly insisted, usually shaped majority judicial opinions. What were conceived to be appalling events and conditions outside the courtroom inevitably created growing conformist pressures across the country, and a heightened spirit of nativism, anti–radicalism, and vigilantism. They also weighed heavily on judges and justices in federal as well as state courts. In fact, they triggered ill-informed fears and severe overreactions in the three branches of government, encouraging draconian measures, scare-mongering official actions, and great public apprehension about America's enemies, all of which led to the blurring of that critical distinction between criminal conduct and normative political activities. Accordingly, in the parlous years around World War I and the Cold War, it became a crime to be a member of, even a sympathizer with, left-of-center organizations.

The resultant toxic culture of conformity made it apparent that judicial victories for freedom of expression, regardless of when they occurred, were not engraved in stone. They were subject to fluctuations triggered by crises that seemingly demanded national emergency legislation and executive actions and when implemented would trump the belief that individual liberties and minority rights were beyond the reach of the state. Consequently, it took about a half-century before the Court majority was prepared to admit that conspiracy and Communist Party membership should not necessarily be conflated. In the comparable emergency period following 9/11 attacks and the Twin Towers debacle, the demonology was reframed, substituting Muslims for radicals and communists and aligning Muslims and terrorists. It would be regrettable to equate terrorists with anarchists, syndicalists, or communists, though arguably similarities do exist, as they would be for all marginalized groups in periods of crisis.

Popular and governmental identification of individuals in such groups with an organization sharing their views in whole or in part defies neat categorization and is highly schematic, but it is a recurrent episode in the nation's political pathology. As a consequence, the principle of individual culpability, for one, is greatly compromised, especially during crises times. "Guilt by association" became a systemic political and legal commonplace for well over a half-century. It has a comparable match in recent federal statutory provisions prohibiting a person from giving the ambiguous "material support" to suspect groups labeled "terrorist."[4] To remind the reader, after World War I, thousands of foreign nationals were rounded up by federal agents and were held responsible not only for own involvement in any criminal activity, but also for the organizations with which they were associated. Arguably, the events of 1919–1920 bear little resemblance to the human mapping of over 100,000 Japanese–Americans by executive order in 1941 or to the provision for detention camps in Section 2of the 1950 McCarran Act, or secret detentions of Muslim Americans, both citizens and foreign nationals, 1,200 of whom were taken into custody following 9/11. However, one may contend that a modest analogy can be made.

In effect, whatever dreary period the reader selects, one may cite parallels: secrecy about the identity of those detained, registration and detention of foreign nationals, frequent denial of counsel, anonymity of accusers, denial of the right to confront them, arrests and convictions on the basis of minimal or non-existing evidence, use of questionable evidence, guilt by association, indifference toward of Fourth Amendment provisions such as the probable cause standard for searches and seizure, and resurrection of the idea of the referential guilt application in conspiracy doctrine. Time-honored legal protections were ignored— toward alleged anarchists, syndicalists, socialists, communists, and to Muslims in the aftermath of the Twin-Towers destruction. Relating to the last, the parallels are startling: profiling and harassment of those having Muslim names and dress codes, covert hearings, covert undisclosed deportations, covert disappearances into the judicial or prison systems, undisclosed evidence linking those of Arab or Muslim identity to "terrorist organizations," non-disclosures for the reason of national security, eavesdropping on constitutionally privileged lawyer–client conversation in those instances when an attorney would be allowed.

A rough correspondence may be found as well between the surveillance of communists, their homes, and Party venues from the early Thirties into the late Sixties and of Muslim mosques and communities following 9/11 attacks. Or the FBI's investigations of political activities leading up to and including COINTELPRO and its expanded power to wiretap or infiltrate Muslim meetings, mosques, and organizations, and conduct covert operations against them. There are further startling comparisons: the listings of the Attorney General, the HUAC and the FBI, each maintaining its own record of suspect organizations after the World War II into the Cold War years; and the listing of possibly a hundred thousand Muslim names, citizen, and non-citizen alike, that would eventually be added to the terrorist lists compiled by various government agencies. Then there was the disquieting statutory resemblance. The ambiguous words of "material support," as signaling violation of the law, may be found in both the 1996 Anti-Terrorism Act and the 2001 Patriot Act. The 1950 McCarran Act, and the 2001

Conclusion

Patriot Act by inference, authorized indefinite detention, deportation of aliens, secret searches without warrant or probable cause. Admittedly in the post-September 11 years, the desire to prevent future harm was grounded in more realistic probabilities than in the past. However, the same encroachments on protected expression, assembly, and press have been featured.

Statutory parallels also illustrating this most recent rush to judgment are equally striking. Preceding their passage, each measure would be tarted up with old tropes and panicked neologisms and rushed through the political branches in periods of peril. These statutes matched the 1917 Espionage Act, for one, in being swiftly and overwhelmingly passed, reflecting the willingness of both the public and lawmakers to accept serious encroachments on freedom of expression to block the anti-war activities of radical aliens. Both the 1940 Smith Act and the McCarran Act of a decade later likewise were stampeded through Congress, as was the 1996 Anti-Terrorism Act in reaction to the bombing of the Oklahoma City federal building, and the 2001 Patriot Act was enacted without congressional committee debate and by a resounding vote; that is, a few key senators met with the administration, a brief debate in Congress followed, and many of those voting to approve the measure had not read or understood it. The statute and the overwhelming congressional vote—356 to 66 in the House and one "no" vote in the Senate—were the swift and unreflective response to the destructive attack in lower Manhattan. These tallies approximated the votes for the other measures cited, each of which to one degree or another inflicting wounds on fundamental liberties.

One consequence of each of these statutes became oppressively clear: the casual disregard of restrictions designed to protect the perpetuation of a crisis mindset in the public, which justified retention, even enlargement, of official powers. Equally apparent was the converse outcome, namely, curtailment of fundamental liberties, most discernibly for the unsheltered and the powerless. However, a caveat is in order. The Palmer Raids turned up no actual bombers who could be prosecuted, the Loyalty Review Board (established by Truman's executive order), according to Seth Richardson, its chairman, found not a single instance of espionage or sabotage in the hundreds of cases it reviewed, and the recent preventive detention program produced only a few who would be charged. Not that actual bombers were absent in 1919, or that actual terrorist and terrorist attacks failed to materialize. In February 1993, explosions occurred at the World Trade Center in New York City, and charges were filed against "Sheikh Omar" (Omar Abdel Rahman) and over a dozen other defendants. Some of the instigators of 9/11 attacks were imprisoned. However, indictments and convictions were relatively few, considering the scale and sweep of the arrests.

To conclude, questions about the limits of government intervention, always entwined with the balancing of individual free expression and social control, remain as problematic today as they had across some seven decades. Quantum leaps in the expansion of executive prerogatives inevitably took place in parlous times. Congressional acceptance of such expansion was in inevitable attendance, and co-partnership decisions of the federal courts were usual features as well. The fact of agreement among the three branches of government does raise questions about our esteemed constitutional design of separation of powers and checks and balances.

The fact of acquiescence, deference, or outspoken approval of the ex-cathedra actions and pronouncements of one branch of government by the others is not an uncommon phenomenon and was hardly limited to the last hundred years. In fact as early as 1799, during the crisis over the Alien and Sedition Acts, James Madison offered up the following admonitory observation: "[t]he fetters imposed on liberty at home have ever been forged out of the weapons provided for defense against real, pretended, or imaginary dangers from abroad."[5] Speaking in Jerusalem in 1987 just short of two centuries after Madison, Justice Brennan, addressing identical concerns, astutely summed up the fortunes of the First Amendment:

> There is considerably less to be proud about, and a good deal to be embarrassed about, when one reflects on the shabby treatment civil liberties have received in the United States during times of war and perceived threats to its national security ... After each perceived security crisis ended, the United States has remorsefully realized that the abrogation of civil liberties was unnecessary. But it has proven unable to prevent itself from repeating the error when the next crisis came along.[6]

Wise and cautionary words, they are entirely relevant to this study and may be well remembered today.

Notes

1. Learned Hand, for one, stated it well, in a letter to Chafee (Quoted in Gerald Günther, *Learned Hand: The Man and the Judge* (New York: Alfred A. Knopf, 1994), 169 and in his "Spirit of Liberty" speech (1960), 165.

2. Oren Gross, "Chaos and Rules: Should Responses to Violent Crises Always Be Constitutional?" *Yale Law Journal* 112 (2003): 1029.
3. Arthur Miller, Politics, *Democracy and the Supreme Court* (Westport, CT: Greenwood, 1985), 208.
4. David Cole and Jules Lobel, *Less Safe, Less Free: Why America Is Losing the War on Terror* (New York: Norton, 2007), 48.
5. Anon. [Jefferson], "Political Reflections," in the Aurora General Advertiser, February 23, 1766.
6. Quoted in Bollinger and Stone, *Eternally Vigilant: Free Speech in the Modern Era* (Chicago, IL: University of Chicago Press, 2002), 16; see also Christopher Wolfe, *The Rise of Modern Judicial Review* (New York: Basic Books, 1986), 278.

Index

Advocacy of action, 253, 263
Alien Act, 8
Alien and Sedition Acts, 314
Alien Registration Act (the Smith Act), 104, 124, 169, 224
American Anarchist Fighters
  Wall Street bombings, 24
American Bar Association (ABA), 4, 260
  anti-communist strictures, 145
American Civil Liberties Union (ACLU), 136
American Communist Party, 178
American Defense Society, 21, 26
American Federation of Labor (AFL), 102, 125
Americanism, 276
American Jewish Congress (AJC), 136
American Labor Party, 219
American League for Peace and Democracy, 113
American Library Association, 145
American Medical Association, 145
Americans for Democratic Action, 134
Anarchism, 4
Anarchists, 223
  disloyal, 9
  peaceable, 3
  The Warren Court, 223
Anglo-American law, 169
Anti-alien sentiments, 9
Anti-communism, 109
Anti-Fascist Refugee Committee, 202
Anti-German, 44
Anti-immigrant sentiments, 8–9
Anti-Irish, 44
Anti-radicalism, 58, 73, 275
Anti-syndicalism measures, 64
Anti-Terrorism Act, 312–313

Anti-war speech, 47
Arbitrary imposed sanctions, 247–248
A Voice in the Wilderness, 13–14

Bad tendency
  freedom of speech doctrine, 60
  standard, 62
  test, 89
Beilan v Board of Public Education (1958), 209
Better America Foundation (BAF), 74
Bill of rights, 99, 135, 190, 192
  protection, 38
Board of Trustees
  privilege against self-incrimination, 157
Bolshevik Revolution (1917), 12, 57
  Socialist Party, 76
Bolshevism, 22
Breach of peace, 135–137
Broyles Commission, 122
Bureau of Investigation (BI), 12
  General Intelligence Division and, 22

California
  advocated criminal syndicalism, 81
  agricultural districts, 70
  anti-radical laws, 80
  criminal syndicalism law, 29
  District Court of Appeals, 81
  Labor Party, 81
  Red-hunting assemblyman, 118
  state syndicalism acts of, 93
  Un-American Activities Committee, 118
Canwell Committee, 156
Capitalist classes, 7
Certiorari, 242, 252, 271

Chicago
 Industrial Workers of the World (IWW), 5
Chief Justice, 260, 274
Citizenship
 Expatriation Act, 187
 right of American, 101
Civil Service Commission, 198
Civil Service law, 280
Classical Marxist, 246
Cold War years, 241
Comintern (Communist International)
 Seventh Congress of, 107
 Third Period (1928–1935), 107
Common law
 Espionage Act, 43
 principles of right and justice, 43
 standard of, 78
Communist, 221
 classics, 264
 Communist front, 278
Communist Control Act of 1954, 150, 155, 189
Communist front organization, 197, 207, 211, 272
Communist infiltration, 244, 271
Communist Labor Party (CLP), 26, 72, 80
 anti-war left-wingers, 30
Communist Party (CP), 26, 90, 215, 218, 225, 239, 242, 260
 advocated criminal syndicalism, 93
 advocated Marxism–Leninism, 145
 "American" movement, 72
 communism and academic freedom, 123
 communist-action organization, 147
 Communist Control of Act of August 1954, 150
 communist front organization, 113
 communistic affiliations, 112
 Communist Manifesto of 1840s, 168
 communists and communist espionage, 152
 constitutional principles, 101
 criminal conspiracy, 168, 175
 equal rights for all, 96
 equal rights for the Negroes, 96
 espionage groups, 142
 left-wing, 154
 legislation against communism, 189
 McCormack–Dickstein Committee of 1934–1935, 111
 membership in, 154, 199
 National Board, 168
 National Committee, 174
 under the pre-Civil War anti-insurrection law, 95
 revolutionary theory of Marxism, 95
 State statute, 279
 subversive organization or subversive persons, 277
 Taft–Hartley Act of 1947, 144
Communist Party USA (CPUSA), 175, 194
Communist Political Association, 108
Communist propaganda, 160
Communist Socialism, 78
Concrete action, 253
Congress, 3, 9, 214, 229, 239, 243, 260, 268
 constitutional right, 47
 contempt of, 273
 First Amendment, 80
 Fourteenth Amendment, 80
 freedom of speech, 47, 60
 Internal Security Act/ McCarran Act, 146
 rights of individual, 48
 Section 9 of the Hatch Act 1939, 123
 Subversive Activities Control Act (SACA), 146
Congress of Industrial Organizations (CIO), 102
Conspiracy
 charge, 50
 under the Espionage Act, 49
 express proof of, 49
 lawfully guilty of, 46
 nature of criminal, 83
Constitution
 draft law, 46
 First Amendment to, 46
 Fourteenth Amendment, 65
 fundamental principles of, 47
 individual's rights, 62
 principles of, 84
 State law, 66
Constitutional privilege, 210
Counter-Intelligence Program (COINTELPRO), 188
Criminal syndicalism laws, 81, 120

Index

Daughters of the America Revolution (DAR), 21, 74
Denaturalization, 227, 228
Department of Defense Industrial Security Program, 221
Department of Health, Education and Welfare (HEW), 217
Department's Industrial Security Program, 223
Deportation, 4, 6, 224
Direct action, 5
Disloyal advice, 10
Draft law, 13, 14

Education Policies Commission of the National Education Association (NEA), 158
Eighth Amendment, 227
Emergency Detention Act, 148
Emergency Relief Act, 123
Engineering and Research Corporation (ERCO), 221
English-speaking freedom, 17
Espionage
  atomic Soviet Union, 143
  Communist Party groups, 142
  communists and communist, 152
  Soviet Union, 151
Espionage Act, 9, 10, 17, 124, 313
European conflict
  United States from intervening in, 44, 108
  Wobbly pacifism and anti-capitalist rhetoric, 23
Executive Order, 203
  Japanese–Americans by, 310
Expatriation Act, 187
ex post facto action, 224
External enamel epithelium, 13, *13*

Farm Equipment Workers (FEW), 241
Federal Bureau of Investigation (FBI), 238
  investigation of Communist Party, 138
  security index, 149
Federal Security Agency (FSA), 198
Feinberg Law, 208
Fifth Amendment, 98, 156, 158, 188, 209
  communists, 114, 186, 210, 214, 215
  equal protection of the law, 278

federal investigatory committees, 190
privilege against self-incrimination, 196
First Amendment, 75, 89, 249
  against abridgment by United States, 104
  American liberties, 196
  Bolshevik revolution, 57
  Chicago ordinance, 136
  defendant's rights, 179
  freedom of expression, 98
  freedom of speech law abridging, 166
  freedoms, 179
  free speech revolution, 90
  guarantees of freedom of speech, 192
  interest-weighing approach, 167
  non-communist, 166
  press clause, 92
  protected political activity, 173
  protection of freedoms, 310
  Red Flag laws, 307
  right of free speech, 77
  rights, 98, 137, 280, 281, 309
  Section 3 of Espionage Act 1917, 58
  Sedition Act 1918, 57–58
  States by the Fourteenth, 278
  Taft Court, 308
  United States Constitution, 62
Florida Supreme Court, 276
Food and Drug Administration, 217
Foreign Agents Registration Act, 169
Fourteenth Amendment, 90, 91, 135
  against abridgment by a state, 104
  American radicals and radicalism, 92
  criminal syndicalism law, 92
  equal protection clauses of, 82
  freedom of press, 92
  freedom of speech, 82, 83, 97
  press clause, 92
  violation of, 83
Fourth Circuit Court, 260
Freedom of expression, 98, 309
  anti-radicalism, 70
Freedom of press, 63, 66
  Fourteenth Amendment, 92
Freedom of speech, 3, 7, 8, 46
  anti-war speech, 47
  bad tendency
    doctrines, 60, 99
    test, 89
  constitutional guarantees of, 51, 53
  constitutional right, 47

319

constitutional rights, 94
draft law, 47
Espionage Act, 46–48
under the Espionage Act, 46, 47
false statement, 62–63
First Amendment, 46–48
  guarantees of, 192
Fourteenth Amendment, 82, 83
High Court, 65
individual rights and preferred
  speech, 100
intent and bad tendency test, 48
invasion of, 182
law abridging, 166
under the "obstructions," 62
Oregon statute, 93
power of the state, 97
and press, 51
privileges of, 66
right of free speech, 74, 90, 91
rights of individual, 48, 49
split decision, 61
thinking, 48
French Communist Party, 152

General Intelligence Division (GID), 12

Hand-Vinson formula, 182
Hatch Act, 141
High Court
  criminal or civil conspiracy
    indictments against Bridges, 103
  freedom of speech, 65
  kangaroo court proceedings, 107
Hitler–Stalin Pact, 179
Holmes–Brandeis danger formula, 182
House Special Committee on Un-
  American Activities (HUAC), 102,
  110, 113, 209, 214, 238, 265
  anti-communist zealotry of, 114
  Committee for clearance, 122
Hunting license, 243

Identical statutes, 4
Illinois
  legislature's Broyles Commission, 122
  Sedition Act of 1919, 31
Immigrants
  Alien Enemy Act, 101
  Alien Registration Act (the Smith
    Act) of 1940, 104, 124

citizenship, 101
  Irish Catholic working class, 191
  Naturalization Act of 1906, 101
Immigration Act, 226
Immigration and Nationality Act, 187
Immigration and Naturalization Act,
  144, 150
Immigration and Naturalization Service
  (INS), 225, 226
Immunity Act, 189
Incompetency, 209
Individual disloyal utterances, 10
Individual's rights, 62
  and preferred speech, 100
Industrial Workers of the World
  (IWW), 5, 11, 12, 70, 82
  anarchists and syndicalists, 23
  anti-criminal syndicalist state
    statutes, 83
  in Chicago, 5
  draft and Espionage statutes, 50
  members, and communists
    denaturalized, 105
  post-war strikes, 22
  State Police, raided radical, 32
Interior's Education Department, 219
Internal dangers, 225
Internal Security (McCarran) Act,
  143, 144, 146, 194, 217–218,
  225, 226
Internal subversion/foreign aggression,
  218
International Labor Defense, 95
International Workers Order (IWO),
  202

Judicial activism, 250
Judicial unanimity, 207–208
Justice Department Authorization Act
  of 1941, 124

Labor Management Reporting and
  Disclosure Act of 1959, 144
Labor union
  membership, 168
Landrum–Griffin Act, 190
Latin maxim, 7
Left-wing socialists, 8
Legal murder of 1887, 4
Loyalty oath, 211, 213, 231
Loyalty Review Board, 198, 203, 313

Index

Loyalty–security program, 141, 240, 259
Lusk laws, 32

Magnuson Act of l950, 144
Marxist–Leninist economic and political theories, 172
McCarran Act, 146–148, 152, 186, 189, 220, 225–226, 312
McCarran–Walter Act, 150, 186, 187
Medicare Act, 260
Michigan Criminal Syndicalism Act, 31
Milwaukee Leader, 14, 15
Montana
    Federal Sedition Act of 1918, 30
    "reign of terror" against of, 37
Moral character, 231, 233
Muffled terms, 214
Mundt–Nixon bill, 170
Municipal colleges, 209–210
Murder for Murder, 2

NAACP, 273
National Civil Liberties Bureau, 10
National Defense Committee
    The Common Enemy, 74
Nationalism and war
    Alien Act, 8
    American Bar Association, 4
    anarchism, 4
    anarchist, 1
        disloyal, 9
    anti-alien sentiments, 9
    anti-immigrant sentiments, 8–9
    Bolshevik Revolution (1917), 12
    capitalist classes, 7
    congress, 3
    Criminal Anarchy Act, 2
    deportation, 4
    direct action, 5
    disloyal advice, 10
    Draft law, 13, 14
    English-speaking freedom, 17
    Espionage Act, 9
    free speech, 3, 7, 8
    identical statutes, 4
    individual disloyal utterances, 10
    Industrial Workers of the World (IWW), 5, 11, 12
    Latin maxim, 7
    left-wing socialists, 8
    non-mailable, 14, 15
    Non-Partisan League, 6
    pacifists, 8
    political action, 5
    political agitation, 16
    post-war Germany, 11
    professional murderer, 3
    radical aliens, 1–3
    revolutionary sentiment, 11
    Russian revolution, 11
    ruthless brutality, 8
    Sedition Act, 10
    socialists, 4, 5
Nationality Act, 228
National Labor Relations Act of 1936, 144
National Labor Relations Board (NLRB), 116, 144, 165
National security, 216, 218, 220, 266
National Security League, 21, 26
    secret communist conspiracy, 74
Naturalization, 227
New York
    anti-radical campaigns, 32
    anti-Red activism, 70
    Board of Higher Education, 156
    Communist Party membership, 154
    Criminal Anarchy Act of 1902, 76, 124
    criminal anarchy statute, 81
    Espionage Act, 124
    Joint Legislative Committee Investigating Seditious Activities, 70, 76
    legislative committee, 76
    Penal Code, 137
    radical movements, 70
    Red conspiracy, 70
    State's Civil Service Law as Section 3022, 156
    State's Education Law and Civil Service Law, 281
    State's 1949 Feinberg Act, 279
    statute, 76
New York Call, 14
Non-mailable, 14, 15
Non-Partisan League, 6, 34, 64
Noto, 265

Ober Act, 119
Ohio's Criminal Syndicalism Act, 119
Oklahoma taxpayers, 211
Organize, 252, 253, 260

Pacifists, 8
Palmer Raids, 313
Party official, 263
Patriot Act, 312–313
Peaceable anarchists, 3
Pennsylvania Supreme Court, 229
People's Commissariat of Internal Affairs (NKVD), 112
Personal conference, 222
Personal rights, 213
Personnel Security Board (PSB), 221, 222
Pertinency issue, 265
Plan Bloody Revolution, 22
Political action, 5
Political agitation, 16
Postmaster General, 13
Post-war Germany, 11
Prejudices
  against Socialists and Anarchists, 44
Pro communist decisions, 250
Professional murderer, 3
Public interests, 268
Public professions, 232

Radical aliens, 1–3
  United States, 4
Red Flag, 26
  law, 28
  measures in US, 28
Red Flag law, 120, 154, 307
Red-hunting campaign, 109
Red Menace, 259. *See also* Red Scare
Red Monday, 265, 275, 308
  advocacy, 252
  Advocacy of action, 253
  arbitrary imposed sanctions, 247–248
  certiorari, 242, 252
  classical Marxist, 246
  Cold War years, 241
  communist infiltration, 244
  Communist Party, 239, 242, 247
  concrete action, 253
  Congress, 239, 243
  Farm Equipment Workers (FEW), 241
  FBI, 238
  federal loyalty–security program, 240
  First Amendment, 249
  HUAC, 238, 242
  hunting license, 243
  judicial activism, 250

  organize, 252, 253
  pro communist decisions, 250
  second-string communists, 250
  Secretary of State Dean Acheson, 240
  security risk, 241
  Senate Appropriations Committee, 239
  service, 241
  Smith Act, 254
  sole purpose, 243
  states rights, 238
  subversive activity, 248
  subversive organizations, 246
  subversive persons, 246
  Taft–Hartley Act, 237
  trial court, 251
Red Scare, 37, 133
  in American society, 135
Refugee Committee, 202
Revolution and terrorism, 180
Revolutionary sentiment, 11
Right of free speech, 74, 90, 91
  constitutional rights, 94
  Oregon statute, 93
Right of petition, 46
Rights of individual, 48
Russia
  American intervention in, 59
  Communist International (Comintern), 32, 107
  communist parties of 1919 to act, 71
  Communist Party, 72
  detention of communists in, 148
  German invasion of, 179
  heroes of revolutionary, 108
  Russian Revolution, 58, 71
  Russo–German Pact, 152
  Union of Russian Workers, 23
Russian Revolution, 11, 71
Ruthless brutality, 8. *See also* Wobblies

Scales, 260, 263, 264
School Code, 122
Second-string communists, 250
Secretary of State Dean Acheson, 240
Secret Service, 22
Section 3 of Espionage Act 1917, 58, 59
Security risks, 223, 241, 260
Sedition Act, 7, 10, 57–59, 153
Sedition law
  arrests of radicals, 37

Index

Select Committee on Un-American Activities of the State Senate, 155
Selective Service Draft Law of 1917, 51
Self-incrimination, 210, 214, 215
Senate Appropriations Committee, 239
Senate Internal Security Committee (SISC), 133
 Interlocking Subversion in Government Departments, 142
Senate Internal Security Subcommittee (SISS), 117, 186
Senate's Permanent Subcommittee on Investigations, 151
Sixth Circuit Court of Appeals, 226–227, 268
Slochower v. Board of Higher Education of New York City (1956), 210
Smith Act, 124, 141, 168, 169, 172, 173, 185, 187, 254, 260
 leadership clause of, 264
Socialist Party
 anti-sedition measures, 32
 Bolshevik Revolution, 76
 Conscription Act, 46
 Convention of June 1919, 32
 doctrinal division in, 71
 First Amendment, 46
 Foreign Language Federations, 71
 left wing, 76, 77
 Lusk laws, 32
 mad march of Red fascism, 73
 militant unionism, 76
 pro-Bolshevik membership, 21, 26
 Red Radical Movement, 73
 right-wing and left-wing, 33
 Section 3 of Espionage Act, 45
 sedition bills, 73
Socialists, 4, 5
 left-wing, 8
Socialist Workers Party (SWP), 125
Sole purpose, 243
Soviet Union
 American Communist Party, 126
 atomic bomb test, 143
 atomic espionage, 143
 espionage for the, 192
 Soviet–American relations, 133
 Soviet espionage, 151
Special Inquiries, 260
Stare decisis, 176
State Civil Service Commission, 219
State's Ober Act (1949), 207
States rights, 238
State's Security Risk Act, 218
State University of New York (SUNY), 280
Subject under inquiry, 274
Subversive Activities Control Act, 119, 146, 223, 226
Subversive Activities Control Board (SACB), 146, 189
Subversive activity, 248, 268
Subversive organizations, 231, 246, 277
Subversive persons, 246, 277
Subversives, 211, 223
Supreme Court
 free speech, 136
 struggle against Un-American Activities, 135
Sympathetic association, 219

Taft Court, 308
Taft–Hartley Act of 1947, 144, 165, 190, 214, 237
Tax exemption, 211
Trial court, 251

Union of Russian Workers, 23
 State Police, raided radical, 32
United Public Workers (UPW), 198
United States
 American Anarchist Fighters, 24
 America's socialists/communists, 49
 anti-immigrant sentiments, 8–9
 anti-radical forces, 21
 anti-radicalism, 38
 anti-Red campaigning, 25
 anti-sedition law, 1919, 29
 Bill of rights, 38
 Bureau of Investigation (BI), 22
 California's criminal syndicalism law, 29
 Capitol Hill, 110, 111
 Committee on Appropriation, 116
 communist movement in, 111, 142, 146
 Congress
  constitutional right, 47
  First Amendment, 80
  Fourteenth Amendment, 80
  freedom of speech, 47, 60
  Internal Security Act/ McCarran Act, 146

323

rights of individual, 48
Section 9 of the Hatch Act 1939, 123
Subversive Activities Control Act (SACA), 146
conspiracy haunting, 37
conspiracy to violate, 24, 33
Constitution
  Fourteenth Amendment, 65
  individual's rights, 62
  principles of, 84
  State law, 66
contemporary statutes, 49
Criminal Anarchy Act, 32
Disloyalty Act, 31
enlistment service of, 31
Espionage Act of 1917, 24, 26, 29, 33
European conflict, 23
First Amendment, 62
  against abridgment by, 104
House Committee on the Judiciary, 110
House Committee on Un-American Activities, 174
House Special Committee on Un-American Activities (HUAC), 102, 110, 113
Illinois' Sedition Act of 1919, 31
Immigration Act of 1918, 27
Immigration and Naturalization Service (INS), 103, 104
intelligence information, FBI, 109
international communism, 133
Justice Department, 28
  Alien Registration Act (the Smith Act) of 1940, 104
Labor Management Reporting and Disclosure Act of 1959, 144
Legislature power, 78
liberty and civilization., 25
mail-letter bombings, 24, 28
May Day, 29
McCormick–Dickstein Committee, 111
Michigan Criminal Syndicalism Act, 31
Montana's Federal Sedition Act of 1918, 30
National Labor Relations Act of 1936, 144
National Labor Relations Board, 116
Naturalization Act 1906, 84, 85

Oval Office, 109
Palmer raids, 27
  disease of evil thinking, 37
  post-war raiding, 27
  recruiting and enlistment service of, 48
Red aggression, 133
Red Flag laws, 28, 154
Reds-in-Government, 112
Report on the Communist Party of, 143
Republican on the Committee, 113
revolution in America, 22
riots in New York and Cleveland, 25
satrap party, 180
Second Circuit Court of Appeals, 171
Secretary of Labor, 103
Secret Service, 22
Sedition Acts of 1918, 26, 29
selective draft law, 35
Senate Foreign Relations Committee, 116
Senate Internal Security Committee, 142
Smith Act of 1940, 110
Soviet–American relations, 133
Special Committee on Un-American Activities, 112
Supreme Court, 98
  struggle against Un-American Activities, 135
terrorist bombings of 1919, 26
Wall Street bombings, 24, 28
White House
  anti-communist practices, 109
  campaign to eliminate communists in government, 188
  Immigration and Naturalization Service, 187
Use of Mails, 12–13

Vice of vagueness, 276
Voorhis Act of 1940, 123, 147, 169

The Warren Court, 259, 281
  Alien Registration Act, 224
  American Labor Party, 219
  communist, 221
  communist front, 207
  communist party, 215
  congress, 214

Index

constitutional privilege, 210
denaturalization, 227, 228
deportation, 224
Eighth Amendment, 227
Feinberg Law, 208
Fifth Amendment Communist, 210
HUAC, 209, 214
Immigration Act, 226
incompetency, 209
internal subversion/foreign aggression, 218
judicial unanimity, 207–208
moral character, 231, 233
national security, 216
personal rights, 213
public professions, 232
security risks, 223
self-incrimination, 210
State's Ober Act (1949), 207
Taft–Hartley Act, 214
tax exemption, 211
writ of habeas corpus, 225
Well-worn pattern, 260
Western Pennsylvania Communist Party, 229
White Court
revolutionary acts, 45
Wide-ranging inquisition, 220
Wobblies, 5, 6, 8. *See also* Industrial Workers of the World (IWW)
Workers (Communist) Party, 106
Workers Party of America, 224
World War I, 7–8
World War II, 226, 231
World-wide communism, 283
Writ of habeas corpus, 225

Young Communist League, 90, 151